Lecture Notes in Artificial Intelligence　　3755

Edited by J. G. Carbonell and J. Siekmann

Subseries of Lecture Notes in Computer Science

Preface

Data mining has been an area of considerable research and application in Australia and the region for many years. This has resulted in the establishment of a strong tradition of academic and industry scholarship, blended with the pragmatics of practice in the field of data mining and analytics. ID3, See5, RuleQuest.com, MagnumOpus, and WEKA is but a short list of the data mining tools and technologies that have been developed in Australasia. Data mining conferences held in Australia have attracted considerable international interest and involvement.

This book brings together a unique collection of chapters that cover the breadth and depth of data mining today. This volume provides a snapshot of the current state of the art in data mining, presenting it both in terms of technical developments and industry applications. Authors include some of Australia's leading researchers and practitioners in data mining, together with chapters from regional and international authors.

The collection of chapters is based on works presented at the Australasian Data Mining conference series and industry forums. The original papers were initially reviewed for the workshops, conferences and forums. Presenting authors were provided with substantial feedback, both through this initial review process and through editorial feedback from their presentations. A final international peer review process was conducted to include input from potential users of the research, and in particular analytics experts from industry, looking at the impact of reviewed works.

Many people contribute to an effort such as this, starting with the authors! We thank all authors for their contributions, and particularly for making the effort to address two rounds of reviewer comments. Our workshop and conference reviewers provided the first round of helpful feedback for the presentation of the papers to their respective conferences. The authors from a selection of the best papers were then invited to update their contributions for inclusion in this volume. Each submission was then reviewed by at least another two reviewers from our international panel of experts in data mining.

A considerable amount of effort goes into reviewing papers, and reviewers perform an essential task. Reviewers receive no remuneration for all their efforts, but are happy to provide their time and expertise for the benefit of the whole community. We owe a considerable debt to them all and thank them for their enthusiasm and critical efforts.

Bringing this collection together has been quite an effort. We also acknowledge the support of our respective institutions and colleagues who have contributed in many different ways. In particular, Graham would like to thank Togaware (Data Mining and GNU/Linux consultancy) for their ongoing infrastructural support over the years, and the Australian Taxation Office for its support of data mining and related local conferences through the participation of its staff. Simeon acknowledges the support of the University of Technology, Sydney. The Australian Research Council's Research Network on Data Mining and Knowledge Discovery, under the leadership of Professor John Roddick, Flinders University, has also provided support for the associated conferences, in particular providing financial support to assist student participation in the conferences. Professor Geoffrey Webb, Monash University, has played a supportive role in the development of data mining in Australia and the AusDM series of conferences, and continues to contribute extensively to the conference series.

The book is divided into two parts: (i) state-of-art research and (ii) state-of-art industry applications. The chapters are further grouped around common sub-themes. We are sure you will find that the book provides an interesting and broad update on current research and development in data mining.

November 2005   Graham Williams and Simeon Simoff

Organization

Many colleagues have contributed to the success of the series of data mining workshops and conferences over the years. We list here the primary reviewers who now make up the International Panel of Expert Reviewers.

AusDM Conference Chairs

Simeon J. Simoff, University of Technology, Sydney, Australia
Graham J. Williams, Australian National University, Canberra

PAKDD Industry Chair

Graham J. Williams, Australian National University, Canberra

International Panel of Expert Reviewers

Mihael Ankerst	Boeing Corp., USA
Michael Bain	University of New South Wales, Australia
Rohan Baxter	Australian Taxation Office
Helmut Berger	University of Technology, Sydney, Australia
Michael Bohlen	Free University Bolzano-Bozen, Italy
Jie Chen	CSIRO, Canberra, Australia
Peter Christen	Australian National University
Thanh-Nghi Do	Can Tho University, Vietnam
Vladimir Estivill-Castro	Giffith University, Australia
Hongjian Fan	University of Melbourne, Australia
Eibe Frank	Waikato University, New Zealand
Mohamed Medhat Gaber	Monash University, Australia
Raj Gopalan	Curtin University, Australia
Warwick Graco	Australian Taxation Office
Lifang Gu	Australian Taxation Office
Hongxing He	CSIRO, Canberra, Australia
Robert Hilderman	University of Regina, Canada
Joshua Zhexue Huang	University of Hong Kong, China
Huidong Jin	CSIRO, Canberra, Australia
Paul Kennedy	University of Technology, Sydney, Australia
Weiqiang Lin	Australian Taxation Office
John Maindonald	Australian National University
Mark Norrie	Teradata, NCR, Australia
Peter O'Hanlon	Westpac, Australia

Table of Contents

Part 1: State-of-the-Art in Research

Methodological Advances

Data Linkage

Text Mining

Temporal and Sequence Mining

Part 2: State-of-the-Art in Applications

Health

Finance and Retail

Generality Is Predictive of Prediction Accuracy

Geoffrey I. Webb[1] and Damien Brain[2]

[1] Faculty of Information Technology,
Monash University, Clayton, Vic 3800, Australia
`webb@infotech.monash.edu.au`
[2] UTelco Systems,
Level 50/120 Collins St Melbourne, Vic 3001, Australia
`damien.brain@utelcosystems.com.au`

Abstract. During knowledge acquisition it frequently occurs that multiple alternative potential rules all appear equally credible. This paper addresses the dearth of formal analysis about how to select between such alternatives. It presents two hypotheses about the expected impact of selecting between classification rules of differing levels of generality in the absence of other evidence about their likely relative performance on unseen data. We argue that the accuracy on unseen data of the more general rule will tend to be closer to that of a default rule for the class than will that of the more specific rule. We also argue that in comparison to the more general rule, the accuracy of the more specific rule on unseen cases will tend to be closer to the accuracy obtained on training data. Experimental evidence is provided in support of these hypotheses. These hypotheses can be useful for selecting between rules in order to achieve specific knowledge acquisition objectives.

1 Introduction

In many knowledge acquisition contexts there will be many classification rules that perform equally well on the training data. For example, as illustrated by the version space [1], there will often be alternative rules of differing degrees of generality all of which agree with the training data. However, even when we move away from a situation in which we are expecting to find rules that are strictly consistent with the training data, in other words, when we allow rules to misclassify some training cases, there will often be many rules all of which cover exactly the same training cases. If we are selecting rules to use for some decision making task, we must select between such rules with identical performance on the training data. To do so requires a learning bias [2], a means of selecting between competing hypotheses that utilizes criteria beyond those strictly encapsulated in the training data.

All learning algorithms confront this problem. This is starkly illustrated by the large numbers of rules with very high values for any given interestingness measure that are typically discovered during association rule discovery. Many systems that learn rule sets for the purpose of prediction mask this problem by making arbitrary choices between rules with equivalent performance on the

G.J. Williams and S.J. Simoff (Eds.): Data Mining, LNAI 3755, pp. 1–13, 2006.

training data. This masking of the problem is so successful that many researchers appear oblivious to the problem. Our previous work has clearly identified that it is frequently the case that there exist many variants of the rules typically derived in machine learning, all of which cover exactly the same training data. Indeed, one of our previous systems, The Knowledge Factory [3, 4] provides support for identification and selection between such rule variants.

This paper examines the implications of selecting between such rules on the basis of their relative generality. We contend that learning biases based on relative generality can usefully manipulate the expected performance of classifiers learned from data. The insight that we provide into this issue may assist knowledge engineers make more appropriate selections between alternative rules when those alternatives derive equal support from the available training data.

We present specific hypotheses relating to reasonable expectations about classification error for classification rules. We discuss classification rules of the form $Z \to y$, which should be interpreted as all cases that satisfy conditions Z belong to class y. We are interested in learning rules from data. We allow that evidence about the likely classification performance of a rule might come from many sources, including prior knowledge, but, in the machine learning tradition, are particularly concerned with *empirical* evidence—evidence obtained from the performance of the rule on sample (training) data. We consider the learning context in which a rule $Z \to y$ is learned from a *training set* $D'=(x_1', y_1'), (x_2', y_2'), \ldots, (x_n', y_n')$ and is to be applied to a set of previously unseen data called a *test set* $D=(x_1, y_1), (x_2, y_2), \ldots, (x_m, y_m)$. For this enterprise to be successful, D' and D should be drawn from the same or from related distributions. For the purposes of the current paper we assume that D' and D are drawn independently at random from the same distribution and acknowledge that violations of this assumption may affect the effects that we predict.

We utilize the following notation.

- $Z(I)$ represents the set of instances in instance set I covered by condition Z.
- $E(Z \to y, I)$ represents the number of instances in instance set I that $Z \to y$ misclassifies (the absolute error).
- $\varepsilon(Z \to y, I)$ represents the proportion of instance set I that $Z \to y$ misclassifies (the error) $= \frac{E(Z \to y, I)}{|I|}$.
- $W \gg Z$ denotes that the condition W is a proper generalization of condition Z. $W \gg Z$ if and only if the set of descriptions for which W is true is a proper superset of the set of descriptions for which Z is true.
- $NODE(W \to y, Z \to y)$ denotes that there is no other distinguishing evidence between $W \to y$ and $Z \to y$. This means that there is no available evidence, other than the relative generality of W and Z, indicating the likely direction (negative, zero, or positive) of $\varepsilon(W \to y, D) - \varepsilon(Z \to y, D)$. In particular, we require that the empirical evidence be identical. In the current research the learning systems have access only to empirical evidence and we assume that $W(D')=Z(D') \to NODE(W \to y, Z \to y)$. Note that $W(D')=Z(D')$ does not preclude W and Z from covering different test cases at classification time and hence having different test set error. We utilize the

notion of *other distinguishing evidence* to allow for the real-world knowledge acquisition context in which evidence other than that contained in the data may be brought to bear upon the rule selection problem.

We present two hypotheses relating to classification rules $W \rightarrow y$ and $Z \rightarrow y$ learned from real-world data such that $W \gg Z$ and $NODE(W \rightarrow y, Z \rightarrow y)$.

1. $Pr(|\varepsilon(W \rightarrow y, D) - \varepsilon(true \rightarrow y, D)| < |\varepsilon(Z \rightarrow y, D) - \varepsilon(true \rightarrow y, D)|) > Pr(|\varepsilon(W \rightarrow y, D) - \varepsilon(true \rightarrow y, D)| > |\varepsilon(Z \rightarrow y, D) - \varepsilon(true \rightarrow y, D)|)$. That is, the error of the more general rule, $W \rightarrow y$, on unseen data will tend to be closer to the proportion of cases in the domain that do not belong to class y than will the error of the more specific rule, $Z \rightarrow y$.
2. $Pr(|\varepsilon(W \rightarrow y, D) - \varepsilon(W \rightarrow y, D')| > |\varepsilon(Z \rightarrow y, D) - \varepsilon(Z \rightarrow y, D')|) > Pr(|\varepsilon(W \rightarrow y, D) - \varepsilon(W \rightarrow y, D')| < |\varepsilon(Z \rightarrow y, D) - \varepsilon(Z \rightarrow y, D')|)$. That is, the error of the more specific rule, $Z \rightarrow y$, on unseen data will tend to be closer to the proportion of negative training cases covered by the two rules[1] than will the error of the more general rule, $W \rightarrow y$.

Another way of stating these two hypotheses is that of two rules with identical empirical and other support,

1. the more general can be expected to exhibit classification error closer to that of a *default rule*, $true \rightarrow y$, or, in other words, of assuming all cases belong to the class, and
2. the more specific can be expected to exhibit classification error closer to that observed on the training data.

It is important to clarify at the outset that we are not claiming that the more general rule will invariably have closer generalization error to the default rule and the more specific rule will invariably have closer generalization error to the observed error on the training data. Rather, we are claiming that relative generality provides a source of evidence that, in the absence of alternative evidence, provides reasonable grounds for believing that each of these effects is more likely than the contrary.

Observation. With simple assumptions, hypotheses (1) and (2) can be shown to be trivially true given that D' and D are idd samples from a single finite distribution $\mathcal{D}$.

Proof.

1. For any rule $X \rightarrow y$ and test set D, $\varepsilon(X \rightarrow y, D) = \varepsilon(X \rightarrow y, X(D))$, as $X \rightarrow y$ only covers instances $X(D)$ of D.
2. $\varepsilon(Z \rightarrow y, D) = \frac{E(Z \rightarrow y, Z(D \cap D')) + E(Z \rightarrow y, Z(D - D'))}{|Z(D)|}$
3. $\varepsilon(W \rightarrow y, D) = \frac{E(W \rightarrow y, W(D \cap D')) + E(W \rightarrow y, W(D - D'))}{|W(D)|}$
4. $Z(D) \subseteq W(D)$ because Z is a specialization of W.

---

[1] Recall that both rules have identical empirical support and hence cover the same training cases.

5. $Z(D \cap D') = W(D \cap D')$ because $Z(D') = W(D')$.
6. $Z(D - D') \subseteq W(D - D')$ because $Z(D) \subseteq W(D)$.
7. from 2-6, $E(Z \rightarrow y, Z(D \cap D'))$ is a larger proportion of the error of $Z \rightarrow y$ than is $E(W \rightarrow y, W(D \cap D'))$ of $W \rightarrow y$ and hence performance on D' is a larger component of the performance of $Z \rightarrow y$ and performance on $D - D'$ is a larger component of the performance of $W \rightarrow y$. □

However, in most domains of interest the dimensionality of the instance space will be very high. In consequence, for realistic training and test sets the proportion of the training set that appears in the test set, $\frac{|D \cap D'|}{|D|}$, will be small. Hence this effect will be negligible, as performance on the training set will be a negligible portion of total performance. What we are more interested in is off-training-set error. We contend that the force of these hypotheses will be stronger than accounted for by the difference made by the overlap between training and test sets, and hence that they do apply to off-training-set error. We note, however, that it is trivial to construct no-free-lunch proofs, such as those of Wolpert [5] and Schaffer [6], that this is not, in general, true. Rather, we contend that the hypotheses will in general be true for 'real-world' learning tasks. We justify this contention by recourse to the similarity assumption [7], that in the absence of other information, the greater the similarity between two objects in other respects, the greater the probability of their both belonging to the same class. We believe that most machine learning algorithms depend upon this assumption, and that this assumption is reasonable for real-world knowledge acquisition tasks. Test set cases covered by a more general but not a more specific rule are likely to be less similar to training cases covered by both rules than are test set cases covered by the more specific rule. Hence satisfying the left-hand-side of the more specific rule provides stronger evidence of likely class membership.

A final point that should be noted is that these hypotheses apply to individual classification rules — structures that associate an identified region of an instance space with a single class. However, as will be discussed in more detail below, we believe that the principle is nonetheless highly relevant to 'complete classifiers,' such as decision trees, that assign different regions of the instance space to different classes. This is because each individual region within a 'complete classifier' (such as a decision tree leaf) satisfies our definition of a classification rule, and hence the hypotheses can cast light on the likely consequences of relabeling sub-regions of the instance space within such a classifier (for example, generalizing one leaf of a decision tree at the expense of another, as proposed elsewhere [8]).

2   Evaluation

To evaluate these hypotheses we sought to generate rules of varying generality but identical empirical evidence (no other evidence source being considered in the research), and to test the hypotheses' predictions with respect to these rules.

We wished to provide some evaluation both of whether the predicted effects are general (with respect to rules with the relevant properties selected at random)

Table 1. Algorithm for generating a random rule

1. Randomly select an example x from the training set.
2. Randomly select an attribute a for which the value of a for x (a_x) is not *unknown*.
3. If a is categorical, form the rule $IF\, a = a_x\, THEN\, c$, where c is the most frequent class in the cases covered by $a = a_x$.
4. Otherwise (if a is ordinal), form the rule $IF\, a\# a_x\, THEN\, c$, where $\#$ is a random selection between $\leq$ and $\geq$ and c is the most frequent class in the cases covered by $a\# a_x$.

as well as whether they apply to the type of rule generated in standard machine learning applications. We used rules generated by C4.5rules (release 8) [9], as an exemplar of a machine learning system for classification rule generation.

One difficulty with employing rules formed by C4.5rules is that the system uses a complex resolution system to determine which of several rules should be employed to classify a case covered by more than one rule. As this is taken into account during the induction process, taking a rule at random and considering it in isolation may not be representative of its application in practice. We determined that the first listed rule was least affected by this process, and hence employed it. However, this caused a difficulty in that the first listed rule usually covers few training cases and hence estimates of its likely test error can be expected to have low accuracy, reducing the likely strength of the effect predicted by Hypothesis 2.

For this reason we also employed the C4.5rules rule with the highest cover on the training set. We recognized that this would be unrepresentative of the rule's actual deployment, as in practice cases that it covered would frequently be classified by the ruleset as belonging to other classes. Nonetheless, we believed that it provided an interesting exemplar of a form of rule employed in data mining.

To explore the wider scope of the hypotheses we also generated random rules using the algorithm in Table 1.

From the *initial rule*, formed by one of these three processes, we developed a *most specific rule*. The most specific rule was created by collecting all training cases covered by the initial rule and then forming the most specific rule that covered those cases. For a categorical attribute a this rule included a clause $a \in X$, where X is the set of values for the attribute of cases in the random selection. For ordinal attributes, the rule included a clause of the form $x \leq a \leq z$, where x is the lowest value and z the highest value for the attribute in the random sample.

Next we found the set of all *most general rules*—those rules R formed by deleting clauses from the most specific rule S such that $cover(R) = cover(S)$ and there is no rule T that can be formed by deleting a clause from R such that $cover(T) = cover(R)$. The search for the set of most general rules was performed using the OPUS complete search algorithm [10].

Then we formed the:

Random Most General Rule: a single rule selected at random from the most general rules.

Combined Rule: a rule for which the condition was the conjunction of all conditions for rules in the set of most general rules.

Default Rule: a rule with the antecedent *true*.

For all rules, the class was set to the class with the greatest number of instances covered by the initial rule. All rules other than the default rule covered exactly the same training cases. Hence all rules other than the default rule had identical empirical support.

We present an example to illustrate these concepts. We utilize a two dimensional instance space, defined by two attributes, A and B, and populated by training examples belonging to two classes denoted by the shapes • and ⋆. This is illustrated in Fig. 1. Fig. 1(a) presents the hypothetical initial rule, derived from some external source. Fig. 1(b) shows the most specific rule, the rule that most tightly bounds the cases covered by the initial rule. Note that while we have presented the initial rule as covering only cases of a single class, when developing the rules at differing levels of generality we do not consider class information. Fig. 1(c) and (d) shows the two most general rules that can be formed by deleting

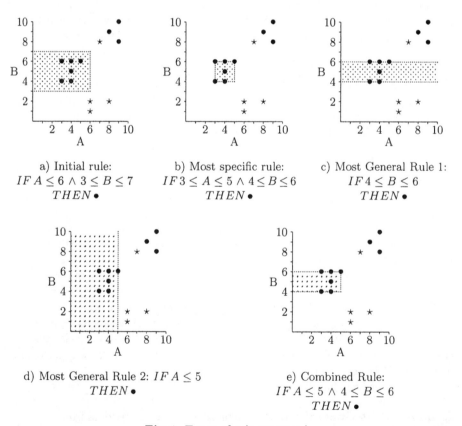

a) Initial rule:
$IF\ A \leq 6 \land 3 \leq B \leq 7$
$THEN \bullet$

b) Most specific rule:
$IF\ 3 \leq A \leq 5 \land 4 \leq B \leq 6$
$THEN \bullet$

c) Most General Rule 1:
$IF\ 4 \leq B \leq 6$
$THEN \bullet$

d) Most General Rule 2: $IF\ A \leq 5$
$THEN \bullet$

e) Combined Rule:
$IF\ A \leq 5 \land 4 \leq B \leq 6$
$THEN \bullet$

Fig. 1. Types of rule generated

Table 2. Generality relationships between rules

More Specific	More General
most specific rule	combined rule
most specific rule	random most general rule
most specific rule	initial rule
combined rule	random most general rule

different combinations of boundaries from the most specific rule. Fig. 1(d) shows the combined rule, formed from the conjunction of all most general rules. The generality relationships between these rules are presented in Table 2.

Note that it could not be guaranteed that any pair of these rules were strictly more general or more specific than each other as it was possible for the most specific and random most general rules to be identical (in which case the set of most general rules would contain only a single rule and the initial and combined rules would also both be identical to the most specific and random most general rules. It was also possible for the initial rule to equal the most specific rule even when there were multiple most general rules. Also, it was possible for no generality relationship to hold between an initial and the combined or the random most general rule developed therefrom.

We wished to evaluate whether the predicted effects held between the rules of differing levels of generality so formed. It was not appropriate to use the normal machine learning experimental method of averaging over multiple runs for each of several data sets, as our prediction is not about relationships between average outcomes, but rather relationships between specific outcomes. Further, it would not be appropriate to perform multiple runs on each of several data sets and then compare the relative frequencies with which the predicted effects held and did not hold, as this would violate the assumption of independence between observations relied on by most statistical tools for assessing such outcomes. Rather, we applied the process once only to each of the following 50 data sets from the UCI repository [11]:

> abalone, anneal, audiology, imports-85, balance-scale, breast-cancer, breast-cancer-wisconsin, bupa, chess, cleveland, crx, dermatology, dis, echocardiogram, german, glass, heart, hepatitis, horse-colic, house-votes-84, hungarian, allhypo, ionosphere, iris, kr-vs-kp, labor-negotiations, lenses, long-beach-va, lung-cancer, lymphography, new-thyroid, optdigits, page-blocks, pendigits, pima-indians-diabetes, post-operative, promoters, primary-tumor, sat, segmentation, shuttle, sick, sonar, soybean-large, splice, switzerland, tic-tac-toe, vehicle, waveform, wine.

These were all appropriate data sets from the repository to which we had ready access and to which we were able to apply the combination of software tools employed in the research. Note that there is no averaging of results. Statistical analysis of the outcomes over the large number of data sets is used to compensate for random effects in individual results due to the use of a single run.

3   Results

Results are presented in Tables 3 to 5. Each table row represents one of the combinations of a more specific and more general rule. The right-most columns present win/draw/loss summaries of the number of times the relevant difference between values is respectively positive, equal, or negative. The first of these columns relates to Hypothesis 1. The second relates to Hypothesis 2. Each win/draw/loss record is followed by the outcome of a one-tailed sign test representing the probability of obtaining those results by chance. Where rules **x** and **y** are identical for a data set, or where one of the rules made no decisions on the unseen data, no result has been recorded. Hence not all win/draw/loss records sum to 50.

Table 3. Results for initial rule is C4.5rules rule with most coverage

x	**y**	$\|\alpha - x\| > \|\alpha - y\|$ w:d:l	p	$\|\beta - x\| < \|\beta - y\|$ w:d:l	p
Most Specific	Combined	27:15: 5	< 0.001	21:15:11	0.055
Most Specific	Random MG	29:14: 4	< 0.001	23:14:10	0.017
Most Specific	Initial	33:10: 4	< 0.001	28:10: 9	0.001
Combined	Random MG	8: 9: 0	0.004	8: 9: 0	0.004

Note: x represents the accuracy of rule **x** on the test data. y represents the accuracy of rule **y** on the test data. β represents the accuracy of rules **x** and **y** on the training data (both rules cover the same training cases and hence have identical accuracy on the training data). α represents the accuracy of the default rule on the test data.

Table 4. Results for initial rule is C4.5rules first rule

x	**y**	$\|\alpha - x\| > \|\alpha - y\|$ w:d:l	p	$\|\beta - x\| < \|\beta - y\|$ w:d:l	p
Most Specific	Combined	16:13: 9	0.115	17:13: 8	0.054
Most Specific	Random MG	19:10: 9	0.044	20:10: 8	0.018
Most Specific	Initial	20: 9: 9	0.031	21: 9: 8	0.012
Combined	Random MG	5: 5: 1	0.109	5: 5: 1	0.109

See Table 3 for abbreviations.

Table 5. Results for initial rule is random rule

x	**y**	$\|\alpha - x\| > \|\alpha - y\|$ w:d:l	p	$\|\beta - x\| < \|\beta - y\|$ w:d:l	p
Most Specific	Combined	26: 5:12	0.017	21: 5:17	0.314
Most Specific	Random MG	26: 5:12	0.017	21: 5:17	0.314
Most Specific	Initial	26: 5:12	0.017	21: 5:17	0.314
Combined	Random MG	0: 2: 1	1.000	1: 2: 0	1.000

See Table 3 for abbreviations.

As can be seen from Table 3, with respect to the conditions formed by creating an initial rule from the C4.5rules rule with the greatest cover, all win/draw/loss comparisons but one significantly (at the 0.05 level) support the hypotheses. The one exception is marginally significant ($p = 0.055$).

Where the initial rule is the first rule from a C4.5rules rule list (Table 4), all win/draw/loss records favor the hypotheses, but some results are not significant at the 0.05 level. It is plausible to attribute this outcome to greater unpredictability in the estimates obtained from the performance of the rules on the training data when the rules cover fewer training cases, and due to the lower numbers of differences in rules formed in this condition.

Where the initial rule is a random rule (Table 5), all of the results favor the hypotheses, except for one comparison between the combined and random most general rules for which a difference in prediction accuracy was only obtained on one of the fifty data sets. Where more than one difference in prediction accuracy was obtained, the results are significant at the 0.05 level with respect to Hypothesis 1, but not Hypothesis 2.

These results appear to lend substantial support to Hypothesis 1. For all but one comparison (for which only one domain resulted in a variation in performance between treatments) the win/draw/loss record favors this hypothesis. Of these eleven positive results, nine are statistically significant at the 0.05 level. There appears to be good evidence that of two rules with equal empirical and other support, the more general can be expected to obtain prediction accuracy on unseen data that is closer to the frequency with which the class is represented in the data.

The evidence with respect to Hypothesis 2 is slightly less strong, however. All conditions result in the predicted effect occurring more often than the reverse. However, only five of these results are statistically significant at the 0.05 level. The results are consistent with an effect that is weak where the accuracy of the rules on the training data differs substantially from the accuracy of the rules on unseen data. An alternative interpretation is that they are manifestations of an effect that only applies under specific constraints that are yet to be identified.

4   Discussion

We believe that our findings have important implications for knowledge acquisition. We have demonstrated that in the absence of other suitable biases to select between alternative hypotheses, biases based on generality can manipulate expected classification performance. Where a rule is able to achieve high accuracy on the training data, our results suggest that very specific versions of the rule will tend to deliver higher accuracy on unseen cases than will more general alternatives with identical empirical support. However, there is another trade-off that will also be inherent in selecting between two such alternatives. The more specific rule will make fewer predictions on unseen cases.

Clearly this trade-off between expected accuracy and cover will be difficult to manage in many applications and we do not provide general advice as to how this should be handled. However, we contend that practitioners are better off aware of this trade-off than making decisions in ignorance of their consequences.

Pazzani, Murphy, Ali, and Schulenburg [12] have argued with empirical support that where a classifier has an option of not making predictions (such as when used for identification of market trading opportunities), selection of more specific rules can be expected to create a system that makes fewer decisions of higher expected quality. Our hypotheses provide an explanation of this result. When the accuracy of the rules on the training data is high, specializing the rules can be expected to raise their accuracy on unseen data towards that obtained on the training data.

Where a classifier must always make decisions and maximization of prediction accuracy is desired, our results suggest that rules for the class that occurs most frequently should be generalized at the expense of rules for alternative classes. This is because as each rule is generalized it will trend towards the accuracy of a default rule for that class, which will be highest for rules of the most frequently occurring class.

Another point that should be considered, however, is alternative sources of information that might be brought to bear upon such decisions. We have emphasized that our hypotheses relate only to contexts in which there is no other evidence available to distinguish between the expected accuracy of two rules other than their relative generality. In many cases we believe it may be possible to derive such evidence from training data. For example, we are likely to have differing expectations about the likely accuracy of the two alternative generalizations depicted in Fig. 2. This figure depicts a two dimensional instance space, defined by two attributes, A and B, and populated by training examples belonging to two classes denoted by the shapes • and ⋆. Three alternative rules are presented together with the region of the instance space that each covers. In this example it appears reasonable to expect better accuracy from the rule depicted in Fig. 2b than that depicted in Fig. 2c as the former generalizes toward a region of the instance space dominated by the same class as the rule whereas the latter generalizes toward a region of the instance space dominated by a different class.

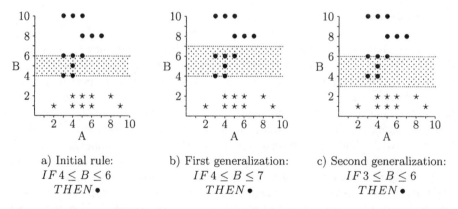

a) Initial rule:
$IF\ 4 \leq B \leq 6$
$THEN\ •$

b) First generalization:
$IF\ 4 \leq B \leq 7$
$THEN\ •$

c) Second generalization:
$IF\ 3 \leq B \leq 6$
$THEN\ •$

Fig. 2. Alternative generalizations to a rule

While our experiments have been performed in a machine learning context, the results are applicable in wider knowledge acquisition contexts. For example, interactive knowledge acquisition environments [3, 13] present users with alternative rules all of which perform equally well on example data. Where the user is unable to bring external knowledge to bear to make an informed judgement about the relative merits of those rules, the system is able to offer no further advice. Our experiments suggest that relative generality is a factor that an interactive knowledge acquisition system might profitably utilize.

Our experiments also demonstrate that the effect that we discuss is one that applies frequently in real-world knowledge acquisition tasks. The alternative rules used in our experiments were all rules of varying levels of generality that covered exactly the same training instances. In other words, it was not possible to distinguish between these rules using traditional measures of rule quality based on performance on a training set, such as information measures. The only exception was the data sets for which the rules at differing levels of generality were all identical. In all such cases the results were excluded from the win/draw/loss record reported in Tables 3 to 5. Hence the sum of the values in each win/draw/loss record places a lower bound on the number of data sets for which there were variants of the initial rule all of which covered the same training instances. Thus, for at least 47 out of 50 data sets, there are variants of the C4.5rules rule with the greatest cover that cover exactly the same training cases. For at least 38 out of 50 data sets, there are variants of the first rule generated by C4.5rules that cover exactly the same training cases. This effect is not a hypothetical abstraction, it is a frequent occurrence of immediate practical import.

In such circumstances, when it is necessary to select between alternative rules with equal performance on the training data, one approach has been to select the least complex rule [14]. However, some recent authors have argued that complexity is not an effective rule quality metric [8, 15]. We argue here that generality provides an alternative criterion on which to select between such rules, one that allows for reasoning about the trade-offs inherent in the choice of one rule over the other, rather than providing a blanket prescription.

5   On the Difficulty of Measuring Degree of Generalization

It might be tempting to believe that our hypotheses could be extended by introducing a measure of magnitude of generalization together with predictions about the magnitude of the effects on prediction accuracy that may be expected from generalizations of different magnitude.

However, we believe that it is not feasible to develop meaningful measures of magnitude of generalization suitable for such a purpose. Consider, for example, the possibility of generalizing a rule with conditions *age* < 40 and *income* < 50000 by deleting either condition. Which is the greater generalization? It might be thought that the greater generalization is the one that covers the greater number of cases. However, if one rule covers more cases than another then there will be differing evidence in support of each. Our hypotheses do not relate to this situation. We are interested only in how to select between alternative rules when the only source of evidence about their relative prediction performance is their relative generality.

If it is not possible to develop measures of magnitude of generalization then it appears to follow that it will never be possible to extend our hypotheses to provide more specific predictions about the magnitude of the effects that may be expected from a given generalization or specialization to a rule.

6   Conclusion

We have presented two hypotheses relating to expectations regarding the accuracy of two alternative classification rules with identical supporting evidence other than their relative generality. The first hypothesis is that the accuracy on unseen data of the more general rule will be more likely to be closer to the accuracy on unseen data of a default rule for the class than will the accuracy on unseen data of the more specific rule. The second hypothesis is that the accuracy on previously unseen data of the more specific rule will be more likely to be closer to the accuracy of the rules on the training data than will the accuracy of the more general rule on unseen data.

We have provided experimental support for those hypotheses, both with respect to classification rules formed by C4.5rules and random classification rules. However, the results with respect to the second hypothesis were not statistically significant in the case of random rules. These results are consistent with the two hypotheses, albeit with the effect of the second being weak when there is low accuracy for the error estimate for a rule derived from performance on the training data. They are also consistent with the second hypothesis only applying to a limited class of rule types. Further research into this issue is warranted.

These results may provide a first step towards the development of useful learning biases based on rule generality that do not rely upon prior domain knowledge, and may be sensitive to alternative knowledge acquisition objectives, such as trading-off accuracy for cover. Our experiments demonstrated the frequent existence of rule variants between which traditional rule quality metrics, such as an information measures, could not distinguish. This shows that the effect that we discuss is not an abstract curiosity but rather is an issue of immediate practical concern.

Acknowledgements

We are grateful to the UCI repository donors and librarians for providing the data sets used in this research. The breast-cancer, lymphography and primary-tumor data sets were donated by M. Zwitter and M. Soklic of the University Medical Centre, Institute of Oncology, Ljubljana, Yugoslavia.

References

1. Mitchell, T.M.: Version spaces: A candidate elimination approach to rule learning. In: Proceedings of the Fifth International Joint Conference on Artificial Intelligence. (1977) 305–310
2. Mitchell, T.M.: The need for biases in learning generalizations. Technical Report CBM-TR-117, Rutgers University, Department of Computer Science, New Brunswick, NJ (1980)
3. Webb, G.I.: Integrating machine learning with knowledge acquisition through direct interaction with domain experts. Knowledge-Based Systems 9 (1996) 253–266
4. Webb, G.I., Wells, J., Zheng, Z.: An experimental evaluation of integrating machine learning with knowledge acquisition. Machine Learning 35 (1999) 5–24
5. Wolpert, D.H.: On the connection between in-sample testing and generalization error. Complex Systems 6 (1992) 47–94
6. Schaffer, C.: A conservation law for generalization performance. In: Proceedings of the 1994 International Conference on Machine Learning, Morgan Kaufmann (1994)
7. Rendell, L., Seshu, R.: Learning hard concepts through constructive induction: Framework and rationale. Computational Intelligence 6 (1990) 247–270
8. Webb, G.I.: Further experimental evidence against the utility of Occam's razor. Journal of Artificial Intelligence Research 4 (1996) 397–417
9. Quinlan, J.R.: C4.5: Programs for Machine Learning. Morgan Kaufmann, San Mateo, CA (1993)
10. Webb, G.I.: OPUS: An efficient admissible algorithm for unordered search. Journal of Artificial Intelligence Research 3 (1995) 431–465
11. Blake, C., Merz, C.J.: UCI repository of machine learning databases. [Machine-readable data repository]. University of California, Department of Information and Computer Science, Irvine, CA. (2004)
12. Pazzani, M.J., Murphy, P., Ali, K., Schulenburg, D.: Trading off coverage for accuracy in forecasts: Applications to clinical data analysis. In: Proceedings of the AAAI Symposium on Artificial Intelligence in Medicine. (1994) 106–110
13. Compton, P., Edwards, G., Srinivasan, A., Malor, R., Preston, P., Kang, B., Lazarus, L.: Ripple down rules: Turning knowledge acquisition into knowledge maintenance. Artificial Intelligence in Medicine 4 (1992) 47–59
14. Blumer, A., Ehrenfeucht, A., Haussler, D., Warmuth, M.K.: Occam's Razor. Information Processing Letters 24 (1987) 377–380
15. Domingos, P.: The role of Occam's razor in knowledge discovery. Data Mining and Knowledge Discovery 3 (1999) 409–425

Visualisation and Exploration of Scientific Data Using Graphs

Ben Raymond and Lee Belbin

Australian Government, Department of the Environment and Heritage,
Australian Antarctic Division, Channel Highway,
Kingston 7050, Australia
ben.raymond@aad.gov.au

Abstract. We present a prototype application for graph-based exploration and mining of online databases, with particular emphasis on scientific data. The application builds structured graphs that allow the user to explore patterns in a data set, including clusters, trends, outliers, and relationships. A number of different graphs can be rapidly generated, giving complementary insights into a given data set. The application has a Flash-based graphical interface and uses semantic information from the data sources to keep this interface as intuitive as possible. Data can be accessed from local and remote databases and files. Graphs can be explored using an interactive visual browser, or graph-analytic algorithms. We demonstrate the approach using marine sediment data, and show that differences in benthic species compositions in two Antarctic bays are related to heavy metal contamination.

1   Introduction

Structured graphs have been recognised as an effective framework for scientific data mining — e.g. [1, 2]. A graph consists of a set of nodes connected by edges. In the simplest case, each node represents an entity of interest, and edges between nodes represent relationships between entities. Graphs thus provide a natural framework for investigating relational, spatial, temporal, and geometric data [2], and give insights into clusters, trends, outliers, and other structures. Graphs have also seen a recent explosion in popularity in science, as network structures have been found in a variety of fields, including social networks [3, 4], trophic webs [5], and the structures of chemical compounds [6, 7]. Networks in these fields provide both a natural representation of data, as well as analytical tools that give insights not easily gained from other perspectives.

The Australian Antarctic Data Centre (AADC) sought a graph-based visualisation and exploration tool that could be used both as a component of in-house mining activities, as well as by clients undertaking scientific analyses.

The broad requirements of this tool were:

1. *Provide functionality to construct, view, and explore graph structures, and apply graph-theoretic algorithms.*

G.J. Williams and S.J. Simoff (Eds.): Data Mining, LNAI 3755, pp. 14–27, 2006.

2. *Able to access and integrate data from a number of sources.* Data of interest typically fall into one of three categories:
   - databases within the AADC (e.g. biodiversity, automatic weather stations, and state of the environment reporting databases). These databases are developed and maintained by the AADC, and so have a consistent structure and are directly accessible.
   - flat data files (including external remote sensed environmental data such as sea ice concentration [8], data collected and held by individual scientists, and data files held in the AADC that have not yet been migrated into actively-maintained databases).
   - web-accessible (external) databases. Several initiatives are under way that will enable scientists to share data across the web (e.g. GBIF [9]).
3. *Be web browser-based.* A browser-based solution would allow the tool to be integrated with the AADC's existing web pages, and thus allow clients to explore the data sets before downloading. It would also allow any bandwidth-intensive activities to be carried out at the server end, an important consideration for scientists on Antarctic bases wishing to use the tool.
4. *Have an intuitive graphical interface* (suitable for a general audience) that would also provide sufficient flexibility for more advanced users (expected to be mostly internal scientists).
5. *Integrated with the existing AADC database structure.* To allow the interface to be as simple as possible, we needed to make use of the existing data structures and environments in the AADC. For example, the AADC keeps a data dictionary, which provides limited semantic information about AADC data, including the measurement scale type (nominal, ordinal, interval, or ratio) of a variable. This information would allow the application to make informed processing decisions (such as which dissimilarity metric or measure of central tendency to use for a particular variable) and thus minimise the complexity of the interface.

A large number of software packages and algorithms for graph-based data visualisation have been published, and a summary of a selection of graph software is presented in Table 1 (an exhaustive review of all available graph software is beyond the scope of this paper). Existing software that we were aware of met some but not all of our requirements. The key feature that seemed to be missing from available packages was the ability to construct a graph directly from a data source (i.e. to create a graph that provides a graphical portrayal of the information contained in a data source). Two notable exceptions are GGobi [10] and Zoomgraph [11]. However, GGobi is intended as a general-purpose data visualisation, and has relatively limited support for structured (nodes and edges) graphs. Zoomgraph's graph construction is driven by scripting commands. For our general audience, we desired that the graph construction be driven by a graphical interface, and not require the user to have any knowledge of scripting or database (e.g. SQL) commands.

This paper describes a prototype tool that implements the requirements listed above. The key novelty of this tool is the ability to rapidly generate a graph

Table 1. A functional summary of a selection of graph software. BG: the package provides functionality for constructing graphs from tabular or other data (manual graph construction excluded); DB,WS: direct access to data from databases/web services; L&D: provides tools for the layout and display of graphs; A: provides algorithms for the statistical analysis of graphs; Int.: interface type; BB: is web browser-based. †Small graphs only. ‡Designed for large graphs. *Limited functionality when run as an applet.

Package	BG	DB	WS	L&D	A	Int.	BB	Summary
GGobi[10]	✓	✓	✗	✓†	✗	GUI	✗	General data visualisation system with some graph capabilities
Zoomgraph[11]	✓	✓	✗	✓‡	✓	Text	✓*	Zoomable viewer with database-driven back end
UCINET[29]	✓			✓	✓	GUI	✗	Popular social network analysis package
Pajek[28]	✗			✓‡	✓	GUI	✗	Analysis and visualization of large networks
Tulip[32]	✗			✓‡	✓	GUI	✗	Large graph layout and visualisation
LGL[33]	✗			✓‡	✗	GUI	✓	Large graph layout
GraphViz [34]	✗			✓	✗	Text	✗	Popular layout package
SUBDUE[14]	✗			✗	✓	Text	✗	Subgraph analysis package

structure from a set of data, without requiring SQL or other scripting commands. The tool can be used to create and explore graph structures from a variety of data sources. The graphical interface has been written as a Flash application; the server-side code is written in ColdFusion (our primary application development environment). The interface can also accept text-based commands for users wishing additional flexibility.

2   Methods

The exploratory analysis process can be divided into three main stages — graph construction; visual, interactive exploration; and the application of specific analytical algorithms. In practice, these components would be used in an interactive, cyclical exploratory process. We discuss each of these aspects in turn.

2.1   Graph Construction

Currently, data can be accessed from one or more local or remote databases (local in this context means "within the AADC") or user files. Accessing multiple data sources allows a user to integrate their data with other databases, but is predictably made difficult by heterogeneity across sources. We extract data from local databases using SQL statements; either directly or mediated by graphical widgets. Local files can be uploaded using http/get and are expected to be in comma-separated text format. Users are encouraged to use standardised column names (as defined by the AADC data dictionary), allowing the semantic advantages of the data dictionary to be realised for file data. Remote databases can be accessed using web services. Initially we have provided access only to GBIF data [9] through the DiGIR protocol. Data from web service sources are described by XML schema, which can be used in a similar manner to the data dictionary to provide limited semantic information.

To construct a graph representation of these data, the user must specify which variables are to be used to form the nodes, and a means of forming edges between nodes. Nodes are formed from the discrete values (or n-tuples) of one or more variables in the database. The graphical interface provides a list of available data sources, and once a data source is selected, a list of all variables provided by that data source. This information comes from the column names in a user file or database table, or from the "concepts" list of a DiGIR XML resource file. Available semantic information is used to decide how to discretise the node variables. Continuous variables need to be discretised to form individual nodes. A simple equal-interval binning option is provided for this purpose. Categorical or ordinal (i.e. discrete) variables need no discretisation, and so this dialogue is not shown unless necessary.

Once defined, each node is assigned a set of attribute data. These data are potentially drawn from all other columns in the database. The graphical interface allows attribute data to be drawn from a different data source provided that the sources can be joined using a single variable. More complex joins can be achieved using text commands. Attribute data are used to create the connectivity of the graph. Nodes that share attribute values are connected by edges, which are optionally weighted to reflect the strength of the linkage between the nodes. The application automatically chooses a weighting scheme that is appropriate to the attribute data type; this choice can be overridden by the user if desired.

Once data sources and variables have been defined, the application parses the node attributes to create edges, and builds an XML (in fact GXL, [12]) document that describes the graph. The graph can be either visually explored, or processed with one of many graph-based analytic algorithms.

2.2   Graph Visualisation

Graph structures are displayed to the user in an interactive graph browser. The browser is a modified version of the Touchgraph LinkBrowser [13], which is an open-source Java tool for graph layout and interaction. Layout is accomplished using a spring-model method, in which each edge is considered to be a spring, and the node positions are chosen to minimise the global energy of the spring system. Nodes also have mutual repulsion in order to avoid overlap in the layout.

While small graphs can reasonably be displayed in their entirety, large graphs often cannot be displayed in a comprehensible form on limited screen real estate. We solve this problem by allowing large graphs to be explored as a dynamic series of smaller graphs (see below). We discuss alternative approaches, such as hierarchical views with varying level of detail, in the discussion.

Interaction with the user is achieved through three main processes: node selection, neighbourhood adjustment, and edge manipulation. The displayed graph is focused on a selected node. The neighbourhood setting determines how much of the surrounding graph is displayed at any one time. This mechanism allows local regions of a graph to be displayed. Edge manipulation can be done using a slider that sets the weight threshold below which edges are not displayed. It is difficult to judge *a priori* which edges to filter out, as weak edges can obscure the graph structure in some cases but may be crucial in others. A practical solution is to create a graph with relatively high connectivity (many weak links), and then allow the user to remove links in an interactive manner.

The graph layout is done dynamically, and changes smoothly as the user varies the interactive settings. The graph layout uses various visual properties of the nodes and edges to convey information, including colour, shape, label, and mouse-over popup windows. We also allow attributes of the nodes to set the graph layout. This is particularly useful with spatial and temporal data.

An alternative visualisation option is to save the XML document and import it into the user's preferred graph software. This might be appropriate with extremely large graphs, since this visualisation tool does not work well with such graphs.

2.3   Analytical Tools

The fields of graph theory and data mining have developed a range of algorithms that assess specific properties of graph structures, including subgraph analyses (e.g. [14, 15, 16, 17, 18]), connectivity and flow [7], graph simplification [5, 19], clustering, and outlier detection [20, 21]. Many of the properties assessed by these tools have interpretations in terms of real-world phenomena (e.g. [22, 23, 24]) that are not easily assessed from non-graph representations of the data. These provide useful analytical information to complement existing scientific analyses, and also the possibility of building graphs based on analyses of other graphs.

A simple but very useful example is an operator that allows the similarity between two graphs to be calculated. We use an edge-matching metric, equal to the number of edges that appear in both graphs, as a fraction of the total number of unique edges in the two graphs (an edge is considered to appear in both graphs if the same two nodes appear in both graphs, and they are joined by an edge in both graphs). This provides a simple method for exploring the relationships between graphs, and also a mechanism for creating graphs of graphs: given a set of graphs, one can construct another graph $\mathcal{G}$ in which each graph in the set is represented by a node. Using a graph similarity operator, one can calculate the similarity between each pair of graphs in the set, and use this similarity information to create weighted edges between the nodes in $\mathcal{G}$. The visualisation tool allows a node in a graph to be hyperlinked to another graph, so that each node in a graph of graphs can be explored in its own right. We demonstrate these ideas in the Results section, below.

We have chosen not to implement other algorithms at this stage, concentrating instead on the graph construction and visual exploratory aspects. We raise future algorithm development options in the Discussion section, below.

3   Results

We use a small Antarctic data set to demonstrate the graph construction and visualisation tools in the context of an exploratory scientific investigation.

Australia has an on-going research programme into the environmental impacts of human occupation in Antarctica (see http://www.aad.gov.au/default.asp?casid=13955). A recent component of this programme was an investigation into the relationships between benthic species assemblages and pollution near Australia's Casey station [25]. Marine sediment samples were collected from two sites in Brown Bay, which is adjacent to a disused rubbish tip and is known to have high levels of many contaminants. Samples were collected at approximately 30 m and 150 m from the tip. Control samples were collected from two sites in nearby, uncontaminated O'Brien Bay. Four replicate samples were collected from two plots at each site, giving a total of 32 samples. Sediment samples were collected by divers using plastic corers and analysed for fauna (generally identified to species or genus level) and heavy metal concentrations (Pb, Cd, Zn, As, Cr, Cu, Fe, Ni, Ag, Sn, Sb). These metals are found in man-made products (e.g. batteries and steel alloys) and can be used as indicators of anthropogenic contamination. Details of the experimental methods are given in [25].

This data set has a very simple structure, comprising a total of 14 variables: site_name, species_id, species_abundance, and measured concentrations of the 11 metals listed above. Site latitude and longitude were not recorded but the site_name string provides information to the site/plot/replicate level (see Fig. 1 caption). All of the above information appears in one database table. The species_id identifier links to the AADC's central biodiversity database, which provides additional information about each species (although we do not use this additional information in the example presented here). Standard practice would normally also see a separate table for the sample site details, but in this case there are only a small number of sample sites that are specific to this data set.

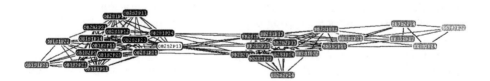

Fig. 1. A graph of Antarctic marine sample sites, linked by their species attribute data. Sites can be separated into two clusters on the basis of their species, indicating two distinct types of species assemblage. The white node is the "focus" node (see text); other colours indicate the number of distinct species within a site, ranging from grey (low) to black (high). Sites from contaminated Brown Bay (*right cluster*) have less species (less diversity) than sites from uncontaminated O'Brien Bay (*left cluster*). Node labels are of the form *XBySsPpr* and denote the position of the sample in the nested experimental hierarchy. BB*y* denotes samples from one of two locations in Brown Bay and OB*y* denotes O'Brien Bay; *s* denotes the site number within location; *p* denotes the plot number within site; and *r* denotes the core replicate number within plot.

Despite the simplicity of the data set, there are a large number of graphs that can be generated. The key questions to be answered during the original investigation related to spatial patterns in species assemblages, and the relationships of any such patterns to contamination (heavy metal concentrations).

Spatial patterns in species assemblages can be explored using sites as nodes, and edges generated on the basis of species attribute data. To create this graph, we needed only to select site_name as entities, and species_id as attributes in the graphical interface. Both of these variables were recognised by the data dictionary as categorical, and so no discretisation was needed. An edge weighting function suitable for species data was selected. This function is based on the Bray-Curtis dissimilarity, which is commonly used with ecological data:

$$w_{ij} = 1 - \sum_k \frac{|x_{ik} - x_{jk}|}{(x_{ik} + x_{jk})} \; , \tag{1}$$

where w_{ij} denotes the weight of the edge from node i to node j, and x_{ik} denotes the kth attribute of node i.

The resultant graph is shown in Fig. 1. Weak edges have been pruned, leaving a core structure of two distinct clusters of sites: the left-hand cluster corresponds to sites from O'Brien Bay; the right-hand cluster Brown Bay. This strong clustering suggests that the species assemblages of the two bays are distinct. As well as this broad two-cluster structure, the graph provides other information about the species composition of the sites. Each cluster shows spatial autocorrelation — that is, samples from a given site in a given bay are most similar to other samples from the same site (e.g. BB3 nodes are generally linked to other BB3 nodes). The colouring of the nodes reflects the number of species within a site (grey=low, black=high), and indicates that the contaminated Brown Bay sites have less species diversity than the uncontaminated O'Brien Bay sites.

An alternative view of the data can be generated by swapping the definitions for entity and attribute, giving a graph of species_id nodes with edges calculated on the basis of site_id attribute data. Fig. 2 shows four snapshots of this graph. These were captured during an interactive exploration of the graph, during which weak edges were progressively removed from the graph. The sequence of graphs shows the emergence of two clusters of nodes within the graph, and confirms the presence of two broad species assemblages. However, the most commonly-observed species (darkest node colours) lie in the centre of the graph, with two sets of less-commonly observed species on the left and right peripheries of the graph. This indicates that the central species are seen across a range of sites (and hence have links to the majority of species) whereas the species on the peripheries of the graph are seen at restricted sets of sites. This may have implications if we wish to characterise the environmental niches of species. We can investigate further by interactively adjusting the visible neighbourhood of the graph. Fig. 3a shows the same graph as Fig. 2b but focused on the *GammIIA* species node, and with only the immediate neighbours of that node made visible. This species has direct links to only four other species, and was seen at relatively few sites. This suggests that *GammIIA* might only be present in certain

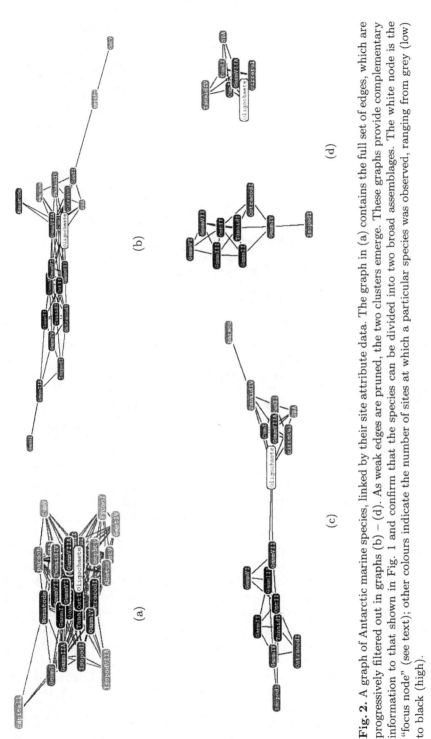

Fig. 2. A graph of Antarctic marine species, linked by their site attribute data. The graph in (a) contains the full set of edges, which are progressively filtered out in graphs (b) – (d). As weak edges are pruned, the two clusters emerge. These graphs provide complementary information to that shown in Fig. 1 and confirm that the species can be divided into two broad assemblages. The white node is the "focus node" (see text); other colours indicate the number of sites at which a particular species was observed, ranging from grey (low) to black (high).

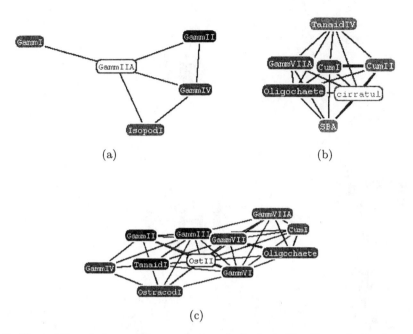

Fig. 3. Three different views of the species graph shown in Fig. 2b, each showing only the immediate neighbours of the focus node. (a) and (b) are focused on *GammIIA* and *cirratul*, species from the periphery of the original graph, while (c) is focused on the more central *OstII*. The white node is the "focus node" (see text); other colours indicate the number of sites at which a particular species was observed, ranging from grey (low) to black (high). *GammIIA* and *cirratul* have fewer neighbours and were seen at fewer sites than *OstII*, indicating that *OstII* is less specialised in its preferred environment than *GammIIA* and *cirratul*.

environmental conditions. A similar argument applies to *cirratul* (Fig. 3b). However, those species that are more central in the graph (e.g. *OstII*) are connected to many other species and were seen at many sites and are therefore less specialised in terms of their preferred environment.

Having established some patterns in species assemblages, we wish to explore the relationships between these patterns and measured metal contamination. A convenient method for this is through the graph similarity operator. We generated a second graph of sites, using chromium as attribute data (graph not shown), and made an edge-wise weight comparison between the site-species graph and the site-chromium graph. The result is shown in Fig. 4. The structure of this graph is identical to that in Fig. 1, but the colouring of the edges indicates the weight similarity. Darker grey indicates edges that have similar weights in both the site-species and site-chromium graphs. Edges within the O'Brien Bay and Brown Bay clusters are generally well explained by chromium (i.e. similar within-cluster chromium values). More notably, the edges linking the O'Brien Bay cluster to the Brown Bay cluster are not well explained in terms of chromium. Similar results were obtained using the other metal variables,

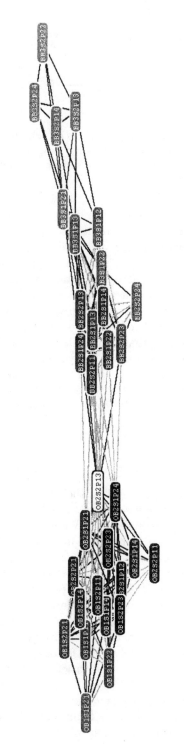
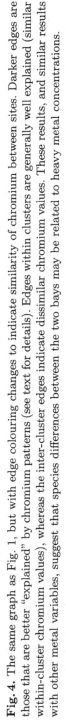

Fig. 4. The same graph as Fig. 1, but with edge colouring changes to indicate similarity of chromium between sites. Darker edges are those that are better "explained" by chromium patterns (see text for details). Edges within clusters are generally well explained (similar within-cluster chromium values), whereas the inter-cluster edges indicate dissimilar chromium values. These results, and similar results with other metal variables, suggest that species differences between the two bays may be related to heavy metal concentrations.

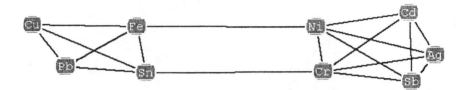

Fig. 5. A graph of graphs. Each node represents an entire subgraph — in this case, a graph of sites linked by a metal attribute. This graph of graphs indicates that the spatial distributions of copper, lead, iron, and tin are similar, and different to those of nickel, chromium, and the other metals.

supporting the notion that the differences in the benthic species assemblages of these bays is related to heavy metal contamination.

Finally, we use a graph of graphs to explore the similarities between the spatial patterns of the various heavy metals. We generated 11 graphs, one for each metal, using sites as entities and the metal as attribute data. The pairwise similarities between each of these graphs were calculated. Fig. 5 shows the resultant graph, in which each node represents an entire site-metal graph, and the edges indicate the similarities between those graphs. The graph suggests that copper, lead, iron, and tin are distributed similarly, and that their distribution is different to that of nickel, chromium, and the other metals. This was confirmed by inspecting histograms of metal values at each location: values of copper, lead, iron, and tin were higher at one of the Brown Bay locations (the one closest to the tip) than the other, whereas the remaining metals showed similar levels at each of the two Brown Bay locations.

4   Discussion

Graphs have been previously been recognised for their value in data mining and exploratory analyses. However, existing software tools for such analyses (that we were aware of) did not meet our requirements. We have outlined a prototype web-based tool that builds graph structures from data contained in databases or files, and presents the graphs for visual exploration or algorithmic analysis.

The construction phase requires the user to define the variables that will be used to form the graph nodes. While there may be certain definitions that are logical or intuitive in the context of a particular database (for example, it is probably intuitive to think of species as nodes when exploring a database of wildlife observations), the nodes can in fact be an arbitrary combination of any of the available variables. This is a powerful avenue for interaction and flexibility, as allows the user to interpret the data from a variety of viewpoints, a key to successful data mining.

Our interest in graph-based data mining is focused on relatively small graphs (tens to hundreds of nodes). This is somewhat unusual for graph-based data mining, which often looks to accomodate graphs of thousands or even millions of nodes. Our focus on small graphs is driven by our application to Antarctic scientific data. Such data are extremely costly to acquire and so many of the data sets that are of interest to us are of relatively small size (generally, tens to thousands of observations). Our goal is to obtain maximum insight into the information provided by these data. This is facilitated by the ability to rapidly generate a number of graphs and interpret a given dataset from a variety of viewpoints,as noted above. Furthermore, the visualisation tool that we have chosen to use provides a high degree of interactivity in terms of the layout of the graph, which further enhances the user's insight into the data. However, this visualisation tool is best suited to relatively small graphs, as the dynamic layout algorithm becomes too slow for more than about a hundred nodes on a standard PC. Other visualisation tools, specifically designed for large graphs (e.g. [19, 26, 27]) might be useful for visualising such graphs. FADE [19] and MGV [26] use hierarchical views that can range from global structure of a graph with little local detail, through to local views with full detail. We note that the constraint on graph size lies with the visualisation tool and not the algorithm that we use to generate the graph from the underlying data. We have successfully used our graph generation procedures on a database of wildlife observations comprising approximately 150000 observations of 30 variables — quite a large data set by Antarctic scientific standards!

One of the notable limitations of our current implementation is the requirement that attribute data be discrete. (Edges are only formed between nodes that have an exact match in one or more attributes). Continuous attributes must be discretised, which is both wasteful of information and can lead to different graph structures with different choices of discretisation method. Discretisation is potentially particularly problematic for Antarctic scientific data sets, which tend not only to be relatively small but also sparse. Sparsity will lead to few exact matches in discretised data, and to graphs that may have too few edges to convey useful information. Future development will therefore focus on continuous attribute data.

Many other packages for graph-based data exploration exist, and we have incorporated the features of some of these into our design. The GGobi package [10] has a plugin that allows users to work directly with databases. GGobi also ties into the open-source statistical package R to provide graph algorithms. Zoomgraph [11] takes the same approach. This is one method of providing graph algorithms without the cost of re-implementation. Another is simply to pass the graph to the user, who can then use one of the many freely-available graph software packages (e.g. [28, 29, 30, 31]). Yet another approach, which we are currently investigating, is the use of analytical web services. Our development has been done in Coldfusion, which can make use of Java and can also expose any function as a web service. This may allow us to deploy functions from an existing Java graph library such as Jung [31] as a set of web services. This approach would have the advantage that external users could also make use of the algorithms, by passing their GXL files via web service calls.

The software discussed in this paper is available from http://aadc-maps. aad.gov.au/analysis/gb.cfm.

References

1. Washio, T., Motoda, H.: State of the art graph-based data mining. SIGKDD Explorations: Newsletter of the ACM Special Interest Group on Knowledge Discovery & Data Mining **5**(1) (2003) 59–68
2. Kuramochi, M., Desphande, M., Karypis, G.: Mining Scientific Datasets Using Graphs. In: Kargupta, H., Joshi, A., Sivakumar, K., and Yesha, Y. (eds): Next Generation Data Mining. MIT/AAAI Press (2003) 315–334
3. Brieger, R.L.: The analysis of social networks. In: Hardy, M., Bryman, A. (eds): Handbook of Data Analysis. SAGE Publications, London (2004) 505–526
4. Lusseau, D., Newman, M.E.J.: Identifying the role that individual animals play in their social networks. Proceedings of the Royal Society of London B **271** (2004) S477–S481
5. Luczkovich, J.J., Borgatti, S.P., Johnson, J.C., and Everett, M.G.: Defining and measuring trophic role similarity in food webs using regular equivalence. Journal of Theoretical Biology **220**(3) (2003) 303–321
6. Yook, S.-H., Oltavai, Z.N., and Barabási, A.-L.: Functional and topological characterization of protein interaction networks. Proteomics **4** (2004) 928–942
7. De Raedt, L., Kramer, S.: The level wise version space algorithm and its application to molecular fragment finding. In: Proceedings of the Seventeenth International Joint Conference on Articial Intelligence. Morgan Kaufmann, San Francisco (2001) 853–862
8. Comiso, J.: Bootstrap sea ice concentrations for NIMBUS-7, SMMR and DMSP SSM/I. Boulder, CO, USA: National Snow and Ice Data Center (1999, updated 2002)
9. Global Biodiversity Information Facility, http://www.gbif.net
10. Swayne, D.F., Buja, A., Temple Lang, D.: Exploratory visual analysis of graphs in GGobi. In: Proceedings of the 3rd International Workshop on Distributed Statistical Computing, Vienna (2003)
11. Adar, E., Tyler, J.R.: Zoomgraph. http://www.hpl.hp.com/research/idl/projects/graphs/
12. Winter, A., Kullbach, B., Riediger, V.: An overview of the GXL graph exchange language. In Diehl, S. (ed.): Software Visualization. Lecture Notes in Computer Science, Vol. 2269. Springer-Verlag, Berlin Heidelberg New York (2002) 324–336
13. Shapiro, A.: Touchgraph. http://www.touchgraph.com
14. Cook, D.J., Holder, L.B.: Graph-based data mining. IEEE Intelligent Systems **15**(2) (2000) 32–41
15. Kuramochi, M., Karypis, G.: Finding frequent patterns in a large sparse graph. In: Berry, M.W., Dayal, U., Kamath, C., Skillicorn, D.B. (eds.): Proceedings of the Fourth SIAM International Conference on Data Mining, Florida, USA. SIAM (2004)
16. Cortes, C., Pregibon, D., Volinsky, C.: Computational methods for dynamic graphs. J. Computational and Graphical Statistics **12** (2003) 950–970
17. Inokuchi, A., Washio, T., Motoda, H.: Complete mining of frequent patterns from graphs: mining graph data. Machine Learning **50** (2003) 321–354
18. Yan, X., Han, J.: CloseGraph: Mining closed frequent graph patterns. In: Getoor, L., Senator, T.E., Domingos, P., Faloutsos, C. (eds.): Proceedings of the Ninth ACM SIGKDD International Conference on Knowledge Discovery and Data Mining, Washington, DC, USA. ACM (2003) 286–295

19. Quigley, A., Eades, P.: FADE: graph drawing, clustering, and visual abstraction. In: Marks, J. (ed.): Proceedings of the 8th International Symposium on Graph Drawing. Lecture Notes in Computer Science, Vol. 1984. Springer-Verlag, Berlin Heidelberg New York (2000) 197–210

20. Shekhar, S., Lu, C.T., Zhang, P.: Detecting graph-based spatial outliers: algorithms and applications (a summary of results). In: Provost, F., Srikant, R. (eds.): Proceedings of the Seventh ACM SIGKDD International Conference on Knowledge Discovery and Data Mining (2001) 371–376

21. Noble, C.C., Cook, D.J.: Graph-based anomaly detection. In: Getoor, L., Senator, T.E., Domingos, P., Faloutsos, C. (eds.): Proceedings of the Ninth ACM SIGKDD International Conference on Knowledge Discovery and Data Mining, Washington, DC, USA. ACM (2003) 631–636

22. Girvan, M., Newman, M.E.J.: Community structure in social and biological networks. Proc. Natl. Acad. Sci. USA **99** (2002) 7821–7826

23. Drossel, B., McKane, A.J.: Modelling food webs. In: Bornholdt, S., Schuster, H.G. (eds.) Handbook of Graphs and Networks: From the Genome to the Internet. Wiley-VCH, Berlin (2003) 218–247

24. Moody, J.: Peer influence groups: identifying dense clusters in large networks. Social Networks **23** (2001) 216–283

25. Stark, J.S., Riddle, M.J., Snape, I., Scouller, R.C.: Human impacts in Antarctic marine soft-sediment assemblages: correlations between multivariate biological patterns and environmental variables at Casey Station. Estuarine, Coastal and Shelf Science **56** (2003) 717–734

26. Abello, J., Korn, J.: MGV: a system for visualizing massive multi-digraphs. IEEE Transactions on Visualization and Computer Graphics **8** (2002) 21–38

27. Wills, G.J.: NicheWorks — interactive visualization of very large graphs. J. Computational and Graphical Statistics **8**(2) (1999) 190–212

28. Batagelj, V., Mrvar, A.: Pajek - Program for Large Network Analysis. http://vlado.fmf.uni-lj.si/pub/networks/pajek/

29. Borgatti, S., Chase, R.: UCINET: social network analysis software. http://www.analytictech.com/ucinet.htm

30. Bongiovanni, B., Choplin, S., Lalande, J.F., Syska, M., Verhoeven, Y.: Mascotte Optimization project. http://www-sop.inria.fr/mascotte/mascopt/index.html

31. White, S., O'Madadhain, J., Fisher, D., Boey, Y.-B.: Java Universal Network/Graph Framework. http://jung.sourceforge.net

32. Auber, D.: Tulip — A Huge Graph Visualization Framework. http://www.tulip-software.org/

33. Adai, A.T., Date, S.V., Wieland, S., Marcotte, E.M.: LGL: creating a map of protein function with an algorithm for visualizing very large biological networks. Journal of Molecular Biology **340**(1) (2004) 179–190

34. Ellson, J., North, S.: Graphviz - Graph Visualization Software. http://www.graphviz.org/

A Case-Based Data Mining Platform

Xingwen Wang and Joshua Zhexue Huang

E-Business Technology Institute,
The University of Hong Kong, Pokfulam Road, Hong Kong
{xwwang, jhuang}@eti.hku.hk

Abstract. Data mining practice in industry heavily depends on experienced data mining professionals to provide solutions. Normal business users cannot easily use data mining tools to solve their business problems, because of the complexity of data mining process and data mining tools. In this paper, we propose a case-based data mining platform, which reuses the knowledge captured in past data mining cases to semi-automatically solve new similar problems. We first extend generic data mining model for knowledge reuse. Then we define data mining case. And then we introduce this platform in detail from its storage bases, functional modules, user interface, and application scenario. Theoretically, this platform can simplify data mining process, reduce the dependency on data mining professional, and shorten business decision time.

Keywords: Data Mining, Knowledge Reuse, Case-Based Reasoning, Case-Based Data Mining Platform.

1 Introduction

Data mining is a technique of extracting useful but implicit knowledge from large amounts of data. It has been widely used to solve business problems, such as, customer segmentation, customer retention, credit scoring, product recommendation, direct marketing campaigns, cross selling, fraud detection, and so on [2]. These problems are ubiquitous in most companies regardless of their size. Data mining has been an important technique applied in current business decision.

Data mining process is not trivial. It consists of many steps, such as, business problem definition, data collection, data preprocessing, modelling, and model deployment [4]. In each step, different techniques may be applied. For example, during the modelling, techniques such as association analysis, decision trees, neural networks, regression, clustering, and time sequence analysis can be used. On the other hand, many commercial data mining tools, such as, Clementine, Enterprise Miner, and Intelligent Miner, have been widely used to solve data mining problems. Even though they have provided user-friendly graphical interfaces to drag-and-drop algorithms to form a processing flow, the prerequisite to successfully conduct a data mining process is that the user should know what those algorithms can do, how to make use of them sequentially, and how to set the parameters.

Because of the complexity of data mining process and data mining tools, normal business users cannot easily use data mining tools to solve their business problems.

G.J. Williams and S.J. Simoff (Eds.): Data Mining, LNAI 3755, pp. 28–38, 2006.

Data mining practice in industry heavily depends on experienced data mining professionals to provide solutions. For the rarity of data mining professionals, data mining practice has become quite expensive and time-consuming.

In this paper, we propose a case-based data mining platform. It makes use of the knowledge captured in past data mining cases to formulate semi-automatic data mining solutions for typical business problems. Knowledge reuse is the key to this case-based data mining platform. In order for knowledge reuse, we should concern the issues, such as, what is the reusable knowledge in data mining process, how to represent the reusable knowledge, and how to take the reusable knowledge into use. In the remainder of this paper, we will first discuss the extensions of generic data mining model for knowledge reuse in Section 2. We will define data mining case in Section 3. In Section 4, we will have a look on this case based data mining platform on its storage base, functional modules, user interface, and application scenario. In the last section, we will give a brief conclusion.

2 Extending Data Mining Model for Knowledge Reuse

Data mining, as a technique, has been investigated for several decades. The generic data mining model can be simply described as using historical data to generate useful model. This generic model has often been extended for certain purposes or in certain application domains. For example, Kotasek and Zendulka [6] have taken domain knowledge into consideration in their data mining model, the MSMiner [11] has integrated ETL and data warehouse into its data mining model, and the CWM [8] has treated data mining as one of its analysis functions. Here, in order for knowledge reuse, we also need to extend this generic data mining model.

The first extension is to relax the algorithms resided in data mining system. That is, data mining algorithms can be externally implemented and can be called by a data mining system. Actually, this kind of extension has been widely implemented in data mining library such as visual basic data mining library [12] and WEKA [14]. The purpose that we recall it here is to show the roadmap of our model's extensions. Meanwhile, in order to relax the dependence of data mining system with its input and output, we use a data base to externally store its input data, and a model base to externally store its output models. Thus, a data mining system has associated a data storage base, an algorithm storage base, and a model storage base.

The second extension is to use processing flows generated in past data mining solutions to solve new similar problems. Even though data mining, as a whole, has its well-understood processing steps, a concrete data mining's processing flow may vary with others when they belong to different industry types, or they have different data mining tasks, or they have different expectations on output model. For example, the process of building a customer classification model for automobile industry may be quite different with the process of building a prediction model for telecommunication industry. This kind of processing flow shows the information, such as, what data have been used in the process, what operators have been involved, what model(s) has been generated, and most importantly, how these data, operators, and model(s) are connected in a sequence. On the contrary, to the applications which have the same industry type, the same data mining task, and the same expectation on output model, the processing flows will be quite similar. Based on these facts, when we deal with a new problem, we can use a similar case's processing flow as template to solve it.

At this time, it is not ready yet to take a past case's processing flow to reuse, because the issue about how to get a right case at right time is not concerned. This issue is a problem of similarity-based retrieval. That is, we compare the similarity scores of new problem with the past cases, and then we select the most similar case as the right one to help solve the new problem. For this requirement on similarity-based retrieval, we need further to define some meaningful and comparable attributes to calculate similarity scores. Generally, these attributes include industry type, problem type, business objective, data mining goal, and other, which can determine a data mining case's processing flow at a general level. For simplifying the description, we use the term of data mining task to enclose these meaningful and comparable attributes. Data mining task is attached on the data mining system to retrieve similar data mining cases. It is also the third extension to generic data mining model.

Now, we can illustrate the data mining model that we have extended. As shown in Figure 1, the central part of this data mining model is a process builder. It retrieves similar cases based on data mining task, loads data from the data base, calls operators from operator base, reuses processing flows to generate model(s) for new data mining problem, and outputs model(s) to model base.

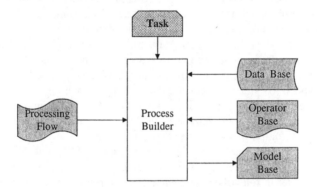

Fig. 1. Extended Data Mining Model for Knowledge Reuse

This data mining model has used the concept of case-based reasoning (CBR). Case-based reasoning [1] is a sub-field of Artificial Intelligence (AI). It has been widely used to solve the problems such as configuration, classification, planning, prediction, and so on [13]. From the perspective of case-based reasoning, this data mining model has taken knowledge retrieval and knowledge reuse into consideration, it has also figured out the content of data mining cases. In the next section, we will have a close look on data mining case.

3 Data Mining Case

From case-based reasoning perspective, a case is a knowledge container [9]. A case should be defined and represented at an operable level. In this section, we will introduce data mining case definition and representation.

From above discussion, we can see that a data mining case consists of five parts: the task, the data, the operator, the model, and the processing flow. Here, we will further define the detailed contents of every part. As shown in Figure 2, data mining case is defined with tree structure in several levels. The first level has included the task, the data, the operator, the model and the processing flow part. In the following, we will concern other levels' contents.

To data mining task, as mentioned before, it includes the elements of industry type, problem type, business objective, data mining goal, company name, and department name. Among them, the first four elements are used for similarity assessment, while the later two elements are used for case grouping.

To the data in this data mining case, what we include is the information about data storage and metadata. The general situation about data storage is that the data are stored in a database or a data warehouse, whereas the data contain many tables, and a table contains many fields. Based on this situation, we describe the data with more three levels: the first level corresponds to the data (a set of tables), the second level corresponds to the table, and the third level corresponds to the field. At each level, there are many other elements, such as, the name, the type, and so on. In a data mining case, the original data and the intermediate data generated in the data mining process all are stored. So, in a data mining case, there are several data description parts.

To the operator in data mining case, it has the elements such as its path, name, category, function, input, parameters, output, and guideline. Here, the operator guideline is used to record the reusable knowledge concerned with the context of an operator on such question as why this operator is required. Furthermore, different operator has different parameters. Thus, we separate operator parameter from operator itself and define it as next level elements. Operator parameter includes the elements such as its name, type, value type, and so on. Among them, the parameter guideline is an important part. It is used to record the reusable knowledge concerned with the internal issues of an operator on such questions as what parameters are required, and how to set their values under certain conditions.

To the model generated in data mining process, we will not define the model's representation format. We just use PMML [5] language to represent model. PMML has become an industry standard. So, in data mining case, the model includes the elements of model type, model parameter, PMML code path, and PMML code name.

Finally, the processing flow describes connective relations of the data, the operators, and the model(s). So, the numbers of the data, operators, and models have been included as the elements of processing flow. The most important part of the processing flow is connections. A connection has an input ID, an operator ID, and an output ID. A data mining case only has one processing flow, and correspondingly, a processing flow corresponds to a data mining case.

As to case representation, we use XML to represent our data mining case. XML is easy to extend and exchange. In our work, the corresponding data mining case representation language (DMCRL) has been defined. The XML-based DMCRL is easy to extend to represent all kinds of data mining cases and easy to integrate with PMML.

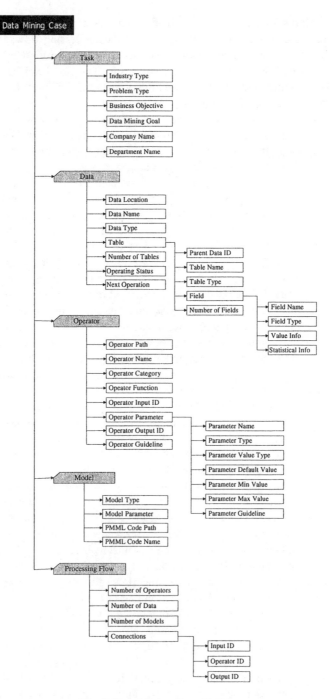

Fig. 2. Date Mining Case Model

4 Case-Based Data Mining Platform

4.1 Storage Bases and Functional Modules

After defining data mining case, we would like to modify the extended data mining model, which has been shown in Figure 1, to draw the architecture of this case-based data mining platform, as shown in Figure 3. Compared with the extended data mining model, the task part and processing flow part have been obliterated and they have been enclosed into data mining case, while data mining case is represented with DMCRL and stored in DMCRL repository. At the same time, the process builder has also changed as a case builder.

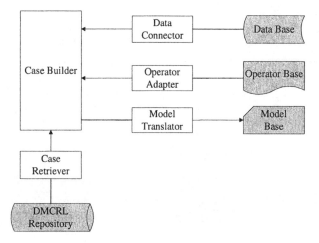

Fig. 3. Architecture of Knowledge Based Data Mining Platform

In this platform, there are four storage bases and five functional modules. The four storage bases are data base, operator base, model base, and DMCRL repository. Among them, the data base, the operator base, and the model base are respectively used to store the data, the operator, and the model. Even though the descriptive parts of the data, the operator, and the model have been encoded in DMCRL, their physical parts are still stored in these storage bases. The DMCRL repository is used to store the data mining cases, which have been represented with DMCRL. The DMCRL repository is also the knowledge base to this platform, because the reusable knowledge of data mining process has been encoded in data mining case, represented with DMCRL, and stored in DMCRL repository.

The five functional modules are case builder, case retriever, data connector, operator adaptor, and model translator. Among them, the case builder is the central functional module. It is used to conduct the data mining process with the supports of other functional modules. The case retriever is used to retrieve the similar case(s) from the DMCRL repository after setting the data mining task. The data connector is used to connect the data base with the case builder. The connector can be the commonly used ODBC or JDBC. The operator adaptor is used to interface the operators with the case builder. Because the operators may be implemented by third parts, we should design the corresponding adaptors to all the operators from different providers. Lastly, the model translator is used to translate the model into the PMML-represented format.

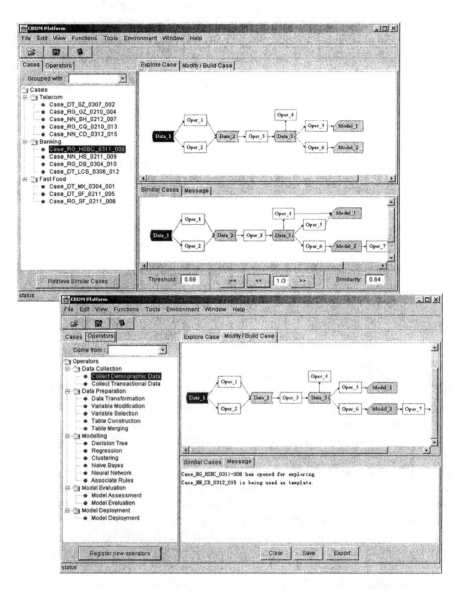

Fig. 4. Main User Interface

4.2 User Interface

The main user interface of this platform is illustrated as Figure 4. Here, the main user interface is the one of case builder, while the other four functional models are dialog-based interface. On its upper part, we can see there are three functional sub-windows. From left to right, and from top to bottom, the three windows respectively are case management window, case exploring window, and similar case management window. Coupled with these three windows, there are three tabbed windows. As shown in the lower part, they are respectively operator management window, case building window, and message window. Thus, there are totally six functional windows.

The case management window is used to organize the cases. The cases can be grouped from different aspects, such as, industry type, business objective, data mining goal, as well as company name and department name. The operator management window is used to organize and register operators. The operators can be the data mining libraries from third parts. The case exploring window is used to explore the case's content in detail. The case will be displayed with graphical flow in case exploring window. The user can view these aspects, such as, what data have been used, what operators have been involved, and what model(s) has been generated. The case building window is used to build the new case. Besides exploring a concrete case, we can modify the processing flow or build a new processing flow from scratch in case building window. The similar case management window is used to manage the similar cases. We assume we can get more than one similar case at similar case retrieval. The similar case management window is used to navigate all the similar cases to view. Meanwhile, there is a threshold to set the criterion of similarity and control the number of retrieved similar cases. The last window is the message window, which is used to log the messages generated in the data mining process.

These six windows can communicate one and another. For example, from the case management window, we can select a specific case to explore its content in case exploring window, to retrieve its similar cases and display in similar case management window, or to be used as template to modify in case building window. From the similar case management window, we can select a specific case to explore in the case exploring window or modify in the case building window.

4.3 Application Scenario

Basically, the application scenarios of this platform include case exploring, model building, and model deployment. Among them, the model building is the main application scenario and will be explained here. As shown in figure 5, the activity diagram of model building is illustrated. Suppose a new data mining case is needed to conduct on this platform, the user needs to do the steps:

1. Click *"Retrieve Similar Case"* button, which is located at the bottom of case management window, to open *"Case Retriever"* dialog.

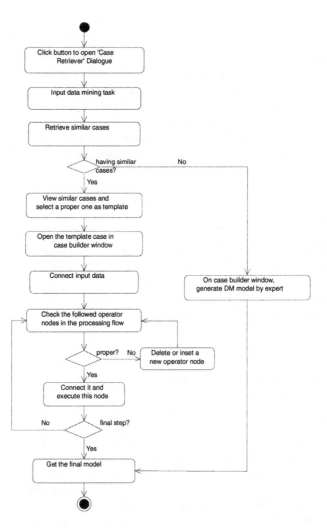

Fig. 5. Activity Diagram of Model Building

2. Input data mining task on case retriever. The elements of data mining task have been listed on case retriever. The user needs to set the values of these elements by directly inputting or selecting from combo boxes.
3. Click "*Retrieve*" button on case retriever to retrieve similar case from DMCRL repository. We assume there are enough cases stored in DMCRL repository. The number of retrieved similar case depends on the threshold value of similarity. The threshold value can be adjusted on the bottom of similar case management window.
4. If there is no similar case, an expert is required to conduct the data mining process on case builder window. Under this situation, this platform is worked as a common data mining platform. On the other hand, if several similar cases have been

retrieved, they will be display in similar case management window. The user can view them one by one and select a proper one as template to solve the new problem. About the proper case, the general situation is that the most similar case is the proper one.

5. When a proper similar case is selected as template, it will be opened in case builder window. For the convenience in further description, the processing flow displayed in case building window of Figure 5 will be used as example to describe from now on.

6. In case building window, right-click on *Data_1* node to invoke data connector. With data connector, we connect current problem's input data to this platform. On data connector, the user can set input data's location, name, type, and other information.

7. Right-click the followed *Oper_1* node to invoke operator adapter. From operator adaptor, the user can first check this operator's usability by viewing its category, function, and guidelines. If it is not a proper operator, the user needs to delete it or insert a new operator ahead of it. If it is a proper operator, the user needs to connect it by setting its path, name, input ID, parameters, and output ID. At setting the operator's parameters, we can refer the parameter's guideline to see how to set its value. After setting all the required values of the operator, the user can execute it.

8. Do in the same way to check and execute the rest operator nodes. A note is that, between two successive operators, there is a data node. This data node is the output of former operator and is also the input of successive operator. The user can view, or save, or export this intermediate data. At the rear part, some intermediate model will be generated. The user can view it first and then decide to accept or discard it. When the final model has been generated, the application scenario of model building is end.

From this application scenario, we can see that the reusable knowledge, either the whole processing flow, the operator guideline, or the parameter guideline, are very helpful to solve a new data mining problem. These knowledge are worked as a supervisor aside of the user. They can eliminate many perplexities for user, such as, what steps should be taken, what operators should be used, how the parameters should be set, and so on.

5 Conclusion

Data mining is a complex and time-consuming process. Data mining practice in industry heavily depends on data mining professionals to provide solutions. In this paper, we have proposed a case-based data mining platform, which reuses the knowledge captured in the past data mining cases to solve new similar problems. This platform is under developing. The XML-based data mining case representation language has been defined, and the storage bases, the functional modules and the user interface have been designed. From its application scenario, we can see that this platform can eliminate many perplexities, such as, what steps should be taken, what operators should be used, how the parameters should be set, and so on. A normal business user can easily and quickly use the knowledge encoded in data mining cases to conduct their data mining practice on this platform. Compared with other systems, this case-based data mining platform will simplify data mining process, reduce the dependency on data mining professional, and shorten business decision time.

Acknowledgement

This work is conducted with the support of Innovation and Technology Fund (ITS/110/002), Innovative Technology Commission, Hong Kong SAR.

References

1. Aamodt, A. and Plaza, E. (1994), "Case-Based Reasoning: Foundational Issues, Methodological Variations, and System Approaches", *AI Communications*, Vol. 7(1), pp.39-59.
2. Berson, A., Simith, S., and Thearling, K., (1999), *Building Data Mining Applications for CRM*, McGraw-Hill, Inc., New York.
3. Cox, E., (2002), "A Protocycling Methodology For Knowledge-Based Data Mining Projects", *PC AI Magazine*, Vol. 16(3), pp. 21-31.
4. CRISP-DM Group (2000), *Cross Industry Standard Process for Data Mining (CRISP-DM) Version 1.0*, http://www.crisp-dm.org/.
5. Data Mining Group (2001), *Predictive Model Markup Language (PMML) Version 2.0*, http://www.dmg.org/pmml-v2-0.htm
6. Kotasek P. and Zendulka J. (2002), "Describing the Data Mining Process with DMSL", in: Manolopoulos, Y. and N´avrat, P. (Eds), Proceedings of the ADBIS 2002 Communications, Bratislava, Slovak Republic, September 2002, pp.131-140.
7. Krishnaswamy, S., and Zaslavasky, A., (2001), "Towards Data Mining Service on the Internet with a Multiple Service Provider Model: An XML Based Approach", *Journal of Electronic Commerce Research*, Vol. 2(3), pp. 103 –130.
8. Object Management Group (2000), *Common Warehouse Metamodel (CWM)*, http://www.omg.org/cwm/
9. Richter, M. M. (1995), "The Knowledge Contained in Similarity Measures", invited talk at the *International Conference on Case-based Reasoning (ICCBR'95)*.
10. SAS whitepaper (1999), *SAS Enterprise Miner 4.3*, http://www.sas.com/
11. Shi Zhongzhi, You Xiangtao, Ye Shiren, and Gong Xiujun, (2000), "General Multi-Strategy Data Mining Platform – MSMiner", *Smart Engineering System Design: Neural Networks, Fuzzy Logic, Evolutionary Programming, Data Mining and Complex Systems*, ASME Press, New York.
12. VBDM.Net Consultant (2002), *Visual Basic Data Mining .Net*, http://www.visual-basic-data-mining.net/
13. Watson, I. (1997), *Applying Case-Based Reasoning: Technical for Enterprise Systems*, Morgan Kaufmann Publishers, Inc.
14. Witten, I. H. and Frank, E. (2000), *Data mining: Practical machine learning tools and techniques with Java implementations*, Morgan Kaufmann, San Francisco.

Consolidated Trees: An Analysis of Structural Convergence

Jesús M. Pérez, Javier Muguerza, Olatz Arbelaitz,
Ibai Gurrutxaga, and José I. Martín

Dept. of Computer Architecture and Technology, University of the Basque Country,
M. Lardizabal, 1, 20018 Donostia, Spain
{txus.perez, j.muguerza, olatz.arbelaitz,
ibai.gurrutxaga, j.martin}@ehu.es
http://www.sc.ehu.es/aldapa

Abstract. When different subsamples of the same data set are used to induce classification trees, the structure of the built classifiers is very different. The stability of the structure of the tree is of capital importance in many domains, such as illness diagnosis, fraud detection in different fields, customer's behaviour analysis (marketing), etc, where comprehensibility of the classifier is necessary. We have developed a methodology for building classification trees from multiple samples where the final classifier is a single decision tree (Consolidated Trees). The paper presents an analysis of the structural stability of our algorithm versus C4.5 algorithm. The classification trees generated with our algorithm, achieve smaller error rates and structurally more steady trees than C4.5 when using resampling techniques. The main focus on this paper is showing how Consolidated Trees built with different sets of subsamples tend to converge to the same tree when the number of used subsamples is increased.

1 Introduction

Many examples of the use of resampling techniques —oversampling or undersampling— with different objectives can be found in bibliography. A very important application of resampling is to use it in order to equilibrate the class distribution in databases with class imbalance [12],[18]. In many areas, such as medicine, fraud detection, etc; cases of one of the classes can be difficult to obtain. This leads very often to class imbalance in the data set which, in general, does not even coincide with the distribution expected in reality. A similar case is the one of databases with non-uniform cost, where the misclassification cost is not the same for the whole confusion matrix. In these cases, if the algorithm does not take into account the cost-matrix in the induction process, the use of resampling techniques to make some errors become more important than others can be a way of introducing such a cost in the learning algorithm [9]. On the other hand, for some databases the use of machine learning algorithms is computationally too expensive due to their memory requirements. In these cases resampling can be used for size reduction [4],[16]. We can not forget one of the most extended uses of resampling techniques: the

G.J. Williams and S.J. Simoff (Eds.): Data Mining, LNAI 3755, pp. 39 – 52, 2006.

construction of multiple classifiers such as bagging, boosting, etc; able to obtain larger accuracy in the classification [1],[3],[6],[10].

In all the mentioned cases, subsamples obtained by resampling the original data set will be given to the learning algorithm in order to build a classifier. This resampling affects severely the behaviour of the classification algorithms [12]. Classification trees are not an exception. Classification trees induced from slightly different subsamples of the same data set are very different in accuracy and structure [8]. This weakness is called unsteadiness or instability. The stability is of capital importance in many domains, such as illness diagnosis, fraud detection in different fields, customer's behaviour analysis (marketing), etc, where comprehensibility of the classifier is necessary [7]. As Turney found working on industrial applications of decision tree learning, "the engineers are disturbed when different batches of data from the same process result in radically different decision trees. The engineers lose confidence in the decision trees even when we can demonstrate that the trees have high predictive accuracy" [17]. Some authors [7],[17] have measured the stability of a classifier observing if different instances agree in the prediction made for each case of the test set (logical stability or variance). However, since the explanation of a tree comes from its structure we need a way of building structurally steady classifiers in order to obtain a convincing explanation (physical stability or structural stability).

This paper presents an analysis of the structural stability of decision trees built using the Consolidated Trees' Construction algorithm (CTC). The CTC algorithm, opposite to other algorithms that work with many subsamples (bagging, boosting), induces a single tree, therefore it does not lose the comprehensibility of the base classifier. A measure of similarity between two induced classifiers (tree's structures) will be used in order to evaluate the structural stability of the algorithm. The structural analysis done shows that the algorithm has a steadier behaviour than C4.5 [15], obtaining this way a steadier explanation. In this paper the main focus is done in showing how the trees built with the proposed algorithm tend to become more similar when the number of subsamples used to build them increases. In some domains, they converge to the same instance of tree even if different subsamples are used.

The discriminating capacity of the CTC algorithm has already been evaluated in previous works [13],[14]. These works show that the classification trees generated using the CTC algorithm achieve smaller error rates than the ones built with C4.5, giving this way a better quality to the explanation.

The paper proceeds with a description of our methodology for building classification trees, Section 2. In Section 3, the description of the data set and the experimental set-up is presented. This paper includes a summary of the results of our previous work in Section 4. Section 5 presents the analysis of the structural stability and convergence of the structure of trees built with CTC algorithm. Finally, Section 6 is devoted to summarise the conclusions and further work.

2 Consolidated Trees' Construction Algorithm

Consolidated Trees' Construction algorithm (CTC) uses several subsamples to build a single tree. This technique is radically different from bagging, boosting, etc. The consensus is achieved at each step of the tree's building process and only one tree is built.

The different subsamples are used to make proposals about the feature that should be used to split in the current node. The split function used in this work is the gain ratio criterion (the same used by Quinlan in C4.5). The decision about which feature will be used to make the split in a node of the Consolidated Tree (CT) is accorded among the different proposals. The decision is made by a voting process node by node. Based on this decision, all the subsamples are divided using the same feature. The iterative process is described in Algorithm 1.

The algorithm starts extracting a set of subsamples (*Number_Samples*) from the original training set. The subsamples can be obtained based on the desired resampling technique (*Resampling_Mode*).

Decision tree's construction algorithms, usually divide the initial sample in several data partitions. In our algorithm, LS^i contains the data partitions created from each subsample S^i.

Algorithm 1. Consolidated Trees' Construction Algorithm (CTC)

Generate *Number_Samples* subsamples (S^i) from S with *Resampling_Mode* method.
CurrentNode := *RootNode*
for i := 1 to *Number_Samples*
    LS^i := $\{S^i\}$
end for
repeat

> **for** i := 1 to *Number_Samples*   Decision in
>   *CurrentS^i* := *First(LS^i)*   each subsample
> LS^i := LS^i - *CurrentS^i*
>   Induce the best split $(X,B)^i$ for *CurrentS^i*
> **end for**

> Obtain the consolidated pair (X_c, B_c), based on $(X,B)^i$, $1 \le i \le$ *Number_Samples*
> **if** $(X_c, B_c) \ne$ *Not_Split*
>   Split *CurrentNode* based on (X_c, B_c)
>   **for** i := 1 to *Number_Samples*
>   Divide *CurrentS^i* based on (X_c, B_c) to obtain n subsamples $\{S_1^i, ... S_n^i\}$
> LS^i := $\{S_1^i, ... S_n^i\}$ + LS^i Force in all
>   **end for**   subsamples
>   **else** consolidate *CurrentNode* as a leaf   (Consolidate)
> **end if**

CurrentNode := *NextNode*
until $\forall i$, LS^i is empty

In the algorithm, the consolidation of a node is divided in two main parts. The first one where a separate analysis is done in each of the subsamples, and the second one, where based on all the proposals, a decision to consolidate the node is made. At this point, all the subsamples are forced to make the same split.

The pair $(X,B)^i$ is the split proposal for the first partition in LS^i. X is the feature selected to split and B indicates the proposed branches or criteria to divide the data in the current node. X_c is the feature obtained by a voting process among all the proposed *X*. Whereas B_c is the median of the proposed *Cut* values when X_c is continuous and all the possible values of the feature when X_c is discrete.

When a node is consolidated as a leaf node, the a posteriori probabilities associated to it are calculated by averaging the a posteriori obtained from the data partitions related to that node in all the subsamples.

The used resampling technique and the number of subsamples used in the tree's building process are important aspects of the algorithm [16]. There are many possible combinations for the *Resampling_Mode*: size of the subsamples —100%, 75%, 50%, etc; of the original training set —, with replacement or without replacement, stratified or not, etc. In previous works stratified subsamples of 75% and 50% of the original training set and bootstrap samples have been used for experimentation and we have observed that CTC algorithm behaves in a similar manner for all of them. We present in this paper results for stratified subsamples of 75% because the quality of the achieved results is slightly better than it is with other combinations.

Once the consolidated tree has been built, it works the same way a decision tree does.

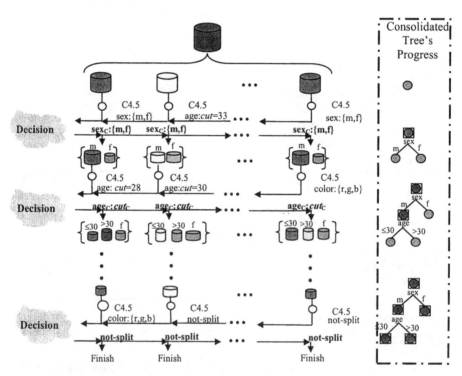

Fig. 1. Example of a Consolidated Tree's (CT) building process based on C4.5 (gain ratio)

We present an example of how a CT tree is built in Fig.1. In the first step, "sex" (*X*) variable with branches "m" and "f" (*B*) is proposed by two of the samples and "age" (*X*) with cut value "33" (*B*) by another one. Whereas in the second step, the proposed variables are "age" for two of the samples and "color" for a third one. If the proportions appearing in the figure are representative of the proportions happening in each step of the CT's building process, X_c will be "sex" in the first step with branches "m" and "f", and "age" in the second one with 30 selected as cut value.

In the last step of the example in Fig. 1, the proposal is not to split the node in two of the partitions and in another one the proposal is to split it using "color" variable. If this proportion is maintained, the final decision will be to consolidate the node as a leaf.

3 Experimental Methodology

Twenty databases of real applications have been used for the experimentation. Most of them belong to the well known UCI Repository benchmark [2]. The Segment domain has been used for experimentation in two different ways: taking into account the whole set of data (*segment2310*) and conserving the training/test division of the original data set (*Segment210*). The *Faithful* database is a real data application from our environment, centred in the electrical appliance's sector. Table 1 shows the wide range of characteristics of the used domains: the number of patterns (*N. of patterns*) goes from 148 to 24,507, the number of features (*N. of features*) from 4 to 57 and the number of classes of the dependent variable (*N. of classes*) from 2 to 15.

Table 1. Description of experimental domains

Domain	N. of patterns	N. of features	N. of classes
Breast-W	699	10	*2*
Heart-C	303	13	2
Hypo	3163	25	2
Lymph	*148*	18	4
Credit-G	1000	20	2
Segment210	210	19	7
Iris	150	*4*	3
Glass	214	9	7
Voting	435	16	2
Hepatitis	155	19	2
Soybean-L	290	35	*15*
Sick-E	3163	25	2
Liver	345	6	2
Credit-A	690	14	2
Vehicle	846	18	4
Breast-Y	286	9	2
Heart-H	294	13	2
Segment2310	2310	19	7
Spam	4601	*57*	2
Faithful	*24507*	49	2

The CTC methodology has been compared to the C4.5 tree building algorithm Release 8 of Quinlan, using the default parameter settings. Both kinds of trees have been pruned, using the pruning algorithm of the C4.5 R8 software, to situate both systems in a similar zone in the learning curve [11],[19]. We can not forget that developing too much a classification tree leads to a greater probability of overtraining. The validation methodology used in this experimentation has been to execute 5 times a 10-fold stratified cross validation [11]. In each of the folds of the cross-validation 100 stratified subsamples have been extracted, always without replacement and with size of 75% of the training sample in the corresponding fold. These subsamples have been used to build both kinds of trees, CT and C4.5.

For CTC algorithm the subsamples have been used disjointedly to build the trees, which has led to different number of instances of CTs when varying the *Number_Samples (N_S)* parameter: $N\_S = 5$ (20 trees), $N\_S = 10$ (10 trees), $N\_S = 20$ (5 trees), $N\_S = 30$ (3 trees), $N\_S = 40$ (2 trees) and $N\_S = 50$ (2 trees). This means that for each fold, 42 Consolidated Trees have been built.

For C4.5 algorithm different options have been tried:

- $C4.5_{100}$ consists on building a tree with each one of the 100 subsamples mentioned before, generated undersampling the training set (fold). The amount of information of the original training set used by each algortihm is different in this case: a CT sees more information than a C4.5 tree, which can lead to differences in accuracy. This has led us to design another comparison, where both algorithms use the same information ($C4.5_{union}$).
- The sample used to induce each one of the $C4.5_{union}$ trees will be the union of the subsamples used to build the corresponding CT. So, in this experimentation the information handled by both algorithms is the same. In this case as many C4.5 trees as CTs are built.
- Related to the previous one we made a third comparison among C4.5 and CTC algorithm where the C4.5 trees have been built directly from the training data belonging to each fold of the 10-fold cross-validation ($C4.5_{not\ resampling}$). We can not forget that this case can not be used when resampling is required. However we think the comparison is interesting to appreciate correctly the achieved error rates.

The number of C4.5 trees generated is larger than the number of CT trees. We have generated 100 $C4.5_{100}$ trees, 42 $C4.5_{union}$ trees (same amount that CT trees) and one $C4.5_{not\ resampling}$ in each fold.

With this information we can quantify the number of trees generated for the wide experimentation described in this section. For each of the 20 databases, 5 runs of 10 folds have been generated, so, for CTC algorithm, 42,000 trees have been built, and for C4.5 algorithm, 100,000 ($C4.5_{100}$) + 42,000 ($C4.5_{union}$) + 100 ($C4.5_{not\ resampling}$).= 142,100 trees.

4 Summary of Previous Work

This section is devoted to present the results of different comparisons made among the two algorithms (C4.5 and CTC).

The analysis has been made from two points of view: error and structural stability. In order to evaluate the structural stability, a structural distance among the trees that are being compared has been defined: *Common*. This structural measure is based on a pair to pair comparison, *Similarity*, among all the trees of the set. This function

(*Similarity*) counts the common nodes among two trees. It is calculated starting from the root and covering the tree, level by level. If two nodes coincide in the feature used to make the split, the proposed branches or stratification and the position in the tree, they will be counted as common nodes. When a different node is found the subtree under that node is not taken into account. For a set of trees T_{set}, with m trees the *Common* value is calculated as the average value of all the possible pair to pair comparisons (Equation 1):

$$Common(T_{set}) = \frac{2}{m(m-1)} \sum_{\substack{k,l=0 \\ k<l}}^{m-1} Similarity(T_k, T_l)$$

(1)

From a practical point of view, *Common* quantifies structural stability of the classification algorithm, whereas the error would quantify the quality of the explanation given by the tree. Evidently an improvement in structural stability must be supported with a reasonable error rate. Our main goal has been to increase stability with no loss in accuracy.

As a summary of previous work we can say that the behaviour of the CTC algorithm improves when the value of *Number_Samples* increases. When this value is 20 or greater, the results for CTC are better in average than results for any of the versions of C4.5. Table 2 shows the results of the comparison of CTC (with N_S = 30), C4.5$_{100}$, C4.5$_{union}$, and C4.5$_{not\_resampling}$.

Values related to Error and *Common* are given (column R.Dif is always calculated as the relative difference among the CTC results and the results of C4.5). The table shows that in 16 (C4.5$_{100}$), 17 (C4.5$_{union}$) and 9 (C4.5$_{not\_resampling}$) domains out of 20,

Table 2. Average results of Error and *Common* for every domain. CTC (N_S = 30), C4.5$_{100}$ (C4.5$_1$), C4.5$_{union}$ (C4.5$_u$) and C4.5$_{not\_resampling}$ (C4.5$_{n\_r}$) are shown.

	Error						Common			
	CTC	C4.5$_1$	R.Dif	C4.5$_u$	R.Dif	C4.5$_{n\_r}$	R.Dif	CTC	C4.5$_1$	C4.5$_u$	C4.5$_{n\_r}$
Breast-W	5.58	6.06	-7.99	6.26	-10.87	5.63	-0.99	2.94	1.67	19.47	2.38
Heart-C	23.12	24.57	-5.88	27.94	-17.23	23.96	-3.48	7.36	1.46	16.11	3.18
Hypo	0.72	0.78	-7.30	1.23	-41.13	0.71	1.31	3.97	2.63	24.34	3.39
Lymph	20.01	22.02	-9.11	24.83	-19.42	20.44	-2.09	7.95	2.10	17.71	3.23
Credit-G	28.03	28.28	-0.89	32.71	-14.29	28.50	-1.64	12.25	2.33	42.97	4.42
Segment2210	12.72	13.71	-7.20	12.75	-0.26	13.61	-6.52	5.38	1.96	8.19	1.95
Iris	4.63	6.29	-26.35	6.63	-30.14	5.75	-19.39	2.80	2.06	5.87	3.20
Glass	30.26	32.48	-6.83	30.28	-0.07	31.55	-4.08	6.62	2.65	17.27	6.01
Voting	3.42	4.17	-17.87	5.47	-37.49	3.41	0.41	4.45	2.19	22.21	4.21
Hepatitis	20.70	20.68	0.11	22.03	-6.03	20.29	2.01	4.06	0.85	12.23	3.25
Soybean-L	11.18	13.53	-17.37	10.92	2.34	11.02	1.46	15.54	6.18	22.95	12.14
Sick-E	2.32	2.21	4.93	2.91	-20.22	1.96	18.54	7.73	4.75	16.74	8.13
Liver	33.94	35.90	-5.46	35.15	-3.44	35.31	-3.88	7.06	1.19	13.57	3.17
Credit-A	14.82	14.81	0.03	18.42	-19.58	14.51	2.11	6.04	2.14	26.19	3.92
Vehicle	27.82	28.30	-1.70	26.55	4.80	27.61	0.76	18.30	7.11	32.97	13.57
Breast-Y	26.78	28.35	-5.52	34.47	-22.30	25.81	3.78	2.23	0.75	34.99	1.16
Heart-H	21.38	20.89	2.35	22.45	-4.75	21.02	1.69	4.50	1.41	25.05	1.66
Segment2310	3.39	3.96	-14.49	3.20	5.74	3.24	4.46	22.54	10.20	29.31	14.84
Spam	7.31	7.73	-5.46	7.96	-8.17	7.25	0.74	16.69	4.55	27.87	9.97
Faithful	1.48	1.50	-1.61	2.42	-38.92	1.48	-0.18	10.76	6.54	52.86	8.18
Average 75%	14.98	15.81	-6.68	16.73	-14.07	15.15	-0.25	8.46	3.24	23.44	5.60

the error is smaller for CTC than for C4.5. The statistically significant differences (paired t-test [5],[6]), with 95% confidence level, have been marked in italics. The differences are statistically significant in 11 databases for C4.5$_{100}$, and 10 databases for C4.5$_{union}$. In the databases where results for C4.5$_{100}$ or C4.5$_{union}$ are better, the differences are not statistically significant. The differences with results of C4.5$_{not\_resampling}$ are never statistically significant being the behaviour of CTC better in average. So we can ensure that the discriminating capacity of CTC algorithm is at least as good or better than the one of C4.5. In this situation, it is worth the comparison of the structural stability of the different classifiers. Achieving greater structural stability will mean that CT trees have better explaining capacity. The data show that CTs achieve higher structural stability than C4.5$_{100}$ (in average 8.46 compared to 3.24) and C4.5$_{not\_resampling}$ (in average 8.46 compared to 5.60).

Looking to the values of *Common* obtained for C4.5$_{union}$ we could say that they achieve higher structural stability than CTC (*Common* is in average 23.44 compared to 8.46) but this happens because complexity of C4.5$_{union}$ trees is an order of magnitude larger than the complexity of CTs. In environments where explanation and therefore stability is important so complex trees are not useful. Moreover, being the error smaller for CTC, the principle of parsimony of the model makes worse the C4.5$_{union}$ option. More information about this experimentation can be found in [14].

Therefore, we can say that in average, classification trees induced with CTC algorithm have lower error rate than those induced with C4.5, and they are structurally steadier. As a consequence they provide a wider and steadier explanation, that allows to deal with the problem of the excessive sensitivity classification trees have to resampling methods.

5 Analysis of Convergence

We have observed that the value of *Common* for CT trees increases with the number of used subsamples. This means that the CT trees tend to have a larger common structure when *Number_Samples* increases. This is a desirable behaviour but it could be due to the higher complexity of the trees (this was the case of C4.5$_{union}$ in previous section). In order to take into account the parsimony principle we have normalised the *Common* value in respect to the trees' size (number of internal nodes). We will denominate this measure *%Common* and it will quantify the identical fraction of two or more trees.

The information in Fig 2. belongs to one run of the 10 fold cross-validation for *Breast-W* database. The curves represent the values of *%Common* in each one of the folds when the *Number_Samples* parameter varies. We will give some clues for better understanding the figure: obtaining a value of 100% for *%Common* in a set of trees means that all the compared trees are equal; obtaining a value of 90% means that in average the compared trees have 90% of the structure identical.

Each line in Fig. 2 represents for CTC algorithm (left side) and C4.5 algorithm (right side), the evolution of *%Common* when the number of samples used to build the trees increases in one fold. The number of trees compared in each fold varies with *Number_Samples* parameter. For $N\_S = 5$, 20 trees are compared in each fold and it

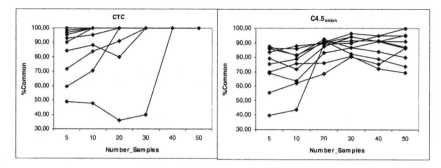

Fig. 2. Structural convergence of CTC and C4.5$_{union}$ for the *Breast-W* domain

can be observed that the CTs have in average 90% or more of the structure common in 6 folds out of 10; and in the fold with worst results the compared trees have 50% of the structure equal. As the number of samples used to build the CTs increases, the percentage of the trees that is equal increases in most of the folds. Concretely, when the number of samples used is 40 or greater, all the trees in the 10 folds are identical. We can say in this case that the CT trees converge structurally in $N\_S = 40$. This means that for $N\_S = 40$ or greater, the tree built with CTC will be always the same independently of the used subsamples. For C4.5$_{union}$ trees (right side), we can not observe any convergence when increasing the number of samples used to build them.

After this analysis we could say that Fig. 2 shows the structural convergence of CTC algorithm in *Breast-W* domain (There is not convergence for C4.5$_{union}$).

As a summary, we can say that for *Breast-W* database, CTs converge to an unique tree after a certain value of *Number_Samples*, whereas C4.5 trees show a greater structural variation.

If we analyse the results of the 20 databases (see Table 3 where averages of the 5 runs and 10 folds for *%Common* are presented), for most of them (15 databases for $N\_S = 50$, and similar values for the rest) CT trees have larger common structure than C4.5 trees, that is to say, the behaviour of CTC is better than the behaviour of C4.5$_{union}$, For some values of *Number_Samples* parameter, relative improvements up to 50% are achieved.

After studying the results in Fig. 2 and Table 3, it seems that from a certain value of *Number_Samples* parameter the tree obtained with CTC algorithm will be always the same.

In the previous analysis all the comparisons have been done among trees with the same value of *Number_Samples* parameter and we have observed that the value of *%Common* increases with this parameter. This suggests us a new question: will also the structure of CTs built with different values of *Number_Samples* be similar? In this case, we could say that CT trees are gradually changing towards a specific tree while *Number_Samples* increases. To answer this question we present the study of Fig. 3.

Fig. 3 shows the values *%Common* for CTC (continuos lines), C4.5$_{union}$ (dashed lines) and C4.5$_{100}$ (triangles, *Number_Samples* parameter does not make any sense in this case), so that, for each case an idea of the percentage of the tree that remains common is given.

Table 3. Results of *%Common* for every domain. C4.5$_{100}$, CTC and C4.5$_{union}$.

%Common	C4.5$_{100}$	CTC						C4.5$_{union}$					
		5	10	20	30	40	50	5	10	20	30	40	50
Breast-W	60	87	95	97	98	99	99	73	78	86	89	89	89
Heart-C	13	26	36	47	52	55	64	14	19	28	34	36	39
Hypo	56	70	74	80	89	94	92	42	51	52	57	57	57
Lymph	30	59	72	80	86	84	91	59	67	76	76	78	80
Credit-G	8	15	20	29	32	37	44	12	16	22	26	30	30
Segment210	19	25	31	37	39	35	45	26	33	41	45	56	47
Iris	69	82	84	87	90	87	92	64	70	77	74	76	81
Glass	15	22	25	27	28	26	28	24	31	41	44	43	46
Voting	53	72	84	91	92	90	92	51	58	67	69	72	70
Hepatitis	16	33	43	50	55	61	58	20	26	35	41	45	50
Soybean-L	31	46	53	64	70	69	72	52	60	66	69	72	74
Sick-E	46	53	56	59	63	65	67	18	17	18	18	22	21
Liver	7	9	13	17	21	24	27	6	9	17	19	23	24
Credit-A	23	30	36	48	53	58	55	20	24	30	35	38	39
Vehicle	14	15	17	20	21	23	23	18	21	24	25	29	32
Breast-Y	21	39	50	57	70	76	81	26	38	52	58	61	66
Heart-H	24	34	40	52	60	63	68	31	28	34	35	40	43
Segment2310	29	35	40	44	49	49	50	31	36	43	46	51	56
Spam	5	9	11	13	15	16	16	6	9	10	10	15	15
Faithful	18	29	30	31	36	39	31	7	7	9	10	11	11
Average	28	40	45	51	56	57	60	30	35	41	44	47	48

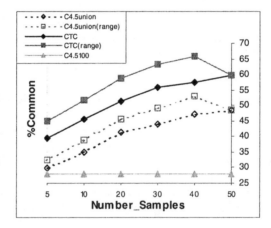

Fig. 3. Averages of *%Common* for CTC, C4.5$_{100}$ and C4.5$_{union}$ (5 times 10 folds, 20 databases)

For each database, average *%Common* values of the 5 runs and 10 folds are calculated and every point in the graphic represents the average of the 20 databases. For CTC and C4.5$_{union}$ two studies are presented. In the first one, trees built with identical values for *Number_Samples* parameter are compared (diamonds). In the second one, called "range" in Fig. 3, trees with different values of *Number_Samples* are compared (squares). In this case the point corresponding to $N\_S = 20$ represents the *%Common* value obtained from the comparison of every tree built with $N\_S \geq 20$. Being this value (59) larger than *%Common* (51) means that there are trees built with 30, 40 or 50 subsamples that when compared to the trees built with 20 subsamples all together, they are even more similar than the trees built with 20 subsamples among them.

On the other hand, it can be observed that the trees built using CTC have a larger common structure than the rest. In average we can say that for any value of *Number_Samples*, CTC results are better than C4.5$_{union}$ results in at least 10%. In the case of C4.5$_{100}$, the behaviour is much worse. Besides, being the values of CTC "range" larger than values of CTC, we can assert that independently of the value used for *Number_Samples* parameter, similar structures are reached, so, we can say that even if different subsamples are used to build trees, the obtained structures are similar. This makes the explanation of the classification steady when varying the *Number_Samples* parameter. If we look to the graphics in Fig. 2 it seems that for *Breast-W* database, when *Number_Samples* is greater than 40 all the trees are identical. This does not happen in all databases but looking to the tendencies of the average (Fig. 3), we could think that it will exist for each database a value of *Number_Samples* with the same properties.

The data in Table 3 has given us the idea of studying the number of folds (*#folds*) where all the trees converge exactly to the same tree for the different values of *Number_Samples*. Centring the analysis in CTC, we can differentiate three kinds of behaviours (clusters) among the analysed databases: domains where for the majority of folds (*#folds* ≥ 25, since the total number of folds is 50) all the trees converge to the same one (Cluster1: *Breast-W, Hypo, Lymph, Iris, Voting, Breast-Y*), domains with an intermediate number of folds that converge to the same tree (Cluster2: *Heart-C, Hepatitis, Soybean-L, Heart-H, Sick-E, Credit-A*), and domains where for the analysed values of *Number_Samples* this situation never happens (Cluster3: *Credit-G, Segment210, Glass, Liver, Vehicle, Segment2310, Spam, Faithful*). This division shows that even if CTC algorithm seems to converge for all the databases, the number of samples needed to converge is domain dependent.

Table 4 shows the results of the mentioned analysis for CTC and C4.5$_{union}$.

Table 4. Analysis of converging folds (*#folds*) and *%Common (%Com)* for CTC and C4.5$_{union}$ for different values of *Number_Samples (N_S)*

N_S		CTC						C4.5$_{union}$					
		5	10	20	30	40	50	5	10	20	30	40	50
#folds	Cluster1	1.83	8.00	21.00	31.00	36.00	38.00	0.00	0.00	0.50	1.00	4.67	4.83
	Cluster2	0.00	0.00	0.50	1.67	5.17	5.50	0.00	0.00	0.00	0.00	0.50	0.83
	Cluster3	0.00	0.00	0.00	0.00	0.00	0.00	0.00	0.00	0.00	0.00	0.00	0.00
%Com	Cluster1	68.33	76.36	82.01	87.44	88.16	91.08	52.61	60.37	68.37	70.39	72.10	73.87
	Cluster2	36.94	44.06	52.99	58.63	61.70	64.08	25.68	28.96	35.29	38.64	42.14	44.28
	Cluster3	19.81	23.36	27.38	30.16	31.16	33.14	16.21	20.31	25.79	28.37	32.08	32.59

When trying to understand the values in the upper part of Table 4 (*#folds*), it has to be taken into account that we use very hard conditions to count an unity: all the trees built for a certain value of *Number_Samples* have to be identical. For example, if we look to the data for *Breast-W* database in Fig.2, (results belong to 1 run 10 folds), when N_S = 20 the values of *%Common* in the 10 folds are: 35.71; 80.00; 90.91; and for the remaining seven 100.00. This means that in seven folds all the compared trees are identical. In this case the value of *#folds* would be 7. The values shown in the table are averages of the databases belonging to the corresponding cluster but taking into account the 50 folds of the 5 runs. Notice that even if the number of converging folds is sometimes very small, this does not mean that the trees are completely different; the average common part of the compared trees (lower part of the table: *%Com*) is still important.

Table 4 shows that the number of converging folds increases with the parameter *Number_Samples* for both algorithms. On the other hand, values obtained for CTC are always much better than values for C4.5$_{union}$ in the 3 clusters. Besides, in every database the error of the CT trees is smaller than error of C4.5$_{union}$ or C4.5$_{100}$ trees and, as it can be observed in Table 2, most of the domains in Cluster1 are among the databases where the differences are statistically significant.

The same kind of analysis has been done for trees built with C4.5$_{100}$ option. The number of folds where all the trees converge to the same one is in this case 0 for every database. The percentage of average common structure (*%Common*) is 28% (See Table 3); even lower than the values obtained for CT trees with *Number_Samples*=5 (40%).

Therefore the CTC algorithm provides a wider and steadier explanation with smaller error rates.

6 Conclusions and Further Work

In order to afford the unsteadiness classification trees suffer when small changes in the training set happen, we have developed a methodology for building classification trees: Consolidated Trees' Construction Algorithm (CTC), being the objective to maintain the explanation without losing accuracy. This paper focuses on the study of the structural convergence of the algorithm.

The behaviour of the CTC algorithm has been compared to C4.5 for twenty databases, 19 from the UCI Repository and one database from a real data application from our environment.

The results show that CT trees tend to converge to a single tree when *Number_Samples* is increased and the obtained classification trees achieve besides, smaller error rates than C4.5. So we can say that this methodology builds structurally more steady trees, giving stability to the explanation and with smaller error rate, so, with higher quality in the explanation. This is essential for some specific domains: medical diagnosis, fraud detection, etc.

Observing the results in structural stability we can conclude that the number of samples required to achieve the structural convergence varies depending on the database. We are analysing the convergence for larger values of the parameter *Number_Samples* in order to find the needed number of samples to achieve the convergence in each database. In this sense, the use of different parallelisation techniques (shared memory and distributed memory computers) will be considered due to the increase of computational cost.

Analysis of the results obtained for both algorithms with other instantiations of *Resampling_Mode* parameter can also be interesting.

The reasons that lead to three different clusters of domains in convergence need to be analysed. The analysis of the influence of the pruning in the error and the bias/variance decomposition can be interesting in this study.

The CTC algorithm provides a way to deal with the need of resampling the training set. Anyway, we are working in quantifying the influence that changes in the class distribution can have in the CTC algorithm. It would also be interesting the comparison of the results obtained with other techniques that use resampling in order to improve the accuracy of the classifier, such as bagging, boosting, etc., although they completely miss the explaining capacity.

Acknowledgments

The work described in this paper was partly done under the University of Basque Country (UPV/EHU) project: 1/UPV 00139.226-T-15920/2004. It was also funded by the Diputación Foral de Guipuzcoa and the European Union.

We would like to thank the company Fagor Electrodomesticos, S. COOP. for permitting us the use of their data (*Faithful*) obtained through the project BETIKO. The *lymphography* domain was obtained from the University Medical Centre, Institute of Oncology, Ljubljana, Yugoslavia. Thanks go to M. Zwitter and M. Soklic for providing the data.

References

1. Bauer E., Kohavi R.: An Empirical Comparison of Voting Classification Algorithms: Bagging, Boosting, and Variants, Machine Learning, Vol. 36, (1999) 105-139.
2. Blake, C.L., Merz, C.J.: UCI Repository of Machine Learning Databases, University of California, Irvine, Dept. of Information and Computer Sciences. http://www.ics.uci.edu/~mlearn/MLRepository.html (1998).
3. Breiman L.: Bagging Predictors. Machine Learning, Vol. 24, (1996) 123-140.
4. Chan P.K., Stolfo S.J.: Toward Scalable Learning with Non-uniform Class and Cost Distributions: A Case Study in Credit Card Fraud Detection, Proceedings of the 4th International Conference on Knowledge Discovery and Data Mining, (1998) 164-168.
5. Dietterich T.G.: Approximate Statistical Tests for Comparing Supervised Classification Learning Algorithms, Neural Computation, Vol. 10, No. 7, (1998) 1895-1924.
6. Dietterich T.G.: An Experimental Comparison of Three Methods for Constructing Ensembles of Decision Trees: Bagging, Boosting, and Randomization, Machine Learning, Vol. 40, (2000) 139-157.
7. Domingos P.: Knowledge acquisition from examples via multiple models. Proc. 14th International Conference on Machine Learning Nashville, TN (1997) 98-106.
8. Drummond C., Holte R.C.: Exploiting the Cost (In)sensitivity of Decision Tree Splitting Criteria, Proceedings of the 17th International Conference on Machine Learning, (2000) 239-246.
9. Elkan C.: The Foundations of Cost-Sensitive Learning, Proceedings of the 17th International Joint Conference on Artificial Intelligence, (2001) 973-978.
10. Freund, Y., Schapire, R. E.: Experiments with a New Boosting Algorithm, Proceedings of the 13th International Conference on Machine Learning, (1996) 148-156.

11. Hastie T., Tibshirani R. Friedman J.: The Elements of Statistical Learning. Springer-Verlang (es). ISBN: 0-387-95284-5, (2001).
12. Japkowicz N.: Learning from Imbalanced Data Sets: A Comparison of Various Strategies, Proceedings of the AAAI Workshop on Learning from Imbalanced Data Sets, Menlo Park, CA, (2000).
13. Pérez J.M., Muguerza J., Arbelaitz O., Gurrutxaga I.: A new algorithm to build consolidated trees: study of the error rate and steadiness, Proceedings of the conference on Intelligent Information Systems, Zakopane, Poland, (2004).
14. Pérez J.M., Muguerza J., Arbelaitz O., Gurrutxaga I., Martín J.I.: Behaviour of Consolidated Trees when using Resampling Techniques, Proceedings of the 4th International Workshop on Pattern Recognition in Information Systems, PRIS, Porto, Portugal, (2004).
15. Quinlan J.R.: C4.5: Programs for Machine Learning, Morgan Kaufmann Publishers Inc.(eds), San Mateo, California (1993).
16. Skurichina M., Kuncheva L.I., Duin R.P.W. Bagging and Boosting for the Nearest Mean Classifier: Effects of Sample Size on Diversity and Accuracy, LNCS Vol. 2364. Multiple Classifier Systems: Proc. 3th Inter. Workshop, MCS , Cagliari, Italy, (2002) 62-71.
17. Turney P. Bias and the quantification of stability. Machine Learning, 20 (1995), 23-33.
18. Weiss G.M., Provost F.: Learning when Training Data are Costly: The Effect of Class Distribution on Tree Induction, Journal of Artificial Intelligence Research, Vol. 19, (2003) 315-354.
19. Windeatt T., Ardeshir G.: Boosted Tree Ensembles for Solving Multiclass Problems, LNCS Vol. 2364. Multiple Classifier Systems: Proc. 3th Inter. Workshop, MCS , Cagliari, Italy, (2002) 42-51.

K Nearest Neighbor Edition to Guide Classification Tree Learning: Motivation and Experimental Results

J.M. Martínez-Otzeta, B. Sierra, E. Lazkano, and A. Astigarraga

Department of Computer Science and Artificial Intelligence,
University of the Basque Country, P. Manuel Lardizabal 1,
20018 Donostia-San Sebastián, Basque Country, Spain
ccbmaotj@si.ehu.es
http://www.sc.ehu.es/ccwrobot

Abstract. This paper presents a new hybrid classifier that combines the Nearest Neighbor distance based algorithm with the Classification Tree paradigm. The Nearest Neighbor algorithm is used as a preprocessing algorithm in order to obtain a modified training database for the posterior learning of the classification tree structure; experimental section shows the results obtained by the new algorithm; comparing these results with those obtained by the classification trees when induced from the original training data we obtain that the new approach performs better or equal according to the Wilcoxon signed rank statistical test.

Keywords: Machine Learning, Supervised Classification, Classifier Combination, Classification Trees.

1 Introduction

Classifier Combination is an extended terminology used in the Machine Learning [20], more specifically in the *Supervised Pattern Recognition* area, to point out the supervised classification approaches in which several classifiers are brought to contribute to the same task of recognition [7]. Combining the predictions of a set of component classifiers has been shown to yield accuracy higher than the most accurate component on a long variety of supervised classification problems. To do the combinations, various strategies of decisions, implying these classifiers in different ways are possible [32, 15, 7, 27]. Good introductions to the area can be found in [9] and [10].

Classifier combination can fuse together different information sources to utilize their complementary information. The sources can be multi-modal, such as speech and vision, but can also be transformations [14] or partitions [5, 2, 22] of the same signal.

The combination, mixture, or ensemble of classification models could be performed mainly by means of two approaches:

G.J. Williams and S.J. Simoff (Eds.): Data Mining, LNAI 3755, pp. 53–63, 2006.

- Concurrent execution of some paradigms with a posterior combination of the individual decision each model has given to the case to classify [31]. The combination can be done by a voting approach or by means of more complex approaches [11].
- Hybrid approaches, in which the foundations of two or more different classification systems are implemented together in one classifier [14]. In the hybrid approach lies the concept of reductionism, where complex problems are solved through stepwise decomposition [28].

In this paper, we present a new hybrid classifier based on two families of well known classification methods; the first one is a distance based classifier [6] and the second one is the classification tree paradigm [3] which is combined with the former in the classification process. The k-NN algorithm is used as a preprocessing algorithm in order to obtain a modified training database for the posterior learning of the classification tree structure. This modified database can lead to the induction of a tree different from the one induced according to the original database. The two major differences are the choice of a different split variable at some point in the tree, and the different decision about pruning at some depth. We show the results obtained by the new approach and compare them with the results obtained by the classification tree induction algorithm (ID3 [23]).

The rest of the paper is organized as follows. Section 2 reviews the decision tree paradigm, while section 3 presents the K-NN method. The new proposed approach is presented in section 4 and results obtained are shown in section 5. Final section is dedicated to conclusions and points out the future work.

2   Decision Trees

A *decision tree* consists of nodes and branches to partition a set of samples into a set of covering decision rules. In each node, a single test or decision is made to obtain a partition. The starting node is usually referred as the root node. An illustration of this appears in Figure 1. In the terminal nodes or leaves a decision is made on the class assignment. Figure 2 shows an illustrative example of a Classification Tree obtained by the mineset software from SGI.

In each node, the main task is to select an attribute that makes the best partition between the classes of the samples in the training set. There are many different measures to select the best attribute in a node of the decision trees: two works gathering these measures are [19] and [16]. In more complex works like [21] these tests are made applying the linear discriminant approach in each node. In the induction of a decision tree, an usual problem is the overfitting of the tree to the training dataset, producing an excessive expansion of the tree and consequently losing predictive accuracy to classify new unseen cases. This problem is overcome in two ways:

- weighing the discriminant capability of the attribute selected, and thus discarding a possible successive splitting of the dataset. This technique is known as "prepruning".

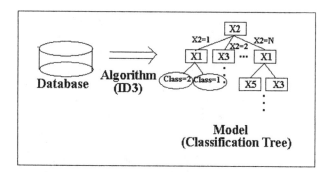

Fig. 1. Single classifier construction. Induction of a Classification Tree.

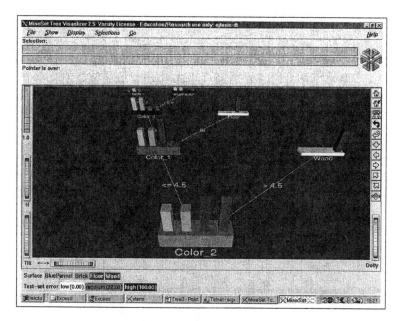

Fig. 2. Example of a Classification Tree

– after allowing a huge expansion of the tree, we could revise a splitting mode in a node removing branches and leaves, and only maintaining the node. This technique is known as "postpruning".

The works that have inspired a lot of successive papers in the task of the decision trees are [3] and [23]. In our experiments, we use the well-known decision tree induction algorithm, ID3 [23].

3   The K-NN Classification Method

A set of pairs $(x_1, \theta_1), (x_2, \theta_2), \ldots, (x_n, \theta_n)$ is given, where the x_i's take values in a metric space X upon which is defined a metric d and the θ_i's take values in the set $\{1, 2, \ldots, M\}$ of possible classes. Each θ_i is considered to be the index of the category to which the ith individual belongs, and each x_i is the outcome of the set of measurements made upon that individual. We use to say that "x_i belongs to θ_i" when we mean precisely that the ith individual, upon which measurements x_i have been observed, belongs to category θ_i.

A new pair (x, θ) is given, where only the measurement x is observable, and it is desired to estimate θ by using the information contained in the set of correctly classified points. We shall call

$$x'_n \in x_1, x_2, \ldots, x_n$$

the nearest neighbor of x if

$$\min d(x_i, x) = d(x'_n, x), \quad i = 1, 2, \ldots, n$$

The NN classification decision method gives to x the category θ'_n of its nearest neighbor x'_n. In case of tie for the nearest neighbor, the decision rule has to be modified in order to break it. A mistake is made if $\theta'_n \neq \theta$.

An immediate extension to this decision rule is the so called k-NN approach [4], which assigns to the candidate x the class which is most frequently represented in the k nearest neighbors to x. In Figure 3 , for example, the 3-NN decision rule would decide x as belonging to class θ_o because two of the three nearest neighbors of x belongs to class θ_o.

Much research has been devoted to the K-NN rule [6]. One of the most important results is that K-NN has asymptotically very good performance. Loosely speaking, for a very large design set, the expected probability of incorrect classifications (error) R achievable with K-NN is bounded as follows:

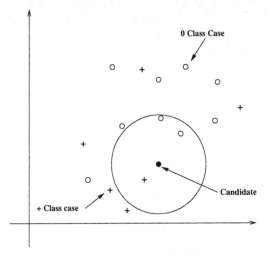

Fig. 3. 3-NN classification method. A voting method has to be implemented to take the final decision. The classification given in this example by simple voting would be class=circle.

$$R^* < R < 2R^*$$

where R^* is the optimal (minimal) error rate for the underlying distributions $p_i, i = 1, 2, \ldots, M$.

This performance, however, is demonstrated for the training set size tending to infinity, and thus, is not really applicable to real world problems, in which we usually have a training set of about hundreds or thousands cases, too little, anyway, for the number of probability estimations to be done.

More extensions to the k-NN approach could be seen in [6, 1, 25, 17]. More effort has to be done in the K-NN paradigm in order to reduce the number of cases of the training database to obtain faster classifications [6, 26].

4   Proposed Approach

In boosting techniques, a distribution or set of weights over the training set is maintained. On each execution, the weights of incorrectly classified examples are increased so that the base learner is forced to focus on the hard examples in the training set. A good description of boosting can be found in [8].

Following the idea of focusing in the hard examples, we wanted to know if one algorithm could be used to boost a different one, in a simple way. We have chosen two well-known algorithms, k-NN and ID3, and our approach (in the following we will refer to it as k-NN-boosting) works as follows:

- Find the incorrectly classified instances in the training set using k-NN over the training set but the instance to be classified
- Duplicate the instances incorrectly classified in the previous step
- Apply ID3 to the augmented training set

Let us note that this approach is equivalent to duplicate the weight of incorrectly classified instances, according to k-NN.

In this manner, the core of this new approach consists of inflating the training database adding the cases misclassified by the k-NN algorithm, and then learn the classification tree from the new database obtained. It has to be said that this approach increases the computational cost only in the model induction phase, while the classification costs are the same as in the original ID3 paradigm.

Modifying the instance distribution in the training dataset, two major effects can be obtained:

- Election of a different variable to split at some node
- Change in the decision about pruning the tree at some point

4.1   Change in the Variable to Split

Let us suppose the training set is formed by twelve cases, six of them belonging to class A and the remaining six to class B.

In figure 4 is depicted an example on the change of information gain after the edition of the training set. The number in parentheses are in the form (#instances

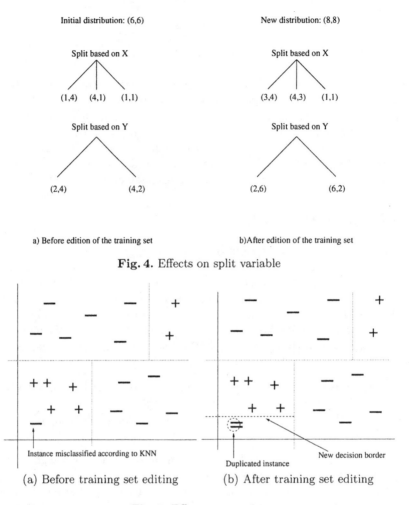

Fig. 4. Effects on split variable

(a) Before training set editing   (b) After training set editing

Fig. 5. Effects on pruning

belonging to A,#instances belonging to B). In the left side it is shown the original training set, along with the partitions induced by the variables X and Y. The information gain if X is chosen is $(1 - 0.7683) = 0.2317$, and if Y is chosen instead is $(1 - 0.9183) = 0.0817$. So, X would be chosen as variable to split. After the training set edition, as showed in the right side of the figure, four instances are duplicated, two of them belonging to class A, and the remaining two to class B. Now, the information gain if X is chosen is $(1 - 0.9871) = 0.0129$, and if Y is chosen instead is $(1 - 0.8113) = 0.1887$. Variable Y would be chosen, leading to a different tree.

4.2   Change in the Pruning Decision

In figure 5 is shown an example where a change in the pruning decision could be taken into account. In the left subfigure, before the edition of the training set with duplication of cases misclasified by k-NN, the density of examples belonging to class "-" is very low, so a new split in the tree is not considered. But, after the duplication of the lonely instance, the density of examples belonging to its class grows, making possible a further split of the tree and the building of different decision borders.

If the two sources of instability above mentioned were generated at random, no improvement in the final accuracy might be expected. We wanted to test if instability generated according to the cases misclasified by other algorithm (k-NN) could lead to a improvement over the accuracy yielded by the original ID3. In the next section are the experimental results we obtained.

5   Experimental Results

Ten databases are used to test our hypothesis. All of them are obtained from the *UCI Machine Learning Repository* [2]. These domains are public at the Statlog project WEB page [18]. The characteristics of the databases are given in Table 1. As it can be seen, we have chosen different types of databases, selecting some of them with a large number of predictor variables, or with a large number of cases and some multi-class problems.

Table 1. Details of databases

Database	Number of cases	Number of classes	Number of attributes
Diabetes	768	2	8
Australian	690	2	14
Heart	270	2	13
Monk2	432	2	6
Wine	178	3	13
Zoo	101	7	16
Waveform-21	5000	3	21
Nettalk	14471	324	203
Letter	20000	26	16
Shuttle	58000	7	9

In order to give a real perspective of applied methods, we use 10-Fold Cross-validation [29] in all experiments. All databases have been randomly separated into ten sets of training data and its corresponding test data. Obviously all the validation files used have been always the same for the two algorithms: ID3 and our approach, k-NN-boosting. Ten executions for every 10-fold set have been carried out using k-NN-boosting, one for each different K ranging from 1 to 10. In Table 2 a comparative of ID3 error rate, as well as the best and worst performance of k-NN-boosting, along with the average error rate among the ten first values of K, used in the experiment, is shown. The cases when k-NN-boosting outperforms ID3 are drawn in boldface. Let us note that in six out of ten databases the average of the ten sets of executions of k-NN-boosting outperforms ID3 and in two of the remaining four cases the performance is similar.

Table 2. Rates of experimental errors of ID3 and k-NN-boosting

Database	ID3 error	k-NN-boosting (best)	K value	k-NN-boosting (worst)	K value	Average (over all K)
Diabetes	29.43	**29.04**	5	32.68	10	31.26
	± 0.40	±**1.78**		±0.87		± 1.37
Australian	18.26	**17.97**	6	19.42	1	18.55
	± 1.31	±**0.78**		± 1.26		± 0.32
Heart	27.78	**21.85**	1	27.78	6	**25.48**
	± 0.77	±**0.66**		± 3.10		±**3.29**
Monk2	53.95	**43.74**	4	46.75	5	**45.09**
	±5.58	±**5.30**		± 0.73		±**1.03**
Wine	7.29	**5.03**	2	5.59	1	**5.04**
	±0.53	±**1.69**		±**1.87**		±**0.06**
Zoo	3.91	**2.91**	4	3.91	1	**3.41**
	±1.36	±**1.03**		±1.36		±**0.25**
Waveform-21	24.84	**23.02**	5	25.26	8	**24.22**
	±0.25	±**0.27**		± 0.38		± **0.45**
Nettalk	25.96	**25.81**	7	26.09	10	**25.95**
	± 0.27	±**0.50**		± 0.44		±**0.01**
Letter	11.66	**11.47**	2	11.86	9	11.66
	± 0.20	±**0.25**		± 0.21		± 0.02
Shuttle	0.02	0.02	any	0.02	any	0.02
	±0.11	±0.11		± 0.11		±0.00

In nine out of ten databases there exists a value of K for which k-NN-boosting outperforms ID3. In the remaining case the performance is similar. In two out of ten databases even in the case of the worst K value with respect to accuracy, k-NN-boosting outperforms ID3, and in other three they behave in a similar way. In Table 3 the results of applying the Wilcoxon signed rank test [30] to compare the relative performance of ID3 and k-NN-boosting for the ten databases tested are shown. It can be seen that in three out of ten databases (Heart, Monk2 and Waveform-21) there are significance improvements under a confidence level of 95%, while no significantly worse performance is found in any database for any K value.

Let us observe that in several cases where no significant difference can be found, the mean value obtained by the new proposed approach outperforms ID3, as explained above.

In order to give an idea about the increment in the number of instances that this approach implies, in Table 4 the size of the augmented databases is drawn. The values appearing in the column labeled $K = n$ corresponds to the size of the database generated from the entire original database when applying the first step of k-NN-boosting. As it can be seen, the size increase is not very high, and so it does not really affect to the computation load of the classification tree model induction performed by the ID3 algorithm.

K-NN-boosting is a model induction algorithm belonging to the classification tree family, in which the k-NN paradigm is just used to modify the database the tree structure is learned from. Due to this characteristic of the algorithm, the

Table 3. *K*-NN-boosting vs. ID3 for every K. A ↑ sign means that *k*-NN-boosting outperforms ID3 with a significance level of 95% (Wilcoxon test).

Database	K=1	K=2	K=3	K=4	K=5	K=6	K=7	K=8	K=9	K=10
Diabetes	=	=	=	=	=	=	=	=	=	=
Australian	=	=	=	=	=	=	=	=	=	=
Heart	↑	=	=	=	=	=	=	=	=	=
Monk2	↑	↑	↑	↑	=	=	↑	↑	↑	↑
Wine	=	=	=	=	=	=	=	=	=	=
Zoo	=	=	=	=	=	=	=	=	=	=
Waveform-21	=	=	=	=	↑	=	=	=	↑	=
Nettalk	=	=	=	=	=	=	=	=	=	=
Letter	=	=	=	=	=	=	=	=	=	=
Shuttle	=	=	=	=	=	=	=	=	=	=

Table 4. Sizes of the augmented databases

Database	Original size	K=1	K=2	K=3	K=4	K=5	K=6	K=7	K=8	K=9	K=10
Diabetes	768	1014	990	1003	987	987	976	977	973	972	969
Australian	690	928	916	916	909	905	895	893	894	897	890
Heart	270	385	375	365	360	360	364	359	360	363	366
Monk2	432	552	580	580	588	604	590	575	565	564	565
Wine	178	219	236	227	238	232	234	238	236	229	237
Zoo	101	103	123	108	106	109	111	113	117	120	122
Wavef.-21	5000	6098	6129	5930	5964	5907	5891	5851	5848	5824	5824
Nettalk	14471	15318	15059	15103	15065	15085	15069	15077	15056	15059	15061
Letter	20000	20746	20993	20799	20889	20828	20857	20862	20920	20922	20991
Shuttle	58000	58098	58111	58096	58108	58111	58112	58111	58120	58129	58133

performance comparison is done between the ID3 paradigm and our proposed one, as they work in a similar manner.

6   Conclusions and Further Work

In this paper a new hybrid classifier that combines Classification Trees (ID3) with distance-based algorithms is presented. The main idea is to augment the training test duplicating the badly classified cases according to *k*-NN algorithm. The underlying idea is to test if one algorithm (*k*-NN) could be used to boost a different one (ID3), acting over the distribution of the training examples and then causing two effects: the choice of a different variable to split at some node, and the change in the decision about pruning or not a subtree.

The experimental results support the idea that such boosting is possible and deserve further research. A more complete experimental work on more databases as well as another weight changing schemas (let us remember that our approach is equivalent to double the weight of misclassified instances) could be subject of exhaustive research.

Further work could focus on other classification trees construction methods, as C4.5 [24] or Ocl [21].

An extension of the presented approach is to select among the feature subset that better performance presents by the classification point of view. A Feature Subset Selection [12, 13, 26] technique can be applied in order to select which of the predictor variables should be used. This could take advantage in the hybrid classifier construction, as well as in the accuracy.

Acknowledgments

This work has been supported by the University of the Basque Country under grant 1/UPV00140.226-E-15412/2003 and by the Gipuzkoako Foru Aldundia OF-761/2003.

References

1. D. Aha, D. Kibler, and M. K. Albert. Instance-based learning algorithms. *Machine Learning*, 6:37–66, 1991.
2. C. L. Blake and C. J. Merz. UCI repository of machine learning databases, 1998.
3. L. Breiman, J. Friedman, R. Olshen, and C. Stone. *Classification and Regression Trees*. Monterey, CA: Wadsworth, 1984.
4. T. M. Cover and P. E. Hart. Nearest neighbor pattern classification. *IEEE Trans. IT-13*, 1:21–27, 1967.
5. R. G. Cowell, A. Ph. Dawid, S. L. Lauritzen, and D. J. Spiegelharter. *Probabilistic Networks and Expert Systems*. Springer, 1999.
6. B. V. Dasarathy. Nearest neighbor (nn) norms: Nn pattern recognition classification techniques. *IEEE Computer Society Press*, 1991.
7. T. G. Dietterich. Machine learning research: four current directions. *AI Magazine*, 18(4):97–136, 1997.
8. Y. Freund and R. E. Schapire. A short introduction to boosting. *Journal of Japanese Society for Artificial Intelligence*, 14(5):771–780, 1999.
9. J. Gama. *Combining Classification Algorithms*. Phd Thesis. University of Porto, 2000.
10. V. Gunes, M. Ménard, and P. Loonis. Combination, cooperation and selection of classifiers: A state of the art. *International Journal of Pattern Recognition*, 17:1303–1324, 2003.
11. T. K. Ho and S. N. Srihati. Decision combination in multiple classifier systems. *IEEE Transactions on Pattern Analysis and Machine Intelligence*, 16:66–75, 1994.
12. I. Inza, P. Larrañaga, R. Etxeberria, and B. Sierra. Feature subset selection by bayesian networks based optimization. *Artificial Intelligence*, 123(1-2):157–184, 2000.
13. I. Inza, P. Larrañaga, and B. Sierra. Feature subset selection by bayesian networks: a comparison with genetic and sequential algorithms. *International Journal of Approximate Reasoning*, 27(2):143–164, 2001.

14. R. Kohavi. Scaling up the accuracy of naive-bayes classifiers: a decision-tree hybrid. In *Proceedings of the Second International Conference on Knowledge Discovery and Data Mining*, 1996.
15. Y. Lu. Knowledge integration in a multiple classifier system. *Applied Intelligence*, 6:75–86, 1996.
16. J. K. Martin. An exact probability metric for decision tree splitting and stopping. *Machine Learning*, 28, 1997.
17. J. M. Martínez-Otzeta and B. Sierra. Analysis of the iterated probabilistic weighted k-nearest neighbor method, a new distance-based algorithm. In *6th International Conference on Enterprise Information Systems (ICEIS)*, volume 2, pages 233–240, 2004.
18. D. Michie, D. J. Spiegelhalter, and C. C. (eds) Taylor. Machine learning, neural and statistical classification, 1995.
19. J. Mingers. A comparison of methods of pruning induced rule trees. *Technical Report. Coventry, England: University of Warwick, School of Industrial and Business Studies*, 1, 1988.
20. T. Mitchell. *Machine Learning*. McGraw-Hill, 1997.
21. S. K. Murthy, S. Kasif, and S. Salzberg. A system for the induction of oblique decision trees. *Journal of Artificial Intelligence Research*, 2:1–33, 1994.
22. J. Pearl. Evidential reasoning using stochastic simulation of causal models. *Artificial Intelligence*, 32(2):245–257, 1987.
23. J. R. Quinlan. Induction of decision trees. *Machine Learning*, 1:81–106, 1986.
24. J. R. Quinlan. *C4.5: Programs for Machine Learning*. Morgan Kaufmann Publishers, Los Altos, California, 1993.
25. B. Sierra and E. Lazkano. Probabilistic-weighted k nearest neighbor algorithm: a new approach for gene expression based classification. In *KES02 proceedings*, pages 932–939. IOS press, 2002.
26. B. Sierra, E. Lazkano, I. Inza, M. Merino, P. Larrañaga, and J. Quiroga. Prototype selection and feature subset selection by estimation of distribution algorithms. a case study in the survival of cirrhotic patients treated with TIPS. *Artificial Intelligence in Medicine*, pages 20–29, 2001.
27. B. Sierra, N. Serrano, P. Larrañaga, E. J. Plasencia, I. Inza, J. J. Jiménez, P. Revuelta, and M. L. Mora. Using bayesian networks in the construction of a bi-level multi-classifier. *Artificial Intelligence in Medicine*, 22:233–248, 2001.
28. B. Sierra, N. Serrano, P. Larrañaga, E. J. Plasencia, I. Inza, J. J. Jiménez, P. Revuelta, and M. L. Mora. Machine learning inspired approaches to combine standard medical measures at an intensive care unit. *Lecture Notes in Artificial Intelligence*, 1620:366–371, 1999.
29. M. Stone. Cross-validation choice and assessment of statistical procedures. *Journal Royal of Statistical Society*, 36:111–147, 1974.
30. F. Wilcoxon. Individual comparisons by ranking methods. *Biometrics*, 1:80–83, 1945.
31. D. Wolpert. Stacked generalization. *Neural Networks*, 5:241–259, 1992.
32. L. Xu, A. Kryzak, and C. Y. Suen. Methods for combining multiple classifiers and their applications to handwriting recognition. *IEEE Transactions on SMC*, 22:418–435, 1992.

Efficiently Identifying Exploratory Rules' Significance

Shiying Huang and Geoffrey I. Webb

School of Computer Science and Software Engineering,
Monash University, Melbourne VIC 3800, Australia
{Shiying.Huang, Geoff.Webb}@infotech.monash.edu.au

Abstract. How to efficiently discard potentially uninteresting rules in exploratory rule discovery is one of the important research foci in data mining. Many researchers have presented algorithms to automatically remove potentially uninteresting rules utilizing background knowledge and user-specified constraints. Identifying the significance of exploratory rules using a significance test is desirable for removing rules that may appear interesting by chance, hence providing the users with a more compact set of resulting rules. However, applying statistical tests to identify significant rules requires considerable computation and data access in order to obtain the necessary statistics. The situation gets worse as the size of the database increases. In this paper, we propose two approaches for improving the efficiency of significant exploratory rule discovery. We also evaluate the experimental effect in impact rule discovery which is suitable for discovering exploratory rules in very large, dense databases.

Keywords: Exploratory rule discovery, impact rule, rule significance, interestingness measure.

1 Introduction

Exploratory rule discovery techniques seek multiple models which are able to efficiently describe the potentially interesting inter-relationships among attributes in a database. Searching for multiple models instead of a single model often results in numerous spurious or uninteresting rules.

How to automatically discard statistically insignificant rules has been an important issue in research of exploratory rule discovery. Several papers have been devoted to this topic. Bay and Pazzani [4], Liu et. al [10] and Webb [15], developed techniques for identifying insignificant rules with qualitative attributes only (or descretized quantitative attributes). Aumann and Lindell [2] and Huang and Webb [8] both did research on exploratory rule significance with undescretized quantitative attributes as consequent.

When filtering insignificant exploratory rules regarding quantitative attributes, the rule discovery systems have to go through the database several times so as to collect the necessary parameters for the significance test. Moreover, considerable CPU time has to be spent on data access and looking for

G.J. Williams and S.J. Simoff (Eds.): Data Mining, LNAI 3755, pp. 64–77, 2006.

the set of records which is covered by the antecedent of a rule. For example, it has been shown by Huang and Webb [8] that the time spent for discovering the top 1000 significant impact rules is on the whole much more than that spent on discovering the top 1000 impact rules without using any filter, especially when most of the top 1000 impact rules are insignificant. A technique for improving the efficiency of the insignificance filter is presented in the same paper by introducing the triviality filter. The anti-monotonicity of triviality was utilized to effectively prune the search space.

There is an immediate need for improving the efficiency of the insignificance filter for distributional-consequent exploratory rule discovery, even after the introduction of the triviality filter. In this paper, we propose two approaches for efficiency improving in exploratory rule discovery, which can result in substantial reduction of the computation for discovering significant rules. Although the demonstration is done on impact rule discovery, these techniques can also be recast for other exploratory rule discovery tasks.

The paper is organized as follows: In section 2, we introduce the concept and notations of exploratory rule discovery. Existing techniques for discarding insignificant exploratory rules are introduced in section 3, followed by the brief description of impact rule discovery in section 4. The techniques for improving the efficiency are presented in section 5. In section 6, we provide experimental results and evaluations. Conclusions are drawn in section 7.

2   Exploratory Rule Discovery

Traditional machine learning systems discover a single model from the available data that is expected to maximize the accuracy or some other specific measures of performance on unknown future data. Predictions or classifications are then done on the basis of this single model [15]. Examples include the decision tree [12], the decision rules [11], and the Naive-Bayes classifier. However, alternative models exist that perform equally well as those which are selected by the systems. Thus, it is not always sensible to choose only one of the"best" models in some cases. The criteria for deciding whether a model is best or not also varies with the context of application. Exploratory rule discovery techniques are proposed to overcome this problem by searching for multiple models which satisfy certain constraints and presenting all these models to the user. Thus, the users are provided with alternative choices. Better flexibility is achieved herewith.

Exploratory rule discovery techniques [8] are classified into propositional rule discovery which seeks rules with qualitative attributes or discretized quantitative attributes only and distributional-consequent rule discovery which seeks rules with quantitative attributes as consequent. The status of performance such quantitative attributes are described with their distributions. *Association rule discovery* [1], *contrast sets discovery* [4] are examples of propositional exploratory rule discovery, while *impact rule discovery* [13] and *quantitative association rule discovery* [2] both belong to the class of distributional-consequent rule discovery. It is argued that distributional-consequent rules are able to provide better descriptions of the interrelationship between quantitative attributes and qualitative attributes.

Here are some notions of exploratory rule discovery that we are to use in this paper:

1. A *dataset* is a finite set of *records*
2. For propositional rule discovery, a *record* is an element to which we apply Boolean predicates called conditions, while for distributional-consequent rule discovery, a record is a *pair* $< c, v >$, where c is the nonempty set of Boolean conditions, and v is a set of values for the quantitative variables in whose distribution the users are interested.
3. A rule is in the form of $A \rightarrow C$. For propositional rules, both A and C are conjunctions of Boolean conditions. The status of such rule is described by interestingness measures like the *support* and the *confidence*. Contrarily, for distributional-consequent rule discovery, A is a conjunction of Boolean conditions while C is a nonempty set of target quantitative variables in which the users are interested. The quantitative variables are described by distributional statistics. We prefer using $A \rightarrow target$ to denote a distributional-consequent rule instead, for the purpose of avoiding confusion.
4. Rule $A \rightarrow C$ is a parent of $B \rightarrow C$ if $A \subset B$. If $|A| = |B| - 1$, then the second rule is a direct parent of the first one, otherwise, it is a grandparent of the first rule.
5. We use the notion $coverset(A)$, where A is a conjunction of conditions, to represent the set of records that satisfy the condition (or set of conditions) A. If a record x is in $coverset(A)$, we say that x is *covered* by A. If A is $\emptyset$, $coverset(A)$ includes all the records in the database.
6. $Coverage(A)$ is the number of records covered by A. $coverage(A) = |coverset(A)|$.

3   Insignificant Exploratory Rules

As is mentioned before, exploratory rule discovery searches for multiple models in a database, and may lead to discovering spurious or uninteresting rules. How to decrease the number of resulting rules becomes a problem of concern. One approach is up to the users to define a suitable set of constraints which may be utilized so that the algorithm can automatically discard some potentially uninteresting rules. Another approach is to perform comparison within resulting rules, so as to present the users with a more compact set of models. Techniques regarding automatically removing potentially uninteresting rules are summarized by Huang and Webb [8].

3.1   Improvement

Filtering insignificant rules using statistical tests is one of the interesting topics of research. By using this technique we perform significance tests among rules and discard those which happen to appear interesting only by chance. To provide a clear idea of insignificant rules, we will at first introduce the concept of rule *improvement* defined by Bayardo et al. [5]. *Confidence improvement* which is used as an example, defined a minimum improvement in confidence that a propositional rule must exhibit in order to be regarded as potentially interesting:

$$imp(A \rightarrow C) = min(\forall A' \subset A, confidence(A \rightarrow C)$$
$$- confidence(A' \rightarrow C))$$

It is argued that setting a minimum improvement is desirable in discarding potentially uninteresting exploratory rules. However, the values used for comparison are derived from samples instead of from the total population. There is the problem that the observed improvement provides only an estimate of the true improvement, and if no account is taken of the quality of that estimate, so it is likely to result in poor decisions.

Rule filtering techniques regarding the significance of rules concern about the statistically significance of the improvement, rather than the values of interestingness measures. Statistical tests are done with resulting rules and those within expectation (or without enough surprisingness) are automatically removed. Such techniques may lead to type-1 error, which result in accepting spurious or uninteresting rules and type-2 error, which result in rejecting rules that are not spurious. A technique for statistically sound exploratory rule discovery is proposed by Webb [15] using a holdout set to validate the resulting rules.

3.2 Statistical Significance of Rules

Chi-square test is a widely used test for identifying propositional rule independence. Liu et al. [10] did research on association rules with a fixed attribute as consequent. They used a chi-square test to decide whether the antecedent of a rule is independent from its consequent or not, accepting only rules whose antecedent and consequent are positively correlated, thus, discarding rules which happen to appear interesting by chance. The rules discarded by using an independent test are referred to as insignificant rules.

Consider the following Boolean-consequent rules:

$$A \rightarrow C[support = 60\%, confidence = 90\%]$$
$$A\&B \rightarrow C[support = 45\%, confidence = 91\%]$$
$$A\&D \rightarrow C[support = 46\%, confidence = 70\%]$$

There is a high possibility that the conditions B and C are conditionally independent given A, thus the second rule provides little interesting information. According to Liu et al., the third rule does not bear interesting information, either. It should also be discarded, because the condition D is negatively correlated to condition C, given A. Bay and Pazzani [4] also made use of Chi-square test to decide the significance of *contrast sets*. Webb [15] proposed a statistically sound technique for filtering insignificant rules, using the Fisher exact test and a hold out set.

Aumann and Lindell [2] and Huang and Webb [8] both proposed ideas for filtering insignificant distributional-consequent exploratory rules. In this paper, we use the definition proposed by the latter.

Definition 1. *significant impact rule An impact rule $A \rightarrow target$ is significant if the distribution of its target is significantly improved in comparison with the target distribution of any of its direct parents'. The measure for the target distribution can be the mean, the variance etc.*

$$significant(A \rightarrow target) = \forall x \in A, dist(coverset(A))$$
$$\gg dist(coverset(A - x) - coverset(A))^1$$

An impact rule is insignificant *if it is not* significant.

Definitions of insignificant propositional exploratory rules are provided by Liu et al. [10] and Bay and Pazzani [4].

In this paper, the mean of the target attribute over $coverset(A)$ is used as the interestingness measure to be compared for the impact rule. Statistical test is done to decide whether the target means of two samples are significantly different from each other.

4   K-Most-Interesting Impact Rule Discovery and Notations

The impact rule discovery algorithm we adopt is based on the OPUS [14] algorithm, which enable the successfully discovery of the top k impact rules that satisfy a certain set of constraints.

We characterized the terminology of k-most-interesting impact rule discovery to be used in this paper as follows:

1. An impact rule is in form of $A \rightarrow target$, while the target is describe by the following measures: *coverage, mean, variance, maximum, minimum, sum* and *impact*.
2. *Impact* is an interestingness measure suggested by Webb [13][2]: $impact(A \rightarrow target) = (mean(A \rightarrow target) - \overline{targ}) \times coverage(A))$.
3. A k-most-interesting impact rule discovery task is a 7-tuple: $KMIIRD(\mathcal{C}, \mathcal{T}, \mathcal{D}, \mathcal{M}, \lambda, \mathcal{I}, k)$.
   $\mathcal{C}$: is a nonempty set of Boolean conditions, which are the set of available conditions for impact rule antecedents.
   $\mathcal{T}$: is a nonempty set of the variables in whose distribution we are interested.
   $\mathcal{D}$: is a nonempty set of records, which is called the database. A record is a pair $< c, v >, c \subseteq C$ and v is a set of values for $\mathcal{T}$.

---

[1] The token "$\gg$" is used to denote **significantly improved**, and $dist(\mathcal{R})$ is used to represent the distribution of the target variable over the set of records $\mathcal{R}$.

[2] In this formula, $mean(A \rightarrow target)$ denotes the mean of the *targets* covered by A, and $coverage(A)$ is the number of the records covered by A.

Table 1. OPUS_IR_Filter

```
Algorithm: OPUS_IR_Filter(Current, Available, M)

1. SoFar := ∅
2. FOR EACH P in Available
   2.1 New := Current ∪ P
   2.2 IF New satisfies all the prunable constraints in M except the nontrivial [8]
       constraint THEN
       2.2.1 IF any direct subset of New has the same coverage as New THEN
                 New → relevant stats is a trivial rule
                 Any superset of New is trivial, so do not access any children of this node,
                 go to step 2.
       2.2.2 ELSE IF the mean of New → relevant stats is significantly higher than all its
             direct parents THEN
                 IF the rule satisfies all the other non-prunable constraints in M
                    THEN record Rule to the ordered rule_list
                 OPUS_IR_Filter(New, SoFar, M)
                 SoFar := SoFar ∪ P
       2.2.3 END IF
   2.3 END IF
3. END FOR
```

$\mathcal{M}$: is a set of constraints. There are two types of constraints *prunable* and *unprunable constraints*. *Prunable constraints* are constraints that you can derive useful bounds for search space pruning and still ensures the completeness of information. Examples include the anti-monotone, the succinct constraints [7], or the convertible constraints [9]. Constraints which are not prunable are *unprunable constraints*

λ: $\{X \rightarrow Y\} \times \{D\} \rightarrow \mathcal{R}$ is a function from rules and databases to value and define a interestingness metric such that the greater the value of $\lambda(X \rightarrow Y, \mathcal{D})$ the greater the interestingness of this rule given the database.

$\mathcal{I}$: is the set of impact rules that can be derived from $\mathcal{D}$, whose antecedents are conjunctions of one or more conditions in C, whose targets are members of $\mathcal{T}$, and which satisfy the constraints in $\mathcal{M}$.

k: is a user specified integer number denoting the number of rules in the ultimate solution for this task.

The original algorithm for impact rule discovery with filters are described in table 1. In this table, *current* is the set of conditions, whose supersets are currently being explored. *Available* is the set of conditions that may be added to *current*. By adding every condition in *available* to *current* one by one, we form the antecedent of the *current rule*: $New \rightarrow target$, which will be referred to later as *current_rules*. *Rule_list* is an ordered list of the top-k interesting rules we have encountered.

5   Efficient Identification of Exploratory Rule Significance

5.1   Deriving Difference Set Statistics Without Data Access

According to the algorithm in table 1 and definition 1, we have to compare the mean of current rule with the means of all its direct parents' in order to decide whether a rule is *significant* or not. The set difference operations necessary for this purpose requires excessive data access and computation. However with the status of current rule and all its parent rules known, we will be able to derive the statistics of the difference sets for performing the significance test, without additional access to the database. The following lemma validates this statement.

Lemma 1. *Suppose we are searching for impact rules from a database $\mathcal{D}$. If $A \subset B$, and $coverset(A) - coverset(B) = \mathcal{R}$, where A and B are both conjunction of conditions, $\mathcal{R}$ is a set of records from $\mathcal{D}$. If the mean and variance of the target attribute over $coverset(A)$ and $coverset(B)$ are known, as well as the cardinality of both record sets, the mean and variance of the target attribute over set $\mathcal{R}$ can be derived without additional data access.*

Proof. Since $coverset(A) - coverset(B) = \mathcal{R}$, it is obvious that

$$|\mathcal{R}| = coverage(A) - coverage(B) \tag{1}$$

$$mean(\mathcal{R}) = \frac{coverage(A) \times mean(A \rightarrow target) - coverage(B) \times mean(B \rightarrow target)}{|\mathcal{R}|} \tag{2}$$

$$variance(A \rightarrow target) = \frac{\sum_{x \in coverset(A)} (target(x) - mean(A \rightarrow target))^2}{coverage(A) - 1} \tag{3}$$

$$variance(B \rightarrow target) = \frac{\sum_{x \in coverset(B)} (target(x) - mean(B \rightarrow target))^2}{coverage(B) - 1} \tag{4}$$

$$\sum_{x \in coverset(A)} target(x) = mean(A \rightarrow target) \times coverage(A) \tag{5}$$

$$\sum_{x \in coverset(B)} target(x) = mean(B \rightarrow target) \times coverage(B) \tag{6}$$

From 3, 4, 5 and 6 it is feasible to derive the following equation:

$$\sum_{x \in \mathcal{R}} target(x)^2 = \sum_{x \in coverset(A)} target(x)^2 - \sum_{x \in coverset(B)} target(x)^2$$
$$= variance(A \rightarrow target) \times (coverage(A) - 1)$$
$$+ mean(A \rightarrow target)^2 \times coverage(A)$$
$$- variance(B \rightarrow target) \times (coverage(B) - 1)$$
$$- mean(B \rightarrow target)^2 \times coverage(B) \tag{7}$$

$$\sum_{x \in \mathcal{R}} target(x) = \sum_{x \in coverset(A)} target(x) - \sum_{x \in coverset(B)} target(x) \tag{8}$$

Thus,

$$variance(\mathcal{R}) = \frac{\sum_{x \in \mathcal{R}} (target(x) - mean(\mathcal{R}))^2}{|\mathcal{R}| - 1}$$
$$= \frac{\sum_{x \in \mathcal{R}} target(x)^2}{|\mathcal{R}| - 1} - \frac{2mean(\mathcal{R}) \sum_{x \in \mathcal{R}} target(x)}{|\mathcal{R}| - 1} + \frac{|\mathcal{R}| mean(\mathcal{R})^2}{|\mathcal{R}| - 1}$$

Since all the parameters in the right hand side of the equation are already known, we are able to derive all the necessary statistics for doing significance test without accessing the records in $\mathcal{R}$. The lemma is proved.

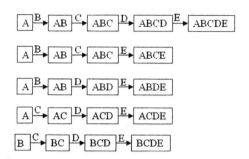

Fig. 1. The parallel intersection Approach for $ABCDE$

Note: in this proof, mean($A \to target$) denotes the target mean of the records covered by rule $A \to target$, variance($A \to target$) denotes the target variance of the records covered by rule $A \to target$, while mean($\mathcal{R}$) denotes the target mean of the records in record set $\mathcal{R}$, and variance($\mathcal{R}$) represents the target variance of the records in $\mathcal{R}$.

By deriving the difference set statistics from the statistics of the *parent_rule* and *New $\to$ target* in table 1, we are able to save data access and computation for collecting the statistics for performing the significance test, thus improve the efficiency of the search algorithm.

5.2   The Circular Intersection Approach

Parallel Intersection Approach. According to the definition of significant impact rules, we compare the current rule with all its *direct parents* to identify its significance. In the original OPUS_IR_Filter algorithm, the procedure described in figure 1 is employed to find the *coverset* of every direct parent of the current rule which is being explored. Each arrow in figure 1 represents an intersection operation. When deciding whether a rule with 5 conditions, namely A, B, C, D and E on the antecedent is significant or not, the algorithm has to go through 16 intersection operations! We refer to this approach as the *parallel intersection* approach.

By examining figure 1, we notice that there are considerable overlaps in the *parallel intersection approach*. For example, by using the parallel intersection approach, we have to do the same intersection of *coverset(A)* and *coverset(B)* three times, when searching for *coverset($ABCD$)*, *coverset($ABCE$)* and *coverset($ABDE$)*. There must be a way in which two of these operations can be omitted.

Circular Intersection Approach. we propose the approach of *circular intersection* which is shown in figure 2[3]. In this approach, intersections are done in two stages. Firstly, in the *forward stage*, intersections are done from condition A to condition E one at a time, and the results are kept in memory. Then we

---

[3] Each dashed arrow in figure 2 and figure 3 points to the outcome of that specific intersection operation and does not represent an actual operation.

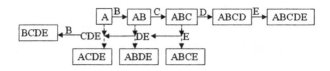

Fig. 2. The circular intersection approach flow for $ABCDE$

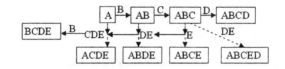

Fig. 3. The circular intersection approach for $ABCDE$ when *current* is $ABCD$

do intersections from the last condition E back to the second one B, which is referred to as the *backward stage*. During the backward stage, the *coverset* of each direct parent of the current rule is found. By introducing the circular intersection approach, the number of intersection operations required for identifying the significance of current rule is reduced to only 10.

Complexity. Using the parallel intersection approach, the number of intersection operations for iterating through all the subsets is:

$$(n - 2) \times n + 1,$$

where n is the maximum number of conditions on the rule antecedent. The complexity is $O(n^2)$.

After introducing the circular intersection approach, the intersection operations for iterating through all the subsets are:

$$3n - 5.$$

The complexity is $O(n)$. However, practically the difference in running time will not be so dramatic, since we have introduced the triviality filter, which enables the pruning of the search space. Both the parallel intersection procedure and the circular intersection procedure will probably stop at anytime when it is identified that the current rule is a trivial rule.

The two approaches (the difference set statistics derivation approach and the circular intersection approach) mentioned above can combine with each other so as to achieve higher efficiency. We can save one more intersection operation by introducing the difference set statistics derivation technique in section 5.1. Suppose that we are deciding whether the rule $A\&B\&C\&D\&E \rightarrow target$ is significant or not. Now that the statistics of one of its parent $A\&B\&C\&D \rightarrow target$ is known, thus we don't have to derive the statistics of *coverset*($ABCD$) once again. Hereby, one intersection operation can also be saved by following the procedure shown in figure 3 according to lemma 1. The number of necessary intersection operations is reduced to

$$3n - 6.$$

Table 2. Improved OPUS_IR_Filter

```
Algorithm: OPUS_IR_Filter(Current, Available, parent_rule, M)

1 SoFar := ∅;
2 FOR EACH P in Available
  2.1 New := Current ∪ P
  2.2 IF New satisfies all the prunable constraints in M except the nontrivial
      constraint THEN
    2.2.1 Derive the statistics of coverset(Current) − coverset(New), according to lemma
          1.
    2.2.2 IF the mean of New     →     target is not significantly improved comparing to
          coverset(Current) − coverset(New) THEN
                go to step 2.2.4;
    2.2.3 ELSE use the circular intersection to comparing the mean of New → target with
          the mean of its direct parents other than parent_rule
      2.2.3.1 IF the mean New     →     target is significantly improved comparing to all its
              direct parents THEN
              record New → target to rule_list;
              OPUS_IR_Filter(New, SoFar, New → target);
              SoFar := SoFar ∪ P ;
      2.2.3.2 END IF;
    2.2.4 END IF;
  2.3 END IF;
3 END FOR
```

The new algorithm for impact rule discovery with filters is shown in table 2. In this table, the *parent_rule* is the corresponding rule for the node whose children we are currently exploring. The antecedent of *parent_rule* is *current*.

6   Experimental Evaluations

In order to explain how the techniques introduced in this paper can practically improve the efficiency of rule discovery, we did our experiments by applying the new algorithm to 10 databases chosen from the UCI Machine Learning repository [6] and the UCI KDD archives [3]. The databases are described in table 3. We applied 3-bin equal-frequency discretization to map all the quantitative attributes, except the target attribute, into qualitative ones. The significance level

Table 3. Basic information of the databases

database	records	attributes	conditions	Target
Abalone	4117	9	24	Shuckedweight
Heart	270	13	40	Max heart rate
Housing	506	14	49	MEDV
German credit	1000	20	77	Credit amount
Ipums.la.97	70187	61	1693	Total income
Ipums.la.98	74954	61	1610	Total income
Ipums.la.99	88443	61	1889	Total income
Ticdata2000	5822	86	771	Ave. income
Census income	199523	42	522	Wage per hour
Covtype	581012	55	131	Elevation

we chose to decide the significance of impact rules is 0.05. The minimum coverage for discovered impact rules is set to 0.01, which is very low. The running time shown in the figures and tables are CPU time spent for the algorithms to search for top 1000 significant impact rules with the highest impact on a computer with two PIII 933MHz processors, 1.5G memory, and 4G virtual memory.

We ran our original algorithm without the two efficiency improving techniques. For databases *abalone, heart, housing, German credit* and *ipmus.la.97*, which are relatively smaller, we set the maximum number of conditions on

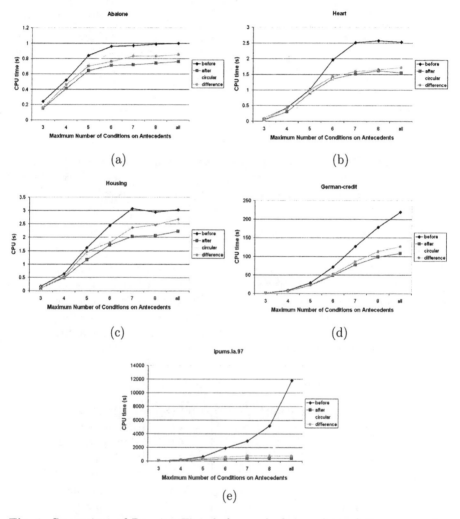

Fig. 4. Comparison of Running Time before and after applying data access saving techniques for (a) *abalone*, (b) *heart*, (c) *housing*, (d) *German credit*, and (e) *ipums.la.97* with maximum number of conditions allowed on rule antecedent set to 3-8, and with no restriction on maximum number of conditions allowed on rule antecedent

the rule antecedents from 3 to 8, and then run the program with no limit on the maximum number of conditions allowed on rule antecedents. After this, the difference set statistics derivation approach and the circular intersection approach are introduced respectively, before the efficient algorithm in table 2 is ran following the same procedure. For *ipmus.la.98, ipmus.la.99, ticdata2000, census income* and *covtype*, which are relatively larger databases, we only ran the programs with maximum number of conditions allowed on rule antecedents set to 3, 4, and 5. We plot the allowed number of maximum conditions on antecedents

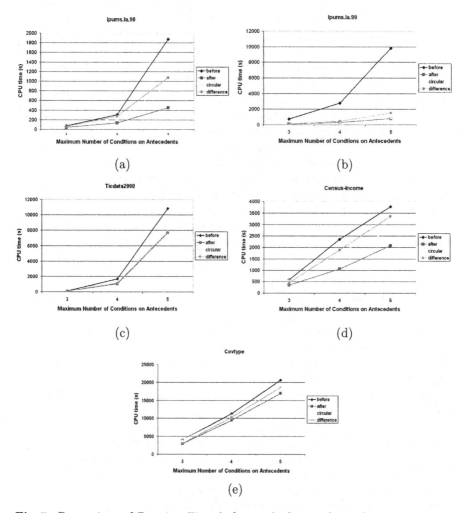

Fig. 5. Comparison of Running Time before and after applying data access saving techniques for (a) *Ipums.la.98*, (b) *ipums.la.99*, (c) *Ticdata2000*, (d) *Census income*, and (e) *covtype* with maximum number of conditions allowed on rule antecedent set to 3, 4 and 5

against required running time for these programs to discover the top 1000 significant impact rules in figure 4 and 5. The lines with square dots show the changes in CPU time for algorithms with neither of these efficiency improving techniques. The lines with round dots show the results for algorithm with difference set statistics derivation only, while the lines with triangular dots denote the trends brought by the algorithms with the circular intersection approach only. The results for algorithm with both techniques introduced are plotted using the lines with diamond dots.

Almost every database undergoes considerable reduction in running time after the introduction of these two efficiency improving approaches. The differences in efficiency increases with the maximum number of conditions allowed on rule antecedent. When there is no limit on the maximum number of conditions on rule antecedent, CPU time spent for the OPUS_IR_Filter algorithm with the two efficiency improving techniques applied to search for top 1000 significant impact rules in *ipums.la.97* is less than one sixth of that necessary for OPUS_IR_Filter without introducing the techniques. However, necessary running time is also influenced by other factors including the size of the databases, the proportion of trivial rules in the top 1000 impact rules, and the proportion of significant rules.

After examining the effects of these two efficiency improving techniques independently, we come to the conclusion that the difference statistics derivation technique works better in some databases like *census income*; while the circular intersection approach has a greater effect on databases including *ipums.la.98*. However, the differences in effect are associated with several subtle factors including the order in which the available conditions are ranked as the input of algorithm, and the order in which different parent rules are compared with the current rule to be assessed.

7   Conclusion

The large number of resulting rules has long been a handicap for exploratory rule discovery. Many techniques have been proposed to reduce the set of resulting rules to a manageable size. Removing statistically insignificant rules is one of those techniques that are popular. Such techniques lead to considerable decrease in the resulting number of exploratory rules. However, performing statistical tests to identify the significance of a rule requires considerable data access and computation. We proposed two techniques in this paper, which can improve the efficiency of rule discovery by deriving difference set statistics without additional references to the data, and by reducing the redundancy of intersection operations. We implemented the techniques in k-most-interesting impact rule discovery, which is suitable for distributional-consequent exploratory rule discovery in very large, dense databases. Experimental results show a substantial improvement in efficiency after applying these techniques.

References

1. Rakesh Agrawal, Tomasz Imielinski, and Arun N. Swami. Mining association rules between sets of items in large databases. In Peter Buneman and Sushil Jajodia, editors, *Proceedings of the 1993 ACM SIGMOD International Conference on Management of Data*, pages 207–216, Washington, D.C., 26–28 1993.
2. Y. Aumann and Y. Lindell. A statistical theory for quantitative association rules. In *Knowledge Discovery and Data Mining*, pages 261–270, 1999.
3. S. D. Bay. The uci kdd archive [http://kdd.ics.uci.edu], 1999.
4. S. D. Bay and M. J. Pazzani. Detecting group differences: Mining contrast sets. In *Data Mining and Knowledge Discovery*, pages 213–246, 2001.
5. Roberto J. Bayardo, Jr., Rakesh Agrawal, and Dimitrios Gunopulos. Constraint-based rule mining in large, dense databases. *Data Min. Knowl. Discov.*, 4(2-3):217–240, 2000.
6. C. L. Blake and C. J. Merz. UCI repository of machine learning databases, 1998.
7. J. Han and M. Kamber. *Data mining : concepts and techniques*. Morgan Kaufmann, 2001.
8. Shiying Huang and Geoffrey I. Webb. Discarding insignificant rules during impact rule discovery in large database. In *SIAM Data Mining Conference, 2005, Newport Beach, USA*.
9. Jiawei han Jian Pei and Laks V.S. Lakshmanan. Mining frequent itemsets with convertible constraints. In *Proceedings of the 17th International Conference on Data Engineering*, page 433. IEEE Computer Society, 2001.
10. B. Liu, W. Hsu, and Y. Ma. Pruning and summarizing the discovered associations. In *Knowledge Discovery and Data Mining*, pages 125–134, 1999.
11. R. S. Michalski. A theory and methodology of inductive learning. In R. S. Michalski, J. G. Carbonell, and T. M. Mitchell, editors, *Machine Learning: An Artificial Intelligence Approach*, pages 83–134. Springer, Berlin, Heidelberg, 1984.
12. J. R. Quinlan. *C4.5: programs for machine learning*. Morgan Kaufmann Publishers Inc., 1993.
13. G. I. Webb. Discovering associations with numeric variables. In *Proceedings of the seventh ACM SIGKDD international conference on Knowledge discovery and data mining*, pages 383–388. ACM Press, 2001.
14. Geoffrey I. Webb. OPUS: An efficient admissible algorithm for unordered search. *Journal of Artificial Intelligence Research*, 3:431–465, 1995.
15. G. I. Webb. Statistically sound exploratory rule discovery, 2004. To be published.

Mining Value-Based Item Packages – An Integer Programming Approach

N.R. Achuthan[1], Raj P. Gopalan[2], and Amit Rudra[3]

[1] Department of Mathematics and Statistics,
Curtin University of Technology, Kent St, Bentley WA 6102, Australia
archi@maths.curtin.edu.au
[2] Department of Computing, Curtin University of Technology,
Kent St, Bentley WA 6102, Australia
raj@cs.curtin.edu.au
[3] School of Information Systems,
Curtin University of Technology, Kent St, Bentley WA 6102, Australia
Amit.Rudra@cbs.curtin.edu.au

Abstract. Traditional methods for discovering frequent patterns from large databases assume equal weights for all items of the database. In the real world, managerial decisions are based on economic values attached to the item sets. In this paper, we first introduce the concept of the value based frequent item packages problems. Then we provide an integer linear programming (ILP) model for value based optimization problems in the context of transaction data. The specific problem discussed in this paper is to find an optimal set of item packages (or item sets making up the whole transaction) that returns maximum profit to the organization under some limited resources. The specification of this problem allows us to solve a number of practical decision problems, by applying the existing and new ILP solution techniques. The model has been implemented and tested with real life retail data. The test results are reported in the paper.

1 Introduction

As organizations accumulate vast amounts of data from day to day operations, the prospect of finding hidden nuggets of knowledge has greatly increased [19]. Traditional inventory systems help a retailer keep track of items in stock and to replenish specific items as they fall below certain levels. The issue these days is not just replenishing the stock on the shelves but also grouping them according to their perceived association with items that attract the attention of customers. Using past sales data, the associations among frequent items can be determined efficiently by current algorithms. The methods for finding the frequent patterns involve different types of partial enumeration schemes where all items are given equal importance. However, in most business environments, items are associated with varying values of price, cost, and profit. So, the relative importance of items differs significantly. Kleinberg et al. [1] noted that frequent patterns and association rules extracted from real life data would be of use to business organizations only if they solve problems in the microeconomic context of the business. Brijs et al. [2] suggest that patterns in the data are interesting only to the extent to which

G.J. Williams and S.J. Simoff (Eds.): Data Mining, LNAI 3755, pp. 78–89, 2006.

they can be used in the decision making process of the enterprise. For example, the management of a supermarket could be interested in identifying combinations of items that generate the maximum profit and requires physical storage space within certain limits. Another example is finding association rules where the items are most profitable or have the lowest margin.

Many such real-world problems can be expressed as optimization problems that maximize or minimize a real valued function. In this paper, we will focus on one such optimization problem in the context of transaction data and refer to it as *value based frequent item packages problem.* A package consists of items that are usually sold together. The aim is to find a set of items that can be sold as part of various packages to realize the maximum profit overall for the business.

Data mining research in the last decade has produced several efficient algorithms for association rule mining [3] [4] [5], with potential applications in financial data analysis, retail industry, telecommunications industry, and biomedical data analysis. However, literature on the use of these algorithms to solve real-world problems is limited [2]. Ali et al [6] reported the application of association rules to reducing fall-out in the processing of telecommunication service orders. They also used the technique to study associations between medical tests on patients. Viveros et al [7] applied data mining to health insurance data to discover unexpected relationships between services provided by physicians and to detect overpayments.

Most of the data mining algorithms developed for transaction data give equal importance for all the items. However, in a real business, not all the items are of equal value and many management decisions are made based on the money value associated with the items. The value may be in terms of the profit made or cost incurred or any other utility function defined on the items. Recent works by Aumann and Lindel [18] and Webb [17] discuss the quantitative aspects of association rules and tackle the problem using a rule based approach. More recently, Brij et al [2] developed a zero-one mathematical programming model for determining a subset of frequent item sets that account for total maximum profit from a pre-specified collection of frequent item sets with certain restrictions on the items selected. They used this model for the market basket analysis of a supermarket. Demiriz and Bennett [8] have successfully used similar optimization approaches for semi-supervised learning.

Mathematical programming has been applied as the basis for developing some of the traditional techniques of data mining such as classification, feature selection, support vector machines, and regression [9] [8]. However, these techniques do not address the value based business decision problems arising in the context of data mining and knowledge discovery. To the best of our knowledge, except for [2], mathematical modeling approach to classes of real world decision problems that integrate patterns discovered by data mining has not been reported so far. In this paper, we address this relatively unexplored research area and propose a new mathematical model for some classes of the value based frequent item packages problem. We contend that frequently occurring and profitable baskets are of greater importance to the retailer than just frequent subsets of transactions. The items that occur in a transaction can be packaged together or alternatively sold as individual items. We consider the expected minimum revenue, minimum and maximum number of items in the optimal item packages, and storage constraint pertinent to a real life retailer.

The structure of the rest of this paper is as follows: In Section 2, we define relevant terms used in transaction data, frequent item sets and association rule mining. In Section 3, we consider a general version of the optimal item packages problem and present an integer linear programming formulation for the same. In Section 4, we illustrate the model by a sample profit optimal item packages problem, provide its ILP formulation and the result of processing it using the commercial mathematical programming software (CPLEX). Finally, we conclude our paper in Section 5 providing pointers for further work.

2   Transaction Data – Notations and Definitions

Transaction data refers to information about transactions such as the purchases in a store, each purchase described by a transaction ID, customer ID, date of purchase, and a list of items and their prices. A web transaction log is another example in which each transaction may denote a user id, web page and time of access.

Let T denote the total number of transactions. Let $I = \{1, 2, ..., N\}$ denote the set of all potential items that may be included in any transaction and more precisely the items included in the tth transaction may be denoted by I_t, a subset of I, where t ranges from 1 to T.

The *support* s of a subset X of the set I of items, is the percentage of transactions in which X occurs. A set of items X is a *frequent item set* if its support s is greater than or equal to a minimum support threshold specified by the user. An *association rule* is of the form $\mathbf{X} \Rightarrow \mathbf{Y}$, where X and Y are frequent item sets that do not have any item in common. We say that $\mathbf{X} \Rightarrow \mathbf{Y}$ has *support* s if s% of transactions includes all the items in X and Y, and *confidence* c if c% of transactions containing the items of X also contains the items of Y. A valid association rule is one where the support s and the confidence c are above user-defined thresholds for support and confidence respectively. Association rules [10] [11] [12] identify the presence of any significant correlation in a given data set.

3   Optimal Item Packages Problem

Brijs et al [2] considered a market basket analysis problem for finding an optimal set of frequent item sets that returns the maximum profit and proposed a mixed integer linear programming (MILP) formulation of their problem. Their model proposed maximizing the profit function of frequent item set X, i.e.

$$\max \sum_{X \in L} M(X) * P_X - \sum_{i \in N} \text{Cost}_i * Q_i \,,$$

where N is the set of all items and L is the set of all frequent item sets X; M(X) is gross sales margin generated by X; and $P_X, Q_i \in \{0,1\}$ are decision variables; subject to $\sum_{i \in N} Q_i = ItemMax$, where i is a basic item and *ItemMax* is the maximum threshold set for the number of items in X.

We generalize their problem specification to include different types of resource restrictions and develop an integer linear programming formulation for the same. The *Optimal Item Packages Problem* (OIPP) is to choose a set of frequent item sets that we term as item packages, so as to maximize the total net profit subject to conditions on maximum storage space for selected items and minimum total revenue from the selected frequent item sets. Our formulation of the problem is much more flexible compared to Brij et al's [2], as the model can adapt to not only different resource restrictions but also to various bounds on the number of items to be included in the final selection. For example, it can specify the minimum and maximum number of elements in the final solution.

3.1 Motivation for OIPP

In many real-life businesses, a transaction may consist of a specific set of items forming a package. For example, while buying a car, a customer's choice may be made easier by having a number of fixed packages offered by the supplier. In some other businesses, it may not make sense to separate any item from a given package; e.g. medical procedures, travel packages etc.

Alternatively, a vendor may be interested in finding out from previous sales as to which, if any, set of items exist that could be offered as a package. This packaging of items (or products) could potentially offer him certain amount of profit under a number of resource constraints. For instance, the resource constraints could be available stocking space, budget (minimum cost or maximum profit), quantity (that needs to be sold) etc. He may be further interested in doing a sensitivity analysis as to how far the resources can be stretched while the given solution remains optimal. Again, in another instance, the vendor may like to see how a change in a certain resource affects his profitability (for example, if he is able to organize a little more space for storage or invest a little more money). For a travel bureau, a constraint could be time-oriented resources (like, a travel consultant's time),

OIPP: For a given database $\{I_t \subset I : 1 \le t \le T\}$, let $\{X_j : 1 \le j \le k\}$ be a pre-specified list of k frequent item sets. Let f_j and n_j respectively denote the number of transactions that exactly include X_j (i.e. $f_j = |\{t: I_t = X_j\}|$) and the number of items in X_j, $1 \le j \le k$. The constant b_{ij} assumes the value 1 whenever item i is a member of the frequent item set X_j, $i \in I$, $1 \le j \le k$. Let p_j denote the revenue made by the frequent item set X_j whenever X_j forms a transaction. Let c_i denote the cost incurred (per unit) while selecting item i, $1 \le i \le N$. Let s_i denote the storage space (in appropriate units) required per unit for item i whenever the item is selected. Furthermore, let S denote the total available storage space. Find, a subset $\hat{I}$ of $\{i: 1 \le i \le N\}$ and a subset F of the set of frequent item sets $\{X_j : 1 \le j \le k\}$ such that they satisfy the following properties:

1. The number of items in $\hat{I}$ is bounded below and above by positive integers N_L and N_U respectively;

2. A frequent item set X_j is selected in F if and only if X_j is covered by $\hat{I}$, that is, $X_j \subseteq \hat{I}$;

3. The total storage space required for the selected items of $\hat{I}$ does not exceed the available space of S units;
4. The total revenue made by frequent item sets of F is at least Minrev ;
5. The net profit (total revenue – the total cost) is maximized.

We now provide an ILP model for the OIPP described above. Let y_i denote the 0-1 decision variable that assumes value 1 whenever item i is chosen. Let z_j denote the 0-1 decision variable that assumes value 1 whenever the frequent item set X_j is covered by the set of selected items, that is, by the set of items $\{ i: y_i = 1 \}$.

Lower and upper bound constraints:
$$N_L \le \sum_{i=1}^{N} y_i \le N_U \tag{1}$$

Occurrence constraint of X_j:
$$\sum_{i \in X_j} y_i - n_j z_j \ge 0, \quad 1 \le j \le k \tag{2}$$

Item storage space constraint:
$$\sum_{j=1}^{k} (\sum_{i=1}^{N} b_{ij} s_i) f_j z_j \le S \tag{3}$$

Lower bound constraint on revenue:
$$\sum_{j=1}^{k} p_j f_j z_j \ge \text{Minrev} \tag{4}$$

Restrictions on variables: $y_i = 0$ or 1, $z_j = 0$ or 1 $\tag{5}$

Objective function: Maximize $\sum_{j=1}^{k} p_j f_j z_j - \sum_{j=1}^{k} (\sum_{i=1}^{N} b_{ij} c_i) f_j z_j$ $\tag{6}$

In this value based frequent item set problem the input information regarding X_1, ..., X_k , p_j, f_j , s_i and c_i must be extracted through data mining of frequent item sets. For the above model (1) – (6), the constraints and the objective function may be validated as follows:

Let the set of selected items to cover all the selected frequent item sets be denoted by $\hat{I} = \{ i: y_i = 1 \}$. It is easy to see that $|\hat{I}| = \sum_{i=1}^{N} y_i$ and the constraint (1) provides the lower and upper bound restrictions on this number. The number of items common to the set $\hat{I}$ and the frequent item set X_j is given by $\sum_{i \in X_j} y_i$. Whenever $\sum_{i \in X_j} y_i = |X_j|$ = n_j , the set $\hat{I}$ covers the frequent item set X_j . The constraint (2) ensures that the decision variable z_j is 1 if and only if the frequent item set X_j is covered by $\hat{I}$. In this case note that F=$\{ X_j : z_j = 1\}$ is the collection of frequent item sets selected. The storage space required by an item i of the selected item sets in F is $\sum_{j=1}^{k} b_{ij} s_i f_j z_j$, for $1 \leq i \leq N$. The constraint (3) expresses the upper bound restriction on the available storage space viz. S. The contribution made by the frequent item set X_j to the profit may be expressed as $p_j f_j z_j$ where $z_j = 1$ if and only if X_j is covered by the set $\hat{I}$. The constraint (4) ensures a minimum revenue contribution from the set of all covered frequent item sets. The constraints of (5) express the 0-1 restrictions of the decision variables y_i and z_j. The objective function in (6) maximizes the total profit contribution expressed as the total net revenue.

4 Experimental Results

To verify our ILP formulation of the OIPP, we implemented and experimentally tested our model with real life market transaction data obtained from a Belgian retail store [16]. The dataset (retail.txt) stores five months of transaction data collected over four separate periods.

Retail data characteristics:

Total number of transactions	88,163
Item ID range	1- 16470
Number of items (N)	3,151
Total number of customers	5,133
Average basket size	13
Data collection period	5 months total (in four separate periods)

For further details of the data refer to [16]. Since not all characteristics of the data are publicly available (presumed to be confidential), we supplemented them with values for such fields as storage space required per item (s_i), revenue from selling item package X_j (p_j) and cost attributed to item i (c_i).

4.1 Data Preparation Stages

As discussed in section 3, before building the ILP model of the market data we need to know the data characteristics. Therefore, the data is preprocessed using the following steps to prepare it for input to the mathematical programming software:

1. Each transaction record is organized as an ascending sequence of item Ids;
2. A count of the number of items (n_j) in each transaction is inserted as the first field of the record;
3. The records in the database are then sorted in ascending order according to the count of items and then by the item Ids as minor keys;
4. Finally, the distinct frequent transactions are listed with their frequencies (f_j). In the present context, a transaction is frequent if its frequency is greater than or equal to 2. Note that the total number of distinct frequent transactions (item sets) is denoted by k.
5. This final dataset is fed to a program (createLP) which builds the ILP model corresponding to the current problem.

This model is then submitted to a mathematical programming application to be solved as an ILP with binary integer variables (y_i's and z_j's).

[We used C++ programs (for steps 1 – 5 above) to process the input retail market basket dataset and produced the output in appropriate format. As our ILP formulation assumes data mining activities as a pre-step, discussions regarding the preprocessing done by these programs are unnecessary.]

4.2 Sample Optimal Package Selection Problem

To help explain our methodology, we use an example problem and work it through the different stages of finding the optimal profit from the given dataset. Consider the following dataset consisting of 5 sales transactions involving 7 items.

$X_1 = \{7\}$, $X_2 = \{1, 2\}$, $X_3 = \{5, 6\}$, $X_4 = \{12, 13\}$ and $X_5 = \{2, 6, 12, 13\}$

Table 1 below, shows the characteristics of various items (sp_i – selling price, $prof_i$ – profit per unit); while Table 2 presents the details of each item package.

Table 1. Characteristics of items in the sample dataset

Item	1	2	5	6	7	12	13
s_i	0.2	0.3	0.25	0.3	0.15	0.3	0.2
c_i	2.5	3.1	4.5	3.7	2.1	3.5	2.5
$s.p._i$	3.2	3.9	6.7	4.9	2.6	4.0	3.1
$prof_i$	0.7	0.8	2.2	1.2	0.5	0.5	0.6

Table 2. Processed sample dataset for creating the ILP model

Count of items (n_j)	Number of transactions (f_j)	Item package (X_j)	Package revenue ($p_{j*} f_j$)	Package storage ($\sum s_{i*} f_j$)	Package cost ($\sum c_{i*} f_j$)
1	200	7	520	30	420
2	231	1 2	1640.1	115.5	1293.6
2	34	5 6	394.4	18.7	278.8
2	341	12 13	2421	170.5	2046
4	11	2 6 12 13	174.9	12.1	140.8

The first column shows the number of items in the packages viz. n_j; the second shows the frequency (f_j); while the third shows the individual items that make up each item package. The last three columns show the computed aggregates for each package.

The createLP program, outlined in step 5 above, processes the formatted dataset (steps 1-4) and produces the corresponding ILP model (Fig. 1) to the sample dataset. This model is then solved using CPLEX, a commercial package for solving all kind of linear programs. Fig. 2 presents the output from the package.

We notice (Fig. 2) that the optimal value i.e. the maximal profit, obtained under the given constraints of 100 units of storage space and satisfying the minimum revenue of

```
\Problem name: sample.lp

Maximize

  100z1 + 346.5z2 + 115.6z3 + 375.1z4 + 34.1z5

Subject To
-1z1 +y7 >= 0
-2z2 +y1 +y2 >= 0                          Max.storage
-2z3 +y5 +y6 >= 0                          constraint
-2z4 +y13 +y12 >= 0
-4z5 +y2 +y6 +y12 +y13 >= 0

  30z1 + 115.5z2 + 18.7z3 + 170.5z4 + 12.1z5 <= 100

                                                        Min. revenue
  520z1 +1640.1z2 +394.4z3 +2421.1z4 +174.9z5 >= 600   constraint

  y1 +y2 +y5 +y6 +y7 +y12 +y13 >= 5        lower & upper
  y1 +y2 +y5 +y6 +y7 +y12 +y13 <= 10       bounds

Binaries
  z1 z2 z3 z4 z5
  y1 y2 y5 y6 y7 y12 y13
End
```

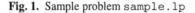

Fig. 1. Sample problem $\mathtt{sample.lp}$

```
Integer optimal solution:  Objective =    2.4970000000e+002
Solution time =     0.03 sec.  Iterations = 0  Nodes = 0

CPLEX> dis sol var -
Variable Name            Solution Value
z1                             1.000000
z3                             1.000000
z5                             1.000000
y7                             1.000000
y2                             1.000000
y5                             1.000000
y6                             1.000000
y13                            1.000000
y12                            1.000000

All other variables in the range 1-12 are zero.
```

Fig. 2. Solution of sample ILP using CPLEX

$600 is $249.70. The three best item packages to stock are X_1, X_3 and X_5 which correspond to the binary decision variables z_1, z_3 and z_5 respectively. Further, the particular items in the optimal set to store are 7, 2, 5, 6, 12 and 13 (corresponding to the decision variables y_7 y_2 y_5 y_6 y_{12} y_{13}. The remaining item packages and items do not participate in the optimal solution.

We now present the results from the retail dataset as described at the beginning of the section. We note that the number of distinct frequent item sets, namely k = 929. To build the model, for each item i, we have randomly generated the corresponding selling price (sp_i), cost price (c_i) and storage space (s_i) with its profit around 25%.

Given a certain maximum storage space, the retailer might like to find out the optimum profit (and item packages) against a maximum number of items to be put on the shelves. He might also be curious as to how the profit varies if he is able to acquire more storage space. To show how easily this can be achieved using our ILP formulation, we varied the values for S, the maximum storage space parameter, from 1000 to 4000 and varied the upper limit for the number of items to be shelved i.e. N_U from 20 to 500. The resulting ILP was then submitted to CPLEX 9.0 to calculate the value of the net profit function (z). Table 3 shows the effect of changing the maximum number of items (N_U) has on the objective.

Table 3. Profit function and time (in seconds) for varying storage space (S) and number of items (N_U)

	N_U	20	50	100	150	200	300	400	450	500
S=4000	Profit	22,697	27,996	32,323	34,646	36,320	39,281	39,384	39,381	39,384
	Time	0.24	0.24	0.23	0.26	0.23	0.24	0.22	0.12	0.11
S=3000	Profit	22,697	27,996	32,323	34,646	36,320	39,281	39,281	39,328	39,328
	Time	0.25	0.22	0.23	0.26	0.22	0.24	0.22	0.35	0.34
S=2000	Profit	22,697	27,996	32,323	34,646	36,320	38,315	38,423	38,423	38,423
	Time	0.25	0.22	0.23	0.26	0.21	0.22	0.23	0.23	0.23
S=1000	Profit	22,697	27,996	32,323	34,556	35,564	35,636	35,636	35,636	35,636
	Time	0.25	0.22	0.23	0.38	0.41	0.23	0.23	0.23	0.23

We then chart (Figure 3) the observations to visualize the effects of max. storage and N_u on the value of the objective, z. We observe that while increasing the number of items does increase the net profit quite substantially, after a certain stage the rate or amount of change in the same is not significant, eventually peaking and remaining so in spite of increasing resources (storage space or number of items stored). This observation could be of value to the retailer as he can clearly visualize the expected changes in profit by changing certain parameters as need be. Similarly, one can study the effect of varying the limits of other resources and study their effects on the profitability function.

For our experiments, we used an AMD Athlon XP2100 PC with a CPU clock of 2.1 GHz having 512 MB of RAM running Windows 2000. Our experiments show very encouraging results as all of them are achieved in a sub-second response time. This proves that our method of solving such problems is very much viable.

Limitations. The model presented in the previous sections has been tested with a reasonable size dataset. However, it is not without its limitations. While the number of transactions (T) could be very large (limited by how large an integer can be on a specific system), for the given data varying the minimum number of items (N_L) could increase the number of possible combinations of items and thereby could affect the solving time. This is dependant on environmental factors like available memory, storage and CPU speed. CPLEX could not solve this problem, using the above PC configuration, when all non-frequent transactions were included within a reasonable time viz. 8 hours.

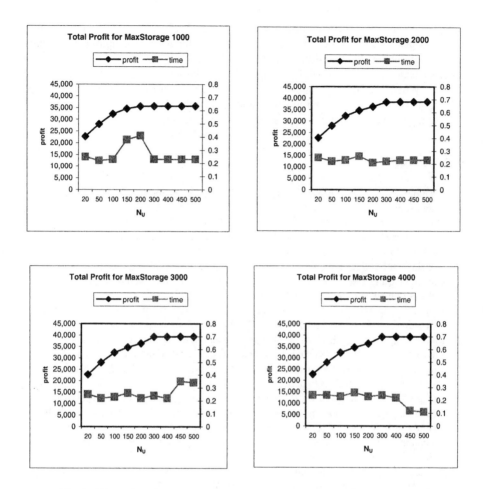

Fig. 3. Effect of varying max storage and max number of items on the objective

5   Conclusions

In this paper, we have introduced a general class of problems called the value based optimal item package problem that can support real world business decisions using data mining. The solutions to these problems require the combination of mathematical modeling with data mining and knowledge discovery from large transaction data. We formulated a generic problem using the mixed integer linear programming model and implemented it using real life transactional data from a retail store. Our specification provides scope for using a large number of methodologies available in the literature to solve the value based frequent item set problems.

It is well known that the general integer linear programming problem is NP hard. In addition, in many practical applications of the frequent item set problem, the parameters like N, the number of items and T, the number of transactions in the data base may be very large. When N and T are not very large, we can use some of the standard commercial software products such as CPLEX to solve the model proposed in this paper. Furthermore, future research can be focused on developing specially designed branch and cut algorithms [13] [14] [15], branch and price algorithms and/or efficient heuristics and probabilistic methods to solve our ILP formulations of these models. When N and T are large, the future research can explore the possibility of solving these models restricted to some random samples drawn from the database and developing methods of estimating the required information.

References

1. Kleinberg, J., Papadimitriou, C., Raghavan, P.: A Microeconomic View of Data Mining. Data Mining and Knowledge Discovery. Vol. 2 (1998) 311-324
2. Brijs, T., Swinnen, G., Vanhoof, K, Wets, G.: Building an Association Rules Framework to Improve Product Assortment Decisions. Data Mining and Knowledge Discovery. Vol. 8 (2004) 7-23
3. Gopalan, R.P., Sucahyo, Y.G.: High Performance Frequent Patterns Extraction using Compressed FP-Tree. Proceedings of SIAM International Workshop on High Performance and Distributed Mining (HPDM04), Orlando, USA (2004)
4. Han, J., Pei, J., Yin, Y.: Mining Frequent Patterns without Candidate Generation. Proceedings of ACM SIGMOD, Dallas, TX (2000)
5. Liu, J., Pan, Y., Wang, K., Han, J.: Mining Frequent Item Sets by Opportunistic Projection. Proceedings of ACM SIGKDD, Edmonton, Alberta, Canada (2002)
6. Ali, K., Manganaris, S., Srikant, R.: Partial Classification using Association Rules. Proceedings of KDD-97, Newport Beach, California (1997)
7. Viveros, M.S., Nearhos, J.P., Rothman, M.J.: Applying Data Mining Techniques to a Health Insurance Information System. Proceedings of VLDB-96, Bombay, India, (1996)
8. Demiriz, A., Bennett, K.P.: Optimization Approaches to Semi-Supervised Learning. In Complementarity: Applications, Algorithms and Extensions. Kluwer Academic Publishers, Boston (2001) 121-141
9. Bradley, P., Gehrke, J., Ramakrishnan, R., Srikant, R.: Scaling Mining Algorithms to Large Databases. Communications of the ACM. Vol. 45 (2002) 38-43
10. Fayyad, U.M., Piatetsky-Shapiro, G., Smyth, P., Uthurusamy, R.: Advances in Knowledge Discovery and Data Mining. MIT Press, Cambridge, MA (1996)
11. Han, J., Kamber, M.: Data Mining: Concepts and Techniques. Morgan Kaufmann Publishers, San Francisco (2001)
12. Hand, D., Mannila, H., Smyth, P.: Principles of Data Mining. MIT Press, Cambridge, MA (2001)
13. Achuthan, N.R., Caccetta, L., Hill, S.P.: A New Subtour Elimination Constraint for the Vehicle Routing Problem. E.J.O.R. Vol. 91 (1996) 573-586
14. Achuthan, N.R., Caccetta, L., Hill, S.P.: Capacitated Vehicle Routing Problem: Some New Cutting Planes. Asia-Pacific Journal of Operational Research. Vol. 15 (1998) 109-123
15. Achuthan, N.R., Caccetta, L., Hill, S.P.: An Improved Branch and Cut Algorithm for the Capacitated Vehicle Routing Problem. Transportation Science. Vol. 37 (2003) 153-169
16. Brijs T., Swinnen G., Vanhoof K., and Wets G. The Use of Association Rules for Product Assortment Decisions: A Case Study, in: Proceedings of the Fifth International Conference on Knowledge Discovery and Data Mining, San Diego (USA), August 15-18, (1999) 254-260

17. Webb, G.   Discovering Associations with Numeric Variables. Proceedings of the Knowledge Discovery in Databases (KDD 01), San Francisco (USA), (2001) 383-388.
18. Aumann, Y., Lindell, Y.   A Statistical Theory for Quantitative Association Rules. Proceedings of the Knowledge Discovery in Databases (KDD 99), San Francisco (USA), (1999) 262-270
19. Marakas, G. M. Modern Data Warehousing, Mining and Visualization. Prentice Hall, Upper Saddle River, New Jersey (USA). (2003).

Decision Theoretic Fusion Framework for Actionability Using Data Mining on an Embedded System

Heungkyu Lee[1], Sunmee Kang[2], and Hanseok Ko[3]

[1] Dept. of Visual Information Processing, Korea University, Seoul, Korea
[2] Dept. of Computer Science, Seokyeong University
[3] Dept. of Electronics and Computer Engineering, Korea University, Seoul, Korea
hklee@ispl.korea.ac.kr, smkang@skuniv.ac.kr,
hsko@korea.ac.kr

Abstract. This paper proposes a decision theoretic fusion framework for actionability using data mining techniques in an embedded car navigation system. An embedded system having limited resources is not easy to manage the abundant information in the database. Thus, the proposed system stores and manages only multiple level-of-abstraction in the database to resolve the problem of resource limitations, and then represents the information received from the Web via the wireless network after connecting a communication channel with the data mining server. To do this, we propose a decision theoretic fusion framework that includes the multiple level-of-abstraction approach combining multiple-level association rules and the summary table, as well as an active interaction rule generation algorithm for actionability in an embedded car navigation system. In addition, it includes the sensory and data fusion level rule extraction algorithm to cope with simultaneous events occurring from multi-modal interface. The proposed framework can make interactive data mining flexible, effective, and instantaneous in extracting the proper action item.

Keywords: Data mining, Embedded data mining, and Speech interactive approach.

1 Introduction

As detailed and accurate data are accumulated and stored in databases at various stages, the large amounts of data in databases makes it almost impractical to manually analyze them for valuable information. Thus, the need for automated analysis and discovery tools to extract useful knowledge from huge amounts of raw data has been urgent. To cope with this problem, data mining methodologies are emerging as efficient tools in realizing the above objectives. Data mining [1][15][11] is the process of extracting previously unknown information in the form of patterns, trends, and structures from large quantities of data. These methodologies are being used in many fields, such as financial, business, medical, manufacturing and production, scientific domains, and the World Wide Web (WWW). Especially, autonomous decision-making process using a data mining approach has been useful in various fields for sourcing efficient and reliable information [3][20].

G.J. Williams and S.J. Simoff (Eds.): Data Mining, LNAI 3755, pp. 90–104, 2006.

In addition, as computer and scientific technologies have improved recently, small size handheld mobile devices such as PDAs, mobile phones, and Auto PCs have been used in various fields of mobile computing and Telexistence technologies more and more. The need to utilize a variety of service applications such as car navigation, MP3/WAV player, car maintenance program, and information center solution connecting to server, on these devices is increasing. However, an embedded hardware system has limited resources that are not enough to handle the large amounts of data, and analyze them. Thus, an embedded technique to resolve this problem is required.

To cope with this problem, we propose a decision theoretic fusion framework that includes the multiple level-of-abstraction approach which combines multiple-level association rules and a summary table as well as active interaction rule generation algorithm for actionability in an embedded car navigation system. In addition, it includes the sensory and data fusion level rule extraction algorithm to cope with simultaneous events occurring from multi-modal interfacing. This embedded system is connected to the data mining server based on the web in order to extract and access the rules and data. This is because the Web not only contains a huge amount of information, but also can provide a powerful infrastructure for communication and information sharing [6][8]. With this data mining server, the proposed system can provide an efficient data representative service as well as actionability to present interactive methods without processing the raw data.

The proposed system is applied to command, control, communication, and intelligent car navigation systems. This provides an efficient speech interactive agent (SIA) rendering smooth car navigation by employing a conversational tool; embedded automatic speech recognition, embedded text-to-speech, and distributed speech recognition modules, all the while enabling safe driving. The embedded car navigation system is extended to provide a user-friendly service and interactive capability by using the conversational tools. The system can reveal the status of the system and its scheduled jobs by actively using the active interaction rule generation algorithm. This is due to the fact that the driver has an access pattern about specific applications that are frequently used. In addition, the information about traffic, weather, news, daily schedules, and car management can provide valuable information to the driver as well as decision-making advice on what action the proposed system should take. Using such information, the speech interactive agent provides efficient interactive methods to operate for the required events.

First, this system uses sensory fusion rules in order to combine multiple events simultaneously occurring from multi-modal sensors such as push-to-talk, remote controller, touch screen, mute, hands-free, external buttons, and application events received from multimedia service applications in the embedded client system. Second, the data fusion framework is provided by using the features extracted from sensory fusion rules. At this time, user access patterns occurring by user driven events operate a specific service application, and are mined and stored in databases on an embedded system for certain periods. This feature provides the means to decide a specific action. The proposed system can connect the Internet server using a CDMA 200 terminal to represent large amounts of information. However, an embedded system has a small sized memory that has not enough space to store a lot of information. To resolve this problem, the multiple level-of-abstraction approach for the multiple-level association rules is applied.

The content of this paper is as follows. The design concept of the proposed system is presented in Section 2. In Section 3, we describe the data mining methodologies based on the decision theoretic fusion framework for actionability. Finally, in Section 4, we provide discussions and conclusive remarks.

2   Architecture of Embedded Car Navigation System

This Section describes the introduction of embedded system on a real car for Telematics service. In addition, speech interactive agent is described as a effective speech interaction tools for safeguard driving and service guide as well as information gathering and generation tools.

2.1   System Overview

The embedded car navigation system provides the various embedded service applications on a car as well as networked service applications via a wireless network using the CDMA 2000 terminal as shown in Figure 1. In our proposed system, we include the interactive techniques using speech interactive agent to provide a speech interaction method as an intelligent interface between human and machine. The speech interactive agent plays a role in combining and processing the information from interface modalities as well as in communicating with the data mining server to provide useful information to the user. This system needs a database to store some valuable information and manage some information. Such an embedded system has limited resources. To resolve this problem, this system stores and manages the multiple

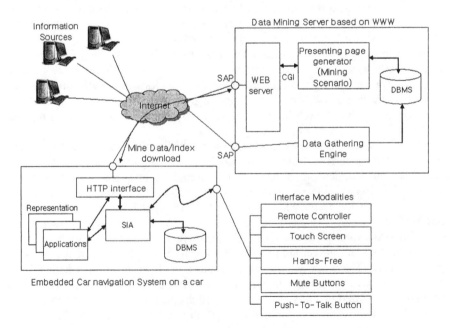

Fig. 1. System architecture overview

level-of-abstraction in the database. The multiple level-of-abstraction information is downloaded, and updated from the data mining server using HTTP (Hyper-Text Transfer Protocol). In addition, this system can manage the user's access patterns providing the user used the service for a certain period. By using this information, the speech interactive agent can speak to the user when the system is first switched on at the start of the day, and the scheduled job should be executed. This information is also managed in the database by using multiple level-of-abstraction.

2.2 Speech Interactive Agent

Conversation is one of the most important factors that facilitate dynamic knowledge interaction. People can have a conversation with a conversational agent that talks with people by using the eASR and eTTS [19] as a combined unit. The speech interaction agent, as a conversational agent [10][16], carries out command and control tasks while interacting with the driver according to the given scenarios on the car navigation system.

As a problem-solving paradigm, the fusion process model using the functional evaluation stage is employed [12]. Although the car navigation system is deterministic, the use of multiple input sensors makes the system complex to cope with various situations. The proposed speech agent is decomposed into three separate processes; composition process of sensory sources, speech signal processing process and decision-making process. As shown in Figure 2, the composition process of sensory sources plays a role in combining input requests and guiding the next-step. The speech signal processing process provides a means of speech interaction using speech recognition and text-to-speech functions. The decision-making process provides a user-friendly interfacing mode using a speech interaction helper function as well as a self-diagnosis function using a speech interaction watch-dog module.

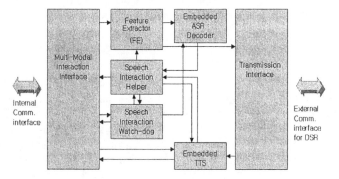

Fig. 2. Speech Interactive Agent (SIA) block diagram

The speech recognition system is classified into the embedded ASR and distributed speech recognition (DSR) system that is used via the wireless network, using a CDMA 2000 terminal. Thus, the feature extractor based on ETSI v1.1.2 has the front-end role of passing the mel-cepstral features to eASR or DSR according to the scenarios without communicating between the speech agent and the application process. The eTTS utters the information when the event is requested by the user and application programs. The "speech interaction helper" provides helper scenarios to the user when a recognition error occurs or an out-of-vocabulary is encountered. The "watch-dog" function monitors the service situation and status of the eASR/eTTS in order to cope with the exception-handling error which can occur when a user pushes the external buttons during the service interval.

Through the use of the speech interactive agent on embedded car navigation system, next Section describes the interactive information generation method using sensor and data fusion on the embedded system and then, the information gathering and generation method via the Web.

3   Decision Theoretic Fusion Framework

This Section provides the base framework for embedded data mining from the raw data to highly processed information. First, raw data is generalized by using the sensor fusion method and then data fusion rules and active interaction rule generation is employed. Finally, the embedded system is connected to the Web for effective data processing and service and user satisfaction.

3.1   Sensory Fusion Rule

To perform the requests for speech interaction, firstly the sensory fusion model can be expressed by

$$Y_i = f(O/K, Y_{i-1}) \tag{1}$$

where i is a number of processing results, O is a observable sensory input, K is a domain knowledge, Y_{i-1} is status information being processed from a previous time and $f()$ is the sensory fusion function to combine the sensory inputs and then control the current requests given the previous situation. The observable sensor input, O is expressed by

$$O = g_1(Mute) \cdot g_2(HF) \cdot g_3(R) \cdot g_4(Ptt) \cdot \prod_{i=0}^{k} g_5(E_i) \tag{2}$$

where M is a mute, HF is a hands-free, R is a remote controller, Ptt is a push-to-talk, E is a event created by service applications, and k is a number of applications being run simultaneously. Each input is independent each other as well as processed parallelly. The variable, $g()$ is a function to observe and detect the sensor input. While a sensory input between g_1 and g_4 is a direct input from a sensor, g_5 is a transmitted input from application programs via the inter-process communication. The sensory inputs can happen simultaneously. However, for the action to be performed promptly it is always one function that is most suitable in a given situation. This is due to the fact that the hardware resource has limitations, and the system can provide the robustness, consistency and efficiency in using a service. Thus, the fusing function, $f()$ should be considered with respect to service quality and usability. In this paper, we apply the rule based decision function as a fusion function of respective inputs. In equation (1), K is a domain specific knowledge to provide combing rules as shown in Table 1. The given rule is decided by considering the service capability, priority and resource limitations, etc. Decision categories are composed of five decision rules. By using this sensory fused rule, data fusion rule is generalized for effective speech interaction in next subsection.

Table 1. The negotiation rule table according to the priority control

Current State / Previous State	eASR is requested	Application TTS is requested	CNS TTS is requested	Hands-Free Button pushed	Mute Button pushed
Hands-Free button enable	Disabled	Disabled	Enabled	Not applicable	Not applicable
Mute button enable	Enabled	Disabled	Enabled	Not applicable	Not applicable
eASR running	Previous eASR exits and new eASR runs	Previous eASR exits and eTTS starts	eASR runs continuously and CNS TTS starts	eASR exits	eASR exits
Application eTTS running	Previous eTTS stops and eASR runs	Previous eTTS stops and new eTTS starts	Application eTTS pauses and CNS TTS starts	eTTS stops	eTTS stops
CNS eTTS running	CNS eTTS starts and eASR runs	Previous CNS eTTS finishs and then application eTTS starts	Previous CNS eTTS stops and new CNS eTTS starts	Don't care	Don't care

3.2 Data Fusion Rules from Interface Modalities

When given the sensory fusion result, the speech agent can decide the action to be performed. Next, the data fusion model for speech interaction can be expressed by

$$Z = H_i(O_i) \cdot I(P) \cdot J(Y), \quad i = 1, ..., 3 \qquad (3)$$

$$H_i(O_i) = h_i(O_i / M_i), \quad i = 1, ..., 3 \qquad (4)$$

where i is the number of speech interaction tools and $H_i(O_i)$ is a speech interaction tool; 1)embedded speech recognition, 2)distributed speech recognition 3)text-to-speech. Thus, the variable, O_1 and O_2 are speech sampling data and O_3 is text data. Thus, $H_i(O_i)$ is decomposed as follows.

$$H_1(O_1) = h_1(O_1 / M_1)$$
$$\cong W_k = \arg \max_j L(O / W_j) \qquad (5)$$

where $h_1(O_1)$ is a pattern recognizer using the maximum a posteriori (MAP) decision rule to find the most likely sequence of words.

$$H_2(O_2) = h_2(O_2 / M_2) = h_2(O_2) \qquad (6)$$

where $h_2(O_2)$ is a front-end feature extractor to pass the speech features into the back-end distributed speech recognition server.

$$H_3(O_3) = h_3(O_3 / M_3) \tag{7}$$

where $h_3(O_3)$ is a speech synthesizer function to read the sentences.

$J(Y)$ is a selecting function to choose a speech interaction tool. The currently selected speech module is just enabled. The variable, M_i is a given specific domain knowledge. M_1 is an acoustic model to recognize the word, M_2 is not used and M_3 is TTS DB. The variable, P is procedural knowledge to provide a user-friendly service such as a helper function. $I(P)$ is a function to guide the service scenario according to the results of the speech interaction tool.

As a result, Z is an action to be performed sequentially. The final decision-making, $Z(t)$ represents the user's history to be processed when the decision is stored for a long period of time. This can provide the statistical information when the user frequently utilizes a specific function.

Sensory fused rules and data fusion rules can be a fusion framework for generation of gathered information. In addition, extension of application service and integration can be easily employed based on this framework. From this information, the generation method of user action statistics is described in next subsection.

3.3 Active Interaction Rule Generation

Users may interact at various service stages and domain knowledge may be used in the form of a higher-level specification of the model, or at a more detailed level. In our system, the speech interactive agent interacts with users using a conversational tool. This user interaction information is applied to data mining which is inherently an interactive and iterative process. This is due to the fact that the user has repeated patterns that he or she frequently uses on specific applications with the car navigation system. By using this information, the speech interactive agent asks the user whether the user wants to perform a specific task, which is the statistical information to be stored and estimated for a period of time according to the procedure in Figure 3. In addition, the speech interactive agent can start a music player automatically according to the days' weather broadcasts if the system has not been used for a long time. This function can be set on or off manually on an application by a user. To obtain some information for specific tasks, the speech interactive agent downloads and updates the mined data from the data mining server via the wireless internet.

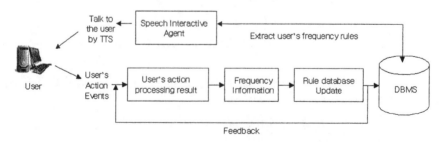

Fig. 3. Active interaction procedure using the user's frequency rule

To extract the features for data mining, the rough set theory [1] is applied. By using the rough set theory, a decision rule induction from an attribute value table is done. The feature extraction algorithm can generate multiple feature sets (reducts). These feature sets are used for predicting the user's action with the primary decision-making algorithm and confirmation algorithm. The primary decision-making algorithm compares the feature values of objects with decision rules. If a matching criterion is found, the decision rule for action of the speech interactive agent is assigned to the specific job. However, the user may not require the specific task to be performed because of lack of confidence if the user is distracted at that time. Thus, the confirmation algorithm is applied using speech interaction tools; speech recognition and text-to-speech. When the user just says "yes", the action is performed according to the rule of the decision-making algorithm.

Table 2. Decision rules for the action

Decision rule 1. IF (F1 = 0) THEN (D = 0)
Decision rule 2. IF (F2 = 1) AND (F3 = NOW) THEN (D = N)
Decision rule 3. IF (F4 = 1) AND (F5 = 1) THEN (D = N)

Table 3. Test sample data

Object No.	F1	F2	F3	F4	F5	D
1,2,3,4,5,6,7	0	X	X	X	X	0
1	1	1	Time	24%	2	1
2	1	1	Time	10%	3	2
3	1	0	X	4%	5	3
4	1	0	X	10%	4	4
5	1	0	X	50%	1	5
6	1	0	X	1%	7	6
7	1	0	X	1%	6	7

We select five features, F1-F5. F1 is the indicator to notify whether the system is in the sleep mode or not. F2 is the indicator to notify whether the object (application ID) is one reserved at the scheduled time or not. F3 is the reserved time if the F2 is set to 1. F4 is the frequency rate when the object is used for some time. F5 is the priority of that application. Table 2 includes 3 decision rules generated with the rule extraction algorithm. The decision rules are followed continually when the F1 is just set to 1. If the matching criterion is met in the next decision rules, decision rule is set to N, which is the object number to be performed by the speech interactive agent. Table 3 depicts a sample data set. When F1 is 1, F2 is 1, and F3 of the object 2 is on time to be executed, the decision rule, D is set to 2. Thus, the object 2 is selected as the one that can be executed. If F3 does not notify by a scheduled time, the decision rule, D is set to 5 because the object number 5 has the highest priority, $F5=1$.

This proposed method gives the intelligence and automation for user satisfaction. In addition, sensory fused rules and data fusion rules can be employed easily on the embedded system, but the amount of this information for user satisfaction is limited. Thus, the previously constructed information on the Web can give the efficient and satisfactory ones to the users. So, the next subsection describes the embedded data mining method using the Web.

3.4 The Association of the Web

An embedded hardware system has not enough memory devices to manage the data because it has a resource limitation problem and low performance capability. Actually, our system has a 512Mbyte working memory (NOR flash memory) and a 256Mbyte Compact Flash (CF) memory. The working memory includes operating system and some files to boot. It cannot store some information permanently. The CF memory includes 200Mbyte map data for car navigation, and 30Mbyte TTS DB. This is due to the cost of car navigation product. However, the user wants to utilize various information and services from a lot of different information sources. To resolve this problem, this system stores and manages only multiple level-of-abstraction. This mined data for multiple-level association rules are performed on the server-side. The data mining server plays a role in performing the Web mining. Mining typical user profiles and URL associations from the vast amount of access logs is an important feature. It deals with tailoring the interaction with Web information space based on information about the users.

The multiple level-of-abstraction is composed of multiple-level association rules and a summary table. The methods for mining associations at a generalized abstraction level by extension of the Apriori algorithm is applied as in [14]. The summary table forms the topic based indexing scheme. It stores basic information about groups of tuples of the underlying relations. This summary table is incrementally updateable and is able to support a variety of data mining and statistical analysis tasks. The summary table forming the indexed file is downloaded from the data mining server when the system is first switched on at the start of the day and the information is changed in the data mining server. The generalization process using attribute-oriented induction approach [14] for summary tables is performed on the server-side. It extracts a large set of relevant data in a database from a low concept level to a relatively high one. Thus, the system does not spend extra calculation time for data mining on an embedded system.

The sample structure of the multiple level-of-abstraction is as shown in Figure 4. It has a hierarchy form to index the data. We use two kinds of mined data; news and traffic information. (a) of Figure 4 depicts the news information. (b) of Figure 4 depicts the traffic information. The summary table basically includes the primary key, data, title, associated URL, and comments. Embedded applications that represent the news and traffic information just display the multiple level-of-abstraction information. If the user wants to see the specific information, that information is downloaded and displayed on the screen by selecting the specific button, or speaking the title. The speech interactive agent requests the URL for information to be sent to the data mining server, then the server sends the requested information in a form of HTML type text using HTTP protocol. The received text information is parsed and passed to the TTS, then the TTS reads this texts.

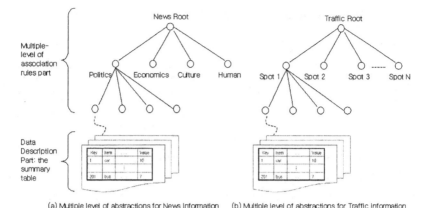

(a) Multiple level of abstractions for News Information   (b) Multiple level of abstractions for Traffic Information

Fig. 4. Multiple level-of-abstraction to manage the news and traffic information

4 Experimental Evaluation

Multimedia Service applications, the Main daemon and the speech interactive agent together are implemented and tested on X-scale 400 Mhz, WindowsCE.NET AutoPC system. 11 Khz speech sampling rate for input and output is used for the speech interactive agent. Each application program and daemon processes communicate between them using IPC method respectively according to the negotiated protocols. On the first time, to test the application programs respectively, the speech interactive agent and simulator are developed. After integrating works are finished, the real car test is evaluated on integrated working environment.

For experimental evaluation of speech based user inter interface such as speech recognition and text-to-speech, respective algorithms are evaluated respectively. First, noise preprocessing algorithm with 2-channel microphone array is applied and implemented for suppressing car noises. The experiments were conducted using the CAR01 corpus from the Speech Information Technology & Industry Promotion Center (SITEC) [23]. This corpus consists of car control and navigation related commands words, isolated digit and connected four digits. As the baseline experiment without any noise reduction method and a single channel noise reduction method using spectral subtraction algorithm (SS) is conducted to compare the performance improvement of the dual-channel noise reduction method.

In 2-channel noise reduction methods, we evaluated some methods using the delay-and-sum beamformer (DS), Griffiths-Jim beamformer (GJ) [4] and eigen-decomposition (EVD) [21]. In addition, we applied the high-pass filter (HP) to cancel the low frequency component of the car environment. But the performance of the EVD method combined with the HP and E-EVD (new two reconstructed signals) method is highly improved. From the results as shown in Table 4 and 5, it is shown that the best performance is obtained when E-EVD method is combined with HP.

Table 4. Word accuracy of various noise reduction methods (%)

Method Channel	Baseline	SS	HP+GJ	HP+DS	HP+ E-EVD
Ch 3 + Ch 5	38.32	57.66	80.66	87.23	89.14
Ch 4 + Ch 7	83.94	85.77	88.50	90.51	91.88

Table 5. PESQ score of various noise reduction methods

Method Channel	Baseline	SS	HP+GJ	HP+DS	HP+ E-EVD
Ch 3 + Ch 5	2.68	2.74	2.74	2.93	2.91
Ch 4 + Ch 7	3.23	3.23	3.19	3.17	3.28

Table 6. Driving tests on a real car

	office	Low-speed	high-speed	average	Car
Off-line	99.69	94.44%	92.10%	-	Avante (1800CC)
Men	-	95.4%	96%	95.7%	EF Sonata, SM5(2000CC)
Women	-	92.5%	93.42%	92.96%	EF Sonata, SM5(2000CC)
Average	-	93.95%	94.71%	94.33%	EF Sonata, SM5(2000CC)

Next, speech recognition experiment is performed. The speech recognition function for the speech interactive agent is classified into embedded ASR and DSR front-end. The total number of recognizable words on embedded ASR is more than about 5,000 words. However, the tree-based dynamic word recognition approach is applied according to the operational scenarios on each multimedia service application. The case of DSR is about 10,000 words for each city. The embedded speech recognition engine is developed and optimized in car noises, and we implemented DSR by using the third-party DSR Software Development Kit (SDK).

For embedded ASR, an isolated word recognizer with dynamic vocabularies to reduce computing time and optimized memory size [15][22] is applied, and speech signals are analyzed within 125ms frame with 10ms lapped into 26th order feature vector that has 13th order MFCCs including log energy and their 1st derivatives. To cope with the car noises, we applied feature compensation scheme based on multivariate Gaussian-Based Cepstral normalization (RATZ) [18], and the hidden Markov model (HMM) based on tied mixture is applied [7][17]. Driving test is performed on a real car as delineated in Table 6. The driving speed was done at a low speed between 20 and 60 Km/H while high speed was between 70 and 110 Km/H. A total of 40 men and women are tested on a Hyundai EF-Sonata and Samsung SM5 car respectively. The number of recognizable words is 100 words on each given scenario respectively.

Finally, text-to-speech experiment is performed. The speech interactive agent has two TTS child-processes. One is related with the CNS, and the other is related with application services. For fast speed on embedded system, the execution time and code sizes of the TTS are also optimized. However, the access time of storage to get the specific tri-phone wave takes a lot of time. It is dependent on the used flash memory.

The sound quality test is evaluated as in Table 7 for men and women in terms of mean-opinion score. The output sampling rate of each version is 16Khz. The TTS 1, 2, 4 and 5 are the various versions of the engines developed for embedded environments. The TTS 1 is 32M in size with a man's voice while the TTS 2 is 64M in size also of a man's voice. The TTS 4 is 32M with a woman's voice. The TTS 5 is 64M with a woman's voice. The TTS 3 is 32M with a woman's voice developed by a benchmark developer. Finally, We applied 16KHz, 40M DB (TTS6) with a woman's voice by compressing 16 KHz, 64M DB. Even if the sampling rate is down and the memory required is more than 8MByte, the sound quality is much better than 16Kz, 32M DB. That is why TTS system has dependency on TTS database for sound quality.

Table 7. MOS(Mean Opinion Score) test for TTS

	TTS1 (32 M)	TTS2 (64 M)	TTS3 (32 M)	TTS4 (32 M)	TTS5 (64 M)	TTS6 (40 M)
Men	2.93125	3.41675	4.00625	3.65625	4.01875	3.95421
Women	2.66875	3.04375	3.25	3.0625	3.44375	3.3478
Avg.	2.8	3.23025	3.628125	3.359375	3.73125	3.651005

Respective modules are integrated based on the behavior of the speech interactive agent. The speech interactive agent is not a best solution for human and machine interface if the usage is not easy. Thus, to provide the efficient tool for speech interaction and improve the performance of speech recognition rate, usability issues are considered. These issues include start button to notify speech recognition, undo function, command mode, verification function, out-of-vocabulary rejection, speech guidance and so on. In our proposed system, following consideration is implemented. Speech recognition start button by pushing the external push to talk (PTT) button is provided. Disabling function of speech recognition is automatically done if the user does not speak any word for 3 seconds after pushing the PTT button. Verification function is applied using TTS to notify the recognition result. Undo function provides the feedback to the previous state by pushing the PTT button again within 1 seconds if the recognition result is failed. Command mode is classified into a global and local command. The user can choose the command mode; expand mode and local mode. Expand mode includes a global and local commands, and local mode includes only a local command. Out-Of-Vocabulary (OOV) rejection is applied to reject the word if there is no one in a given recognition list. Lastly, Speech guidance using the TTS in order to notify the guideline information for the easy use is applied. On this situation, a lot of people used this system for some periods. Mostly used application was road navigation, MP3 player, Radio, and TV in order.

5 Discussions and Conclusions

5.1 Discussions

As the quality of automatic speech recognition (ASR) and text-to-speech (TTS) steadily improves, a variety of multimedia application services using embedded ASR (eASR), distributed speech recognition (DSR) and embedded TTS (eTTS) are being introduced for commercial use. In particular, since the demand of Telematics services is surging, speech interface to interact with human users has become an essential means of the multi-modal interface. As a Telematics client service interface, the eASR, DSR, and eTTS combined as a stand-alone unit provides an easy manipulation interface for command and controlling a car navigation system while the driver can pay attention to safe driving. In addition, as computer technology is improved, small sized computers such as AutoPCs has been utilized in various fields. Thus, by using this embedded system, the user requests and wants to utilize various service applications that they is used on a desktop PC, even while driving a car.

However, an embedded hardware system has a resource limitation and low performance capability. Actually, this condition is not able to represent huge data. Thus, a new architectural model is required in an embedded system. One alternative method is to use the Web. On the server-side, a comprehensive database is first mined, and then all the discovered patterns are stored in a DBMS. On the client-side, some abstraction data and indexes are stored. If the user wants to show specific data, the client obtains that information from a data mining server via the Internet using abstraction data and indexes. Meanwhile, Multimedia files such as music, moving picture files can be presented using data streaming method [5]. In our system, we reduce the memory size by using this concept. Even if a data communication fee per a packet should be paid, compression techniques for transmission packets could reduce the packet size. In addition, this can be resolved according to the policy of service usage. On the other hand, sensor network [12][13] is employed. Distributed sensor network obtain the distinct information by using its own functionality. Finally fused data provides the reliable information processed from competitive and cooperative terms to the users.

Fig. 5. Embedded system using an AutoPC for car navigation

With the above concepts, we designed a framework for command, control, communication, and intelligence environment based on a software agent on an embedded car navigation system, and then implemented it on AutoPC environment as shown in Figure 5. The proposed framework provides the structure to extend the system easily and integrate with other services. It is possible that the core processing such as combining rules from interface modalities, data fusion rules, DBMS processing, and communication tasks are done by the speech interactive agent. In this system, a conversational tool provides advantages in confirming the final decision to use human interactive data mining [3].

5.2 Conclusions

In this paper, we proposed a decision theoretic fusion framework that includes the multiple level-of-abstraction approach combining multiple-level association rules and the summary table, as well as the active interaction rule generation algorithm using the rough set theory for actionability on an embedded car navigation system. In addition, it included the sensory and data fusion level rule extraction algorithm to cope with simultaneous events occurring from multi-modal interface. Using such a decision theoretic fusion framework, a variety of applications can be applied easily to this system in the form of flexible, extensible and transparent ones. We expect that this fusion framework will be able to meet the user's demands and desires.

Acknowledgements

This work was supported by grant No. A17-11-02 from the Korea Institute of Industrial Technology Evaluation & Planning Foundation.

References

[1] A. Kusiak, and et al., "Autonomous Decision-Making: A Data Mining Approach," IEEE Trans. on Information Technology in Biomedicine, Vol. 4, No. 4, December 2000.

[2] B. Delaney, and et al., "A Low-Power, Fixed-Point Front-End Feature Extraction for a Distributed Speech Recognition System," HP Technical Report, HPL-2001-252, 2001.

[3] C. C. Aggarwal, "A Human-Computer Interactive Method for Projected Clustering," IEEE Trans. On Knowledge and Data Engineering, Vol. 16, No. 4, April 2004.

[4] D. R. Campbell, and P. W. Shields, "Speech enhancement using sub-band adaptive Griffiths-Jim signal processing," Speech Communication 39, pp. 97-110, 2003.

[5] G. Brettlecker, H. Schuldt, and R. Schatz. "Hyperdatabases for Peer-to-Peer Data Stream Processing," IEEE International Conference on Web Service, pp.358-366, July 2004.

[6] H. Ashida, and T. Morita, "Architecture of data mining server: DATAFRONT/Server," IEEE SMC '99 Conference Proceedings., Volume: 5 , 12-15 Oct. 1999.

[7] J. Beh and H. Ko, "A Novel Spectral Subtraction Scheme For Robust Speech Recognition: Spectral Subtraction using Spectral Harmonics of Speech," ICME, pp. 633-636, Jul. 2003.

[8] J. Han and et al. "Data mining for Web intelligence," Computer , Volume: 35, Issue: 11, Nov. 2002.

[9] J. Han, Y. Cai, and N. Cercone, "Data-Driven Discovery of Quantitative Rules in Relational Databases," IEEE Trans. on Knowledge and Data Eng., vol. 5, pp.29-40, 1993.

[10] M. Aakay, and et al., "A system for medical consultation and education using multimodal human/machine communication," IEEE Trans. On Information Technology in Biomedicine, Vol 2 , Issue: 4 , Dec. 1998.

[11] M. Chen, and et al., "Data Mining: An Overview from a Database Perspective," IEEE Trans. on knowledge and Data Engineering, Vol. 8, No. 6, December 1996.

[12] R. T. Antony, *Principles of Data Fusion Automation,* Artech house, 1995.

[13] R. R. Brooks and S. S. Iyengar, *MultiSensor Fusion: Fundamentals and Applications with Software*, Prentice Hall, 1998.

[14] R. Srikant and R. Agrawal, "Mining Generalized Association Rules," Proc. 21th Int'l Conf. Very Large Data Bases, pp. 407-419, Sept. 1995.

[15] S. Mitra, and et al., "Data Mining in Soft Computing Framework: A Survey," IEEE Trans. on Neural Networks, Vol. 13, No. 13, January 2002.

[16] S. Takata, S. Kawato, and M Mase, "Conversational agent who achieves tasks while interacting with humans based on scenarios," Robot and Human Interactive Communication Proceedings:11th IEEE International Workshop, 25-27 Sept. 2002.

[17] T. Kim and H. Ko, "Uttrance Verification Under Distributed Detection and Fusion Framework", Eurospeech, pp. 889~892, Sep. 2003.

[18] W. Kim, S. Ahn and H. Ko, "Feature Compensation Scheme Based on Parallel Combined Mixture Model", Eurospeech, pp. 677~680, Sep, 2003.

[19] X. Huang, A. Acero and H. Hon, *Spoken Language Processing*, Prentice Hall PTR, 2001.

[20] Y. Elovici and D. Braha, "A Decision-Theoretic Approach to Data Mining," IEEE Trans on Systems, Man, and Cybernetics – PART A:Systems and Humans, Vol. 33, No. 1, January 2003.

[21] Y. Cao, S. Sridharan, and M. Moody, "Multichannel speech separation by Eigendecomposition and its application to co-talker interference removal," IEEE Transactions on Speech and Audio Processing, vol. 5, no. 3, pp. 209-219, May 1997.

[22] Y. Gong, and Y. Kao, "Implementing a high accuracy speaker-independent continuous speech recognizer on a fixed-point DSP," Proc. of ICASSP, Vol. 6, June 2000.

[23] http://www.sitec.or.kr.

Use of Data Mining in System Development Life Cycle

Richi Nayak[1] and Tian Qiu[2]

[1] School of Information Systems, QUT, Brisbane, QLD 4001, Australia
r.nayak@qut.edu.au
[2] EDS Credit Services, Adelaide, Australia
tian.qiu@eds.com

Abstract. During the life cycle of a software development project, many problems arise. Resolutions to these problems are time consuming and expensive. This paper discusses the use of data mining in solving some of these problems to improve the system development life cycle process. A case study of applying data mining to the software Problem Report management data is also presented. The empirical results demonstrate the capability and benefit of data mining analysis in systems development life cycle.

1 Introduction

The System Development Life Cycle (SDLC) includes various phases during which the defined software products are created or modified [22]. These phases include planning, definition, requirement analysis, design, development, testing and integration, implementation, operation and maintenance. During the SDLC process, huge repositories for configuration management, risk management, project metric report and problem report management are maintained in addition to source code.

These repositories are potential sources of useful information that can be used in improving the SDLC process. Researchers have started using data mining (DM) [5,9,10,11,16,18,21] techniques in this process. Some examples of DM usage are in (1) software maintenance by summarizing and augmenting software changes, (2) software development process by automatically generating test cases and checking their outputs, (3) software reuse by predicting success or failure of components beforehand, and matching and discovering reusable patterns, and (4) project planning and estimation by identifying relationships between human resources and product types.

This paper discusses the capability and benefit of data mining analysis in systems development life cycle. The paper is organised into two parts. The first part includes the discussion on various DM applications in SDLC. The second part presents a case study of applying DM to the software problem report management data.

2 Data Mining Applications in SDLC

Figure 1 illustrates a general framework of applying DM techniques to aid the SDLC process. We have summarised the use of DM in SDLC into two areas: (1) software development process that includes management rule generation, risk assessment and

G.J. Williams and S.J. Simoff (Eds.): Data Mining, LNAI 3755, pp. 105–117, 2006.

software component testing and (2) software reuse and maintenance that includes component discovery, reuse and maintenance.

There are also examples of complementing DM with the use of software engineering (SE) principles. [7] utilised SE principles for the development of clustering architecture implemented on the multi-stage DM process to reduce the processing time. A SE methodology is also used to combine the application of deductive logic for generating intelligence from a collection of SE data [13].

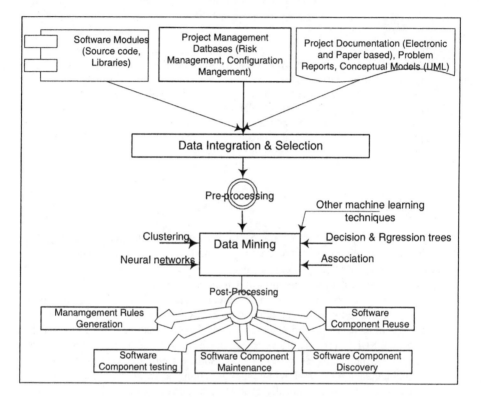

Fig. 1. A general framework showing steps of DM process in SDLC

2.1 Software Development Process

There exist several software development methodologies such as waterfall, incremental, rapid, agile and object-oriented [18]. Usually developers choose a methodology based on their previous experience or according to the managerial decisions. Every organisation collects a meta-data about the applications being developed. A data set can be created based on the methodology used, human resources involved, nature of the application, etc, and finally whether the project has been successful or not. Results of the DM analysis can be used in advising developers on the usage of a methodology according to the nature of the future application, to warn developers about failure stories, and to inform project mangers on human resources planning and scheduling.

DM has been used in detecting error-patterns linked to a certain software component(s). The error patterns in combination with the associated component(s) can give an overview of the problem, and whether this problem in the component is associated with other failures elsewhere in the component hierarchy. [9] used the classification and regression trees algorithm to predict which software modules likely to have faults discovered during operations. They derived the variables from various SDLC repositories and used them as useful predictors of software quality. Software developers need such predictions early in development to enhance software quality.

[16] successfully used regression tree analysis to determine the project size based on the size of individual software components. The size estimation helps in resource planning. [5] used the classification and association data mining to model the complex behaviour of the software development process and created different scenarios for the same project. The generated management rules make the decision-taking process easy for project managers in a similar situation.

Researchers have also used DM in automatic testing of systems. [10] used info-fuzzy network based method to recover the system requirements, to automatically design a minimal set of test cases and to evaluate the correctness of outputs.

2.2 Software Reuse and Maintenance

The use of object oriented analysis and design has skyrocketed in the last decade and contributes greatly to both organizational and commercially available software components. However finding the right component at the right time can be a complex task. Choosing the right library or (module) component can result in an efficient project, but selecting the wrong components can cause unnecessary project delays due to possible software failure and debugging.

Nakkrasae et al. [15] used a neural network technique to classify software components for effective archival and retrieval purposes. This work enables software components details to be stored, classified, and subsequently retrieved for reuse. In the same line, Miller et al [12] utilised DM techniques to discover structural information about legacy programs and constructed a warehouse of program-analysis data to provide support in software reuse and maintenance.

Morisio et al. [14] identified success or failure factors in components by using predictive DM which is aimed at two factors namely human factors and product type. This leads to recommending possible successful components for reuse. Michail [11] used link analysis to find association between library classes and program functions that are typically reused in combination with application classes. Specific rules of how components are associated with library functions through usage are created.

Many software projects fail because components fail and huge resources is wasted in debugging and fixing faulty code. This becomes worse when changes in one part of the program code make other components faulty and unusable based on relationships between the components. Ying et al. [20] applied association mining to determine change patterns – set of files that were changed together frequently in the past – from the change history of the programming codes. The mined change patterns (a set of files) are used as recommendation (to check for correctness) whenever a developer modifies the linked existing code. Shirabad et al [17] investigated decision tree learning to find out the relevant files that are affected by the changes applied to a particular file or a set of files. They used the software maintenance records to provide the training data set in a DM process.

2.3 Data Mining Tools in SDLC

The most commonly used DM techniques in SDLC are decision trees, neural networks and association analysis. A DM tool used in SDLC should be effective to utilise these techniques, easy to use, support data preparation and most importantly, be able to present results in a succinct manner. The general-purpose DM tools such as SAS 'Enterprise Miner' and Statsofts's 'Statistica Data Miner' (known for the user-friendly drag-and-drop workspace and good reporting functions) can be used. There also exits DM tools especially built to assist in SDLC process. An example is EMERALD [4], Enhanced Measurement for Early Risk Assessment of Latent Defects, for assessing reliability risk for software developers and managers. This tool has been used in number of studies, e.g., [19] used EMERALD for predicting fault ranges of software modules with Fuzzy Nonlinear Regression.

2.4 Major Issues Arising with Applications of Data Mining in SDLC

General problems encountered with data such as over-fitting/poor-fitting, missing and noisy values, large size and dimensionality, still remain the same for this domain as others. Some of the issues listed below can be considered as major requirements and challenges for the further evolution of DM technology in SDLC.

Diversity of the Data Types: Large software projects often keep huge amounts of data spread over different non-consolidated repositories such as source code repositories e.g., CVS*; conceptual models of software e.g., UML†; modelling tools e.g., Rational Rose‡; project management tools and documentation tools. Additionally, data collected during a SDLC process reside in many sources such as flat files, relational databases, data warehouses, transactional databases, advance database systems (including object-oriented, object-relational, multimedia and specific application-oriented databases) and the Web. While DM is applicable to any kind of data, the challenges and techniques may vary depending on the repository type.

A DM system must be able to deal with data drawn from different sources and formats. Without proper pre-processing, analysis of data to uncover patterns will be difficult since bad quality data ultimately leads to useless discoveries. The pre-processing module should include the use of simple query languages to extract data from various repositories, integrate, select, assess for quality and convert to the format suitable to the analysis tool.

Mining Methodology and User Interaction Issues: Data residing in many sources also poses a problem in mining of knowledge at multiple levels [8]. This raises the problem of finding associations among these various sets of extracted knowledge. The integration of extracted relationships from various sources is an unresolved issue [18].

---

* CVS is a common method to store source code of a project in a centralized repository.
† Unified Modelling Language is a popular modelling language in SDLC.
‡ An industry standard multi-purpose modelling tool (by IBM) for software projects.

Additionally, a large portion of the SDLC process is based on background knowledge of personnel involved. A DM technique should learn to incorporate the priori knowledge in its process.

Another aspect of DM that can be a problem is the presentation and visualization of the complex results. Output of a mining process is usually a large number of meaningful rules. However the representation of these rules to assist a project manager in making strategic directions requires significant post-processing.

Performance Issues: These include efficiency, scalability, and user effectiveness of data mining algorithms and tools. The performance metrics assessing the appropriateness of DM methods to SDLC includes robustness, scalability, automatic pre-processing capability, reliability, noise tolerance and sensitivity analysis [6]. A DM tool should be able to include all (or majority) of these to get the user satisfaction.

3   A Case Study: Analysis of Problem Report Data

This section describes the application of DM techniques to the software Problem Report (PR) management data of a large global telecommunication company. When a problem is reported, the responsible team can only approximately suggest the efforts (time) to fix the problem based on their previous experience. If the current project is not within their familiar topics, the accuracy of the estimation becomes worse.

The goal of this mining process is to provide estimation of effort to fix when a problem is raised. The results will reveal the hidden relationships in data, such as:

- How long does it take to fix a problem when a particular type of PR is raised?
- What type of project documents needs significant efforts to fix the associated bug?

This will bring great cost savings and benefits to the organisation by the improved control over the PR fixing and an accurate project planing, estimation and progress control. The results will especially be useful to developers in problem reasoning. When a programmer is struggling with a bug, a resolution can be suggested from the knowledge inferred from the previous similar problems stored in PRs.

3.1   Data Pre-processing

The first task in the process is to prepare the data set according to the DM techniques.

Field Selection: The PR data consists of textual information, categorical and numerical fields. Several fields such as *confidential, submitter-ID, environment, fix, release note, audit trail, the associated project name and the PR number* are ignored during mining. These are used in pre-processing and post-processing stages to assist in the selection of data and a better understanding of the rules being found.

Whenever a PR is raised, a project leader will have to find answers for the following questions before taking any action:

- How severe the problem is (customer impact)?
- What is the impact of the problem on project schedule (Cost & Team priority)?
- What type of the problem it is (a Software bug or a design flaw)?

- How long it will take to fix?
- How many people were involved?
- What is the problem description?

Accordingly, attributes such as *Severity (serious, critical* or *non-critical), Priority (high, medium or low), Class (sw-bug, doc-bug, change-request, duplicate, mistaken,* or *support), Arrival-Date, Closed-Date, Responsible,* and *Synopsis* are considered for mining.

The attribute '*Class*' is chosen as the target attribute in order to find out any valuable knowledge of the type of the problem with the rest of the PR attributes. Knowing the relationship between the fix effort and the PR class, a project leader can analyse the fix effort versus the human resources available. This knowledge can now be used in the scheduling and resource planning.

Every PR has an attribute, *State (open, active, analysed, suspended, feedback, resolved and closed),* to indicate the current stage of the PR. Since, the aim of this mining exercise is to find useful knowledge from existing projects, the PRs with a *closed* value in their *State* field are only considered.

The first five fields have fixed input values. *Responsible* attribute is used to calculate how many people were involved to fix the problem. *Association or classification rules* are generated by applying DM techniques on these fields. The *Synopsis* field has text information. It may contain what type of a project document (a piece of code or a support document) that the PR is concerned with. It can be used as a text index. *Text Mining* is considered to analyse this qualitative information.

Data Cleaning: The data set has some noise due to evolution of the data acquisition system and human involvement with the process. An example is the use of different terminologies over the time such as *SW-bug* or *sw-bug* as an input value for *Class* field (Example a, d in Figure 2). A *Time-Zone* field and other new input values have been added later in the system on management request based on the feedback of users after several years of system running.

To handle with the erroneous PRs, attempts are made to recover errors in PRs manually or automatically. If successful, the modified PRs are included in the mining process. For example, *SW-bug* in *Class* field is replaced by *sw-bug* throughout the data. The *Completed-Date* field (that was obsolete after some year of usage) is deleted, and the value (if any) is copied into the *Closed-Date* field.

The PRs, in which an error cannot be recovered precisely, are either discarded or replaced by a '?' if a software can handle the missing values. For example, the instance a in Figure 2 has its closed time earlier than the time being raised. Some PRs do not have all the values stored; such as Example c in Figure 2 has no closed date. An example of inconsistent values is shown in Figure 2 - there is no input for the *Time-Zone* field in a PR recorded before 1998, as the *Time-Zone* field is added in 1998.

Data Transformation: The attributes *Arrival-Date* and *Closed-Date* are transformed to a time-period - identifying the time spent to fix a PR – by taking account the additional information *Time-Zone* and *Responsible*. This transformation resulted in the *Time-to-fix* attribute with continuous values (figure 3). The *Responsible* attribute has the information about personnel engaged in rectifying the problem. We assume that the derived attribute *Time-to-fix* is total time spent to fix a problem if there is only one person involved. The calculated time period from *Arrival-Date* and *Closed-Date* is than multiplied by the number of people yield from the *Responsible* attribute. We have also experimented with discretizing this attribute with cutting points be one day (1), half week (3 days), one week (7), two weeks (14), one month (30) and one quarter (90 days), half year (180 days) and more than one year (360 days). The main reason behind this exercise is to give an approximate estimate. It allows for a minor change in human resource, and being not highly dependent on the exact human resource involved.

PR_ID|Category|Severity|Priority|Class|Arrival-Date|Close-Date|Synopsis

a. 17358|bambam|serious|high|*sw-bug|20:50 May 25 CST 1999|11:35 Mar 24 CST 1999|* STI STR register not being reset at POR
b. 17436|bambam|serious|high|support|18:10 Mar 30 CST 1999|12:00 May 24 CST 1999| sequence_reg varable in the RDR_CHL task is not defined
c. 580 |bingarra|serious|low|doc-bug|10:10 May 31 May 1996| | In URDRT2 of design doc, the word 'last' should be 'first'
d. 6205 |gali|serious|medium|*SW-bug|*14:30 Nov 5 1997|13:14 Dec 1 1997| grouping of options in dialog box

---

Fig. 2. Data examples from the original PR data set

Severity |Priority| Time-to-fix| Class |Synopsis

a. serious, high, 61, sw-bug, STI STR register not being reset at POR
b. serious, high, 56, support, sequence_reg varable in the RDR_CHL task is not defined
c. serious, low, ?, doc-bug, In URDRT2 of design doc, the word 'last' should be 'first'
d. serious, medium, 24, sw-bug, grouping of options in dialog box

---

Fig. 3. Data examples ready for mining

3.2 Data Modelling and Mining

We have chosen three data mining techniques to analyse the PR data:

- Predictive modelling on the PR data to make estimation on the time spent to fix a PR according to the PR properties.
- Link analysis to discover association among various PR characteristics.
- Text mining to analyse *Synopsis* field to find out most representative words in the problem-discussion, showing the major cause of a problem, along with the relationship of each frequent word with other words to show how are they related.

The predictive modelling or classification task builds a model by recognising distinct characteristics of the data set. We have chosen tree induction or decision tree (DT) due to their simplicity, efficiency and capability of dealing with noise and large data. The size of a DT depends on the number of attributes used to construct it. Because the number of attributes in our problem is small, the resulting DT is relatively simple and thus its structure is understood easily by a human analyst.

The link analysis operation exposes samples and trends by predicting correlation of variables in a given data set. We have used the Apriori algorithm [6] to reveal hidden affinity among the variables if a PR report is being raised.

We have used the **C5** [2], **CBA** [1] and the **TextAnalyst** [3] tools for classification, both classification and association, and text mining respectively.

3.3 Assimilation and Analysis of Outputs

Classification and Association Rule Mining: In order to get better rules and to decrease the error rate, several approaches are used. One approach is to stratify the data on the target using the choice-based sampling instead of using random samples. Equal numbers of samples representing each possible value of the target attribute (Class) are chosen for training. This improves the possibility of finding rules that are associated with the small groups of values during training. Another approach is to choose different amounts of PR data as training sets.

We used different training data sets. The first data set (Case 1, Table 1) contains 1224 PRs belonging to a specific software project out of total 11,000 PRs. The second data set (Case 2) contains the equal distributed target values for a medium size of 3400 PRs (about 900 PRs from each value of '*Class*') from all software projects. The third data set (Case 3) contains a large size of 5381 PRs from all software projects. We also performed the randomly selected PRs in 10-fold cross-validation experiments. The cross validation technique splits the whole data set into several subsets (called folds). Let each fold to be the test case and the rest as training sets in turn during training.

Experiments were conducted to test both type of time attribute – manually discretised or continuous values (labelled D or C in Table 1). Table 1 reports the classification mining results on all three cases, the associative rule mining results as Case 4, and (average) 10-fold cross-validation results.

We used two learning engines to discover rules from the PR data set– single support CBA (labelled SS in the Table 1 e.g., Case1-SS) and multiple support CBA (labelled b in the Table 1 e.g., Case1-MS). Constraints, support and confidence, are included in rules to control the quality of results. Confidence is the measure of the strength of a rule that indicates the probability of having consequence(s) in the rules provided that the rule contains certain antecedent(s). Support indicates the number of input data supporting the rule.

Some of the attributes in the data do not have uniform distributions, and many attributes are of very low frequency. Therefore a single support for all attributes is not able to discover important rules. This problem is relieved by setting multiple supports that allow user to choose different minimum supports to different attributes.

In general, all classification results in CBA achieve around 46% error rate in training data set (the lowest is 43.51%, the highest is above 59.10%). Above 51%

correct prediction rate is achieved in testing data set (the lowest has 43.51%, the highest has 58.25%). Another interesting point is that the attempt to improve the accurate prediction in the way of equal-distributed target-value samples does not lead much change; there is only roughly 3% improvement over the final result. The error rates from using multiple supports are higher and the number of extracted rules is lower than those from using single support mining engine.

The continuous time values result better than manually discretized values. This indicates that the discretized values may have resulted in some information loss.

Table 1. CBA Mining Results Summary. Rules are ranked by confidence.

	#Rules	Error rate (%)		Time cost (seconds)	
		Training	Testing	Training	Testing
Case1-SS-D	15	46.16	52.94	1.00	0.08
Case1-SS-C	10	**45.180**	47.56	1.01	0.07
Case1-MS-D	11	47.059	47.49	1.01	0.10
Case1-MS-C	9	45.180	47.56	1.04	0.09
Case2-SS-D	41	57.04	59.95	0.41	1.1
Case2-SS-C	18	**57.39**	58.09	0.44	1.3
Case2-MS-D	21	59.10	58.25	0.44	1.0
Case2-MS-C	12	58.45	58.91	0.45	1.2
Case3-SS-D	20	43.61	44.5	2.2	2.0
Case3-SS-C	15	**43.5**	43.8	2.2	2.0
Case3-MS-D	15	46.5	45.1	1.6	1.9
Case3-MS-C	15	46.5	46.9	1.6	1.6
10-CV-SS-D	22	50.5	52.5	25	
10-CV-SS-C	18	46.05	46.89	25.4	
10-CV-MS-D	17	48.87	49.1	28.9	
10-CV-MS-C	16	**45.02**	45.98	25.3	
Case4-SS-D	15	46.16	N/A	0.60	N/A
Case4-SS-C	10	**45.180**	N/A	0.66	N/A
Case4-MS-D	11	47.059	N/A	0.77	N/A
Case4-MS-C	9	45.180	N/A	1.04	N/A

There is no rule that has confidence value larger than 80%, however they do describe some characters of the PR fixing process. Therefore they are useful for the project management in estimating bug fixing related time issues.

Followings are examples of generated classification rules with CBA:

Rule 1: If *severity= non-critical and Time-to-fix = 3 to 30 days and priority= medium*
    Then *class = doc-bug.* Confidence = 82.7%, Support = 2.7%

Rule 2: If *severity= critical and Time-to-fix = less than 3 days and priority = high*
       Then *class = sw-bug.* Confidence = 75.2%, Support = 2.3%

Overall, the extracted rules infer that the software related bugs can be fixed within 3 days with above 75% confidence if they have high priority and are in critical condition. It may take 3 months to fix the problem if the corresponding priority and severity are graded as medium and serious.

The software **C5** was also used to perform classification data mining. We also utilised boosting and cross validation (Table 2). Boosting is a technique for generating and combining multiple classifiers to give improved predictive accuracy. After a number of trials, several different decision trees or rule sets are combined to reduce error rate for prediction. Boosting takes a longer time to produce the final classifier, and may not always achieve better results than a single classifier approach does, especially when the training data set has noise. Boosting and cross validation techniques do not generate a new rule, but try to find a better rule from the existing results. They only produce better results than the individual trees if the individual trees disagree with one another.

Table 2. C5 Mining Results Summary

	Normal mining		Mining with Boosting		Mining with cross-validation (10-fold)	
	Training	Testing	Training	Testing	Training	Testing
#Rules	51	N/A	N/A.	N/A	57.7	N/A
Error Rate (%) (Rules)	41.5	42.6	41.3	42.6	43.9	42.8
Error Rate (%) (Trees)	40.3	42.5	39.4	42.6	44.1	43.1
Size of tree	141	N/A.	N/A.	N/A	121.9	N/A.
Process Time (seconds)	5.6	0.2	37.7	0.4	41.1	1.1

Some example extracted classification rules with C5 are:

Rule 1: When a PR is in *low priority* and the *time spent is around half a day (0.5 day)* Then the rule has a high probability (87.5% Confidence) to classify a bug to be a *document related bug.*

Rule 2: When a PR is in *medium priority* with *non-critical severity* and the *time spent is around 1.1 day* Then the rule has 84.6% Confidence to classify a bug to be a *document related bug.*

Rule 3: When a PR is in *low priority* and the *time spent for fixing is around 1 week* Then the rule has 83.3% Confidence to classify a bug to be a *software bug.*

In general, all the rule sets achieve around 42% training error rate (the lowest is 40.3%, the highest is 43.9%) and 42.5% test error rate (the lowest is 39.4%, the highest is 44.1%). Both of the rates are better than CBA results. The time efficiency of C5 is also better than CBA.

Text Mining in PR Data: In order to find valuable knowledge from thousands of text, we categorise the pure text into several document types based on specific background knowledge. The result of the text mining together with the rules obtained from classification and association can more accurately predict the time and cost of fixing PRs. The TextAnalyst [3] tool automatically provides a concise and accurate summary of the analysed text and extracts some valuable rules. It builds up a semantic network for the investigation over the PR data.

The semantic network tree of the PR data contains a set of the most important words or word combinations, called *concepts*. Each concept of the semantic network is characterised by a weight value and a set of relationship of this concept to other concepts in the network. Every relationship between concepts is also assigned a weight value. The values of the weights range from 0 to 100, which correspond to the probability that the associated concept is characteristic for the whole PR data.

An interesting result is obtained for SCMP, Software Configuration Management Plan, a support document in every project. Since SCMP is not a main design document for a project with just about tens pages, it has never been considered as a trouble making item. However, the result showed that SCMP has 71% probability of appearing in test related PRs, and 58% probability of appearing in Code related PRs. This result is higher than the result associated with SRS ("Software Requirements Specification", a main development document directly related to software). This indicates that the attention should be paid in designing the SCMP document, and hence reducing the total cost of fixing SCMP related PRs.

Another analysis shows that a test related PR also has a higher weight (36, 100) in document related bugs than a SRS related PR (35, 99) does. This suggests that designers should also focus on the quality of the support and testing related documents along with the product related documents.

3.4   Problems in Performing Mining

The error rates in both CBA and C5 are higher than expected. Although several approaches are attempted to reduce the error such as uniform distribution of values, cross validation, boosting, different size of training set, etc. Unfortunately, the average error rate is only fallen down by 5% from 47% to 42%. The best result is 9% improvement from 46% to 37%. These results indicate that some amount of noise is still existent in data even after dealing with the noise during pre-processing.

The relationships between PRs and human resources within a particular project play a major role. The time needed to fix a bug is different for each project depending upon the actual human resources available. We have used only the *'Responsible'* attribute to indicate the human resource available. Truly, the relationship with the human resources available for past projects is needed to help project leaders to predict time consummations more accurately. The integration of the 'Change Request' data set that records all customer request process may rectify this problem.

Another reason is a non-uniform value distribution in the data set. For example, there are only 342 PRs with *change-request* value in the data set, compared to more than

5900 PRs related to *sw-bug*. Any potential rule associated to *change-request* can be heavily affected due to the presence of large size group with other values. Again the use of additional data sources together with the PR data set can rectify this problem.

We also attempted to use neural networks, there was no significant improvement in accuracy. In addition, it was difficult to interpret the outputs without the use of rule extraction techniques.

4 Conclusion

This paper attempts to show the use of data mining as one of the efficient methods to improve the SDLC process. Data mining can assist software developers by automating some of the development tasks. For example, the fundamental idea behind object-oriented programming is the re-use of components and linkage of objects through class instantiation, polymorphism and abstraction calls. Data mining can help to realise this concept more efficiently.

This paper also explored the use of data mining on a set of data collected during the SDLC process under a real software business environment. Some useful rules are inferred on the time consumption to fix a Problem Report and the relationship between the content and the type of the PR. These rules are in the form of associations, decision trees and semantic trees. The result may help developers in problem reasoning, and project leaders in estimation and planning.

Results of this application indicate that DM has capacity to improve the quality and efficiency of the software development process, even though the scale of this DM task was limited. It will be interesting to apply data mining to different phases of software development such as software quality data and integration of various data and knowledge at multiple levels.

As in many other domains, the benefits and capabilities brought by data mining in SDLC are worth of further investigations.

Acknowledgment

We will sincerely like to thank Mihir Shah, Parita Choksi and Magnus Haugaasen (ITB239: Enterprise Data Mining students at QUT) for conducting a short literature review on DM in SE domain. We will also like to show our gratitude to Dr Anurag Nayak a Senior IT Consultant for providing answers to SDLC related questions.

References

1. CBA, http://www.comp.nus.edu.sg/~dm2/
2. C5.0, http://www.rulequest.com/see5-info.html
3. TextMiner, http://www.megaputer.com/company/index.html
4. EMERALD, http://www.graphicsillustrated.com/reliametrics/products/tools.html
5. Alvarez-Macias J., J. Mata-Vazquez and J. Riquelme-Santos, *Data Mining for the Management of Software Development Process*, IJSEKE, Vol. 14, Issue 6 (2004) 665-695.

6. Chung H and P. Gray, *Current Issues in Data Mining* Journal of Management Information Systems, forthcoming
7. Gerardo B., J. Lee, Y. Choi and M. Lee, *"The K-Means Clustering Architecture in the Multi-Stage Data Mining Process"* , ICCSA 2005, LNCS 3481, pg 71-81,2005.
8. Han J., and M. Kamber, *"Data mining: concepts and techniques"*, Morgan Kaufmann Publishers, 2001.
9. Khoshgoftar T. and E. Allen, "Predicting Fault-Prone Software Modules in Embedded Systems with Classification Trees", International Journal of Reliability, Quality and Safety Engineering, 7(4), 2004.
10. Last M., M. Friedman and A. Kendal, *Using Data Mining for Automated Software Testing,* IJSEKE, Vol 14. Issue 4., 2004.
11. Michail A *Data mining library reuse patterns using generalized association rules* In International Conference on Software Engineering (2000), pp. 167–176.
12. Miller R. and A Gujarathi *Mining for program structure* IJSEKE, vol 9, No 5 (1999) 499-517
13. Mitkas P., "Knowledge Discovery for Training Intelligent Agents: Methodology, Tools and Applications", AIS-ADM 2005, LNAI 3505, pp 2-18, 2005.
14. Morisio M., M. Ezran and C. Tully (2003) *Comments on 'More Success and Failure Factors in Software Reuse"* , IEEE trans on SE, Vol 29, Issue 5. pg 478, 2003.
15. Nakkrasae S.and P. Sophatsathit, *An Rpcl-Based Indexing Approach for SoftwareComponent Classification,* IJSEKE, Vol 14, Issue 5. pg.497-518, 2004
16. Pendharkar P. *An exploratory study of object-oriented software component size determinants and the application of regression tree forecasting models.* Information & Management 42 (2004) 61-73.
17. Shirabad J., T. Lethbridge and S Matwin Applying data mining to software maintenance records In Proceedings of the 2003 conference of the Centre for Advanced Studies on Collaborative research.
18. Sunderhaft, N and Medonca. M. *Mining Software Engineering Data: A Survey,* A DACS state of the art report prepared for air-force Research Laboratory - Rome, NY, 1999.
19. Xu Z., Allen E.B., *Prediction of Software Faults using Fuzzy Nonlinear Regression Modeling,* In 5th IEEE International Symposium on High Assurance Systems Engineering, Nov, 2000, NewMaxico, pp 281-290.
20. Ying A., G. Murphy, R. Ng and C. Carroll. *Predicting Source Code Changes by Mining Change History,* IJSEKE, Vol 30. Issue 9. pg. 574-590, 2004.
21. (eds) Dia H and Webb G. IJSEKE, special issue: Best Papers from SEKE 2003 Workshop on Data Mining for Software Engineering and Knowledge Engineering, Vol 14, No 4, August 2004.
22. The Systems Development Life Cycle Guidance Document. [Accessed   21/6/2005] Available online at: *http://www.usdoj.gov/jmd/irm/lifecycle/table.htm*

Mining MOUCLAS Patterns and Jumping MOUCLAS Patterns to Construct Classifiers

Yalei Hao[1], Gerald Quirchmayr[1,2], and Markus Stumptner[1]

[1] Advanced Computing Research Centre, University of South Australia,
SA5095, Australia
[2] Institut für Informatik und Wirtschaftsinformatik, Universität Wien,
Liebiggasse 4, A-1010 Wien, Austria
Yalei.Hao@postgrads.unisa.edu.au,
Gerald.Quirchmayr@unisa.edu.au, mst@cs.unisa.edu.au

Abstract. This paper proposes a mining novel approach which consists of two new data mining algorithms for the classification over quantitative data, based on two new pattern called *MOUCLAS* (MOUntain function based CLASsification) Patterns and *Jumping MOUCLAS* Patterns. The motivation of the study is to develop two classifiers for quantitative attributes by the concepts of the association rule and the clustering. An illustration of using petroleum well logging data for oil/gas formation identification is presented in the paper. *MPs* and *JMPs are* ideally suitable to derive the implicit relationship between measured values (well logging data) and properties to be predicted (oil/gas formation or not). As a hybrid of classification and clustering and association rules mining, our approach have several advantages which are (1) it has a solid mathematical foundation and compact mathematical description of classifiers, (2) it does not require discretization, (3) it is robust when handling noisy or incomplete data in high dimensional data space.

1 Introduction

Data mining based classification aims to build accurate and efficient classifiers not only on small data sets but more importantly also on large and high dimensional data sets, while the widely used traditional statistical data analysis techniques are not sufficiently powerful for this task[1, 2]. With the development of new data mining techniques on association rules, new classification approaches based on concepts from association rule mining are emerging. These include such classifiers as ARCS[3], CBA[4], LB[5], JEP[6], etc., which are different from the classic decision tree based classifier C4.5[7] and k-nearest neighbor[8] in both the learning and testing phases. To improve ARCS[3], A non-grid-based technique[9] has been further proposed to find quantitative association rules that can have more than two predicates in the antecedent. All the above algorithms are constrained by the framework of binning. Though several excellent discretization algorithms[10, 11] are proposed, a standard approach to discretization has not yet been developed.

G.J. Williams and S.J. Simoff (Eds.): Data Mining, LNAI 3755, pp. 118–129, 2006.
© Springer-Verlag Berlin Heidelberg 2006

Therefore, all the above research issues establish a challenge, which is whether it is possible that an association rule based classifier with any number of predicates in the antecedent can be developed for quantitative attributes by the concepts of clustering which can overcome the limitation caused by the discretization method. In this paper, to resolve the problem, we present a new approach to the classification over quantitative data in high dimensional databases, called *MOUCLAS* (MOUntain function based CLASsification), based on the concept of the fuzzy set membership function. It aims at integrating the advantages of classification, clustering and association rules mining to identify interesting patterns in selected sample data sets.

2 Problem Statement

We now give a formal statement of the problem of *MOUCLAS* Patterns (called *MPs*) and introduce some definitions.

The *MOUCLAS* algorithm, similar to ARCS, assumes that the initial association rules can be agglomerated into clustering regions, while obeying the anti-monotone rule constraint. Our proposed framework assumes that the training dataset D is a normal relational set, where transaction $d \in D$. Each transaction d is described by attributes A_j, $j = 1$ to l. The dimension of D is l, the number of attributes used in D. This allows us to describe a database in terms of volume and dimension. D can be classified into a set of known classes Y, $y \in Y$. The value of an attribute must be quantitative. In this work, we treat all the attributes uniformly. We can treat a transaction as a set of (attributes, value) pairs and a class label. We call each (attribute, value) pair an item. A set of items is simply called an itemset.

In this paper, we propose two novel classifiers, called the *De-MP* and *J-MP*, which exploit the discriminationg ability of *MOUCLAS* Patterns (*MPs*) and *Jumping MOUCLAS* Patterns (*JMPs*).

The *MOUCLAS* Pattern (so called *MP*) has an implication of the form:

$$Cluster(D)_t \rightarrow y,$$

where *Cluster(D)*$_t$ *is a cluster of D,* $t = 1$ to m, and *y* is a class label.

The definitions of *frequency* and *accuracy* of *MOUCLAS* Patterns are defined as following: The *MP* satisfying minimum support is **frequent**, where *MP* has support s if s% of the transactions in D belong to *Cluster(D)*$_t$ and are labeled with class *y*. The *MP* that satisfies a pre-specified minimum confidence is called **accurate**, where *MP* has confidence c if c% of the transactions belonging to *Cluster(D)*$_t$ are labeled with class *y*.

We also adopt the concept of reliability[12] to describe the correlation. The measure of reliability of the association rule $A \Rightarrow B$ can be defined as:

$$\text{reliability} \quad R(A \Rightarrow B) = \left| \frac{P(A \wedge B)}{P(A)} - P(B) \right|$$

Since R is the difference between the conditional probability of B given A and the unconditional of B, it measures the effect of available information of A on the probability of the association rule. Correspondingly, the greater R is, the stronger *MOUCLAS* patterns are, which means the occurrence of *Cluster(D)ᵢ* more strongly implies the occurrence of *y*. Therefore, we can utilize reliability to further prune the selected *frequent and accurate and reliable MOUCLAS* patterns (*MPs*) to identify the truly interesting *MPs* and make the discovered *MPs* more understandable. The *MP* satisfying minimum reliability is **reliable**, where *MP* has reliability defined by the above formula.

Given a set of transactions, *D*, the problems of *De-MP* are to discover *MPs* that have support and confidence greater than the user-specified minimum support threshold (called *minsup*)[13], and minimum confidence threshold (called *minconf*)[13] and minimum reliability threshold (called *minR*) respectively, and to construct a classifier based upon *MPs*.

A Jumping *MOUCLAS* Pattern (*JMP*) can be further defined based on the notion of the Jumping Emerging Pattern[6] (*JEP*) and *MP*. A *JEP* is an itemset whose support increases significantly from 0 in a class (say poisonous class in mushroom data from the UCI repository) to a user-specified value in another class (say edible class). We can then use *JEP* as an index for dimensionality reduction. For each *JEP* in a certain class *y*, only the attributes of the *JEP* will be kept for all the transactions in the class *y*. We then perform the clustering on those transactions.

Let *C* denote the dataset of transaction *d* labeled with class *y* after dimensionality reduction processing by *JEPs*. A *JMP* can be defined as a *cluster_rule* , namely a rule:

$$cluset \rightarrow y,$$

where *cluset* is a set of itemsets from a cluster *Cluster(C)ᵢ*, which is obtained from the clustering on the same class of transactions after dimensionality reduction via JEP, *y* is a class label, *y* ∈ *Y*. Let *JMPset* denote a set of *JMPs* which coresponds to the same *JEP*.

Suppose the number of transactions of C in *cluset* is *cluCount*, the number of tansactions in *C* is *clasCount*, the *support* of transaction *d* belong to *cluset* in *C*, denoted as *subsup*, can be defined by the formula:

$$subsup = \frac{cluCount}{clasCount}$$

Given a set of transactions, *D*, the problems of *J-MP* is to discover all *JMPs* and calculate their *subsup* and construct a classifier based upon *JMPs*.

3   The *MOUCLAS-1* Algorithm

The classification technique, *MOUCLAS-1*, consists of two steps:

1. Discovery of *frequent*, *accurate* and *reliable MPs*.
2. Construction of a classifier, called *De-MP*, based on *MPs*.

The core of the first step in the *MOUCLAS-1* algorithm is to find all *cluster_rules* that have support above *minsup*. Let *C* denote the dataset *D* after dimensionality reduction processing. A *cluster_rule* represents a *MP*, namely a rule:

$$cluset \to y,$$

where *cluset* is a set of itemsets from a cluster $Cluster(C)_t$, *y* is a class label, $y \in Y$. The support count of the *cluset* (called *clusupCount*) is the number of transactions in *C* that belong to the *cluset*. The support count of the *cluster_rule* (called *cisupCount*) is the number of transactions in *D* that belong to the *cluset* and are labeled with class *y*. The *confidence* of a *cluster_rule* is (*cisupCount* / *clusupCount*) × 100%. The support count of the *class y* (called *clasupCount*) is the number of transactions in *C* that belong to the class *y*. The *support* of a *class* (called *clasup*) is (*clasupCount* / |C|) × 100%, where | C | is the size of the dataset *C*.

Given a *MP*, the *reliability* R can be defined as:

$$R(cluset \to y) = \left| \ (cisupCount \ / \ clusupCount) - (clasupCount \ / \ |C|) \ \right| \times 100\%$$

The traditional association rule mining only uses a single *minsup* in rule generation, which is inadequate for many practical datasets with uneven class frequency distributions. As a result, it may happen that the rules found for infrequent classes are insufficient and too many may be found for frequent classes, inducing useless or over-fitting rules, if the single *minsup* value is too high or too low. To overcome this drawback, we apply the theory of mining with multiple minimum supports[14] in the step of discovering the frequent MPs as following.

Suppose the total support is *t-minsup*, the different minimum class support for each class *y*, denoted as $minsup_i$ can be defined by the formula:

$$minsup_i = t\text{-}minsup \times \text{freqDistr}(y)$$

where, freqDistr(y) is the function of class distributions. *Cluster_rules* that satisfy $minsup_i$ are called *frequent cluster_rules*, while the rest are called *infrequent cluster_rules*. If the *confidence* is greater than *minconf*, we say the *MP* is *accurate*.

The first step of *MOUCLAS-1* algorithm works in three sub-steps, by which the problem of discovering a set of *MPs* is solved:

Algorithm: Mining *frequent* and *accurate* and *reliable MOUCLAS* patterns (*MPs*)
Input: A training transaction database, *D*; minimum support threshold ($minsup_i$); minimum confidence threshold (*minconf*); minimum reliability threshold (*minR*)
Output: A set of *frequent, accurate* and *reliable MOUCLAS* patterns (*MPs*)
Methods:
  (1) Reduce the dimensionality of transactions *d*, which efficiently reduces the data size by removing irrelevant or redundant attributes (or dimensions) from the training data, and
  (2) Identify the clusters of database *C* for all transactions *d* after dimensionality reduction on attributes A_j in database *C*, based on the Mountain function, which is a fuzzy set membership function, and specially capable of transforming quantitative values of attributes in transactions into linguistic terms, and
  (3) Generate a set of *MPs* that are both *frequent, accurate* and *reliable*, namely, which satisfy the user-specified minimum support (called $minsup_i$), minimum confidence (called *minconf*) and minimum reliability (called *minR*) constraints.

In the first sub-step, we reduce the dimensionality of transactions in order to enhance the quality of data mining and decrease the computational cost of the *MOUCLAS* algorithm. Since, for attributes A_j, $j = 1$ to l in database, D, an exhaustive search for the optimal subset of attributes within 2^l possible subsets can be prohibitively expensive, especially in high dimensional databases, we use heuristic methods to reduce the search space. Such greedy methods are effective in practice, and include such techniques as stepwise forward selection, stepwise backward elimination, combination of forwards selection and backward elimination, etc. The first sub-step is particularly important when dealing with raw data sets. Detailed methods concerning dimensionality reduction can be found in some papers[15-18].

Fuzzy based clustering is performed in the second sub-step to find the clusters of quantitative data. The Mountain-climb technique proposed by R. R. Yager and D. P. Filev[19] employed the concept of a mountain function, a fuzzy set membership function, in determining cluster centers used to initialize a Neuro-Fuzzy system. The substractive clustering technique[20] was defined as an improvement of Mountain-climb clustering. A similar approach is provided by the DENCLUE algorithm[21], which is especially efficient for clustering on high dimensional databases with noise. The techniques of Mountain-climb clustering, Substractive clustering and Denclue provide an effective way of dealing with quantitative attributes by mountain functions (or influence functions), which has a solid mathematical foundation and compact mathematical description and is totally different from the traditional processing method of binning. It offers us an opportunity of mining the patterns of data from an innovative angle. As a result, part of the research task presented in the introduction can now be favorably answered.

The observation that, a region which is dense in a particular subspace must create dense regions when projected onto lower dimensional subspaces, has been proved by R. Agrawal and his research cooperators in CLIQUE[22]. In other words, the observation follows the concepts of the apriori property. Hence, we may employ prior knowledge of items in the search space based on the property so that portions of the space can be pruned. The successful performance of CLIQUE has again proved the feasibility of applying the concept of apriori property to clustering. It brings us a step further towards the solution of the rest part of the research task, that is, if the initial association rules can be agglomerated into clustering regions, just like the condition in ARCS, we may be able to design a new classifier for the purpose of classification, which confines its search for the classifier to the cluster of dense units of high dimensional space. The answer to the rest research task can contribute to the third sub-step of the *MOUCLAS* algorithm to the forming of the antecedent of *cluster_rules*, with any number of predicates in the antecedent. In the third sub-step, we identify the candidate *cluster_rules* which are actually *frequent* and *accurate* and *reliable*. From this set of *frequent* and *accurate* and *reliable cluster_rules*, we produce a set of *MPs*.

Let I be the set of all items in D, C be the dataset D after dimensionality reduction, where transaction $d \in C$ contains $X \subseteq I$, a k-itemset. Let E denote the set of candidates of cluster_rules, where $e \in E$, *and* F denote the set of frequent cluster_rules. The first step of the *MOUCLAS* algorithm is given in Figure 1 as follows.

The task of the second step in *MOUCLAS-1* algorithm is to use a heuristic method to generate a classifier, named *De-MP*, where the discovered *MPs* can cover D and are organized according to a decreasing precedence based on their confidence and support. Suppose R be the set of *frequent, accurate* and *reliable MPs* which are generated in the past step, and $MP_{default\_class}$ *denotes* the default class, which has the lowest precedence. We can then present the *De-MP* classifier in the form of

$$<MP_1, MP_2, ..., MP_n, MP_{default\_class}>,$$

where $MP_i \in R$, $i = 1$ *to* n, $MP_a \succ MP_b$ if $n \geq b > a \geq 1$ *and* a, $b \in i$, $C \subseteq \cup$ *cluset of* MP_b.

1 X = reduceDim (I); // reduce the dimensionality on the set of all items I of in D
2 *Cluster(C)*$_t$ = genCluster (C); // identify the complete clusters of C
3 **for** each *Cluster(C)*$_t$ **do**
    E = genClusterrules(*cluset, class*); // generate a set of candidate *cluster_rules*
4   **for** each transaction $d \in C$ **do**
5   E_d = genSubClusterrules (E, d); // find all the *cluster_rules* in E whose *cluset* are
                                         supported by d
6   **for** each $e \in E_d$ **do**
7   e. clusupCount++; // accumulate the *clusupCount* of the *cluset* of *cluster_rule e*
8   if d.class = e.class then e.cisupCount++ // accumulate the *cisupCount* of *cluster_rule e*
                                    supported by d
9   **end**
10 **end**
11 $F = \{e \in E \mid e.cisupCount \geq minsup_i\}$; // construct the set of frequent cluster_rules
12 MP = genRules (F); //generate MP using the genRules function by *minconf* and *minR*
13 **end**

14 $MPs = \cup MP$; // discover the final set of *MPs*

Fig. 1. The First Step of the MOUCLAS-1 Algorithm

The second step of the *MOUCLAS-1* algorithm also consists of three sub-steps, by which the *De-MP* classifier is formed:

Algorithm: Constructing *De-MP* Classifier
Input: A training database after dimensionality reduction, C; The set of *frequent and accurate and reliable MOUCLAS* patterns (*MPs*)
Output: *De-MP* Classifier
Methods:
(1) Identify the order of all discovered *MPs* based on the definition of precedence and sequence them according to decreasing precedence order.
(2) Determine possible *MPs* for *De-MP* classifier from R following the descending sequence of *MPs*.
(3) Discard the *MPs* which cannot contribute to the improvement of the accuracy of the *De-MP* classifier and keep the final set of *MPs* to construct the *De-MP* classifier.

In the first sub-step, the *MPs* are sorted in descending order, which has the training transactions surely covered by the *MPs* with the highest precedence when possible in the next sub-step. The sort of the whole set of *MPs* is performed following the definition of *precedence*:

Given two *MPs*, we say that MP_a has a higher precedence than MP_b, denoted as $MP_a \succ MP_b$,

if $\forall MP_a, MP_b \in MPs$, it holds that: the confidence of MP_a is greater than that of MP_b, or if their confidences are the same, but the support of MP_a is greater than that of MP_b, or if both the confidences and supports of MP_a and MP_b are the same, but MP_a is generated earlier than MP_b.

In the second sub-step, we test the *MPs* following decreasing precedence and stop the sub-step when there is no rule or no training transaction. For each *MP*, we scan *C* to find those transactions satisfying the cluset of the *MP*. If the *MP* can correctly classify one transaction, we store it in a set denoted as *L*. Those transactions satisfying the cluset of the *MP* will be removed from *C* at each pass. Each transaction can be identified by a unique ID. The next pass will be performed on the remaining data. A default class is defined at each scan, which is the majority class in the remaining data. At the end of each pass, the total number of errors that are made by the current *L* and the default class are also stored. When there is no rule or no training transaction left, we terminate this sub-step. After this sub-step, every *MP* in *L* *can* correctly classify at least one training transaction in *C*.

In the third sub-step, though we would like to find as many *MPs* as possible to give good coverage of the training transactions in the second sub-step, we prefer strong *MPs* which have relatively high support and confidence, due to their characteristics of corresponding to larger coverage and stronger differentiating power. Meanwhile, we hope that the *De-MP* classifier, consisting of a combination of strong *MPs*, has a

```
1 R = sort(R); // sort MPs based on their precedence
2 for each MP ∈ R in sequence do
3     temp = ∅ ;
4     for each transaction d ∈ C do
5         if d satisfies the cluset of MP then
6             store d.ID in temp;
7             if MP correctly classifies d then
8                 insert MP at the end of L;
9         delete the transaction who has ID in temp from C;
10        selecting a default class for the current L; // determine the default class based on majority class of
                                                         remaining transactions in C
11    end
12    compute the total number of errors of L; // compute the total number of errors that are made by the
                                                  current L and the default class
13 end
14 Find the first MP in L with the lowest total number of errors and discard all the MPs after the MP in L;
15 Add the default class associated with the above mentioned first MP to end of L;
16 De-MP classifier = L
```

Fig. 2. The Second Step of the MOUCLAS Algorithm

relatively smaller number of classification errors, because of greedy strategy. In addition, the reduction of *MPs* can increase the understandability of the classifier. Therefore, in this sub-step, we identify the first *MP* with the least number of errors in *L* and discard all the MPs after it because these *MPs* produce more errors. The undiscarded *MPs* and the default class corresponding to the first *MP* with the least number of errors in *L* form our *De-MP* classifier.

The second step of the *MOUCLAS* algorithm is shown in Figure 2.

In the testing phase, when we classify a new transaction, the first *MP* in *De-MP* satisfying the transaction is used to classify it. In *De-MP* classifier, *default_class*, having the lowest precedence, is used to specify a default class for any new sample that is not satisfied by any other *MPs* as in C4.5[7], CBA[4].

4   The *MOUCLAS-2* Algorithm

The classification technique, *MOUCLAS-2*, consists of two main processes:

1. Discovering of all *JMPs* for each class.
2. Calculating their *subsup* and building a classifier, called *J-MP*, based on *JMPs*.

The core of the *MOUCLAS-2* algorithm is to find all *cluster_rules,* namely the *JMPs*. The *MOUCLAS-2* algorithm works in three sub-steps, by which the problem of discovering *JMPsets* and construction of a classifier is solved:

Algorithm: Mining Jumping *MOUCLAS* Patterns (*JMPs*) and building *J-MP* Classifier

Input: A training transaction database, *D*;

Output: *J-MP* Classifier

Methods:

(1)   Reduce the dimensionality of transactions *d* in each class *y* by the information of the attributes in corresponding *JEPs*, and

(2)   Identify all the clusters of database based on the Mountain function, which is a fuzzy set membership function, and specially capable of transforming quantitative values of attributes in transactions into linguistic terms, and

(3)   Generate *JMPsets* for each class *y* and calculate their *subsup*.

In the first sub-step, detailed method concerning JEP can be found in this paper[6].

The third sub-step of the *MOUCLAS-2* algorithm form the *cluster_rules*, with any number of predicates in the antecedent. It brings us a step further towards the solution of our research challenge. From this set of *cluster_rules* of a class *y*, we produce a set of *JMPs* for the class *y*.

Let *I* be the set of all items in *D* labeled with class *y, C* be the dataset of transaction *d* labeled with class *y* after dimensionality reduction processing by a *JEP*, where transaction $d \in C$ contains $X_i \subseteq I$, a *k*-itemset, and *i* be the number of *JEPs* in the class *y*. Let E denote a set of *cluster_rules* (*JMPset*) of a class *y*, corresponding to a JEP, where $e \in E$.

The first step of the *MOUCLAS-2* algorithm is given in Figure 3 as follows.

1 X = genJEP (I); // generate all the *JEPs* of all the class y in D
2 **for** each class *y* **do**
3   **for** each *JEP* of a same class y **do**
4   Xi = reduceDim (I); // reduce the dimensionality on the set of all items I in D
         labeled with class y based on the attributes of the *JEP*
5   E_i = genClusterrules(*cluset, class*); // generate a set of *cluster_rules, namely
         JMPset,* based on X_i
6   **for** each transaction $d \in C$ **do**
7   **if** one $e \in E_i$ can be supported by *d* **then** *e.cluCount++*; // accumulate the
           cluCount of *cluster_rule e* supported by *d*
8   **end**
9     $subsup_i = \dfrac{e.cluCount}{|C|}$; //calculate the *subsup* of each *JMPset*

10 **end**
11 **end**

12 *JMPs* = $\cup$ E_i; // discover the final set of *JMP*

Fig. 3. The Training Phase of the MOUCLAS-2 Algorithm

1 **for** each transaction $d \in D$ **do**
2   **for** each class *y* **do**
3   **for** each *JMPset* of a same class y **do**
4   **if** *d* satisfies a *JMPset* **then** *e.subsupt++* ; // accumulate the *subsup* of *JMPsets*
                                                supported by d
5   **end**
6   the *subsup_y* of *d* in class *y* = *e.subsupt* ; // calculate the total *subsup* of *d* in
                                                class *y*
7   **end**
8   **if** *subsup_y* is the maximum **then** *d* is labeled as *y*
9   **if** the *subsup* in two or more classes are the same **then** *d* is labeled as the class,
       whose *JMPs* are generated earlier than the others.
10 **if** the *subsup* = 0 **then** *d* is labeled as a default class
11 **end**

Fig. 4. The Testing Phase of the MOUCLAS Algorithm

In the testing phase, The *MOUCLAS-2* algorithm also consists of two sub-steps, by which the *J-MP* classifier can classify test data:

Algorithm: Classification Process of *J-MP* Classifier
Input: A test database, *D*; The set of Jumping *MOUCLAS* patterns (*JMPs*); The *support* of transaction *d* belong to *JMPs* in C (*subsup*)
Output: classification result of test database
Methods:
(1) Determine the *subsup* of each transaction *d* in D in each class.
(2) Classify the test data.

In the first sub-step, we firstly determine whether a *JMPset* can be supported by a transaction $d \in D$. If so, we then sum up the total *subsup* of the transaction d in one class. In this way, the $subsup_y$ of the transaction d in the class y can be obtained, where $y \in Y$. In the second step, the testing transaction d can be labeled as the class y, where the $subsup_y$ is greater than all the others. If the transaction d has the same maximum $subsup_y$ in two classes, then it is labeled as the class, whose *JMPs* are generated earlier than the other.

The classification process of the *MOUCLAS* algorithm is shown in Figure 4.

5 Example of *MOUCLAS* Application in Reservoir Characterization

Oil/gas formation identification is a vital task of reservoir characterization in the petroleum industry, where the petroleum database contains such records (or attributes) as seismic data, various types of well logging data and petrophysical property data whose values are all quantitative.

An illustration of using well logging date for purpose of oil/gas formation identification is illustrated in Figure 5. The well logging data sets include attributes (well logging curves) of GR (gamma ray), RDEV (deep resistivity), RMEV (shallow resistivity), RXO (flushed zone resistivity), RHOB (bulk density), NPHI (neutron porosity), PEF (photoelectric factor) and DT (sonic travel time). Since most of the reservoirs are horizontally and vertically heterogeneous, no depth information is used for training.

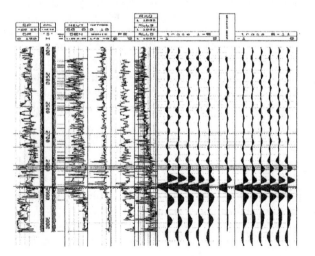

Fig. 5. Quantitative Petroleum Data for MOUCLAS Mining
(note: the dashed indicate the location of oil formation)

One transaction of the database can be treated as a set of the items corresponding to the same depth and a class label (oil/gas formation or not). A hypothetically useful *MP* or *JMP* may suggest a relation between well logging data and the class label of oil/gas formation since. In this sense, a selected set of such *MPs* or *JMPs* can be a useful guide to petroleum engineers to identify possible drilling targets and their depth and thickness at the stage of exploration and exploitation.

MPs and *JMPs* aim at deriving an explicit or implicit heuristic relationship between measured values (well logging data) and properties to be predicted (oil/gas formation or not). The *MOUCLAS* based method is ideally suitable to establish such implicit relationships through proper training. The notable advantage of *MOUCLAS* based algorithms over more traditional processing techniques such as model based well logging analysis is that a physical model to describe the relationship between the well logging data and the property of interest is not needed; nor is an very precise understanding of the physical phenomena of the well logging data. From this point of view, *MOUCLAS* based algorithms provides a complementary and useful technical approach towards the interpretation of petroleum data and benefits petroleum discovery.

6 Conclusions

Two novel classification patterns, the *MOUCLAS* Pattern (*MP*) and the *Jumping MOUCLAS* Pattern (*JMP*) for quantitative data in high dimensional databases, are investigated in this paper. We also propose the algorithm for the discovery of the interesting *MPs* and *JMPs* and construct two new classifiers called *De-MP* and *J-MP*. As a hybrid of classification and clustering and association rules mining, our approach may have several advantages which are (1) it has a solid mathematical foundation and compact mathematical description of classifiers, (2) it does not require discretization, as opposed to other, otherwise quite similar methods such as ARCS are strongly related to, (3) it is robust when handling noisy or incomplete data in high dimensional data space, regardless of the database size, due to its grid-based characteristic. An illustration of application of *MPs* and *JMPs* is presented for the cost effective and intelligent well logging data analysis for reservoir characterization. In the future research, we attempt to carry out experiments on petroleum datasets to establish a relationship between different well logs, seismic attributes, laboratory measurements and other reservoir properties to evaluate performance of the MOUCLAS algorithms proposed in this paper.

Acknowledgement

This work was partially supported by the Australia-China Special Fund for Scientific and Technological Cooperation under grant CH030086.

References

1. Fayyad, U. M., Piatetsky-Shapiro, G., & Smyth, P. From data mining to knowledge discovery: An overview. Advances in knowledge discovery and data mining. AAAI/MIT Press. (1996) 1-34
2. Han, J., & M. Kamber. Data mining: concepts and techniques. Morgan Kaufmann Publishers. (2000)

3. B. Lent, A. Swami, and J. Widom. Clustering association rules. ICDE'97, (1997) 220-231
4. B. Liu, W.Hsu, and Y.Ma. Integrating classification and association rule mining. KDD'98. (1998) 80-86
5. Meretakis, D., & Wuthrich, B. Extending naive Bayes classifiers using long itemsets. Proc. of the Fifth ACM SIGKDD. ACM Press. (1999) 165-174
6. Jinyan Li, Guozhu Dong, Kotagiri Ramamohanarao. Making Use of the Most Expressive Jumping Emerging Patterns for Classification. Knowledge and Information Systems, 3(2):131--145, 2001.
7. Quinlan, J. R. C4.5: Programs for machine learning. San Mateo, CA: Morgan Kaufmann. (1993)
8. Cover, T. M., & Hart, P. E. Nearest neighbor pattern classification. IEEE Transactions on Information Theory, 13. (1967) 21-27
9. R. Skikant and R. Agrawal. Mining quantitative association rules in large relational tables. SIG-MOD'96, (1996) 1-12.
10. Fayyad, U., & Irani, K. Multi-interval discretization of continuous-valued attributes for classification learning. Proc. of the 13th Int'l Conf. on Artificial Intelligence. Morgan Kaufmann. (1993) 1022--1029
11. Dougherty, J., Kohavi, R., & Sahami, M. Supervised and unsupervised discretization of continuous features. Proc. of the Twelfth Int'l Conf. on Machine Learning pp. 94--202. Morgan Kaufmann. (1995)
12. Khalil M. Ahmed, Nagwa M. El-Makky, Yousry Taha: A note on "Beyond Market Baskets: Generalizing Association Rules to Correlations". In The Proceedings of SIGKDD Explorations Volume1, Issue 2, (2000) 46-48
13. Agrawal, R., Srikant, R. Fast algorithms for mining association rules. Proc. of the 20th VLDB (1994) 487- 499
14. Bing Liu, Wynne Hsu, Yiming Ma, "Mining Association Rules with Multiple Minimum Supports" Proceedings of the ACM SIGKDD International Conference on Knowledge Discovery & Data Mining (KDD-99), August 15-18, San Diego, CA, USA (1999)
15. Dong, G., & Li, J. Feature selection methods for classification. Intelligent Data Analysis: An International Journal, 1, (1997)
16. H. Liu and H. Motoda, editors. Feature Selection for Knowledge Discovery and Data Mining. Boston: Kluwer Academic Publishers, (1998)
17. W.Sarawagi and M. Stonebraker. On automatic feature selection. Int'l J. of Pattern Recognition and Artificial Intelligence, 2, (1988) 197-220.
18. R. Kohavi and G. John. Wrappers for feature subset selection. Artificial Intelligence, (1997) 273-324
19. Yager, R. and D. Filev, "Generation of Fuzzy Rules by Mountain Clustering," Journal of Intelligent & Fuzzy Systems, Vol. 2, No. 3, (1994) 209-219
20. Chiu, S. L. Fuzzy model identification based on cluster estimation. Journal of Intelligent and Fuzzy System, 2(3), (1994)
21. A. Hinneburg and D. Keim. An efficient approach to clustering in large Multimedia dataset with noise. KDD'98, (1998) 58-65
22. R. Agrawal, J. Gehrke, D. Gunopulos, and P. Raghavan. Automatic subspace clustering of high dimensional data for data mining applications. SIGMOD'98. (1998)

A Probabilistic Geocoding System Utilising a Parcel Based Address File

Peter Christen[1,*], Alan Willmore[2], and Tim Churches[2]

[1] Department of Computer Science, Australian National University,
Canberra ACT 0200, Australia
peter.christen@anu.edu.au
[2] Centre for Epidemiology and Research, New South Wales Department of Health,
Locked Mail Bag 961, North Sydney NSW 2059, Australia
{awill, tchur}@doh.health.nsw.gov.au

Abstract. It is estimated that between 80% and 90% of governmental data collections contain address information. Geocoding – the process of assigning geographic coordinates to addresses – is becoming increasingly important in application areas that involve the analysis and mining of such data. In many cases, address records are captured and/or stored in a free-form or inconsistent manner. This fact complicates the task of accurately matching such addresses to spatially-annotated reference data. In this paper we describe a geocoding system that is based on a comprehensive high-quality geocoded national address database. It uses a learning address parser based on hidden Markov models to segment free-form addresses into components, and a rule-based matching engine to determine the best matches to the reference database.

1 Introduction

With many businesses, government organisations and research projects collecting massive amounts of data, the techniques collectively known as *data mining* have recently attracted interest both from academia and industry. While there is much ongoing research in data mining algorithms (to extract new and unexpected information from data, build predictive models, or detect outliers and rare events), a large proportion of the time and effort in real world data mining projects is spent understanding the data and in data preparation processes (which may dominate the actual data mining activity) [14]. It is generally accepted [6] that about 20% to 30% of the time and effort in a data mining project is used for data understanding, and about 50% to 70% for data preparation.

In this paper we discuss one issue of data preparation, namely the matching of user data with geocoded reference data (which comprises cleaned and standardised records containing address information plus their geographical location). This *geocode matching* or *geocoding* is needed before any spatial data analysis can be done, and is becoming increasingly important for many data

---

* Corresponding author.

G.J. Williams and S.J. Simoff (Eds.): Data Mining, LNAI 3755, pp. 130–145, 2006.
© Springer-Verlag Berlin Heidelberg 2006

mining projects. The US Federal Geographic Data Committee estimates that geographic location is a key feature in 80% to 90% of governmental data collections [17]. In many cases, addresses are the key to spatially enable data (i.e. to associate data with locations). The aim of geocoding is to generate a geographical location (latitude and longitude) from street address information in the user data. Once geocoded, the data can be used for further processing, for spatial data mining [7], and it can be visualised and combined with other data using Geographical Information Systems (GIS).

The applications of spatial data analysis and mining are widespread. In the health sector, for example, geocoded data can be used to find local clusters of disease. Environmental health studies often rely on GIS and geocoding software to map areas of potential exposure and to locate where people live in relation to these areas. Geocoded data can also help in the planning of new health resources, e.g. additional health care providers can be allocated close to where there is an increased need for such services. An overview of geographical health issues can be found in [1]. Geocoded client data, combined with additional demographic data, can help businesses to better plan marketing and future expansion, and the analysis of historical geocoded data, for example, can show changes in their client base. For national censuses, geocoding can be used to assign people or households to small area units, for example census collection districts, which are then the basis of further statistical analysis.

Geocoding can be seen as a special case of data (or record) linkage, the task of linking records from one or more data sets belonging to the same entity. Most of the time the linkage (or matching) process is challenged by the lack of common unique entity identifiers, and thus becomes non-trivial [3, 8, 18]. In such cases, the available partially identifying information – like names, addresses, and dates of birth – is used to decide if two (or more) records correspond to the same entity. This process is computationally intensive, and linking todays large data collections becomes increasingly difficult using traditional linkage techniques. Within many data mining and data analysis projects, data linkage is needed to integrate, match, or combine information from multiple sources in order to enrich the available data and to allow more detailed analysis.

In the following section we discuss geocoding techniques in more detail, and in Section 3 we present an overview of our geocoding system. The two central technical issues in geocoding are (1) the accurate and efficient matching of user input addresses with the address information stored in the geocoded reference data, and (2) the efficient retrieval of the address location (latitude and longitude) of the matched geocoded records. In order to achieve accurate match results, addresses both in the user data set and the geocoded reference data need to be cleaned and standardised in the same way. We cover this issue in more details in Section 3.1. Address locations can efficiently be retrieved from the geocoded reference data by converting the traditional database tables (or files) into inverted indices, as presented in Section 3.2. In Section 4 we then discuss the geocode matching engine and in Section 5 we present some experimental results. Conclusions and an outlook to future work are given in Section 6.

2   Geocoding

There are two basic scenarios for geocoding user data. In the first, a user wants
to automatically geocode a (large) data set. The geocoding system should find
the *best possible* match for each record in the user data set without human
intervention. Each record needs to be attributed with the corresponding location
plus a *match status* which indicates the accuracy of the match obtained (for
example an exact address match, or a street level match, or a locality level
match). This scenario might become problematic if the user data is not of high
quality (and contains records with missing, incorrect, or out-of-date address
information). Typographical errors are common with addresses, especially when
they are recorded over the telephone, scanned, or manually typed from hand-
written forms. As reported in [13], a match rate of 70% successfully geocoded
records is often considered an acceptable result.

In the second scenario a user interactively wants to geocode a single address
(or a small number of addresses) that may be incomplete, erroneous or unfor-
matted. The system should return the location if an exact match can be found,
or alternatively a list of possible matches, together with a matching status and
a likelihood rating. This geocoding of a single record should be done in (near)
real time (i.e. less than a couple of seconds response time) and be available via
a suitable user interface (for example a Web site).

Standard data (or record) linkage techniques [3, 8, 18], where the aim is to link
(or match) together all records belonging to the same entity, normally classify
the compared record pairs into one of the three classes *matches*, *non-matches*
and *possible matches*, with the latter class containing those record pairs for which
human oversight, also known as *clerical review*, is needed to decide their final
linkage status. This is similar to the second geocoding scenario described above,
where the user is presented with a selection of possible matches (sorted according
to their matching status and likelihood rating).

Many GIS software packages provide for street level geocoding. As a recent
study shows [2], substantial differences in positional error exist between addresses
which are geocoded using street reference files (containing geographic centreline
coordinates, street numbers and names, and postcodes) and the corresponding
true locations. The use of point property parcel coordinates (i.e. the centres or
centroids of properties), derived from cadastral data, is expected to significantly
reduce these positional errors. Figure 1 gives an illustrative example. Even small
discrepancies in geocoding can result in addresses being assigned to, for example, different census collection districts, which can have significant implications
when doing small area analysis. A comprehensive property based database is
now available for Australia: the Geocoded National Address File (G-NAF). It is
presented in details in the following section.

2.1   G-NAF – A Geocoded National Address File

In many countries geographical data is collected by various state and territorial
agencies. In Australia, for example, each state/territory has its own governmental

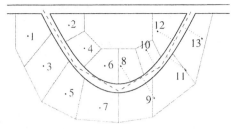

Fig. 1. Example geocoding using property parcel centres (numbers 1 to 7) and street reference file centreline (dashed line and numbers 8 to 13, with the dotted lines corresponding to a global street offset)

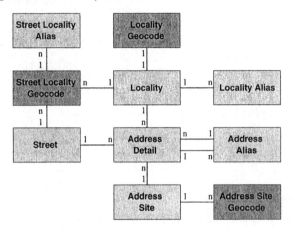

Fig. 2. Simplified G-NAF data model (10 main tables only). Links *1–n* denote one-to-many, and links *1–1* denote one-to-one relationships.

agency that collects data to be used for land planning, as well as property, infrastructure or resource management. Additionally, national organisations like post and telecommunications, electoral rolls and statistics or census bureaus collect their own data. All these data sets are collected for specific purposes, have varying content and might be stored in different formats.

The need for a nation-wide, standardised and high-quality geocoded data set has been recognised in Australia since 1990 [13], and after years of planning, collaboration and development the G-NAF was first released in March 2004. Approximately 32 million address records from 13 organisations were used in a five-phase cleaning and integration process, resulting in a database consisting of 22 normalised tables (or files). Figure 2 shows the simplified data model of the 10 main G-NAF tables. For our project we only used the G-NAF records covering the Australian state of New South Wales (NSW), containing around 4.5 million address, 60,586 street and 5,357 locality records. Table 1 gives an overview of the size and content of the 10 main G-NAF tables used.

The G-NAF is based on a hierarchical model, which stores information about address sites separately from locations and streets. It is possible to have multiple

Table 1. Characteristics of the 10 main G-NAF tables (NSW data only)

G-NAF table	Numbers of records and attributes	Keys (persistent identifiers)
ADDRESS_ALIAS	333,729 / 7	PRINCIPAL_PID ALIAS_PID
ADDRESS_DETAIL	4,585,707 / 34	GNAF_PID LOCALITY_PID STREET_PID ADDRESS_SITE_PID
ADDRESS_SITE	4,499,157 / 7	ADDRESS_SITE_PID
ADDRESS_SITE_GEOCODE	3,872,217 / 15	ADDRESS_SITE_PID
LOCALITY	5,357 / 9	LOCALITY_PID
LOCALITY_ALIAS	575 / 9	LOCALITY_PID ALIAS_PID
LOCALITY_GEOCODE	5,318 / 14	LOCALITY_PID
STREET	60,586 / 6	STREET_PID
STREET_LOCALITY_ALIAS	2,940 / 10	STREET_PID LOCALITY_PID
STREET_LOCALITY_GEOCODE	130,262 / 16	STREET_PID LOCALITY_PID

geocoded locations for a single address, and vice versa, and aliases are available at various levels. Three geocode tables contain location (latitude and longitude) information for different levels. If an exact address match can be found, its location can be retrieved from the ADDRESS_SITE_GEOCODE table. If there is only a match on street level (but not street number), then the STREET_LOCALITY_GEOCODE table will provide an overall street geocode. Finally, if no street level match can be found the LOCALITY_GEOCODE table contains geocode information for cities, towns and suburbs. The street and locality level geocode tables also contain information about the extent of streets and localities, respectively.

3 System Overview

The geocoding system presented in this paper is part of the *Febrl* (Freely Extensible Biomedical Record Linkage) data linkage system [3], that contains modules to clean and standardise data sets which can contain names, addresses and dates; and link and deduplicate such cleaned data. An overview of the *Febrl* geocoding system is shown in Figure 3. The geocoding process can be split into the preprocessing of the G-NAF tables (which is described in detail in Sections 3.1 and 3.2), and the matching with user-supplied addresses as presented in Section 4.

The preprocessing step takes the G-NAF tables and uses the *Febrl* address cleaning and standardisation routines to convert the detailed address values (like street names, types and suffixes, house numbers and suffixes, flat types and numbers, locality names, postcodes, etc.) into a form which makes them consistent with the user data after *Febrl* standardisation. Note that the G-NAF

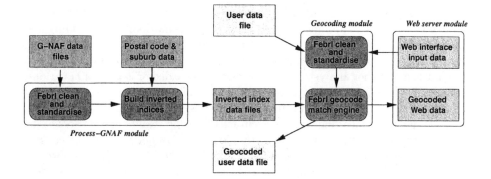

Fig. 3. Overview of the *Febrl* geocoding system

tables already come in a highly standardised form, but the finer details, for example how whitespaces within locality names are treated, make the difference between successful or failed matching. The cleaned and standardised reference records are then inserted into a number of inverted index data structures.

In order to be able to find matches with typographical errors (like in street or locality names), indices based on q-grams (substrings of length q) are built for the main address name fields. If no exact match can be found, for example for a given suburb name, these approximate indices will return the most similar suburb names available in the G-NAF.

Additional data used in the preprocessing step are a postcode-suburb look-up table based on a publicly-available file made available by the Australian postal service (Australia Post), and which can be used to impute missing postcodes or suburb values in the G-NAF locality table; and a look-up table of adjacent postcodes and suburbs, derived from boundary information, which is used to create *neighbouring region* look-up tables.

The geocode matching engine takes as input the inverted indices and the raw user data, which is cleaned and standardised before geocoding is attempted. As shown in Figure 3, the user data can either be loaded from a data file, geocoded and then saved into a new data file, or it can be passed as one or more addresses to the geocoding system via a Web interface. An extension module has been developed by the New South Wales Department of Health which allows geocoded point data derived from such addresses to be immediately visualised as a layer in a Web-based GIS (geographic information system) facility.

The complete *Febrl* system, including the geocoding and Web server modules, is implemented in the object-oriented open source language *Python*[1], which allows rapid prototype development and testing.

3.1 Probabilistic Address Cleaning and Standardisation

A first crucial step when processing both the geocoded reference files and the user data is the cleaning and standardisation of the data (i.e. addresses) used

---

[1] For more information see: http://www.python.org

for geocoding. It is commonly accepted that real world data collections contain erroneous, incomplete and incorrectly formatted information. Data cleaning and standardisation are important preprocessing steps for successful data linkage and geocoding, and must also be carried out before including such data in a data warehouse for further analysis [16]. Data may be recorded or captured in various, possibly obsolete, formats and data items may be missing, out-of-date, or contain errors. The cleaning and standardisation of addresses is especially important for data linkage and geocoding so that accurate matching results can be achieved.

The main task in the cleaning and standardisation of addresses is the conversion of the raw input data into well defined, consistent forms and the resolution of inconsistencies in the manner in which address values are represented or encoded. Rule-based data cleaning and standardisation, as currently used by many commercial systems, can be cumbersome to set up and maintain, and often needs adjustment for new data sets. We have recently developed (and implemented within *Febrl*) probabilistic techniques [4] based on hidden Markov models (HMMs) [15] which achieved better address standardisation accuracy and which seem to be easier to set up and maintain than rule-based address processing software.

A HMM is a probabilistic finite-state machine consisting of a set of observation or output symbols, a finite set of discrete, hidden (unobserved) states, a matrix of transition probabilities between those hidden states, and a matrix of probabilities with which each hidden state emits an observation symbol [15] (this *emission matrix* is also sometimes referred to as an *observation matrix*). In our case, the hidden states of the HMM correspond to the output fields of the standardised addresses.

Training data are representative samples of the input records which have been tokenised into sequences of observation symbols as described below (steps 1 and 2), and then tagged with the hidden state which the (human) trainer thought was most likely to have been responsible for emitting each observation symbol. Maximum likelihood estimates (MLEs) are derived for the HMM transition and emission probability matrices by accumulating frequency counts for each type of state transition and observation symbol from the training records [4]. The HMMs appear to be quite robust with respect to the training set used and quite general with respect to the data sources with which they can be used. As a result, it is quite feasible to add specific training records which are archetypes of unusual address patterns, without compromising the performance of the HMMs on more typical source records.

The *Febrl* approach to address cleaning and standardisation consists of the following three steps.

1. The user input addresses are *cleaned*. This involves converting all letters to lower-case, removing certain characters (such as punctuation), and converting various sub-strings into their canonical form, for example 'c/-', 'c/o' and 'c.of' would all be replaced with 'care_of'. These replacements are based on user-specified and domain-specific substitution tables. Note that these substitution tables can also contain common misspellings for street and locality names, for example, and thus help to increase the matching quality.

2. The cleaned input strings are split into a list of words, numbers and characters, using whitespace as the delimiter. Look-up tables and some hard-coded
rules are then used to assign one or more tags to the elements in this list.
These tags will be the observation symbols in the HMM used in the next step.
3. The list of tags is given to the HMM, assuming that each tag (observation
symbol) has been emitted by one of the hidden states. The *Viterbi* algorithm [15] is then used to find the most likely path through the HMM, and
the corresponding hidden states provide the assignment of the elements from
the input list to the output fields.

Consider for example the address '73 Miller St, NORTH SYDENY 2060', which
will be cleaned in step 1 ('SYDENY' corrected to 'sydney'), and split into a list of
words and numbers, and tagged in step 2. The resulting lists of words/numbers
and tags looks as follows.

```
['73', 'miller', 'street', 'north_sydney', '2060']
['NU', 'UN',    'WT',     'LN'           , 'PC' ]
```

with 'NU' being the tag for numbers, 'UN' the tag for unknown words (not
found in any look-up table or covered by any rule), 'WT' the tag for a word
found in the wayfare (street) type look-up table, 'LN' the tag for a sequence
of words found to be a locality name, and 'PC' the tag for a known postcode. In step 3 the tag list is given to a HMM (like the simple example shown
in Figure 4), which has previously been trained using similar address training
data. The *Viterbi* algorithm will return the most likely path through the HMM
which for the given example will correspond to the following sequence of output
fields.

```
'wayfare number': '73'
 'wayfare name': 'miller'
 'wayfare type': 'street'
'locality name': 'north_sydney'
    'postcode': '2060'
```

Further details of how to efficiently train the HMMs for address (as well as
name) standardisation, and the results of trials with real-world data are given
in [4]. Training of the HMMs is relatively quick compared to the creation of
address parsing rules and does not require any programming skills. For addresses,

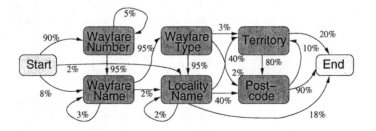

Fig. 4. Simple example address hidden Markov model

our HMM approach produced equal or better standardisation accuracies than the widely-used rule-based system *AutoStan* [10], which uses a re-entrant, regular expression-like pattern matching approach.

3.2   Processing the G-NAF Files

Processing the G-NAF tables consists of two steps, the first being the cleaning and standardisation as described above, and the second step being the building of inverted indices. An inverted index is a keyed hash-table in which the keys are the values from the cleaned G-NAF tables, and the entries in the hash-table are sets with the corresponding PIDs (persistent identifiers, see Table 1) of the values. For example, assume there are four records in the LOCALITY table with the following content (the first line is a header-line with the attribute names).

```
locality_pid,  locality_name,  state_abbrev,  postcode
60310919,      sydney,         nsw,           2000
60709845,      north_sydney,   nsw,           2059
60309156,      north_sydney,   nsw,           2060
61560124,      the_rocks,      nsw,           2000
```

The inverted indices for the three attributes locality_name, state_abbrev and postcode then are (curly brackets denote keyed hash-tables and round brackets denote sets):

```
locality_name_index = {'north_sydney':(60709845,60309156),
                       'sydney':(60310919),
                       'the_rocks':(61560124)}

state_abbrev_index = {'nsw':(60310919,60709845,60309156,61560124)}

postcode_index = {'2000':(60310919,61560124),
                  '2059':(60709845),
                  '2060':(60309156)}
```

The matching engine then finds intersections of the inverted index sets for the values in a given record. For example, a postcode value '2000' would result in a set of PIDs (60310919,61560124) being returned, and when intersected with the PIDs returned for locality name value 'the_rocks' would result in the single PID set (61560124), which corresponds to the original record. The geographic location of this PID can then be looked-up in the corresponding G-NAF geocode index. Table 2 shows the 23 attributes for which inverted indices are built.

For the G-NAF tables containing names, it is possible to create q-gram indices, which can be used for approximate matching. The keys in these indices are not the full values from the G-NAF tables as shown above, but rather substrings of length q (currently bigrams are used, i.e. $q = 2$). Approximate string matching between two strings x and y is performed by finding common

Table 2. G-NAF attributes used for geocode matching

G-NAF table	Attributes used
ADDRESS_DETAIL	flat_number_prefix, flat_number, flat_number_suffix, flat_type, level_number, level_type, building_name, location_description, number_first_prefix, number_first, number_first_suffix, number_last_prefix, number_last, number_last_suffix, lot_number_prefix, lot_number, lot_number_suffix
LOCALITY_ALIAS	locality_name, postcode, state_abbrev
LOCALITY	locality_name, postcode, state_abbrev
STREET	street_name, street_type, street_suffix
STREET_LOCALITY_ALIAS	street_name, street_type, street_suffix

q-grams, and then calculating a similarity value (sometimes called the *Dice co-efficient* [5])

$$sim\_value = 2 \times \left(\frac{qgram(x) \cap qgram(y)}{|qgram(x)| + |qgram(y)|} \right)$$

where $qgram(s)$ is a function which reduces a string s to its set of q-grams. This similarity measure can have values between 0.0 (no q-grams in common) and 1.0 (all q-grams in common, i.e. the strings are the same). A ranked list of all approximate matches that have a similarity value above a user defined threshold are then used in the matching process for a given user record.

3.3   Additional Data Files

Additional information is used in the *Febrl* geocoding system during the preprocessing step to verify and correct (if possible) postcode and locality name values, and in the matching engine to enable searching for matches in neighbouring regions (postcodes and suburbs) if no exact match can be found.

Australia Post publishes a look-up table containing postcode and suburb information[2], which is used when processing the G-NAF locality tables to verify and correct wrong or missing postcodes and suburb names. For example, if a postcode is missing in a record, the Australia Post look-up table can be used to find the official postcode(s) for the suburb in this record, and if this is a unique postcode it can be safely imputed into the record. Similarly, missing suburb names can be imputed if they correspond to a unique postcode.

Other look-up tables are used to find *neighbouring* regions for postcodes and suburbs, i.e. for a given region these tables contain all its neighbours. These adjacency tables were derived from region boundary data using well-known GIS algorithms. Look-up tables of both direct and indirect neighbours (i.e. neighbours of direct neighbours) are used in the geocode matching engine to find matches in addresses where no exact postcode or suburb match can be found.

---

[2] http://www.auspost.com.au/postcodes/

Experience has shown that people often record different postcode or suburb values if a neighbouring postcode or suburb has a higher perceived social status, or if they live close to the border of such regions.

4   Geocode Matching Engine

The geocode matching engine in *Febrl* is based on the G-NAF inverted hash indices, and takes a deterministic but adaptive approach to find an exact match or alternatively one or more approximate matches. Its input is one or many cleaned and standardised user record(s).

The matching engine tries to find an exact match first, but if none can be found it extends its search to neighbouring postcode and suburb regions. First direct neighbouring regions (level 1) are searched, then direct and indirect neighbouring regions (level 2), until either an exact match or a set of approximate matches can been found. In the latter case, either an average location over all the found matches is returned, or a ranked (according to a matching weight) list of possible matches. The following steps explain in more detail (but still at a conceptual level) how the matching engine works.

1. Find the set of address level matches (using street number and suffix) and the set of street level matches (using street name and type). Street names are first searched using exact string comparison, and if no street name match can be found approximate string matching will be applied (using a q-gram index), allowing to find matches with typographical errors.
2. Set the neighbouring search level to 0 (no neighbouring regions are searched).
3. Find the locality level matches (using locality name, qualifier and postcode) according to the current value of the neighbouring search level. Locality names are first searched using exact string comparison, and if no locality name match can be found approximate string matching will be applied (using a q-gram index), allowing to find matches with typographical errors. Postcodes are only used in the matching process if they result in the same matches as the locality names (i.e. if they contribute to these matches). If postcodes result in different matches, they are not used in the final match (this is because postcodes are not fixed locality regions, but can be – and often are – changed by Australia Post for the purposes of expediting delivery of mail).
4. Check for matches between street level and locality level, and if they exist reduce the set of street level matches using the locality level matches, and set a flag *street_locality_match* to true.
5. Check for matches between address level and locality level, and if they exist reduce the set of address level matches using the locality level matches, and set a flag *address_locality_match* to true.
6. Check for matches between address level and street level, and if they exist reduce the set of address level matches using the street level matches, and set a flag *address_street_match* to true.
7. Now a decision needs to be made (if a match has been found or if the neighbouring search level needs to be increased for extended searching), based

on the values of the three matching flags. A match has been found if all three match flags are true, or if there was no address level match and the *street_locality_match* flag is true, or if there was no street level match and the *address_locality_match* flag is true, or if there was no locality level match and the *address_street_match* flag is true. If no match has been found then increase the neighbouring search level –that is, widen the search to adjacent regions – (up to a maximum of 2) and go back to step 3.

8. If several matches have been found, try to refine them using unit, flat and building (or property) information (if such information is available in the user input record).

9. Combine the match(es) from the different levels (basically get their set intersections), and set the final *match level* (to either *address*, *street* or *locality*).

10. Retrieve the coordinates of the match(es) from the corresponding G-NAF geocode index (address site, street/locality or locality). If one match has been found retrieve it's coordinates and return them together with the G-NAF PID (persistent identifier). If several matches were found check if they are within a small area (defined by the user). If so, average their coordinates and return the averaged location together with the list of G-NAF PIDs. If the distances between the matches were large, return a *'Many match'* (without coordinates, only a list of G-NAF PIDs).

11. In some cases a match at a certain level has been found, but no record is available in the corresponding G-NAF geocode index, or a record is available but does not contain coordinates. In this case go to the next higher match level (e.g. from address to street, or from street to locality) and try to retrieve the corresponding coordinates (back to step 10).

12. If no match was found return a *'No match'* match status.

Geocoding of multiple addresses is an iterative process where each record is first cleaned and standardised, then geocoded and written into an output data set with coordinates and a match status added to each record.

5   Experimental Results

We have run experiments with geocoding various administrative health data sets. An address hidden Markov model (HMM) was trained using 1,300 training records, around half of them randomly selected from the NSW *Midwives Data Collection* [11] (MDC) containing data from 1990 to 2000, the other half taken from a NSW *Land and Property Information* (LPI) data set from 2002. Some unusual training records (like rural addresses or addresses with property or institution information) were manually added to increase the standardisation accuracy for such addresses.

Table 3 presents the results of geocoding 10,000 randomly selected LPI free-form addresses (from a data set containing 2,775,134 addresses). Of these 10,000 addresses, 1,799 contained no street number, 407 had no street name and 476 no street type. All addresses had a postcode, and only two contained no locality name. We ran the same experiment with and without approximate indices.

Table 3. Matching results for geocoding 10,000 free-form LPI address records, with $(q = 2)$ and without $(q = 0)$ approximate indices

Match status	Number of records		Percentage	
	$q = 2$	$q = 0$	$q = 2$	$q = 0$
Exact address level match	7,525	7,497	75.27 %	74.97 %
Average address level match	303	303	3.03 %	3.03 %
Many address level match	178	178	1.78 %	1.78 %
Exact street level match	1,160	1,131	11.60 %	11.31 %
Average street level match	17	17	0.17 %	0.17 %
Many street level match	65	62	0.65 %	0.62 %
Exact locality level match	653	680	6.53 %	6.80 %
Average locality level match	1	1	0.01 %	0.01 %
Many locality level match	98	118	0.98 %	1.18 %

Table 4. Comparative matching results for geocoding 873 MDC addresses

Match status	Number of records		Percentage	
	Febrl	Commercial	*Febrl*	Commercial
Exact address level match	746	789	85.45 %	90.38 %
Average address level match	23	-	2.63 %	-
Many address level match	13	-	1.49 %	-
Exact street level match	48	37	5.50 %	4.24 %
Many street level match	3	-	0.34 %	-
Exact locality level match	35	46	4.01 %	5.26 %
Many locality level match	4	-	0.46 %	-
No match	1	1	0.11 %	0.11 %

Table 5. Comparative matching results for geocoding 607 nursing home addresses

Match status	Number of records		Percentage	
	Febrl	Commercial	*Febrl*	Commercial
Exact address level match	265	384	43.66 %	63.26 %
Average address level match	30	-	4.94 %	-
Many address level match	21	-	3.46 %	-
Exact street level match	240	202	39.54 %	33.28 %
Average street level match	1	-	0.16 %	-
Many street level match	4	-	0.66 %	-
Exact locality level match	38	-	6.26 %	-
Many locality level match	8	-	1.32 %	-
No match	0	21	0.00 %	3.46 %

When activated, the approximate indices allowed for up to two typographical errors (i.e. single character insertions, deletions, or substitutions) in street and locality names. As the results show, a total of 93.38% (with approximate indices) and 93.08% (without) exact matches were found at different levels. Using approximate indices resulted in only a slightly improved match quality, but geocoding took much longer. Without approximate indices, the average geocoding time per address was 67 milliseconds; using approximate indices it increased to 269 milliseconds per address (around four times slower).

In Table 4 the results of a geocoding experiment on 873 randomly selected addresses (a 1% sample) from the MDC using the *Febrl* geocoder are compared to a commercial (street centreline based) geocoding system (which only returns exact matches). The *'no match'* address in both cases was for an overseas address. Table 5 shows comparative results on a NSW nursing home data sets containing 607 addresses. For this data set the commercial system achieves a significantly better geocoding quality. This is because nursing homes are often located at street intersections and have corner addresses. Such addresses are currently not handled properly in our geocoding system, as they correspond to two G-NAF address detail records (with the same address site), and cannot be separated properly by our address standardiser.

Note also that the comparison results in Tables 4 and 5 only show the match status, but not the relative accuracy of the coordinates returned. We are planning to do a more detailed analysis on this issue, comparable to the study presented in [2].

6   Conclusions and Future Work

In this paper we have described a geocoding system based on a geocoded national address file. We are currently evaluating and improving this system using raw uncleaned addresses taken from various administrative health related data sets. We are also planning to compare the accuracy of our geocoding system with street-based geocoders, and similar to [2] we expect to obtain more accurate results. Our geocoding system has been published as part of the *Febrl* data linkage system [3] under an open source software license. Readers should note that although our geocoding engine is available for free, the G-NAF reference files which it uses are not freely available, and must be licensed through PSMA [13] or its partner organisations.

Future efforts will be directed towards the refinement of the geocode matching engine to achieve more accurate matching results, as well as improving the performance of the matching engine (i.e. reducing the time needed to match an address). Three other areas of future work include:

- The *Febrl* standardisation routines currently return fields (or attributes) which are different from the ones available in the G-NAF. This makes it necessary to map *Febrl* fields to G-NAF fields within the geocode matching engine. It would be preferable if the *Febrl* standardisation returned the same fields as the ones available in the G-NAF, resulting in explicit field by field comparisons. We are planning to modify the necessary *Febrl* standardisation routines.

- Currently both the G-NAF preprocessing and indexing, as well as the geocode matching engine work in a sequential fashion only. Due to the large data files involved, parallel processing becomes desirable. In the preprocessing step, the G-NAF tables can be processed independently or in a block-wise fashion, distributed over a number of processors, with only the final inverted indices needing to be merged. Geocoding of a large user data file can easily be done in parallel as the cleaning, standardisation and matching of each record is completely independent from all others. An additional advantage of parallelisation is the increased amount of main memory available on many parallel platforms. We are planning to explore such parallelisation techniques and implement them into the *Febrl* system to allow faster geocoding of larger data sets. Additional performance improvements can be achieved by profiling and re-implementing the core computational routines as C language routines called from the Python code (something which Python makes easy to do).
- Corner addresses are stored in the G-NAF as two separate addresses with the same address site PID, but when processed in a user data set this becomes problematic, as the standardisation process is currently not capable of separating the components of a corner address. We aim to work on this issue and add it to a future version of our geocoding system.
- Geocoding uses identifying information (i.e. addresses) which raises privacy and confidentiality issues. Organisations that collect sensitive data (e.g. disease registries) cannot send their data to a third-party geocoding service as this may result in the loss of privacy for individuals involved. It is desirable to develop methods which allow for privacy-preserving geocoding. We aim to develop such methods based on techniques recently described for blindfolded data linkage [5, 9, 12].

Acknowledgements

This work is funded by the NSW Department of Health, Centre for Epidemiology and Research. The authors would like to thank David Horgan (student at the University of Queensland) who worked on a first version of this system while he was a summer student at the ANU. The authors also wish to thank the NSW Department of Lands for facilitating access to the G-NAF for research and development purposes.

References

1. Boulos, M.N.K.: Towards evidence-based, GIS-driven national spatial health information infrastructure and surveillance services in the United Kingdom. International Journal of Health Geographics 2004, 3:1. Available online at: http://www.ij-healthgeographics.com/content/3/1/1
2. Cayo, M.R. and Talbot, T.O.: Positional error in automated geocoding of residential addresses. International Journal of Health Geographics 2003, 2:10. Available online at: http://www.ij-healthgeographics.com/content/2/1/10
3. Christen, P., Churches, T. and Hegland, M.: A Parallel Open Source Data Linkage System. Proceedings of the 8th PAKDD'04 (Pacific-Asia Conference on Knowledge Discovery and Data Mining), Sydney. Springer LNAI-3056, pp. 638–647, May 2004.

4. Churches, T., Christen, P., Lim, K. and Zhu, J.X.: Preparation of name and address data for record linkage using hidden Markov models. BioMed Central Medical Informatics and Decision Making 2002, 2:9, Dec. 2002. Available online at: http://www.biomedcentral.com/1472-6947/2/9/

5. Churches, T. and Christen, P.: Some methods for blindfolded record linkage. BioMed Central Medical Informatics and Decision Making 2004, 4:9, June 2004. Available online at: http://www.biomedcentral.com/1472-6947/4/9/

6. Shearer, C.: The CRISP-DM Model: The new blueprint for data mining. Journal of Data Warehousing, vol. 5, no. 4, pp. 13–22, Fall 2000.

7. Ester, M., Kriegel, H.-P. and Sander, J.: Spatial Data Mining: A Database Approach, Fifth Symposium on Large Spatial Databases (SSD'97). Springer LNCS 1262, pp. 48–66, 1997.

8. Fellegi, I. and Sunter, A.: A Theory for Record Linkage. Journal of the American Statistical Society, 1969.

9. Hok, P.: Development of a Blind Geocoding System. Honours thesis, Department of Computer Science, Australian National University, Canberra, November 2004.

10. *AutoStan and AutoMatch, User's Manuals*, MatchWare Technologies, Kennebunk, Maine, 1998.

11. Centre for Epidemiology and Research, NSW Department of Health. New South Wales Mothers and Babies 2001. NSW Public Health Bull 2002; 13(S-4).

12. O'Keefe, C.M., Yung, M., Gu, L. and Baxter, R.: Privacy-Preserving Data Linkage Protocols. Proceedings of the Workshop on Privacy in the Electronic Society (WPES'04). Washington, DC, October 2004.

13. Paull, D.L.: A geocoded National Address File for Australia: The G-NAF What, Why, Who and When? PSMA Australia Limited, Griffith, ACT, Australia, 2003. Available online at: http://www.g-naf.com.au/

14. Pyle, D.: Data Preparation for Data Mining. Morgan Kaufmann Publishers, Inc., 1999.

15. Rabiner, L.R.: A Tutorial on Hidden Markov Models and Selected Applications in Speech Recognition. Proceedings of the IEEE, vol. 77, no. 2, Feb. 1989.

16. Rahm, E. and Do, H.H.: Data Cleaning: Problems and Current Approaches. IEEE Data Engineering Bulletin, 2000.

17. US Federal Geographic Data Committee. Homeland Security and Geographic Information Systems – How GIS and mapping technology can save lives and protect property in post-September 11th America. Public Health GIS News and Information, no. 52, pp. 21–23, May 2003.

18. Winkler, W.E.: The State of Record Linkage and Current Research Problems. RR99/03, US Bureau of the Census, 1999.

Decision Models for Record Linkage

Lifang Gu[1] and Rohan Baxter[2]

[1] CSIRO ICT Centre,
GPO Box 664, Canberra, ACT 2601, Australia
Lifang.Gu@csiro.au
[2] Australian Taxation Office,
2 Constitution Avenue, Canberra, ACT 2601, Australia
Rohan.Baxter@ato.gov.au

Abstract. The process of identifying record pairs that represent the same real-world entity in multiple databases, commonly known as record linkage, is one of the important steps in many data mining applications. In this paper, we address one of the sub-tasks in record linkage, i.e., the problem of assigning record pairs with an appropriate matching status. Techniques for solving this problem are referred to as decision models. Most existing decision models rely on good training data, which is, however, not commonly available in real-world applications. Decision models based on unsupervised machine learning techniques have recently been proposed. In this paper, we review several existing decision models and then propose an enhancement to cluster-based decision models. Experimental results show that our proposed decision model achieves the same accuracy of existing models while significantly reducing the number of record pairs required for manual review. The proposed model also provides a mechanism to trade off the accuracy with the number of record pairs required for clerical review.

Keywords: data linking, record linkage, probabilistic linking, decision model, clustering, classification.

1 Introduction

Record linkage is the task of identifying records corresponding to the same entity from one or more data sources. Entities of interest include individuals, families, households, companies, or geographic regions. Record linkage has applications in systems for marketing, customer relationship management, fraud detection, data warehousing, law enforcement and government administration.

In many data mining projects it is often necessary to collate information about an entity from more than one data source. If a unique identifier is available, conventional *SQL* 'join' operations in database systems can be used for record linkage, which assumes error-free identifying fields and links records that match exactly on these identifying fields. However, real-world data is 'dirty' and sources of variation in identifying fields include lack of a uniform format, changes over time, misspellings, abbreviations, and typographical errors.

G.J. Williams and S.J. Simoff (Eds.): Data Mining, LNAI 3755, pp. 146–160, 2006.

Record linkage can be considered as part of the *data cleaning* process, which is a crucial first step in the knowledge discovery process [1]. Fellegi and Sunter [2] were the first to introduce a formal mathematical foundation for record linkage. Their original model has since been extended and enhanced by Winkler [3] and others [4, 5, 6].

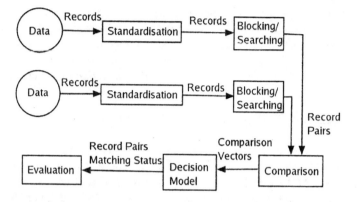

Fig. 1. Information flow diagram of a record linkage system

No matter what technique is used, a number of issues need to be addressed when linking data. Figure 1 shows the information flow diagram of a typical record linkage system as implemented in *TAILOR* [7] and *Febrl* [8].

Often, data is recorded or captured in various formats, and data fields may be missing or contain errors. Standardisation is an essential first step in every linkage process to clean and standardise the data. Since potentially every record in one dataset has to be compared with every record in a second dataset, *blocking* or *searching* techniques are often used to reduce the number of comparisons. These techniques use *blocking variables* to group similar records together and therefore partition the datasets into smaller blocks (clusters). Only records within the same block are then compared in detail using the defined *comparison variables* and *functions*. The comparison vectors generated by such detailed comparison functions are passed to the decision model to determine the final status (match, non-match or possible match) of record pairs. The results of the record linkage can be assessed by the evaluation model.

The main challenges in record linkage are how to achieve both high efficiency and linkage accuracy. Recent developments in information retrieval, database systems, machine learning and data mining have led to improvement in the efficiency and accuracy of record linkage systems [9, 10, 11, 12].

In this paper, we focus on the decision model component of a record linkage system. The linkage accuracy in a record linkage system depends heavily on the decision model. We review several existing decision models and identify problems with these models. An enhanced clustering-based decision model is proposed.

The main contribution of this paper is the development of an enhanced clustering-based decision model as well as the introduction of some performance metrics. The key feature of our proposed decision model, compared to other existing models [7, 13], is that clustering is initially performed based on two clusters (matched and unmatched). A refinement step is then applied to identify record pairs with an uncertain matching status by using a metric introduced in this paper. The enhancement step also provides a mechanism to trade off the linkage accuracy with the amount of clerical review work.

The rest of the paper is organised as follows. Problems and notations are introduced in Section 2. Several existing decision models are reviewed and their limitations are identified in Section 3. In Section 4 we then present our enhanced decision model for addressing some of the identified limitations. Experimental results are described in Section 5 and conclusions are made in Section 6.

2   Definitions, Notation, and Problems

For two data sources A and B, the set of ordered record pairs $A \times B = \{(a, b) : a \in A, b \in B\}$ is the union of two disjoint sets, M where $a = b$ and U where $a \neq b$. The former set, M, is usually referred to as *matched* and the latter set, U, as *unmatched*. The problem is to determine which set each record pair belongs to. In practice, a third set P, *possibly matched*, is often introduced to accommodate situations where the matching status of a record pair cannot be decided with information available from the data sources. If a record pair is assigned to P, a domain expert must manually examine the pair. Here we assume that a domain expert can always identify the correct matching status (M or U) of such a record pair with or without extra information.

Assume that n common fields, $f_1, f_2, \ldots, f_n$, of each record from sources A and B are chosen for comparison. For each record pair $r_{i,j} = (r_i, r_j)$, the field-wise comparison results in a vector of n values, $c_{i,j} = [c_1^{i,j}, c_2^{i,j}, \ldots, c_n^{i,j}]$ where $c_k^{i,j} = C_k(r_i.f_k, r_j.f_k)$ and C_k is the comparison function that compares the values of the record field f_k. The vector, $c_{i,j}$, is called a *comparison vector* and the set of all the comparison vectors is called the *comparison space*. A comparison function C_k is a mapping from the Cartesian product of the domain(s), D_k, for the field f_k to a comparison domain R_k; formally, $C_k : D_k \times D_k \to R_k$. One example of a simple comparison function is

$$C_I(v_1, v_2) = \begin{cases} 0 & \text{if } v_1 = v_2 \\ 1 & \text{otherwise} \end{cases} \tag{1}$$

where $R_I = \{0, 1\}$. The value computed by C_I is called a *binary comparison value*. Two additional types of comparison values produced by comparison functions are *categorical* and *continuous*.

The role of a decision model is to determine the matching status of a record pair given its comparison vector $c_{i,j}$. Depending on the type of comparison values and whether training data is needed, decision models of varying complexity have been proposed in the literature. In the following section, we review some of these existing models.

3   Existing Decision Models

In this section, we review four existing decision models. The probabilistic model described in Section 3.1 was developed in 1969 and is still widely used in the medical and statistical domains. The other three models have been proposed recently to address some of its limitations.

3.1   Error-Based Probabilistic Model

The probabilistic model defined by Fellegi and Sunter [2] assigns a weight $w_k^{i,j}$ for each component of a record pair, i.e.,

$$w_k^{i,j} = \begin{cases} \log(m_k/u_k) & \text{if } c_k^{i,j} = 0 \\ \log((1 - m_k)/(1 - u_k)) & \text{if } c_k^{i,j} = 1 \end{cases} \tag{2}$$

where m_k and u_k are the conditional probabilities of observing that the two values of the field k are the same given that record pair $r_{i,j}$ is a true match and a true non-match respectively. Mathematically, they are defined as:

$$\begin{aligned} m_k &= Prob(c_k^{i,j} = 0 | r_{i,j} \in M) \\ u_k &= Prob(c_k^{i,j} = 0 | r_{i,j} \in U) \end{aligned} \tag{3}$$

It can be seen that the weight $w_k^{i,j}$ is large (positive) for a matched pair and small (negative) for an unmatched pair. A decision is made for each record pair by calculating a composite weight $W(r_{i,j}) = \sum_{k=1}^{n} w_k^{i,j}$, and comparing this value against two threshold values t_1 and t_2 where $t_1 < t_2$. Specifically, the decision is made as follows:

$$\begin{aligned} r_{i,j} &\in M \text{ if } W(r_{i,j}) \geq t_2 \\ r_{i,j} &\in U \text{ if } W(r_{i,j}) \leq t_1 \\ r_{i,j} &\in P \text{ if } t_1 < W(r_{i,j}) < t_2 \end{aligned} \tag{4}$$

The main issue in this model is therefore to determine estimates of the conditional probabilities m_k and u_k for $k = 1, 2, \ldots, n$, as well as estimates of the two thresholds t_1 and t_2. Two methods for estimating the conditional probabilities m_k and u_k were proposed by Fellegi and Sunter [2] under the assumption of independence of these conditional probabilities. Under an assumption weaker than the conditional independence, Winkler [14] proposed to use the EM (Expectation Maximisation) algorithm to estimate these conditional probabilities. However, several different initialisation values should be used for the EM algorithm to find better estimates.

3.2   Cost-Based Probabilistic Model

In the above error-based probabilistic model, the thresholds t_1 and t_2 are estimated by minimising the probability of the error of making an incorrect decision for the matching status of a record pair. This implicitly assumes that all errors are equally costly. However, this is rarely the case in many applications. There-fore, the minimisation of the probability of the error is not the best criterion to use in designing a decision rule because misclassification of different record pairs may have different consequences. For example, when linking a cancer reg-istry database with a hospital database, a missed match might result in a cancer patient being missed important follow-up tests, which has very serious conse-quences, while a false match would result in a non-cancer patient being tested.

Verykios et al. [13] propose a decision model that minimises the cost of making a decision. Specifically, they use a constant error cost Bayesian model to derive the decision rule for a given cost matrix. For record linkage, the cost matrix D is 3×2 in dimension. Let us denote by d_{ij} the cost of making a decision i when the record pair to be compared corresponds to one with an actual matching status j. Here i corresponds to one of the three regions decided by a decision rule in the decision space, namely matched M, possibly matched P, and unmatched U respectively, while j refers to the actual matching status M' and U'. The decision rule is obtained by minimising the mean cost $\overline{d}$, which is written as follows:

$$
\begin{aligned}
\overline{d} = d_{MM'} \cdot Prob(M, M') + d_{MU'} \cdot Prob(M, U') + \\
d_{PM'} \cdot Prob(P, M') + d_{PU'} \cdot Prob(P, U') + \\
d_{UM'} \cdot Prob(U, M') + d_{UU'} \cdot Prob(U, U')
\end{aligned}
\tag{5}
$$

where $Prob(i, j)$ denotes the joint probability that a decision i is taken when the actual matching status is j. By using Bayes theorem and replacing the above probabilities with the *a priori* probabilities of M' and U', and the probability densities of the comparison vectors given the matching status, the above equation can be summarised by a decision rule similar to that of the error-based model described in Section 3.1. The only difference is that the threshold values also depend on the cost matrix (see [13] for details).

3.3   Inductive Learning-Based Decision Model

One of the limitations of the above probabilistic models is that they do not handle continuous or numeric comparison vectors very well. Decision models based on machine learning techniques can overcome this shortcoming. One such decision model is based on inductive learning techniques and can handle all types of comparison vectors [7].

In inductive learning, a training set of patterns, in which the class of each pat-tern is known a priori, is used to build a model that can be used afterwards to predict the class of each unclassified pattern. A training instance has the form of $< x, f(x) >$ where x is a pattern and $f(x)$ is a discrete-value function that repre-sents the class of the pattern x, i.e., $f(x) \in L_1, L_2, \ldots, L_l$ where l is the number of possible classes. In the case of record linkage, x is the comparison vector c, l is 2 (M and U), and $f(c)$ is the corresponding matching status, i.e., $f(c) \in M, U$. One of the popular classification techniques is decision trees, which exploit the regularities among observations in the training data. Predictions are made on the basis of similar, previously encountered situations. The accuracy of this type of decision model depends on the representativeness of the training data.

3.4 Clustering-Based Decision Model

A problem with inductive learning-based decision models is that they rely on the existence of training data. However, training data is not usually available for most real-world applications. Therefore, unsupervised learning methods, such as clustering, have been introduced to the record linkage community since they do not require training data. Elfeky et al. [7] used the *k-means clustering* to group record pairs into three clusters: *matched*, *unmatched*, and *possibly matched*. They also described how to determine the matching status of each cluster once the clustering is completed.

However, the *possibly matched* record pairs do not necessarily form a distinctive cluster in real applications. It is usually assumed that the distribution of comparison values is bimodal. The 3-cluster *k*-means algorithm thus leads to a large cluster of the *possibly matched* record pairs as reported in [7]. This is undesirable for most real-world applications as clerical review is very costly.

4   Enhanced Clustering-Based Decision Model

In Section 3 we have identified limitations with existing decision models. These include the restriction to categorical comparison values, the need for training datasets and the large proportion of record pairs required for clerical review. In this section, we propose an enhanced clustering-based decision model that does not have these limitations.

Based on the observation that record pairs usually form two main clusters in the comparison space, the proposed model uses a clustering algorithm to partition the record pairs into matched and unmatched clusters initially. A third cluster is then formed by record pairs in a fuzzy region between the two main clusters. The matching status of these record pairs in the fuzzy region cannot be determined from the available information and therefore have to be resolved by a domain expert. We refer to this third cluster as the *possibly matched*. We introduce a distance-based metric used for identifying the fuzzy region. The size of the fuzzy region, which can be easily controlled by tuning a threshold parameter, determines the balance between the linkage accuracy and the amount of clerical review work.

4.1 Clustering Algorithms

There are many clustering algorithms [15, 16] available. The most widely used is the k-means clustering [15] because of its easy implementation and computational efficiency when k is small. With the k-means clustering algorithm, the number of clusters has to be given before the start of the algorithm. The k-means algorithm is summarised as follows:

1. Partition the whole dataset into k clusters (the data points are randomly assigned to the clusters). This results in clusters that have roughly the same number of data points.

2. Compute the mean (centroid) of each cluster.
3. For each data point, calculate the distance from the data point to each cluster centroid. If the data point is closest to its own cluster centroid, leave it where it is. If it is not, move it into the closest cluster.
4. Repeat Steps 2 and 3 until no data point moves from one cluster to another.

Good results can be achieved by the k-means clustering algorithm if all points are distributed around k well separated clusters. The shape of these k clusters depends on the distance measure used. For example, if the Euclidean distance metric is used, the shape of the clusters is spherical for 3-dimensional data.

For our decision model, other clustering algorithms, such as model-based clustering [16], can also be used.

4.2   Fuzzy Region Identification

When the initial clustering process is completed, all record pairs are assigned to one of the two main clusters. However, there is usually a grey or fuzzy region where record pairs of true matches and non-matches co-exist. Here we introduce a metric to identify this fuzzy region.

For k-means clustering, the distances of each point to the two cluster centres can be calculated. We denote the distances of point i to the two cluster centres by $d_{i,1}$ and $d_{i,2}$ respectively. Any distance metric, such as Euclidean or Mahalanobis, can be used. Mahalanobis distance differs from Euclidean distance in that it takes into account the correlations of the data set. It gives relatively less weight to variables with large variances. To identify the fuzzy region, we define Δd_i, the relative distance difference of point i to the two cluster centres, as follows:

$$\Delta d_i = \frac{|d_{i,1} - d_{i,2}|}{(d_{i,1} + d_{i,2})/2} \tag{6}$$

where the denominator is the average of $d_{i,1}$ and $d_{i,2}$. If Δd_i is small, point i has approximately same distances to the two cluster centres. Therefore, points with small Δd_i values cannot be assigned to one of the two clusters with certainty and they form the fuzzy region. The size of this fuzzy region can be controlled by a parameter, the threshold T_d, the maximum acceptable relative distance difference. The value of the threshold T_d can be determined based on available resources for manual review and the required accuracy. All points with a Δd value smaller than T_d would be then assigned to the *possibly matched* cluster.

For other clustering algorithms, similar metrics can be defined. For example, the difference of the probabilities of each point belonging to each of the two clusters can be such a metric for model-based clustering.

Our enhanced clustering algorithm can therefore be considered as a normal 2-cluster clustering with an additional refinement step. During this refinement step record pairs in the fuzzy region are reassigned to the *possibly matched* cluster, based on their values of Δd_i and the given threshold value, T_d. As it will be shown in our experiment (Section 5), this provides an effective way of controlling the trade-off between the required linkage accuracy and the proportion of record pairs needed for clerical review.

5   Experimental Results

To evaluate the performance of our clustering-based decision model and compare it to existing decision models, an empirical experiment has been conducted.

5.1   Datasets and Parameters

We use the database generator [17], which is distributed as a part of Febrl package [8], to generate test datasets for our experiment. This tool can generate datasets that contain fields, such as names, addresses, dates etc., based on various frequency tables. It generates *duplicates* of the original records by randomly introducing various modifications, the degrees of which are specified by the corresponding probabilities. We generate 4 datasets and their characteristics are shown in Table 1. Dataset 1 contains 500 original records, each of which has a corresponding duplicate. In dataset 2, the number of records is increased and also an original record can have a maximum of 5 duplicates. In dataset 3, the number of duplicated records is larger than that of the original records. The duplicates of dataset 4 are generated by doubling the default modification probabilities used in dataset 2. Therefore, the difference between an original record and its duplicates in dataset 4 is larger compared to those in dataset 2. Note the number of true matched record pairs (column 5) is larger than the number of duplicates (column 3) for datasets 2, 3 and 4 because of the transitivity of the multiple duplicates.

Table 1. Characteristics of test datasets generated by the Febrl database generator

dataset name	#original records	#duplicate records	#max dups per record	#total true matches	#pairs from blocking	#matched pairs
dataset 1	500	500	1	500	693	459
dataset 2	1,000	1,000	5	2,290	2,782	1,940
dataset 3	2,000	3,000	5	6,924	10,666	5,905
dataset 4	1,000	1,000	5	2,338	2,539	1,639

We applied the 3-pass standard blocking, i.e. 3 rounds of grouping record pairs based on 3 different blocking variables, on all four datasets. The number of record pairs generated by this blocking method for each dataset is shown in column 6 of Table 1. The last column of Table 1 shows the number of true matched record pairs among the record pairs generated by blocking. It can be seen that blocking has efficiently reduced the number of record pair comparisons but also missed some true matched record pairs. In this paper, we do not compare the performance of blocking methods (see [18] for details).

Table 2 shows the comparison variables and the corresponding comparison functions used in our experiment. Most of these comparison functions return binary values except the approximate string comparator, which returns continuous comparison values in the range of $[0.0, 1.0]$. In Febrl, a binary comparison value is converted to the weight using Equation 2 whereas a continuous comparison value is converted to the weight using the following equation:

$$w_k^{i,j} = \begin{cases} \log \frac{m_k}{u_k} - \frac{c_k^{i,j}}{c_{max}} \left(\log \frac{m_k}{u_k} + |\log \frac{1-m_k}{1-u_k}| \right) & \text{if } 0 \leq c_k^{i,j} \leq c_{max} \\ \log \frac{1-m_k}{1-u_k} & \text{if } c_k^{i,j} > c_{max} \end{cases} \quad (7)$$

Table 2. Comparison variables and functions used in the experiment

Comparison Variable	Comparison Function
given name	NYSIIS Encoding String Comparator
surname	Winkler Approximate String Comparator
wayfare name	Winkler Approximate String Comparator
locality name	Key Difference Comparator
postcode	Distance Comparator
age	Age Comparator

where c_{max} is the maximum approximate string difference value tolerated. The disagreement weight is obtained when the comparison value exceeds c_{max} whereas a (partial) agreement weight is calculated for a smaller comparison value.

In our experiment, we compare our clustering-based model to other existing decision models, specifically to the probabilistic decision model implemented in Febrl [8] and the 3-cluster k-means model [7]. Since the probabilistic decision model takes the sum of all weights as input, clustering is also performed on this one dimensional feature. Note that clustering on individual comparison vector components can be easily performed and details are discussed in Section 5.3. All the parameters for the probabilistic decision model are set manually. Specifically, the conditional probabilities m (0.95) and u (0.01), and the maximum string difference value tolerated c_{max} (0.3) are fixed and the threshold values t_1 and t_2 vary in the range of 0 to 20. For clustering-based decision models, we use the k-means clustering algorithm implemented in R [19] and k is equal to 2 and 3 for our record linkage application. The distance threshold value, T_d, used for controlling the size of fuzzy region varies from 0.1 to 1.0.

5.2   Performance Metrics

To compare different decision models, we need some performance metrics. Here we adopt two metrics proposed in [7] and the *recall* metric commonly used in information retrieval [20] to evaluate the decision models.

Let N be the total number of record pairs generated by a blocking method, and $n_{a,b}$ be the number of record pairs whose predicted matching status is a, and whose actual matching status is b, where a is either M, U or P, and b is either M' or U'. For evaluation purposes, we assume that record pairs with a P status can always be correctly classified. The three metrics are defined as follows:

- *AC*: the *accuracy* metric, *AC*, tests how accurate a decision model is. It is defined as the proportion of the correctly classified (both matched and unmatched) record pairs:

$$AC = \frac{n_{M,M'} + n_{U,U'} + n_{P,M'} + n_{P,U'}}{N} \qquad (8)$$

- *PP*: the *PP* metric measures the proportion of record pairs that are classified as *possibly matched* by a decision model, for clerical review:

$$PP = \frac{n_{P,M'} + n_{P,U'}}{N} \qquad (9)$$

– *recall*: the *AC* metric does not distinguish accuracy between the matched and unmatched record pairs since it reflects the total classification accuracy. The original *recall* metric [20] in information retrieval measures the number of relevant documents retrieved as fraction of all relevant documents. Here we use it to measure the accuracy of the decision model for matched record pairs and it is defined as the proportion of all matched record pairs that are classified correctly:

$$recall = \frac{n_{M,M'} + n_{P,M'}}{n_{M,M'} + n_{P,M'} + n_{U,M'}} \tag{10}$$

5.3 Results

Figure 2 shows distributions of the sum of weights (calculated by Equations 2 and 7) among the true matched and unmatched record pairs for our test datasets. It can be seen that the two clusters are separated reasonably well except for

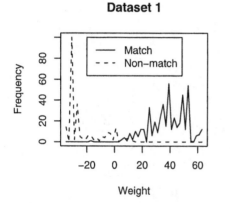
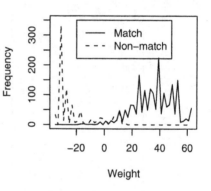
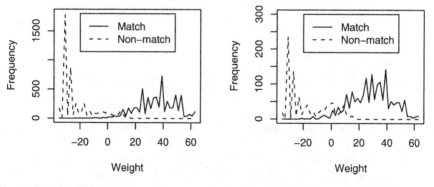

Fig. 2. Weight distributions of true matched and unmatched record pairs of the four test datasets

156   L. Gu and R. Baxter

Table 3. Results of the probabilistic model for $t_1 = 0$ and $t_2 = 10$ and of the k-means clustering models for $k = 2$ and 3

	Decision Model								
	Probabilistic			**Clustering $(k=2)$**			**Clustering $(k=3)$**		
Name	AC	PP	recall	AC	PP	recall	AC	PP	recall
dataset 1	0.989	0.038	0.998	0.980	0.0	0.985	0.981	0.297	0.998
dataset 2	0.973	0.039	0.991	0.955	0.0	0.975	0.997	0.311	0.996
dataset 3	0.982	0.046	0.993	0.963	0.0	0.979	0.998	0.230	0.996
dataset 4	0.961	0.093	0.977	0.919	0.0	0.926	0.996	0.310	0.993

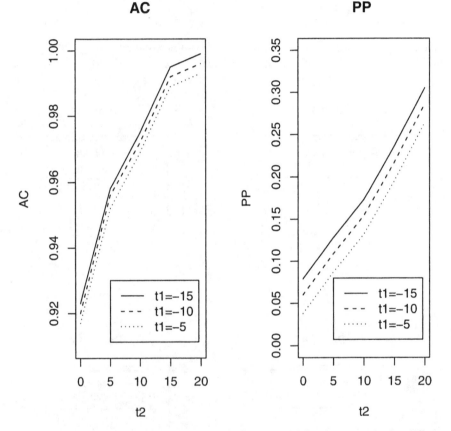

Fig. 3. The AC and PP values of the probabilistic model for dataset 4 under different t_1 and t_2 values

dataset 4. The two clusters overlap in the middle with weight values ranging between -15 and 15 for dataset 4.

We have run the probabilistic decision model on the weights of these datasets and the results under the threshold values $t_1 = 0$ and $t_2 = 10$ are shown in Table 3. It can be seen that dataset 4 has the lowest AC and $recall$ values, and the highest PP value due to larger errors in the duplicate records. Figure 3 shows the AC and PP values of the probabilistic decision model for dataset 4 under different threshold values. It can be seen that the linkage accuracy (AC) increases as t_1 decreases and t_2 increases. But this also leads to an increase in the proportion of record pairs (PP) for manual review. It is also evident that the increase in AC and PP values is greater when t_2 increases, compared to the same amount of decrease in t_1. Similar trends have been observed for the other 3 datasets.

We have also run the k-means clustering algorithm on the same datasets and the results for two- and three-cluster models are also shown in Table 3. Clustering using 3-clusters have resulted in about 23% to 31% of record pairs being classified as possible matches. This is obviously impractical for most real world applications as they often involve large datasets. On the other hand, the accuracy values for the two-cluster case range from 0.919 to 0.980. Such accuracy might be acceptable for some applications, considering that this is done fully automatically and no manual review is required.

If resources for manual review are available, a third cluster can be created by applying our proposed process of identifying record pairs in the fuzzy region for clerical review. Table 4 shows the results of our enhanced model for the four test datasets under different T_d threshold values. It can be seen that the accuracy for dataset 1 increases from 0.980 to 0.999 by assigning about 7% of record pairs for clerical review. Similarly, the accuracy (or *recall*) for dataset 4 also increases from 0.919 to 0.992 by assigning 27% of record pairs for manual review. This provides an effective mechanism to trade-off the *accuracy* and *recall* metrics with the number of record pairs for manual review. In practice, a T_d value in the range of 0.2 to 0.5 is a good starting point, depending on the quality of datasets and available resources for manual review.

Table 4. Results of our enhanced decision model under various threshold values

	Dataset											
	Dataset 1			Dataset 2			Dataset 3			Dataset 4		
T_d	AC	PP	*recall*	AC	PP	*recall*	AC	PP	*recall*	AC	PP	*recall*
0.10	0.993	0.010	0.989	0.964	0.016	0.980	0.969	0.011	0.984	0.931	0.017	0.936
0.20	0.997	0.029	0.998	0.969	0.025	0.984	0.977	0.025	0.987	0.946	0.042	0.953
0.50	0.999	0.071	0.998	0.992	0.078	0.991	0.993	0.077	0.993	0.974	0.113	0.970
0.80	0.999	0.123	0.998	0.997	0.127	0.996	0.997	0.125	0.996	0.988	0.206	0.982
1.00	0.999	0.144	0.998	0.997	0.173	0.996	0.998	0.162	0.997	0.992	0.270	0.988

Comparison of Table 3 with Table 4 shows that our enhanced decision model achieves the same accuracy/recall of the 3-cluster clustering model [7] with a much smaller PP value. For example, to achieve an AC value of 0.997 and a *recall* value of 0.998 for dataset 1, our model assigns only 2.9% of record pairs needed for manual review while the existing 3-cluster clustering model allocates 29.7% of record pairs for manual review. This reinforces our observation that there is not always a distinctive cluster between the matched and unmatched clusters. The existing 3-cluster decision model therefore leads to a large number of record pairs required for manual review. In addition to requiring a smaller number of record pairs for clerical review, our model also offers the flexibility of balancing between accuracy and the percentage of record pairs required for clerical review by tuning the threshold value T_d.

Tables 3 and 4 show that our proposed model achieves higher accuracy (both AC and *recall*) than the simple probabilistic model at similar PP values for dataset 1. For dataset 4, it also achieves better or at least comparable accuracy of simple probabilistic model at similar PP values. Furthermore, our model has only one parameter T_d, which is normalised and can be easily set based on the particular application requirement (accuracy required and resources available), while the probabilistic model has two parameters t_1 and t_2, to be set manually. Finding a good set of t_1 and t_2 values without training data is a challenge for many real-world applications. In addition, the probabilistic model needs to estimate the conditional probabilities m and u for each comparison variable while our model can directly take the output of any comparison function, for example, the output of any approximate string comparison function. Our enhanced model is not restricted to any particular comparison functions and has the potential to be applied directly to the components of the comparison vectors via multi-dimensional clustering. Performance comparison between one-dimensional and multi-dimensional clustering decision models is beyond the scope of this paper and will be the topic of future research.

6   Discussion and Conclusions

In this paper, we have reviewed several existing decision models for record linkage and proposed an enhanced clustering-based decision model. Many existing decision models require good training data, which is not readily available in real-world applications. Our enhanced decision model is based on the unsupervised learning technique and does not need any training data. In addition, we have introduced a metric, which can be used to identify record pairs with an uncertain matching status. These record pairs are classified as possibly matched for clerical review. We have also introduced some metrics for comparing the performances of different decision models.

Current experimental results show that the proposed decision model achieves similar accuracy of the existing clustering-based model, but with a much smaller proportion of record pairs for manual review. Furthermore, our model has a mechanism to control the trade-off between linkage accuracy and the amount of clerical review work.

In the current implementation, clustering is performed on the one dimensional feature. Further work is required to test our methodology on the comparison vector components directly using multi-dimensional clustering. We will also look into incorporating clustering algorithms that can handle categorical comparison values into our model and test the efficacy of the proposed method to categorical comparison values. We are also investigating the possibility of taking into account the different costs for false positives and false negatives when identifying record pairs in the fuzzy region.

Acknowledgements

We thank Warren Jin for useful discussions on fuzzy region identification.

References

1. Fayyad, U., Piatesky-Shapiro, G., Smith, P.: From Data Mining to Knowledge Discovery in Databases (a Survey). AI Magazine **17** (1996) 37–54
2. Fellegi, L., Sunter, A.: A Theory for Record Linkage. Journal of the American Statistical Society **64** (1969) 1183–1210
3. Winkler, W.: The State of Record Linkage and Current Research Problems. Technical Report RR/1999/04, US Bureau of the Census (1999)
4. Jaro, M.: Software Demonstrations. In: Proc. of an International Workshop and Exposition - Record Linkage Techniques, Arlington, VA, USA (1997)
5. Gill, L.: Methods for Automatic Record Matching and Linking and their Use in National Statistics. Technical Report National Statistics Methodological Series No. 25, National Statistics, London (2001)
6. Copas, J., Hilton, F.: Record Linkage: Statistical Models for Matching Computer Records. Journal of the Royal Statistical Society Series A **153** (1990) 287–320
7. Elfeky, M., Verykios, V., Elmagarmid, A.: TAILOR: A Record Linkage Toolbox. In: Proc. of the 18th Int. Conf. on Data Engineering, IEEE (2002)
8. Christen, P., Churches, T., Hegland, M.: Febrl - A Parallel Open Source Data Linkage System. In: Proc. of the 8th Pacific-Asia Conference on Knowledge Discovery and Data Mining (PAKDD'04), Sydney, Australia (2004) 638–647
9. Elfeky, M., Verykios, V.: On Search Enhancement of the Record Linkage Process. In: Proc. of ACM SIGKDD'03 Workshop on Data Cleaning, Record Linkage, and Object Consolidation, Washington DC, USA (2003) 31–33
10. Gu, L., Baxter, R.: Adaptive Filtering for Efficient Record Linkage. In: Proc. of the SIAM Data Mining Conference. (2004) 477–481
11. Bilenko, M., Mooney, R.: Adaptive Duplicate Detection Using Learnable String Similarity Measures. In: Proc. of ACM SIGKDD International Conference on Knowledge Discovery and Data Mining (KDD'03), Washington DC, USA (2003)
12. Jin, L., Li, C., Mehrotra, S.: Efficient Record Linkage in Large Data Sets. In: Proc. of the International Conference on Database Systems for Advanced Applications (DASFAA'03), Kyoto, Japan (2003)
13. Verykios, V., Moustakides, G., Elfeky, M.: A Bayesian Decision Model for Cost Optimal Record Matching. The VLDB Journal (2002)
14. Winkler, W.: Using the EM Algorithm for Weight Computation in the Fellegi-Sunter Model of Record Linkage. In: Proc. of the Section on Survey Research Methods. (1988) 667–671
15. Hartigan, J., Wong, M.: A k-means Clustering Algorithm. Applied Statistics **28** (1979) 100–108
16. Fraley, C., Raftery, A.: Model-Based Clustering, Density Estimation and Discriminant Analysis. Journal of the American Statistical Association **97** (2002) 611–631
17. Christen, P.: Probabilistic Data Generation for Deduplication and Data Linkage. In: Proc. of the 6th International Conference on Intelligent Data Engineering and Automated Learning (IDEAL'05), Brisbane, Australia (2005) 109–116

18. Baxter, R., Christen, P., Churches, T.: A Comparison of Fast Blocking Methods for Record Linkage. In: Proc. of ACM SIGKDD'03 Workshop on Data Cleaning, Record Linkage, and Object Consolidation, Washington DC, USA (2003) 25–27
19. Venables, W., Smith, D.: An Introduction to R (http://www.r-project.org). (2003)
20. Baeza-Yates, R., Ribeiro-Neto, B.: Modern Information Retrieval. Addison Wesley Professional (1999)

Intelligent Document Filter for the Internet

Deepani B. Guruge and Russel J. Stonier

Faculty of Informatics and Communication, Central Queensland University,
Rockhampton, QLD 4702, Australia
deepani@cc.ruh.ac.lk, r.stonier@cqu.edu.au

Abstract. Current major search engines on the web retrieve too many
documents, of which only a small fraction are relevant to the user query.
We propose a new intelligent document filtering algorithm to filter out
documents irrelevant to the user query from the output of internet search
engines. This algorithm uses output of 'Google' search engine as the basic
input and processes this input to filter documents most relevant to the
query. The clustering algorithm used here is based on the fuzzy c-means
with modifications to the membership function formulation and cluster
prototype initialisation. It classifies input documents into 3 predefined
clusters. Finally, clustered and context-based ranked URLs are presented
to the user. The effectiveness of the algorithm has been tested using
data provided by the eighth Text REtrieval Conference (TREC-8) [25]
and also with on-line data. Experimental results were evaluated by using
error matrix method, precision, recall and clustering validity measures.

1   Introduction

The amount of information on the internet has exploded during the past decade
but technologies that allow the full exploitation of the information on the internet
are still in their early stages. Several major search engines on the web retrieve
both relevant and non-relevant material. Then the user has to search manually
for relevant documents by traversing a topic hierarchy, into which a collection
is categorised. As more information becomes available, it is a time consuming
task to search for required relevant information [1]. Even now, users often find
themselves having to wade through several hundred documents in response to
their queries; this situation will only get worse in the future. To bridge this
gap requires new data mining techniques and new processes that can be used
for filtering information from the output produced by the search engines. An
efficient and effective information filtering system can help users of the internet
to control inflow and satisfy their information needs [2].

In practice a user query may not be precisely defined. To deal with this
ambiguity, it is helpful to introduce some 'Fuzziness' into the formulation of the
problem [3, 4, 5].

There has been much new research in the field of document retrieval over the
last ten years. Sugimoto, Hori, and Ohsuga [6] introduced a document retrieval
system based on automatic indexing techniques and statistical methods. Wang

G.J. Williams and S.J. Simoff (Eds.): Data Mining, LNAI 3755, pp. 161–175, 2006.

and Kitsuregawa [7], Thombros and Rijsbergen [8] used cosine similarity to calculate the similarity of a page with a cluster. The similarity of two documents is typically measured by the Jaccard coefficient [9]. The fuzzy k-nearest neighbour algorithm was implemented by Chau and Yeh [10] to classify documents into predefined clusters.

This research focuses on developing an effective document-filtering algorithm that classifies documents into 3 clusters, namely: *closely related*, *related*, and *not related*. It uses methodologies based on fuzzy clustering, automatic indexing and information retrieval techniques [11, 12]. A fuzzy document clustering (FDC) algorithm which is based on the fuzzy c-means algorithm [3, 14] is used to classify input documents into appropriate clusters [15]. Finally latent semantic indexing (LSI) [17] is used to rank documents in the first two clusters based on their context.

We validate the effectiveness of the document filtering algorithm using data provided by the eighth Text REtrieval Conference (TREC-8) [25] and also with on-line data.

2   Web Document Filter

This section describes the modelling steps of the Intelligent Document Filter (IDF). The system architecture given in Figure 1 describes the methodological design of the proposed filtering system.

2.1   Web Document Extractor (WDE)

The WDE (Figure 1) uses Perl module WWW::Mechanize to search the internet using the 'Google' search engine. After removing duplicate links (in Process 4 Figure 1) and filtering all the extracted document-links based on the meta-data that comes along with the links, the documents are downloaded into a temporary directory. Off-line processing is used here to reduce document-accessing time. Then all formatted documents (e.g. .pdf and .doc) are converted to text format. Files in this directory are automatically assigned name-tags and document numbers. These tags and document numbers are used to process these documents. Finally, details of the tags are mapped into the corresponding links.

2.2   Document Indexing

Each term in a document is then labelled with a document number (d_i) and a weight (x_i). A web document X^q with n key terms can therefore be represented as

$$X^q = ((d_i, t_1^q, x_1^q), (d_i, t_2^q, x_2^q), \cdots, (d_i, t_n^q, x_n^q),) \tag{1}$$

where

d_i - is the document number given to each term in document X^q
t_i^q - is the ith key term in document X^q
x_i^q - are the different weights assigned to terms in document X^q
 based on their frequencies.

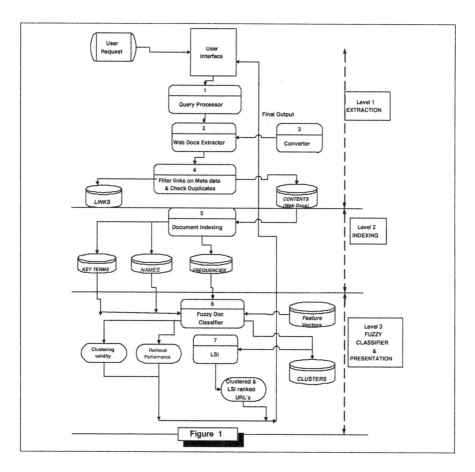

Fig. 1. Main System Architecture

Selecting Key Terms. Terms with low weights (low frequencies) are removed from the key term lists that are formed from the documents in the collection. This is achieved by defining a threshold which is dependent on the size of the document. The threshold is defined as shown below.

```
If  (Doc-size <= 10 KB) then Threshold=1
else if (Doc-size >10 KB) and (Doc-size <40 KB) Threshold=2
else     Threshold=3
```

The system then provides two methods to enter another set of n_1 key terms (including initial query or not) that can refine the initial output produced by the search engine. The system prepares a word list by selecting a few characteristic terms of high frequency from the top 20 documents in the search engine output. The user is able to use terms from this list and input n_1 terms or the user can input their own key terms to the system.

3 Classifier Architecture

This section describes the FDC algorithm (Process 6) which is used to classify documents into predefined clusters, namely: 'closely related', 'related', and 'not related' which we shall refer to as cluster 0, 1 and 2 respectively. This FDC algorithm is based on fuzzy c-means (FCM) of Bezdeck [3, 16] with modifications to the membership function formulation and cluster prototype initialisation [15]. To overcome problems encountered with FCM, a factor sw_{kq} was introduced to the membership function based on the number of user selected key terms appearing in the feature vector and cluster prototype (see Section 3.1). A further problem with FCM in application to document clustering [15] is that the resulting clusters are affected by the weights chosen to initialise cluster prototypes. We use evolutionary algorithms to validate an initialisation of weights or cluster prototype components, see Section 3.3.

3.1 Modified Membership Function

The Factor $sw_{kq} = \dfrac{min(n_q, n_k)}{max(n_q, n_k)}$ which lies in $[0, 1]$, measures the amount of overlap between the components of the feature vector and the cluster prototype, where n_q is the number of selected key terms appearing in document q and n_k is the number of elements in the prototype vector of cluster k. When feature vector and cluster prototype both have the same number of features then the overlap sw_{kq} of 2 vectors is one. In order to make sw_{kq} more effective, initially we assign a smaller number of term-weights into the components of the second and third clusters as shown below. Let CN represent Cluster Number and n_1 the number of user selected terms. If $CN = 0$, initially n_k in Cluster 0 $= n_1$. If $CN = 1$, initially n_k in Cluster 1 $= int(n_1/2) + 1$. If $CN = 2$, initially n_k in Cluster 2 $= int(n_1/2)$. For example, if a particular document contains almost all the user-selected key terms, then n_q and n_k are high in cluster 0 and the documents will be assigned a higher sw_{kq} in cluster 0 than in cluster 1 and 2. By multiplying μ_{kq}^{FCM} with higher sw_{kq} we can assign a higher weight to documents with all the user-selected terms. This gives higher membership value for cluster 0, rather than cluster 1 and 2. The new membership function can be defined as:

$$\mu_{kq}^{new} = \frac{\mu_{kq}^{FCM} \times sw_{kq}}{\sum_{i=0}^{k_1-1} \mu_{iq}^{FCM} \times sw_{iq}} \tag{2}$$

In classical c-means algorithm [7] membership function is defined as

$$\mu_{kq}^{FCM} = \frac{\left(d_{kq}^{-2}(X^q, Z^k)\right)^{1/(p-1)}}{\sum_{k=0}^{k_1-1} \left(d_{kq}^{-2}(X^q, Z^k)\right)^{1/(p-1)}}, \tag{3}$$

where $X^q = [x_1 \cdots x_{n_1}]^T$ is a feature vector and $Z^k = [z_1^k \cdots z_{n_1}^k]^T$ is a prototype vector for cluster k, both have dimension n_1. $d_{kq}^2(X^q, Z^k)$ represents the Euclidean distance between the feature vector X^q and the cluster prototype Z^k. μ_{kq} represents the degree of membership of feature vector X^q in the cluster Z^k, p is any real number greater than 1 [3, 16]. By substituting μ_{kq}^{FCM} in Equation (2) we have

$$\mu_{kq}^{new} = \frac{\left(\dfrac{\left(d_{kq}^{-2}(X^q, Z^k) \right)^{1/(p-1)}}{\sum_{k=0}^{k_1-1} \left(d_{kq}^{-2}(X^q, Z^k) \right)^{1/(p-1)}} \right) \times sw_{kq}}{\sum_{i=0}^{k_1-1} \left[\left(\dfrac{\left(d_{iq}^{-2}(X^q, Z^k) \right)^{1/(p-1)}}{\sum_{k=0}^{k_1-1} \left(d_{iq}^{-2}(X^q, Z^k) \right)^{1/(p-1)}} \right) \times sw_{iq} \right]}. \tag{4}$$

3.2 New FDC Algorithm

1. Initialise all membership values (μ_{kj}) by using Equation 4. Cluster prototypes are initialised before starting the algorithm, see Section 3.3.
2. Compute the new cluster prototypes by using

$$Z^k = \sum_{q=0}^{q_1-1} \mu_{kq} X^q \qquad \text{where } k = 0, \cdots, (k_1 - 1) \tag{5}$$

3. Update μ_{kj}^ℓ to $\mu_{kj}^{\ell+1}$ using

$$\mu_{kj}^{\ell+1} = \frac{\mu_{kq}^{FCM(\ell+1)} \times sw_{kq}}{\sum_{i=0}^{k_1-1} \left(\mu_{iq}^{FCM(\ell+1)} \times sw_{iq} \right)} \tag{6}$$

4. Set $\ell = \ell + 1$, if $|\mu_{kj}^{\ell+1} - \mu_{kj}^\ell| < \epsilon$ stop; else go to step 2.

Finally the FDC assigns feature vector (documents) to a cluster which has maximum membership value in the final FDC results.

3.3 Solution for Initial Z-Values by Evolutionary Algorithm

As stated previously we found that the resulting clusters were greatly affected by the initialisation of prototype centers. It was found by trial and error that if components of the first cluster prototype were initialised with higher values, feature vectors with higher component values would be classified in the first cluster. So we initialised prototypes of cluster 0 and 1 with higher values than cluster 2. We justify this assumption by the use of evolutionary algorithms as shown below.

An evolutionary algorithm (EA) [30], is used to learn the initial values for cluster prototypes. Each individual string in the evolutionary population, is to uniquely represent the entire set of cluster prototypes (Z-values). This can be achieved as follows. Each Z-value is uniquely represented by a real number within the range $[0,1]$. The complete set of N, Z-values for all k_1 clusters (where $k_1 = 3$ for this application) can therefore be represented as a linear individual string a row vector of $N = k_1 \times n_1$ weights,

$$\underset{\sim}{Z} = [\underset{\sim}{Z^1}\, \underset{\sim}{Z^2} \cdots \underset{\sim}{Z^{k_1}}]$$

$$\underset{\sim}{Z^k} = [z_1^k\, z_2^k \cdots z_{n_1}^k]$$

where z_n^k is a real number in the range $[0,1]$ for $n = 1, \cdots, n_1$ and $k = 1, \cdots, k_1$. n_1 and k_1 are number of components in a cluster prototype and number of clusters respectively.

The initial population $P(0) = \{\underset{\sim}{Z_j} : j = 1, \cdots, M\}$, where M is the number of strings (the population size), was determined by choosing the z_n^k as a random real number in $[0,1]$. In determining successive populations a full replacement policy was used, tournament selection with size n_T (typically 2 or 4) was used to select parents in the current generation to produce children for the next generation. An elitism policy was also used with typically two (2) copies of the best string from a current generation passed to the next generation.

Mutation (with probability *pmutation*), was defined as a modified version of the Michalewicz mutation [30], using pseudo code similar to that below :

```
mutate=flip(pmutation); /* flip the biased coin
if (mutate){
        nmutation= nmutation + 1;
        pow=((1.0-padd) * (1.0-padd));
        fact=1.0 * (1.0 - power(MyRandom(),pow));
        if (flip(0.5))
            perturbation = fact * (lower_bound - allelevel);
        else    pertubation = fact *  (upper_bound - allelevel);
        temp = allelevel + pertubation  ;
    }
else    temp = allelevel;
return (temp);
```

where *MyRandom()* is a procedure to generate a random real number in the range $[0,1]$ and for an individual $Z_j(i)$, upper-bound is 1, lower-bound is 0 and allelevel is $Z_j(i)$. The value of parameter *padd* is determined as follows.

```
paddout=gen_no/max_gen;
if (flip(0.5))
        padd = paddout;
else
        padd =  0.995;
```

Classical arithmetic crossover was used to form two children from two parent strings to be then added to the population in the next generation.

The fitness (objective) function for each string was simply determined as the objective function of FCM algorithm [3]. It is

$$J(U, Z) = \sum_{q=1}^{(q_1)} \sum_{k=1}^{(k_1)} (\mu_{kq})^p ||\underset{\sim}{X}^q - \underset{\sim}{Z}^k||^2, \tag{7}$$

where $||\underset{\sim}{X}^q - \underset{\sim}{Z}^k||^2$ represents the Euclidean distance between a feature vector $\underset{\sim}{X}^q$ and a prototype $\underset{\sim}{Z}^k$, μ_{kq} represents the degree of membership of feature vector $\underset{\sim}{X}^q$ in the cluster $\underset{\sim}{Z}^k$, p is any real number greater than 1 and $U = [\mu_{kq}]$ is a $k_1 \times q_1$ fuzzy c-partition matrix. Here $\{X^q : q = 1, ..., q_1\}$ is a set of q_1 feature vectors that is to be partitioned into k_1 clusters. Feature vectors $\underset{\sim}{X}^q = [x_1 \ ... \ x_{n1}]^T$ and cluster prototype $\underset{\sim}{Z}^k = [z_1 \ ... \ z_{n1}]^T$ have dimension n_1, [3]. The objective function (9) uses the sum over the quadratic distances of the data to the prototypes, weighted with their membership degrees and it is to be minimised by the evolutionary algorithm.

The initial population is randomly generated, while ensuring that individual elements in the chromosome are within the range [0,1]. We set length of the chromosome (N) as 30 (3×10) allowing the first 10 elements in the chromosome for initialising components of the first cluster prototype, 11 to 20 elements in the chromosome for initialising components of the second cluster prototype and 21 to 30 elements for initialising components of the third cluster prototype. From these 10 elements allocated for each cluster prototype only $3 \times n_1$ components are used to calculate the fitness of each individual string in the population.

The fitness of each individual was modified to $f_j = \delta J(U, Z)$, where δ denotes a scaling factor to increase the small values of J typically 10^{-3} to values lying in the range [0 100]. Once the new population is generated, the fitness of the new population is evaluated and the fittest individuals are allowed to propagate through subsequent generations. A cross-over rate of 0.6 and mutation-rate of 0.05 was set. The fittest individual, the one with minimum fitness was examined after a preset number of generations.

Using the TREC-8 data, as test data, it was found for random initialisation of the population, that the fittest individual after some a few thousand generations, yielded Z-values for cluster 0 and cluster 1 higher (in the range $0.5 - 0.8$) than the Z-values for cluster 2 (in the range $0.1 - 0.3$).

This analysis justifies our procedure for prototype initialisation, setting values in cluster 0 and 1, higher than the values in cluster 2. For this research we set the values for cluster 0 and 1 in the range $0.6 - 0.8$ and for cluster 2, $0.1 - 0.2$.

4   Content-Based Ranking

After passing through the classifier, documents in clusters 0 and 1 are presented to the next process LSI (Process 7). Latent semantic indexing is used in Process 7 to rank the documents in clusters, cluster 0 and cluster 1 based on their context, in order to allow the user to examine the most relevant documents provided in the initial search engine output before proceeding on to other queries or documents.

Latent semantic indexing uses truncated singular value decomposition (SVD) [17, 18, 19, 20] to estimate the structure in word usage across documents and place documents with similar word usage patterns near each other in the term-document space. LSI starts with a terms (m) by documents (n) matrix A [17, 19]. Process LSI uses documents classified into cluster 0 as training data. In order to construct matrix A, document frequencies (df) of terms in the training corpus are calculated and terms with df less than predetermined threshold are removed. These terms that describe cluster 0 are presented to the user in descending order of importance to reformulate the query. Terms will not be shown in the list if they appear in less than 20% of the documents in cluster 0.

One of the common and usually effective methods for improving retrieval performance in vector methods is to transform the raw frequency of occurrence of a term in a document by some function. Such transformations normally have two components. Each term is assigned a global weight ($G(i)$), indicating its overall importance in the document collection as an indexing term and also transform the term's frequency in the document which is called a local weighting($L(i, j)$) [17, 18, 21]. We can write global and local weighting as,

$$a_{ij} = L(i, j) \times G(i) \tag{8}$$

Results in [18] indicate a log transformation of the local cell entries combined with a global entropy (1-entropy) weight for terms is the most effective term-weighting scheme. In local weighting $log(Term\_frequency + 1)$ takes the log of the raw term frequency, thus dampening effects of large differences in frequencies. Entropy (global weighting) is based on information theoretic ideas and is the most sophisticated weighting scheme. The average uncertainty or entropy of a term is given by

$$\sum_j \frac{p_{ij} \log(p_{ij})}{\log(ndocs)} \quad \text{where} \quad p_{ij} = \frac{tf_{ij}}{gf_i} \tag{9}$$

tf_{ij} is the frequency of term i in document j, gf_i is the total number of times term occurs in the whole collection, $ndocs$ is the number of documents in the document collection. Subtracting the quantity in Equation 9 from a constant assigns minimum weight to terms, which are concentrated in a few documents. Entropy takes into account the distribution of terms over documents [18].

Next, the matrix A is decomposed by using SVD, into three other matrices of special form [17], $A = U \Sigma V^T$. This is a form of factor analysis where one component matrix (U) describes the original row entities as vectors of derived orthogonal factor values, another describes the original column entities (V) in the same way, and third is a diagonal matrix (Σ) containing scaling values such that when the three components are matrix-multiplied, the original matrix is reconstructed [17, 21]. The diagonal matrix contains the monotonically decreasing singular values of A. The first k columns of U and V matrices and the first k (largest) singular values of A are used to construct a rank-k approximation to A, A_k.

The idea is that the A_k matrix, by containing only the first k independent linear components of A, captures the major associational structure in the matrix

and throws out noise. In this reduced model, the closeness of objects is determined by the overall pattern of term usage, so objects can be near each other
regardless of the precise words that are used to describe them, and their description depends on a kind of consensus of their term meanings, thus dampening the
effects of polysemy [18].

In the LSI model, queries are formed into pseudo-documents that specify
the location of the query (q) in the reduced term-document space. The pseudo-
document can be represented by $\hat{q} = q^T U_k \Sigma_k^{-1}$, where q is simply the vector of
words in the users query, multiplied by the appropriate term weights in Equation 8 [17]. Once the query is projected into the term-document space, one
of several similarity measures can be applied to compare the position of the
pseudo-document to the positions of the terms or documents in the reduced
term-document space. The query vector is compared to all document vectors,
and the documents are ranked by their similarity (nearness) to the query. Cosine
similarity measure between the query vector and document vector is used to measure the similarity of documents to the user query [17]. According to the results of
similarity measures, links in clusters 0 and 1 are ranked and returned to the user.

4.1   Choosing the Number of Dimensions

Dimension reduction analysis removes much of the noise, but keeping too few
dimensions would loose important information [17, 18]. The dimensionality of
the feature set needs to be reduced while the maximum amount of information
and pattern in the data set is preserved.

In principal component analysis, the two guidelines for data reduction that
are commonly used in practice, are the Kraiser criterion and the Scree test [23].
The Kraiser criterion retains only factors with eigenvalues greater than one and
the Scree test use a graphical method to select the number of factors. In this
graphical method plotting eigenvalues it is required to find the place where the
smooth decrease of eigenvalues appears to level off to the right of the plot. We
found Scree test was more effective for this system and wrote a small piece of
code to implement this criteria within the working code of the algorithm, so that
off line calculations were not required.

5   Experimental Setup

This section describes the experimental settings we used to test the clustering
validity of the filtering system. Data provided by the eighth Text REtrieval
Conference (TREC -8) [25] and on-line data were used. Specifically, we used
TREC-8 queries with their corresponding collections and relevance judgements
supplied by NIST accessors [26]. Sixteen (16) topics from the TREC topics 401-
450 were randomly selected. They were: 402, 403, 406, 407, 410, 412, 414, 415,
419, 420, 425, 427, 429, 430, 431, 436. These topics were then converted into
queries and ran against the TREC-8 web track (small web) 2 gigabyte, 250,000
document collection. For each topic we used a few relevant documents as training

data and the context of the query was built with the training documents. These words were used to form matrix A in the LSI process. We set the stopping condition (ϵ) for FDC algorithm as 0.001.

6 Performance Evaluation

Retrieval effectiveness of the IDF was tested on Google output and the results were evaluated using, the error matrix method [31] and the two standard measures precision and recall [11]. The performance of the FDC algorithm was tested on TREC-8 data and results were evaluated using precision and recall within the TREC-8 evaluation, as reported by NIST [26].

Clustering Validity Measures. The Xie-Beni (XB) clustering validity measure has been used here to evaluate the clustering results. This measures the overall average compactness and separation of a fuzzy c-partition. Compactness and separation validity function XB is defined as the ratio of compactness π to the separation s, [29].

$$XB = \pi/s = \frac{\sigma/N}{(d_{min})^2} = \frac{\sum_{i=1}^{N}\sum_{j=1}^{N}\mu_{ij}^2||z_i - x_j||^2}{n\min_{i,j}||z_i - z_j||^2} \tag{10}$$

A smaller XB indicates a partition in which all the clusters are overall compact and separate to each other.

In the relevance judgement given in the TREC-data, documents were classified into two classes *relevant* and *non-relevant*, using only titles in the TREC queries. Precision and recall values obtained by running FDC algorithm on TREC-8 data are shown in Figure 2. The graph on the left in Figure 2 shows performance of the FDC algorithm relative to the documents filtered into the cluster 0(*closely related*) and the graph on the right in Figure 2 displays the performance relative to the documents filtered into the clusters 0 and 1 (*related*). In both graphs the median performance of all the TREC-8 systems (pre-results) for corresponding queries are given [27]. The average precision relative to cluster 0 documents was 39% and the average precision relative to cluster 0 and cluster 1 was slightly low (33%). This is because the system classifies documents which are 'related' but 'not closely related' to the the given topic into the cluster 1. We selected only 40 % of the top ranked (in Process 7) documents in the cluster 1. Average precision obtained for different systems for small web track (TREC-8) is in the range (2.9%-38%), [28]. Compared to these results retrieval effectiveness of the FDC algorithm is satisfactory. The average XB value obtain for this test data is low (0.03). A smaller XB indicates a partition in which all the clusters are well separated from each other. Title terms given in the TREC-data were used as n_1 terms input into the classifier. We can improve the performance of the FDC algorithm by reorganising the query based on the context built by the process LSI. By analysing this context the user can input n_1 key terms to the system.

Then *intelligent document filter* was applied to the output from the Google search engine for two initial queries *Genetic Algorithms* and *Evolutionary Algorithms*.

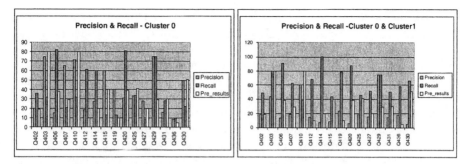

Fig. 2. Precision and Recall for TREC Data set

The first 200 links output by the Google search engine for the initial query *Genetic Algorithms* were selected for testing. Duplicate and non accessible links were removed from the 200 links leaving 87 documents in the set. Documents attached to 87 URLs were downloaded into a temporary directory. This data set is called 'set1' for reference.

The downloaded documents were indexed. Punctuations, numbers and Stop words were also removed, all letters were converted to lowercase, and Porter's stemming algorithm was applied.

Then a set of n_1 key terms/secondary query (including or excluding the initial query used in Google) that can refine the initial output produced by the search engine were selected to prepare feature vectors. The secondary query *Genetic Algorithms for Neural Networks* was used to filter these downloaded documents. The filtered documents were classified into three clusters: *closely related, related, not directly related* to the secondary query. The intelligent document filtering algorithm classified 23 documents as *closely related*, 8 as *related*, 56 as *not directly related* to the secondary query.

Relevance Judgements. The relevance judgement, that is, a classification of the documents for the given query, is determined by a review pooling method. For the purpose of evaluation five experts in the field of Evolutionary Algorithms were asked to evaluate the retrieved document set for the query *Genetic Algorithms for Neural Networks*.

The value of the XB obtained for the data set1 was small (0.075) and that indicates the clusters are overall separate from each other.

The error matrix method [31] was used to evaluate the clustering results. Overall Accuracy (OA) was computed by dividing the sum of the major diagonal elements by the total number of sample elements. OA is a measure of the total match between reference and classification data. Accuracy of each individual category was measured by using producer's accuracy (PA) and user's accuracy (UA). PA is related to the error of omission which is calculated by dividing corresponding major diagonal elements by the total in reference data. UA is related to the errors of commission which is calculated by dividing corresponding major diagonal elements by the total in classification data.

In the following tables, clusters R^1, R^2, R^3 are the document classes classified by human experts and Z^1, Z^2, Z^3 are indicators of clusters produced by the clustering algorithm. Examining the error matrix values in Table 1, it can be observed that the error matrix is diagonally dominant and the overall accuracy measure, $OA = 0.81$ is high. This indicates that a high proportion of data items have been classified correctly. If we consider cluster 1 PA and UA values, under estimation is low, $PA^1 = 1$. But cluster 1 is over estimated $UA^1 = 0.57$ and cluster 2 is under estimated $PA^2 = 0.33$ in the classification data. This is because a few related documents were grouped as *closely related* in classification data. The reason for this is that some documents are very difficult to judge whether they are closely related or related to the user query. In cluster 3 PA and UA values are high. It can be concluded that cluster 3 is not over estimated or under estimated in classification data.

Precision and recall values obtained for the data set1 are given in Table 2. The high recall in cluster 1 indicates that all closely related documents are grouped into cluster 1. High precision and recall in cluster 3 and high PA^3 and UA^3 in Table 1, confirm that the intelligent document filtering algorithm classified most of the non-related documents to the user query perfectly into cluster 3. Precision and recall values for all three clusters are greater than 50% except for the recall value obtained for cluster 2. Effectiveness of the intelligent document filtering algorithm is therefore considered satisfactory. Then intelligent document filtering algorithm was applied to the output from the Google search engine for another initial query. This time *Evolutionary Algorithms* was used as the initial query submitted to the Google search engine. After removing duplicate links, non-accessible links and filtering all links based on meta data attached to each link, 93 documents were downloaded from 200 links in the Google output. This data set is called data 'set2'. These downloaded documents were then filtered by using the secondary query *Evolutionary algorithms for optimization*. The intelligent document filtering algorithm classified 56 documents as *closely related*, 32 as *related*, 5

Table 1. Error matrix for FDC - downloaded data set1

$OA = 0.81$	R^1	R^2	R^3	PA	UA
Z^1	13	5	5	1	0.57
Z^2	0	4	4	0.33	0.50
Z^3	0	3	53	0.86	0.95

Table 2. Precision and recall of FDC for downloaded data set1 and set2

	data set1		data set2	
Cluster No	Precision	Recall	Precision	Recall
1	57	100	57	97
2	50	33	97	55
3	95	86	60	100

as *not directly related* to the secondary query. The value of $XB = 0.034$ obtained for this data set was low, so all clusters are well separated from each other.

Five experts in the field of Evolutionary Algorithms were asked to evaluate the retrieved document set for the query *Evolutionary Algorithms for Optimization*. The error matrix obtained for this data set is given in Table 3. Precision

Table 3. Error matrix for FDC - downloaded data set2

$OA = 0.70$	R^1	R^2	R^3	PA	UA
Z^1	32	24	0	0.97	0.57
Z^2	1	31	0	0.55	0.97
Z^3	0	2	3	1	0.60

and recall values obtained for data set, set2, are given in Table 2. Examining the error matrix values it can be observed that the error matrix is diagonally dominant and the $OA = 0.7$ is high. Therefore a high proportion of data items have been classified correctly. If we consider the PA and UA values of cluster 1 and cluster 2, $PA^1 = 0.97$ is high in cluster 1. So under estimation is low in cluster 1. But an over estimation is introduced in cluster 1, $UA^1 = 0.57$ and an under estimation is introduced in cluster 2, $PA^2 = 0.55$.

As with the data set, set1, a few related documents were classified as *closely related*. As far as the user is concerned this is not a major issue, since all most all the closely related documents were grouped as *closely related* (recall and PA values are high in cluster 1 for both downloaded data sets) and most of the non-related documents were grouped into cluster 3, *not related* (high recall and PA values in cluster 3 for both data sets). Again we conclude that the effectiveness of the intelligent document filter is satisfactory.

7 Conclusions

An intelligent document filtering algorithm for the internet has been presented in this paper. First the fuzzy document clustering algorithm was applied to the TREC-8 data and compared with relevance judgements supplied by NIST accessors. As documents in the TREC data are classified into two clusters *relevant* and *non-relevant*, the output from the FDC algorithm had to be merged into two clusters. This was undertaken in two ways. One was to merge documents in cluster 1 and 2 into a cluster of *non-relevant* documents with cluster 0 recognised as the cluster of *relevant* documents. The other was to merge documents in cluster 0 and cluster 1 into a cluster of *relevant* documents and cluster 2 recognised as the cluster of *non-relevant* documents. It was found that the average precision relative to cluster 0 in the first method was 39% and in the second method lower at 33%. This compares favourably with the average precision which lies between 2.9% and 38%, obtained for different systems applied to cluster the small web track.

We evaluated the performance of the intelligent filtering algorithm with outputs of Google search engine. It was shown using the various measures of error matrix, producer's accuracy, user's accuracy, precision and recall, that retrieval effectiveness of the designed filtering system was satisfactory on the TREC-8 data set and also on the on-line data.

References

1. S. Abuleil and M. Evens, "Building a machine-learning system to categorize Arabic text", Proceedings of Eleventh international conference on intelligent systems:emerging technologies, Boston, Massachusetts USA, 2002.
2. B. Sheth and P. Maes, "Information filtering using software agents", vol.2002: MIT labs-software agents group, 1993-1994.
3. L. X. Wang, "A course in fuzzy systems and control", U.S.A: Prentice Hall, 1997.
4. Chau, R., Yeh, C.H., "A fuzzy Knowledge-based System for cross-lingual text retrieval", Proceedings of Computational intelligence for modelling, control and automation, pp.489-494, ISO Press, 1999.
5. C. H. Oh, K. Honda, and H. Ichihashi, "Fuzzy clustering categorical multivariate data", Proceedings of Joint 9th IFSA word congress and 20th North American Fuzzy Information Processing Society (NAFIPS) international conference, pp.2154-2159, Vancouver, Canada, 2001.
6. M. Sugimoto, K. Hori, and S. Ohsuga, "A document retrieval system for assisting creative research", Proceedings of 3rd International conference on document analysis & recognition, ISBN: 0-8186-7128-9, Montreal, Canada, 1995
7. Y. Wang and M. Kitsuregawa, "Evaluating contents-link coupled web page clustering for web search Results", Proceedings of Eeleventh international conference on information and knowledge management, ISBN:1-58113-492-4, pp.499-506, Virginia, USA, 2002.
8. A. Thombros and C. J. Van Rijsbergen, "Query-sensitive similarity measures for the calculation of inter-document relationships", Proceedings of the international conference on information and knowledge management, ISBN: 1-58113-436-3, pp. 17-24, Georgia, USA, 2001.
9. T. H. Heveliwala, A. Gionis, D. Klein, and P. Indyk, "Evaluating strategies for similarity search on the web", Proceedings of Eleventh international conference on world wide web, ACM 158113-449-5/02/0005, Honolulu, Hawaii, USA, 2002.
10. R. Chau and C. H. Yeh, "Building a concept-based multilingual text retrieval system using fuzzy clustering and classification", Proceedings of international conference on intelligent agents, web technologies and internet commerce- IAWTIC, ISBN:0858898489, pp.418-425, U.S.A, 2001.
11. G. Salton and M. J. McGill, "Introduction to modern information retrieval", ISBN:0-201-12227-8, Addison-Wesley, Singapore: McGraw-Hill international book company, 1984.
12. C. J. Van Rijsbergen, "Information retrieval", London: Butterworths, 1979.
13. M. F. Porter, "An algorithm for suffix stripping", vol. 14, pp.130-137, 1980.
14. L. Zhang, "Comparison of fuzzy c-means algorithm and new fuzzy clustering and fuzzy merging algorithm", University of Nevada, Reno, NV89557 2001.
15. R. J. Stonier and D. B. Guruge, "Building an efficient document detrieval system using fuzzy clustering", Proceedings of First indian international conference on artificial intelligent (IICAI), pp.1014-1027, Hydreabad, India, 2003.
16. C. G. Looney, "Interactive clustering and merging with a new expected value", vol.2002: University of Nevada, Pattern recognition society, Reno, NV 89557, 2002.

17. M. W. Berry, S. T. Dumais, and G. W. O'Brien, "Using linear algebra for intelligent information retrieval", SIAM review, vol.37, pp.573-595, 1995.
18. S. T. Dumais, "Improving the retrieval of information from external sources", Behaviour research methods, instruments and computers, vol.23, pp.229-236, 1991.
19. S. Deerwester, S. T. Dumais, G. W. Furnas, T. K. Landauer, and R. Harshman, "Indexing by latent semantic analysis", Journal of the American society for information science, vol.41, pp. 391-407, 1990.
20. T. K. Landauer and S. T. Dumais, "A solution to plato's problem: The latent semantic analysis theory of the accquisition, induction, and representation of knowledge", Psychological review, vol.104, pp.211-240, 1997.
21. T. K. Landauer, P. W. Foltz, and D. Laham, "An introduction to latent semantic analysis", Discourse processes, vol.25, pp.259-284, 1998.
22. T. K. Landauer, D. Laham, and P. W. Foltz, "Learning human-like knowledge by singular value decomposition: A progress report", Advances in neural information processing systems, vol. 10, pp.45-51, 1998.
23. STATISTICA,"Factor analysis", vol.2003: StatSoft, Inc, 1984-2004.
24. E. Binaghi, P. A. Brivio, P. Ghezzi, and A. Rampini, "A fuzzy set-based accuracy assessment of soft classification", Pattern recognition letters, vol.9, pp.935-948, 1999.
25. E. M. Voorhees, D. Harman,"The eighth Text REtrieval Conference (TREC-8)", Gaithersburg, Maryland, November 16-19,1999.
26. http://trec.nist.gov/
27. A. Berger,J. Lafferty,"The Weaver system for document retrieval", Proceedings of The Eighth Text REtrieval Conference(TREC-8), Gaithersburg, Maryland, November 16-19,1999.
28. D. Hawking,E. M. Voorhees, N. craswell, P. Bailey, "Overview of the TREC-8 web track", Proceedings of The Eighth Text REtrieval Conference (TREC-8), Gaithersburg, Maryland, November 16-19,1999.
29. X.L. Xie, G. Beni,"Validity measures for fuzzy clustering", IEEE transactions on pattern analysis and machine intelligence, vol.13, pp.841-847, 1991.
30. Z. Michalewicz, "Genetic algorithms data structures evolution programs",2nd Ed., Springer Verlag, 1994.
31. E.Binaghi, P.A.Brivio, P.Ghezzi, and A. Rampini,"A fuzzy set-based accuracy assessment of soft classification", Pattern recognition letters, vol.9, pp.935-948, 1999.

Informing the Curious Negotiator: Automatic News Extraction from the Internet

Debbie Zhang and Simeon J. Simoff

Faculty of Information Technology,
University of Technology, Sydney,
Broadway PO Box 123, NSW 2007, Australia
{debbiez, simeon}@it.uts.edu.au

Abstract. Information acquisition and validation play an important role in the decision making process during negotiation. In this chapter we briefly present the framework of a smart data mining system for providing contextual information extracted from the Internet to a negotiation agent. We then present one of its components in more details - an effective automated technique for extracting relevant articles from news web sites, so that they can be used further by the mining agents. Most current techniques experience difficulties in coping with changes in web site structure and formats. The proposed extraction process is completely automatic and independent of web site formats. Proposed technique identifies regularities in both format and content of news web sites. The algorithms are applicable to both single- and multi-document web sites. Since invalid URLs can cause errors in data extraction, we also present a method for the negotiation agent to estimate the validity of the extracted data based on the frequency of the relevant words in the news title. Once the news articles are extracted the next task is to construct sets of given articles. This chapter presents a new procedure for constructing news data sets on given topics. The extracted news data set is further utilised by the parties involved in negotiation. The information retrieved from the data set can support both human and automated negotiators.

1 Introduction

The *curious negotiator* [1] is a multiagent system of competitive agents supporting multi-attribute negotiation where the set of issues is not fixed [2]. The overall goal of its design is to exploit the interplay between contextual information [3] and the development of offers in negotiation conducted in an electronic environment. Current design is illustrated in Fig. 1. Negotiation agents apply the negotiation strategies in the negotiation process [4]. With respect to the curious negotiator the term 'negotiation strategies' includes strategies for developing the set of issues in an offer as well as *identifying, requesting and evaluating contextual information* including determining what information to table as the negotiation proceeds [5]. A negotiation strategy should generally rely on information drawn from the context of the negotiation. The significance of information to the negotiation process was analysed formally in the seminal paper by Milgrom and Weber [6] in which the Linkage Principle,

G.J. Williams and S.J. Simoff (Eds.): Data Mining, LNAI 3755, pp. 176–191, 2006.

relating the revelation of contextual information to the price that a purchaser is pre-pared to pay, was introduced. "Good negotiators, therefore, undertake integrated processes of knowledge acquisition that combine sources of knowledge obtained at and away from the negotiation table. "They learn in order to plan and plan in order to learn" [7]. The grand vision for curious negotiator encapsulates this observation. The mediation agents (labelled as 'mediator' in Fig. 1) assist negotiation agents in the negotiation process. The role of observer agents (labelled as 'observer' in Fig. 1) is to observe and analyse what is happening on the 'negotiation table' and to look for op-portunities particularly from failed negotiations.

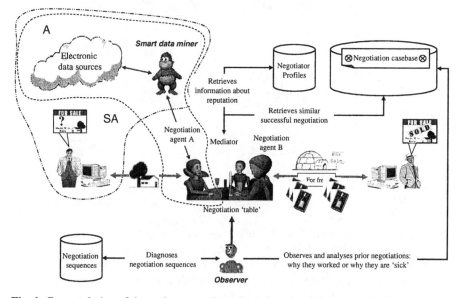

Fig. 1. Current design of the curious negotiator (includes negotiation agent, mediator, observer and the smart data miner)

Successful negotiation relies on an understanding of how to 'play' the negotiation mechanism [5] and on *contextual information*. From a process management point of view, negotiation processes are interesting in that they are knowledge-driven emergent processes that can be fully managed provided that, first, full authority to negotiate is delegated to the agent and, second, sufficient contextual information can be derived from the market data from the sources available on the Internet (news feeds, company white papers, specialised articles, research papers) and other sources by the data mining bots. The dashed lines in Fig. 1 contour two scenarios: "SA" – a semi-automated sce-nario in which the human agent receives and processes contextual information and af-fects the strategies of the negotiation agent, and "A" in which contextual information is distilled and passed to the negotiation agent in a form of parameters that are taken in consideration by the negotiation strategies. The curious negotiator is designed to incorporate data mining and information discovery methods [8] that operate under time constraints, including methods from the area of topic detection and

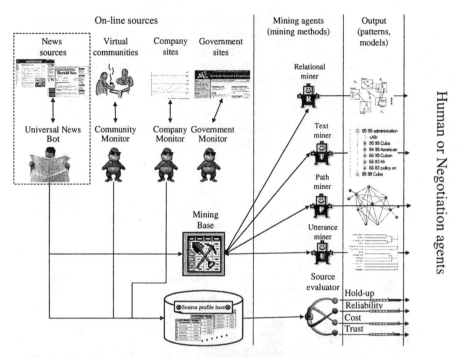

Fig. 2. Smart data mining system for supporting negotiation with contextual information

event tracking research [9]. The idea is encapsulated in the "smart data miner" in Fig. 1. The architecture of this specialised data mining system, which operates in tandem with the human or/and negotiation agent, is shown in Fig. 2. Initially the information is extracted from various sources including on-line news media, virtual communities, company and government web sites.

Extracted information is converted to a structured representation and then both representations are stored in the mining base. They are used for further analysis by different data mining algorithms, including different text and network mining agents. The 'Source profile base', includes a collection of time-stamped data about the behaviour of the approached sources like response time, the number of answered requests, dates when a new layout appears, redirections of requests, types of errors, subscription price, change in subscription price, change of the level of service provided and other parameters. The 'Source evaluator' provides a number of estimates, e.g. 'hold-up', 'reliability', 'cost', 'trust' that evaluate the quality of the data sources from which the patterns have been extracted. These estimates are derived from the related data in the source profile base. This chapter is limited to the techniques that cover the automatic extraction of relevant news articles. Regardless of whether we deal with scenario "SA" or "A", there are a number of challenges in real world negotiations that the smart data mining system needs to address, including (i) critical pieces of information being held in different repositories; (ii) non-standard formats; (iii) changes in formats at the same repository; (iv) possible duplicative, inconsistent and erroneous data. This chapter addresses the first three challenges in the context of providing news

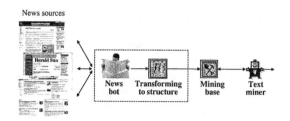

Fig. 3. The news mining portion of the system

to the negotiation table. The scope of the chapter covers the universal news bot shown within the dashed rectangle in Fig. 2 and separately in Fig. 3. The techniques considered in this chapter are applicable for both scenarios; however, the details are beyond the scope of the chapter.

1.1 On-line News Media

Obtaining and verifying information from on-line sources takes time and resources. To reduce the impact of some delay factors on the net, the architecture of the data mining system in Fig. 2 allows not only just-in-time operation, but also 'pre-fetching' some of the information that is expected to be necessary for a scheduled negotiation. In the context of news mining, the news bots fetch the news, which then are transformed into a structured form and both the structured and unstructured data are stored in the mining base (see Fig. 3) for accessing by the mining agents (The fragment selected illustrated in Fig. 3 shows only the text mining agent).

The news sources on the Internet include the web sites of major news papers. The development of algorithms for finding the correct URLs that contain the requested news articles is within the scope of the intelligent crawler research. Major search engines, including Google (shown in Fig. 4) and Yahoo provide functionality for news searching with user provided keywords. These news portals provide convenient interface for humans; answering queries in a way similar to conventional search engine interface (see Fig. 5).

Within the framework of curious negotiator, a generic news bot should be able to retrieve automatically, classify and store the news article obtained by a search engine in an efficient way that can be further used by the other mining agents. The initiation of the process in just-in-time mode can be by the negotiation agent (scenario "A" in Fig. 1) or the human player (scenario "SA" in Fig. 1). In pre-fetch mode, a source monitoring agent is subscribed to the email digests that these sources distribute [10]. These sources include 2-3 sentence news abstract and the corresponding URLs for retrieving the full articles. The trigger for fetching an article can be a negotiation scheduler, using as initial information the topic, the list of items and the description of participants.

However, the automatic retrieval by a computer program of an individual news article from the URL that is obtained either from search results or from the pre-fetched list is a tedious job since the news content can come from different web sites. Different news sources have different layout and format as illustrated by the two examples of news web sites in Fig. 6 and Fig. 7. The layout may vary from time to time even in the news coming from the same source. Hence when automating news retrieval, even for the same news site, it is impractical to develop a static template, as it will stop working when the layout is changed. It is even more impractical (if not impossible) to develop a predefined program (template) for each news web site in the whole Internet. In this chapter we present a more generic approach to retrieve news articles regardless the web site format and bringing them to the smart data mining system of the curious negotiator.

Fig. 4. Example of specialised news search engines web interfaces

Fig. 5. Example of specialised news search engines web interfaces – response to a query

Fig. 6. A version of SMH news site format

Fig. 7. A version of Herald Sun news site format

2 The Universal News Bot Approach

Data extraction process from Web documents is usually performed by software modules called wrappers. As explained in the previous section, hard-coded wrapper based on using static template is tedious, error-prone and difficult to maintain. To overcome this limitation, significant research has been done in the area of wrapper induction. It typically applies machine learning technology to generate wrappers automatically [11, 12]. WIEN is the first wrapper induction system that defined six wrapper classes (templates) to express the structures of web sites [13, 14]. STALKER - a wrapper, more efficient than WIEN [15], treats a web page as a tree-like structure and handles information extraction hierarchically. Gao and Sterling [16] have also done significant work on knowledge-based information extraction from the Internet. However, most of the earlier wrapper techniques were tailored to particular types of documents and none are specific for news content retrieval. The more recent techniques aim on data extraction from general semi-structured documents. The application of general content identification and retrieval methods to news data brings unnecessary overhead in processing. This chapter proposes a technique that detects and takes into account the characteristics of news web pages. Without loss of generality, the approach improves the processing efficiency and requires neither user specified examples nor a priori knowledge of the pages.

2.1 The Data Extraction Method

The data extraction process is divided into three stages. The logical structure of the tagged (in our case, HTML) file is firstly identified and the text, which is most likely to be the news article, is extracted. During the second stage a filter is dynamically built and some extra text is filtered out if multiple documents from the same web site are available. During the third stage extracted data is validated by the developed keyword based validation method. The details are presented below.

2.1.1 Stage 1: Identifying the Logical Structure of the Tagged File

News pages normally not only contain the news article, but more often, also related news headings, the news category, advertisements, and sometimes a search box. Although each web site may have a different format, web pages can always be broken down into content blocks. The layout in which these content blocks are arranged varies considerably across sites. The news article is expected to be the content block which is displayed on the "centre" of the page. Therefore, it is reasonable to assume that *the biggest block of text on the news web page is the news article*. Similar to McKeown et al.'s [17] approach, the biggest block of text is detected by counting the number of words in each block.

Most of web sites employ visible and invisible tables in conjunction with Cascading Style Sheets (CSS) to arrange their logical structures by using HTML table tags [18]. Tables are designed to organize data into logical rows and columns. A table is enclosed within the <table></table> tag. Nested tables are normally used to form a complex layout structure. It is common for news web sites to display advertisements within news articles to attract reader's attention. This is normally done by inserting nested tables that contain advertisements and other contents in the table that contains the news article. The pseudo code of the process is presented in Fig. 8.

2.1.2 Stage 2: Building Internal Filters Dynamically

Although most of news web sites use tables for partitioning content blocks, there are some web sites that use other methods. Also, even for the web pages that use tables as the partition method, the table with the news article may contain a few extra lines of text at the beginning or the end of the article. Therefore, extraction accuracy can be improved by developing algorithms that do not rely on table tag information.

Input: HTML file
Output: The largest body of text contained in a table
Begin
1. Break down the HTML file into a one dimensional array, where each cell contains a line of text or an HTML tag
2. Remove the HTML tags except <table> and </table>
3. Set *table_counter* to 0
4. For each cell in the array:
    a.   if <table> tag is encountered, increase *table_counter* by 1
    b.   if <\table> tag is encountered, decrease *table_counter* by 1
    c.   if it is a text element, append it to the end of **container**[*table_counter*]
5. Return **container**[*i*] that contains the largest body of text by counting the number of words.
End

Fig. 8. Pseudo code of the algorithm for identifying the largest text block

Many web sites use templates to automatically generate pages and fill them with results of a database query, in particular, for news web sites. Hence, news under the same category from the same source is often with the same format. When two or more web pages from same source become available, a filter can be constructed by comparing the extracted text from these pages. The filter contains the common header and tail of the text. The text is compared sentence by sentence from the beginning to the end between two files. Common sentences are regarded as part of web page template. Therefore, they should be removed from the file. The pseudo code of the process is shown in Fig. 9.

Once the filter is generated, text is refined by removing the common header and tail text in the filter. Since the filter is dynamically generated, it is adjusted automatically when the web site format is changed.

2.1.3 Stage 3: Keyword Based Validation
Incorrect and out of date URLs can cause errors in the results of data extraction. Such errors can not be identified by the data extracting methods described in the previous sections. A simple validation method based on keyword frequency is developed to validate the data retrieved by the algorithms in Fig. 8 and Fig. 9.

The basic assumption is that a good news title should succinctly express the article's content. Therefore, the words contained in the news title are expected to be normally among the most frequent words appearing in a news article. Consequently, the words from the news title (except the stop words, which are filtered out) are considered as keywords. For situations when the news title is not available at the time of text extraction, the words in the first paragraph of the extracted data are considered as keywords, based on the assumption that title is always placed at the beginning of an article. The extracted text is regarded as the requested news article if it satisfies the following condition:

Input: two text files from the same web site, each contains a news article
Output: a data structure contains:
    String *URL*
    String *Header*
    String *Tail*
Begin
  1. Remove all the html tags in the files.
  2. Break down the files into one dimensional arrays (a and b), each cell contains a line of text.
  3. For each cell of the array from beginning
      1. if **a**[*i*] == **b**[*i*], append **a**[*i*] at the end of *Header* string
      2. if **a**[*i*] != **b**[*i*], break;
  4. For each cell of the array from the end
      1. if **a**[*i*] == **b**[*i*], insert **a**[*i*] at the beginning of *Tail* string
      2. if **a**[*i*] != **b**[*i*], break
  5. Set the *URL* value to the common part of the URLs of two text files
  Return the data structure that contains *URL*, *Header* and *Tail*.
End

Fig. 9. The pseudo code of dynamic filter generation

$$\min\left(w_1 \frac{l_t}{l_m}, w_2 \frac{n_k}{t_k}, w_3 k_f \right) > th1 \tag{1}$$

where:

l_t	total length
l_m	minimum length (predefined)
n_k	the number of keyword that appears in the text at least once
t_k	total number of keywords
k_f	average keyword frequency
w_1, w_2, w_3	weighting values
$th1$	threshold value (predefined)

The first term in equation (1) considers the total length of the extracted text. If the text length is unreasonably short, the text is unlikely to be a news article. The second term in the equation represents the percentage of the keywords that appeared in the text. The third term in the equation stands for the average frequency of the keywords that appeared in the text. The validation value takes the minimum value of these three and then compares with a predefined threshold to validate if the extracted text is the news article.

3   News Data Set Construction

The news data set for a given specific topic that will be used as the information source for the negotiation table is dynamically constructed from on-line news articles. In stead of simply searching for keywords, the data mining agent constructs the news data set according to the concept related to the given keywords. Similar to using a search engine, the negotiation agent provides a phrase or several keywords to the data mining agent to define the topic of the news it requests. The data mining agent submits the query to a news search engine. In general, large amount of search results are returned. The data mining agent only retrieves the most relevant data evaluated by the keyword frequency and their proximity position. Based on the assumption that a concept can be represented by a set of keywords, which occur frequently inside particular collection of documents, the most frequent keywords (terms) from the retrieved data set are extracted and considered to be related to the same concept. The extracted keywords are resubmitted to the search engine. The process of query submission, data retrieval and keyword extraction is repeated until the search results start to derail from the given topic. The news articles used in this section are extracted from HTML files by the algorithms described in Section 2.

3.1   Key Phrase Extraction

As it is introduced in the previous section, key phrase extraction plays an important role in the data set construction process in this project. Many studies have been conducted in the area of automatic keyword generation from text documents. Most of these methods are based on syntactic analysis using statistical co-occurrence of word types in text and vector space representation of the documents [19]. Hulth [20] suggested the quality of keywords generated by frequency analysis was significantly improved when a domain specific thesaurus is used as a second knowledge source. Therefore, a similar approach that employs a domain specific thesaurus in the key phrase extraction process is adopted in this project. Since the frequently used words represent the topic of a document in greater degree than less frequently used words, the frequency of the words and phrases predefined in the domain thesaurus that appear in the documents are calculated and the top ranked words or phrases are considered as the keywords.

There are many publications on automatic thesaurus construction. We applied a relatively simple approach based on word frequency count. The news articles in many news web sites are organized into the categories of: World, National, Business, Science (Technology), Sport and Entertainment. To build the domain specific thesaurus, a large number of news articles under each category are collected, and each of such categories represents a domain. Fig. 10 shows the steps of building the database of key phases for each category (the domain thesauri). Word stemming problem was resolved by using a simple stemming algorithm by which two words are considered to have the same stem if they have the same beginnings and their endings differ in one or two characters [21]. Stop words are not counted in each document.

Input: document collection of each category
Output: collection of key phases for each category
Begin
    1.   define the initial number of document (*ni*) to be used
    2.   for each category
          a. randomly select *ni* articles from the working category to form document cluster A
          b. randomly select *ni/(total_number_of_category-1)* articles from every other category to form document cluster B
          c. calculate the total frequency of keywords and key phases of clusters A and B
          d. generate the list of most frequent keywords (phrases) of cluster A (list A) and cluster B (list B) according to the ranking of the frequency.
          e. remove the keywords (phrases) in list A if they also appear in list B
          f. increase the number of the articles to be selected by 10%
          g. repeat from a to e to generate a new list of most frequent keywords (phases) and compare with the list generated by the last run. If the difference between two lists is smaller than a predefined threshold, stop the process and the latest list of most frequent keyword (phase) is used as the keywords to define the current working domain.
End

Fig. 10. The pseudo code of domain thesaurus construction

In 2.c of the process in Fig. 10, a sequence of words is defined as a phrase if it satisfies the condition:

$$\frac{f_{seq}}{f_{average}} > th2 \tag{2}$$

where:

f_{seq} frequency of the sequence of words that appears in the same sentence in the whole cluster

$f_{average}$ average frequency of each word in the sequence.

$th2$ threshold value (predefined)

3.2 News Data Set Construction Process

The news data set is constructed by repeating the news retrieval and keyword extraction process. Fig. 11 shows the detail procedure of the construction process. The news data domain is determined by searching the initially provided keywords (phase) in the domain thesauri.

Input: domain thesauri, initial keywords
Output: news data set
Begin
1. determine the domain thesaurus to be used according to the initial keywords
2. search and retrieve the news articles that contain the given keywords.
3. put the retrieved news articles into the news data set container.
4. calculate the total frequency of each keyword and phrase in the domain thesaurus that appears in the articles just retrieved and rank them from most frequent to less frequent.
5. if the ranking of the initial keywords is not higher than a predefined threshold, return the news data set.
6. calculate the total frequency of each keyword and phrase in the domain thesaurus that appears in each article in the whole data set and rank them.
7. select one phrase or two keywords with the highest frequency that have not been used for searching as the new keywords for next search.
8. goto step 2.
End

Fig. 11. The pseudo code of news data set construction for a given concept

4   Experimental Results

Experiments have been conducted in two steps: first to evaluate the news extraction algorithm. Second, a news data set was constructed and manually examined.

4.1   News Extraction

The proposed methods of extracting news articles were evaluated by the experiments using some of the most popular Australian and International news web sites, which are listed in Table 1. 200 pages from each web site were tested. The average processing time for each page was 436 milliseconds on a Pentium 4 1.60 GHz computer. The notions used in the table are explained below:

- *Correct* – on average 0% error rate in the extracted text of a single web page;
- *Minor Error* – on average less than 5% error rate in the extracted text of a single web page;
- *Major Error* – on average between 5% to 30% error rates in the extracted text of a single web page;
- *Error* – on average more than 30% error rate in the extracted text of a single web page

Experiment results show that news articles were mostly extracted properly except BBC News (UK). After a detailed manual analysis of these web pages, it was found

Table 1. News sites for testing the news article extraction algorithm and the results

URL Location	Accuracy [without Filter]	Accuracy [with Filter]
www.smh.com.au/national	Minor Error	Correct
www.smh.com/business	Minor Error	Correct
www.usatoday.com/news/world	Minor Error	Minor Error (Error Rate Reduced)
www.usatoday.com/news/nation	Minor Error	Minor Error (Error Rate Reduced)
http://abcnews.go.com/sections/us	Minor Error	Correct
http://abcnews.go.com/sections/world	Minor Error	Correct
http://money.cnn.com	Correct	Correct
www.cnn.com/ALLPOLITICS/	Minor Error	Correct
www.theaustralian.news.com.au	Correct	Correct
http://news.bbc.co.uk/2/hi/business	Major Error	Minor Error
http://news.bbc.co.uk/2/hi/asia-pacific	Minor Error	Minor Error (Error Rate Reduced)
http://www.reuters.com	Correct	Correct
http://news.ft.com (Financial Times)	Correct	Correct
http://dailytelegraph.news.com.au	Minor Error	Correct
www.iht.com (International Herald Tribune)	Correct	Correct
http://www.dailytimes.com.pk	Correct	Correct
http://news.xinhuanet.com/english	Correct	Correct
http://www.abc.net.au/news	Minor Error	Correct
http://news.ninemsn.com.au	Correct	Correct

that they contained more than one content block in the table that also contains the news article, namely, the news article only occupies one of the table cells. Therefore, more experiments were conducted on this web site by using multiple documents. Experiment results show that the accuracy rate have been improved dramatically. Although during the first step in our process the content block is not correctly classified and other content blocks in the table are also extracted, these extra content blocks are then removed by the filtering process during the second step.

As it is shown in Table 1, by using the dynamically generated filter, the extraction accuracy has been improved considerably. The experiment confirmed the approach, which assumes that the news article is contained in a table formatting structure, and the advertisements and other content block data are embedded in a nested table structure within the news article table, works well. This layout method is commonly used in most news web sites, which makes proposed algorithms and their implementation practically valuable tools.

During the experiments, the threshold value for validation was set to 1. Different combinations of weighting values have been tested. Experiment results showed that the validation process is highly effective. Moreover, the experimental validation results are not sensitive to the choices of weighting values.

4.2   Constructing a News Data Set

An experiment was conducted to build a news data set from keywords "Interest Rate". As there are large amount of news on the internet, this experiment restricted the time frame to 1 week and news sources within Australia.

Domain thesauri were constructed by using 500 articles from each category: World, National, Business, Science (Technology), Sport and Entertainment. After the domain thesauri have been constructed, their data remain the same for the whole experiment.

Table 2 shows the keywords (phases) used for each new search and the number of articles retrieved. The keywords for the next search were extracted from the data in the data set that has been constructed so far instead of the data from the last search results. The search process stops when the initial keywords are no longer in the most frequent keyword list generated from the last search results.

In total, the news data set contains 102 news articles. Each article in the data set was manually examined. Their contents are all within the scope of "interest rate". Once the data set is constructed, it will be further processed and used as the information source for the negotiation agent.

Table 2. The keywords used for each search in a data set construction process

Keywords (phases) Used for the Search	Number of Most Related Articles Retrieved	Most Frequent Keywords
Interest Rate	23	interest rate, housing market, bank, price, bond, finance, loan ...
Housing Market	10	housing market, finance, interest rate, price, value, bank ...
Price, Bank	30	bank, price, interest rate, share, oil, economy, stock ...
Finance, Bond	12	Bond, finance, housing market, interest rate, investor, price ...
Share, Investor	27	Share, investor, housing market, bank, price, finance, value ...

5 Bringing the News to the Negotiation Table

The above described tools can be used directly in the "semi-automatic" negotiation scenario (scenario "SA" in Fig. 11). In this case, the information request can be initiated either by the human participant or by the negotiation agent. In both cases the keywords for initiating the news "hunt" can be extracted out of the negotiation utterances. In the case, when the negotiation agent requests the news, the keywords are filtered automatically from the dialogue and are passed to the news extraction bots (possibly with some weights based on the relative intensity with which they occur during the negotiation). In the "SA" scenario, the body of the article together with a date/time stamp and the source identifier is sufficient, as the information is assessed by the human player. An information table that contains the retrieved news text, validity of the data, most frequent keywords and other parameters is delivered to an information aggregation agent for further processing so that the information can be used by the negotiation agent efficiently. The detailed discussion of the automated utilisation of retrieved information is beyond the scope of this chapter.

6 Conclusions and Future Work

The curious negotiator is our long term work in automated negotiation systems. It will blend 'strategic negotiation sense' with 'strategic information sense' as the negotiation unfolds. This requires a system capable of providing information to the "negotiation table". Smart data mining systems that support the negotiation agents are expected to operate under time-constraints and over dynamically changing corpus of information. They will need to determine the sources of information, the confidence and validity of these sources and a way of combining extracted information (models).

In this chapter, we presented a method to extract relevant news article from news web sites regardless of the format and layout of the source. The article's logical structure is firstly identified by using the table tags in the tagged files. An internal dynamic filter is built to further clean up the data. Finally, a validation method is developed to validate the retrieved data. Experiment results confirm that the overall approach and the corresponding methodology and algorithms can be applied to most news web sites with reasonable accuracy.

In the case when a Web page is not partitioned by table tags, the proposed method relies on the availability of a second document from the same web site. Although using tables for page layout is the most popular method, other content partition methods should also be implemented in the system to improve the extraction accuracy.

Though developed for the curious negotiator, the proposed methods can be applied for content extraction from tagged documents in mobile phone and PDA browsing area. Mobile phone and PDA have relatively slow internet access and a small display area. Therefore, the presented algorithms can be applied for automatic detection and display of articles from news web sites on such devices with improved efficiency and visual effect.

Acknowledgements

This research is supported by the Australian Research Council.

References

1. Simoff, S. J. and J. K. Debenham: Curious negotiator. Proceedings of The Int. Conference on Cooperative Information Agents, CIA-2002, Madrid, Spain, Springer, Heidelberg (2002).
2. Gerding, E. H., D. D. B. van Bragt, et al.: Multi-issue negotiation processes by evolutionary simulation: validation and social extensions. Proceedings Workshop on Complex Behavior in Economics. Aix-en-Provence, France, (2000).
3. Gomes, A. and P. Jehiel: Dynamic process of social and economic interactions: On the persistence of inefficiencies. Journal of Political Economy 113 (3), (2005) 626-667.
4. Kraus, S.: Strategic Negotiation in Multiagent Environments. Cambridge, MA, MIT Press (2001).
5. Ströbel, M.: Design of Roles and Protocols for Electronic Negotiations. Electronic Commerce Research Journal, Special Issue on Market Design (2001).
6. Milgrom, P. and R. A. Weber: Theory of Auctions with Competitive Bidding. Econometrica, 50 (5), (1982) 1089-1122.
7. Watkins, M.: Breakthrough Business Negotiation-A Toolbox for Managers, Jossey-Bass (2002).
8. Hand, D., H. Mannila, et al.: Principles of Data Mining. Cambridge, MA, MIT Press (2001).
9. Franz, M., A. Ittycheriah, et al.: First Story Detection: Combining Similarity and Novelty Based Approaches. In Topic Detection and Tracking Workshop Report, (2001)
10. Simoff, S. J. and J. K. Debenham: Time-constrained support for decision-making in e-market environments. Proceedings of the 6th International Conference of The International Society for Decision Support Systems ISDSS'01, London, UK, (2001), pp 193-206.
11. Chidlovskii, B., J. Ragetli, et al.: Automatic wrapper generation for web search engines. Proceedings of the 1st International Conference on Web-Age Information Management WAIM'00, Springer. (2000).
12. Freitag, D. and N. Kushmerick: Boosted wrapper induction. Proceedings of the 17th National Conference on Artificial Intelligence AAAI-2000. (2000).
13. Kushmerick, N. and B. Grace: The wrapper induction environment. Workshop on Software Tools for Developing Agents, AAAI-98. (1998).
14. Kushmerick, N.: Wrapper induction: Efficiency and expressiveness. Artificial Intelligence 118(1-2): 15-68. (2000)
15. Muslea, I., S. Minton, et al.: STALKER: Learning extraction rules for semistructured, Web-based information sources. Proceedings of AAAI-98 Workshop on AI and Information Integration, Menlo Park, CA, AAAI Press. (1998).
16. Gao, X. and L. Sterling: Semi-structured Data Extraction from Heterogeneous Sources. In T. Bratjevik D. Schwartz, M. Divitini, editor,Internet-based Knowledge Management and Organizational Memories, pages 83--102. Idea Group Publishing. (2000).
17. McKeown, K. R., R. Barzilay, et al.: Columbia multi-document summarization: Approach and evaluation. Proceedings of the Workshop on Text Summarization, ACM SIGIR Conference, DARPA/NIST Document Understanding Conferences (DUC). (2001).

18. Lin, S. H. and J. M. Ho: Discovering informative content blocks from Web documents. Proceedings of the Eighth ACM SIGKDD International Conference on Knowledge Discovery and Data Mining KDD2002, ACM Press. (2002).
19. Salton, G.: Automatic Text Processing:The Transformation, Analysis and Retrieval of Information by Computer. Addison-Wesley, (1989).
20. Hulth, A., J. Karlgren, A. Jonsson, H. Boström and L. Asker: Automatic Keyword Extraction Using Domain Knowledge, Proceedings of Second International Conference on Computational Linguistics and Intelligent Text Processing. *(CICLing 2001)*. Mexico City, February 2001. LNCS 2004, Springer.
21. Andrade M, and A. Valencia: Automatic extraction of keywords from scientific text: application to the knowledge domain of protein families, Bioinformatics (14) 600-607, (1998).

Text Mining for Insurance Claim Cost Prediction

Inna Kolyshkina and Marcel van Rooyen

This project was done in PricewaterhouseCoopers, Sydney, Australia
Phone: +61-2-8266-1429, Fax: +61-2-8286-1429
inna.kolyshkina@au.pwc.com, marcel.van.rooyen@au.pwc.com

Abstract. The paper presents the findings of an industry-based study in the utility of text mining. The purpose of the study was to evaluate the impact of textual information in claims cost prediction. The industrial research setting was a large Australian insurance company. The data mining methodologies used in this research included text mining, and the application of the results from the text mining in subsequent predictive data mining models. The researchers used software of the leading commercial vendors. The research found commercially interesting utility in textual information for claim cost prediction, and also identified new risk management factors.

Keywords: text mining, predictive model, insurance claim prediction, risk management.

1 Introduction

Claims cost prediction is an important focus area for insurance companies. The reason is that proactive case management can significantly reduce the final claims pay-out value. The issue is particularly relevant, when considered that a small number of cases amount to a disproportionately big portion of total claims pay-out value. It follows that small improvements in claims pay-out value prediction, may bring significant financial benefits to insurance companies.

There has been recognition for some time now that data about incidents contain information which allows for a proactive risk management approach (Feyer and Williamson 1998, p.1). The large size of insurance databases is making data mining an increasingly attractive tool for analysis compared to traditional analytical methods (Kolyshkina, Steinberg et al. 2003, p.493). Up to 80% of this data is in unstructured textual format (Feldman 2003, p.481). Realising the potential value of information resident in this textual data, there is growing interest by insurers in the application of new text mining techniques (Feyer, Stout et al. 2001). We refer to an example where text mining analysis of narrative fields about claims, resulted in beneficial claims management and fraud detection in the occupational injury insurance domain (Stout 1998). In the example, the benefits stemmed from information in the textual narrative data, which was not present in the existing coding system.

This paper shows how textual data can be directly included in the claim analysis and used to improve prediction of pay-out value of insurance claims.

G.J. Williams and S.J. Simoff (Eds.): Data Mining, LNAI 3755, pp. 192–202, 2006.
© Springer-Verlag Berlin Heidelberg 2006

The data for the project was provided by a large Australian insurance company. That insurer first wanted to assess the potential value that using text mining facilities could add to the organisation in increasing the precision of claim cost prediction; second to explore the possibilities and benefits of augmenting their existing incident coding system using free text; and thirdly to suggest how text mining could be used for improvement in other areas of the business.

Our approach was to create a model identifying at the time of the incident report, whether the incident would result in a claim pay-out value within the top 10 percent by value, by the end of the next quarter. We assessed the model in terms of the predictive power of textual information on its own, and in terms of textual information adding predictive power to other, non-textual predictors. Predictive power of a model was measured by the cumulative lift the model achieved.

2 Description of Algorithms Used

The researchers used both SAS® Enterprise Miner and SPSS® Clementine text mining software for textual data preparation and text mining. The discovered concepts were similar irrespective of the software package used.

Predictive feature selection and predictive modelling was done using both CART® and TreeNet® (Hastie, Tibshirani et al. 2001). The choice of TreeNet® was because of its high precision in predictive modelling, its effectiveness in selecting predictors, and its resistance to overtraining. CART® models are more easily interpretable than TreeNet® models, therefore the researchers used CART® in conjunction with TreeNet® to assure understandability about the predictive models.

3 Data Description

The first group of data comprised features about claimant demographics, claims pay-out value information, and codings about various aspects of the incident (e.g. about the body part injured). To facilitate the discussion, we name this first group of data TransData. The second group of data which we will name TextData, contained unstructured free-type text fields of about 200 characters each. These fields described the incident and the resulting injury.

Both data groups were identified by claim numbers. The data sets represented all claims reported between 30 September 2002 and 31 March 2004, which were still open at the time of the research. This was an 18 month data history, which provided approximately 56,000 records. The target variable for prediction was a binary indicator (yes/no) of whether or not that injury report had resulted in a claim pay-out value within the top 10 percent by the end of the quarter of the report. The quarter represents a three-month time window of investigation.

4 Description of Analytical Techniques

In Figure 1 we present the research process flow:

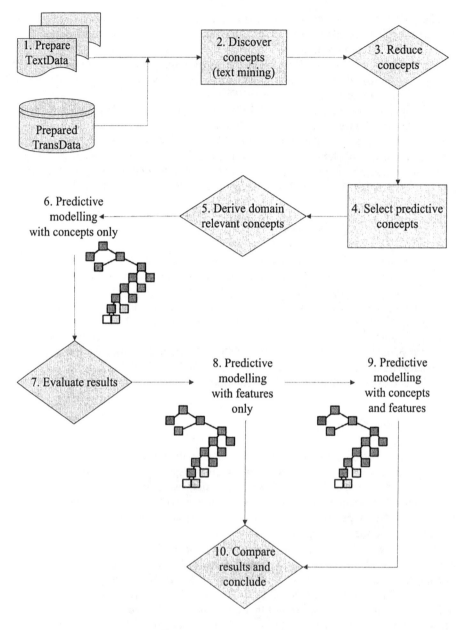

Fig. 1. Research process flow

We will discuss our research process under the following headings. These headings are the same as the labels of the elements of Figure 1.

3.1 Prepare TextData

The process started at point one with the preparation of TextData for text mining. The preparation included routine activities of extracting data, and merging TextData and TransData by the unique claim identity.

3.2 Discover Concepts

We will refer to meaningful words or word combinations resident in the text as "concepts". Text mining is the process of derivation of concepts from unstructured text. This is achieved by applying text mining software to the fields containing free text, where text field is the input and concepts are the outputs. For example, the incident description "the worker fell off horse and broke his leg" may contain such concepts as "worker", "fell off horse", "broken leg".

A concept then leads to creation of the corresponding concept counting variable that assumes the value of n where n is the number of times that the concept is present in the text field. Within this context, text mining can be considered a way of pre-processing unstructured data for use in subsequent modelling. We refer to these concept counting variables from here on as "concept variables".

TextData was mined at point two to derive concept variables. We achieved this by applying SAS ® and SPSS ® text mining software to the data. The mining process was characterised by iterative experimentation to find optimal algorithm settings. These settings included both language and mathematical weightings.

The mining of TextData required not only expertise in the software packages used but also incorporating the subject matter knowledge of the insurance domain.

3.3 Reduce Concepts

About 8000 concepts were discovered in the preceding activity, resulting in a similar number of concept variables. Not only did it prove difficult to make sense of so many concepts, but it would also make subsequent analysis intractable. Further, concepts with a low frequency would not be relevant within our context. Therefore at point three the researchers filtered out those concepts which had a frequency of less than 50 in TextData. After filtering 860 concept variables remained. The issue of the predictive value of concepts now needed resolution. We had prior knowledge about the predictive value of the data features in TransData from existing modelling by the insurer.

3.4 Select Predictive Concepts

The researchers resolved the issue of concept predictability by using TreeNet® at point four to identify the most predictive of the 860 concept variables. We present the nine most predictive concept variables from this step in Table 1. The first column of Table 1 lists the concept variables which were selected by TreeNet®, and the second column states each concept variable's relative predictive importance.

Table 1. Concept importance using TreeNet®

Concept name	Concept importance
LEG	100
LACERATED	99.43
FRACTURE	92.56
STRESS	92.27
EYE	86.56
HERNIA	84.11
TRUCK	82.62
BURN	73.06
LADDER	58
...	...

3.5 Derive Domain-Relevant Concepts

The researchers depended on insurance domain expertise for deriving additional features at point five. This encompassed the grouping and combining of concepts e.g. 'to injure' and 'to hurt' were set as equivalent terms. Concept derivation was assisted by referring to other targets in addition to the predicted target.

3.6 Predictive Modelling with Concepts Only

At point six the researchers built one TreeNet® and one CART® predictive model for claims cost, using only the concept variables as predictors. The purpose of building the models was to discover the predictive potential of the text-derived concepts. TreeNet® models are known to be highly predictive, but difficult to interpret. Decision trees offer more interpretable results in the form of easily understandable split rules. We therefore also built a CART® decision tree model for improving the interpretability of results for the business.

3.7 Evaluate Results

At point seven the researchers evaluated these two models based on the concepts alone by referring to model topology, gains charts, and model accuracy. The TreeNet® model was 75.7% precise on test data. We present the gains charts for the two models in Figure 2:

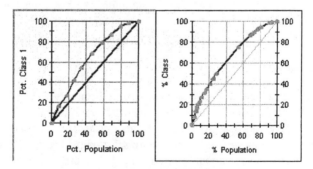

Fig. 2. Gains chart TreeNet® (left)and CART® (right)

From these CART® and TreeNet® gains charts we evaluated that the concepts had predictive potential. We show the reduced model topology from CART® in Figure 3:

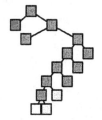

Fig. 3. Topology CART® model using concepts only

CART® tree diagram above is easy to interpret. The first split is on the concept 'eye', followed by 'lacerated', 'stress', 'fracture', 'hernia', 'truck', and 'ladder'. Blue colour indicates lower claim cost while red colour indicates higher claim cost. This topology made domain sense, since eye-related claims have a relatively low cost, as do laceration-related claims.

Table 2. Concept importance using CART®

Concept name	Concept importance
GROUP_EYE	100
GROUP_LACERATED	72.61
FOREIGN BODY	60.85
GROUP_STRESS	60.25
GROUP_FRACTURE	50.45
HERNIA	20.91
KNIFE	14.43
GROUP_LADDER	12.93

In Table 2 we present the most important concepts as identified by this CART® model. The concept names which start with GROUP_, are derived concepts from step five.

3.8 Predictive Modelling with Features Only – Creating a Reference Base

The question of interest for the client was whether adding textual data to the model can improve prediction of claim cost based on existing incident codes. Further, domain experts suggested that textual information may be particularly useful for improving prediction precision where there is high variance in claim pay-out value. This last class of cases was presented in our data by certain injury codes.

To prove that text adds value to the codes, we built two models using only TransData features i.e. there were no concepts in these models. We present the results from these models in section 3.10, where we also compare them to the models which we build at point 9.

The first model we build at point 8 was a CART® model, and we called that model C1. C1 was build using data from all injury codes, in order to maintain understandability for the client across all codes. We built the second model using TreeNet®, and called it called T1. T1 was built using only observations which represented high variance claims pay-out injury codes. This was do demonstrate the potency of concepts in improving predictability in on a high-variance problem.

3.9 Compare Results and Conclude that Concepts Improve Predictive Accuracy

At point nine we build one more CART® model and one more TreeNet® model, also predicting claims pay-out. In these two models we combined TransData features with predictive concept variables from TextData. The combined CART® model (called C2) we built on the same data sets as C1 above. The combined TreeNet® model (called T2) we build on the same data sets as T1 above.

In the next section we will compare the results from these four models, and make inference about the contribution of the concepts to predictive accuracy about claims cost.

3.10 Compare Results and Conclude

We present the gains charts of the C1 and C2 models in Figure 4:

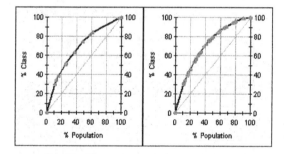

Fig. 4. Gains chart CART® models – C1 left and C2 right

Comparing the two gains charts shows about a 5% increase in predictive performance of C2 over C1. In Figure 5 we present the gains charts of TreeNet® models T1 and T2:

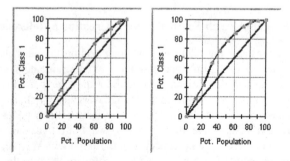

Fig. 5. Gains charts TreeNet® – T1 left and T2 right

The gains chart of T2 shows about a 10% improvement over the gains chart of T1. We note that this improvement is twice as much as the improvement over the full data set (C2 over C1). This is consistent with the idea that textual features add value to claims pay-out prediction in high-variance injury code categories.

We attribute the increase in predictive value of the combined models, to resolution which is added to the models by the addition of the concepts. In Figure 6 we display the additional resolution in the C2 CART® model.

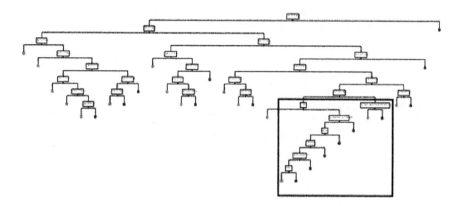

Fig. 6. Additional CART® model resolution from concepts

The binary splits outside the boxed area in Figure 6, are on features from TransData e.g. injury location (part of body), nature of the injury, and mechanism of the injury. The splits inside the square were on concepts from TextData. The concepts found in the square are not covered by the insurer's existing coding system. Examples of such concepts were 'truck', 'roof', and 'ladder'. Such concepts can also be useful in identifying particular industry OH&S issues, which require proactive risk management strategies.

From the above results, the researchers conclude that the combined models had increased predictive precision in claim cost prediction, compared to the models with TransData features only. The conclusion is valid for the full data set, as well as for the high variance data subset.

Mining unstructured textual data therefore did improve the prediction of insurance claims cost. We also discovered new concepts which complement the insurer's existing coding system. The next section contains ideas about how text mining could be used for improving other areas of the insurer's business.

4   Potential Applications of Text Mining by the Insurance Industry

The researchers offer their impressions of some possible uses of text mining in the insurance industry;

o first, we perceive application in an insurer's capital management. Improved prediction about future insurance claims cost, should bring about improvements in the quantification of re-insurance needs. Such quantification about needs will be invaluable in negotiating favourable re-insurance premiums, and terms and conditions, with re-insurers. Further, such quantification should assist with better planning about working capital requirements for that portion of their risk which is not re-insurable;

o a second potential application is where textual data from the incident investigation is available for analysis. Insurers could identify new risk factors, and previously unknown interactions between known risk factors. Such knowledge would enable insurers to develop industry-specific proactive risk management practices with their insured clients, with consequential financial benefits to both parties;

o a third potential application is where textual data is available from after-the-event therapy sessions with victims. Here, text mining could be used to discover concepts about victims' attitude about and perception of risk, leading up to the risk event (Dedobbeleer and Béland 1998). Knowing such psychographic factors will enable insurers to develop industry-specific, proactive behaviour management programs with their clients. Such programs could bring about paradigm shift in the approach to risk management;

o a further potential application is quality control of the application of incident codlings in reporting systems, and for development of new incident reporting and investigation business rules;

o further, in those cases where textual data is available from market research interviews with potential retail insurance customers, text mining can be used to discover consumers' attitudes about, and needs for insurance. Such concepts can then be used for segmenting the retail market simultaneously for attitude and need, using conceptual clustering techniques. Such multi-dimensional market segmentation would enable insurance retailers to develop campaign offers which are much better matched to consumer needs and attitudes, than what is possible, for instance, with demographic segmentation approaches. Such campaign offers will result in better campaign response rates, and improved competitive advantage for insurers (Berry and Linoff 2004) Chapter 4;

o the use of the data mining techniques has been shown to be effective in fraud detection and prevention (Phua, Lee et al. Submitted). Text mining is already being used in the insurance claims fraud discovery and prevention arena (Mailvaganam Accessed February 2005) (Ellingworth and Sullivan Accessed February 2005), and the researchers perceive an underutilised opportunity by the insurance industry. This entails mining unstructured textual data from claimants' contact with the insurer. Such mining would be focused at discovering both known and new concepts from that data, upon which to base both proactive and remedial fraud management.

5 Future Work

The researchers identify a number of issues which require further research. The first is investigating the value of text mining in predicting other targets of interest to the insurance industry. Such other targets could be 'number of days off work', 'cost of medical treatment', or 'exact claim pay-out amount'.

Further, research could extend the modelling time horizon about the target past the current three-month period, to for instance six months or even 12 months. This will enable insurers to accordingly extend their planning horizon about claims cost. Research about the utility of text mining for business rule development and fraud management could be valuable.

Research is also required into some of the opportunities identified in the previous section to:

o quantify the dollar benefits from improved capital management which is realisable from text mining;

o discover new risk factors or interactions between risk factors;

o use text mining as a psychographic profiling and segmenting tool; and

o quantify the monetary benefits from marketing campaigns based upon this psychographic approach compared to traditional marketing approaches.

Acknowledgements

The researchers acknowledge the contributions to this research of Michael Playford and Anne-Marie Feyer, both PricewaterhouseCoopers partners, for offering help and valuable insights. Dominic Roe, consultant PricewaterhouseCoopers, and Bianca Zubac, student UNSW for their assistance in project facilitation and data analysis. SAS Institute and SPSS, both for providing text mining software for the project as well as for assistance and guidance in using text mining software.

References

Berry, M. J. A. and G. S. Linoff (2004). Data Mining Techniques for Marketing, Sales, and Customer Relationship Management. Indianapolis, Wiley.

Dedobbeleer, N. and F. Béland (1998). Is risk perception one of the dimensions of safety climate? Occupational Injury: Risk, Prevention and Intervention. A.-M. Feyer and A. Williamson. London, Taylor & Francis: 73-81.

Ellingworth, M. and D. Sullivan (Accessed February 2005). Text Mining Improves Business Intelligence and Predictive Modelling in Insurance, http://www.dwreview.com/article_sub. cfm?articleId=6995.html. **2005**.

Feldman, R. (2003). Mining Text Data. The Handbook of Data Mining. N. Ye. London, Lawrence Erlbaum Associates: 481-517.

Feyer, A.-M., N. Stout, et al. (2001). "Use of narrative analysis for comparisons of the causes of fatal accidents in three countries: New Zealand, Australia, and the United States." Injury Prevention 7: i15-i20.

Feyer, A.-M. and A. Williamson (1998). Introduction. Occupational Injury: Risk, Prevention and Intervention. A.-M. Feyer and A. Williamson. London, Taylor & Francis: 1-3.

Hastie, T., R. Tibshirani, et al. (2001). The elements of statistical learning: Data mining, inference and prediction. New York, Springer-Verlag.

Kolyshkina, I., D. Steinberg, et al. (2003). Using Data Mining for Modeling Insurance Risk and Comparison of Data Mining and Linear Modeling Approaches. Intelligent and Other Computational Techniques in Insurance: Theory and Applications. A. F. Shapiro and L. C. Jain. London, World Scientific. **Volume 6:** 493-421.

Mailvaganam, H. (Accessed February 2005). Text Mining for Fraud Detection: Creating cost effective data mining solutions for fraud analysis, http://www.dwreview.com/Data_mining/ Effective_Text_Mining.html . **2005**.

Phua, C., V. Lee, et al. (Submitted). "A Comprehensive Survey of Data Mining-based Fraud Detection Research." Submitted.

Stout, N. (1998). Analysis of narrative text fields in occupational injury data. Occupational Injury: Risk, Prevention and Intervention. A.-M. Feyer and A. Williamson. London, Taylor & Francis: 15-20.

An Application of Time-Changing Feature Selection

Yihao Zhang[1], Mehmet A. Orgun[1], Weiqiang Lin[2], and Warwick Graco[2]

[1] Department of Computing, I.C.S.,
Macquarie University Sydney, NSW 2109, Australia
{yihao, mehmet}@ics.mq.edu.au
[2] Australian Taxation Office, Canberra ACT 2601, Australia
{wei.lin, graco.warwick}@ato.gov.au

Abstract. This paper describes a time-changing feature selection[1] framework based on hierachical distribution method for extracting knowledge from health records. In the framework, we propose three steps for time-changing feature selection. The first step is a qualitative-based search, to find qualitative features (or, structural time-changing features). The second step performs a quantitative-based search, to find quantitative features (or, value time-changing features). In the third step, the results from the first two steps are combined to form hybrid search models to select a subset of global time-changing features according to a certain criterion of medical experts. The present application of the time-changing feature selection method involves time-changing episode history, an integral part of medical health records and it also provides some challenges in time-changing data mining techniques. The application task was to examine time related features of medical treatment services for diabetics. This was approached by clustering patients into groups receiving similar patterns of care and visualising the features devised to highlight interesting patterns of care.

Keywords: time-changing data mining, event sequence, time-changing feature selection, hierarchical distribution, health records.

1 Introduction

A huge amount of data is collected every minute in the form of event time-changing sequences. Temporal data mining is concerned with discovering time-changing knowledge from these time-changing sequences. But one of basic problems of time-changing data mining is selecting useful and sufficient features for mining time-changing knowledge. Although a lot of work has been done on discovering time-changing patterns such as periodic patterns and similar patterns in discrete-valued time series (DTS) datasets(e.g. [2], [13]), little attention has been paid to the discovery of time-changing patterns or relationships that involve time-changing feature selection. We believe that time-changing feature selection is an important aspect of time-changing data mining.

In this paper we describe a new framework of time-changing feature selection for discovering patterns from time-changing health records. Time-changing feature selection

---

[1] Feature is also called in other names such as attribute, property and characteristic.

G.J. Williams and S.J. Simoff (Eds.): Data Mining, LNAI 3755, pp. 203–217, 2006.

(also known as time-changing attribute selection) is important to time-changing data mining because each feature component of a time-changing observation is based on time-changing measurements. The goal of time-changing feature selection is to make the error distribution on data mining results of time-changing behaviour (e.g., time-changing pattern, time-changing rules, time-changing cluster and so on.) as small as possible. In fact, the feature space of a large set of time-changing records is large and sparse, making it difficult for time-changing data mining to build good tempora data models. For example time-changing noise (e.g., noise with uncentainty time component) is one of the important problems in time-changing feature selection which makes meaningful time-changing clustering (or, classification) difficult.

The paper is organised as follows. Section 2 is devoted to the discussion of our framework based on hierarchical distribution for time-changing feature selection. In section 3 we are first to explain briefly the background in Medicare area of our application. Then, describe how our selection methods are applied to time-changing medical service health records and discuss the results of our experiments. Section 4 discusses related work and concludes the paper with a brief summary of our contributions.

2   Hierarchical Time-Changing Feature Selection

In this section, we present our hierachical time-changing feature selection method in searching and analysing time-changing features for the purpose of Temporal Data Mining.

For an analysis of a real-world time-changing sequence which may contain different kinds and levels of time-changing features such as complete and partial similarity time-changing features and periodicity time-changing features, we consider two groupings of the time-changing sequence,

1. Qualitative-based feature grouping, and
2. Quantitative-based feature grouping.

Then we combine the results from the above two groupings in a hierarchical fashion to obtain the final global time-changing features for time-changing data mining.

2.1   Some Definitions

We first give definitions for what we mean by time-changing feature, then provide some definitions and notations which will be used later.

Definition 1. *Suppose $O_b = \{f_1, f_2, \ldots, f_d\}$ is an observation with features f_j ($1 \leq j \leq d$), if all or some of the features f_j always vary with time, then feature(s) f_j are called time-changing feature(s). Time-changing feature set T_f of a dataset consists of all features that vary with time.*

Definition 2. *Hierachical time-changing feature selection is a process that chooses an optimal time-changing feature subset according to its time-changing feature selection* *from its qualitative-based feature grouping and quantitative-based feature grouping (a certain criterion).*

Our time-changing sequence analysis method is based on a time series measuring method that represents measurements of similiarity (or, disimiliarity) among (or after transformation) the time series data.

Definition 3. *Suppose we have multiple and/or mulitdimensional time-changing series dataset such as*

$$T = \left\{ \begin{pmatrix} t_1 \\ x_1 \end{pmatrix}, \begin{pmatrix} t_2 \\ x_2 \end{pmatrix}, \begin{pmatrix} t_3 \\ x_3 \end{pmatrix}, \ldots, \begin{pmatrix} t_n \\ x_n \end{pmatrix}, \ldots \right\}$$

where t_i is the time vector component of an observation and x_i is the value vector component of the observation, then we define the multiple and/or mulitdimensional time-gap time series $T_g{}^2$ of T as follows:

$$T_g = \left\{ \begin{pmatrix} t_1 - a_1 \\ x_1 \end{pmatrix}, \begin{pmatrix} t_2 - a_2 \\ x_2 \end{pmatrix}, \begin{pmatrix} t_3 - a_3 \\ x_3 \end{pmatrix}, \ldots, \begin{pmatrix} t_n - a_n \\ x_n \end{pmatrix}, \ldots \right\}$$

where $\{a_1, a_2, \ldots, a_n\}$ are values of a function $f(t)$.[3]

For every successive three time points: t_j, t_{j+1} and t_{j+2}, the triple time-changing value of $\{x_{t_j}, x_{t_{j+1}}, x_{t_{j+2}}\}$ has only nine distinct states. That is, let S_s be the same state as prior one, S_u the go-up (or, stonger) state compared with prior one and S_d the go-down (or, weaker) state compared with prior one. Such as

$$S_1 = \{x_{t_j}, x_{t_{j+1}}, x_{t_{j+2}}\} = \{x_{t_j}, S_u, S_u\},$$

$$S_2 = \{x_{t_j}, x_{t_{j+1}}, x_{t_{j+2}}\} = \{x_{t_j}, S_u, S_s\},$$

$$S_1 = \{x_{t_j}, x_{t_{j+1}}, x_{t_{j+2}}\} = \{x_{t_j}, S_u, S_d\},$$

$$S_1 = \{x_{t_j}, x_{t_{j+1}}, x_{t_{j+2}}\} = \{x_{t_j}, S_s, S_u\},$$

$$S_1 = \{x_{t_j}, x_{t_{j+1}}, x_{t_{j+2}}\} = \{x_{t_j}, S_s, S_s\},$$

$$S_1 = \{x_{t_j}, x_{t_{j+1}}, x_{t_{j+2}}\} = \{x_{t_j}, S_s, S_d\},$$

$$S_1 = \{x_{t_j}, x_{t_{j+1}}, x_{t_{j+2}}\} = \{x_{t_j}, S_d, S_u\},$$

$$S_1 = \{x_{t_j}, x_{t_{j+1}}, x_{t_{j+2}}\} = \{x_{t_j}, S_d, S_s\},$$

$$S_1 = \{x_{t_j}, x_{t_{j+1}}, x_{t_{j+2}}\} = \{x_{t_j}, S_d, S_d\},$$

Then we have the following definition of a state-space $\mathcal{S}$:

Definition 4. *Let $\mathcal{S} = \{s1, s2, s3, s4, s5, s6, s7, s8, s9\} = \{(x_j, S_u, S_u), (x_j, S_u, S_s), (x_j, S_u, S_d), (x_j, S_s, S_u), (x_j, S_s, S_s), (x_j, S_s, S_d), (x_j, S_d, S_u), (x_j, S_d, S_s), (x_j, S_d, S_d)\}$, then $\mathcal{S}$ called state-space. If the triple time-changing value of*

---

[2] Sometimes, **time-gap time series** T_g is episode of an time-changing event.

[3] In most cases we choose $t_i - a_i$ as the Euclidean distance between time component of the same behaviour between observations (e.g., $t_i - t_j$ or $t_i - t_{i+1}$).

$\{x_{t_j}, x_{t_{j+1}}, x_{t_{j+2}}\}$ *are all indepentent to each other, then* $S = \{1, 2, \ldots, N\}$ *is also called a state space.*

The meaning of *Data* is a result of something exhibiting certain regularities, something representing a concept of what was observed. In general, *Data* is a triple such as

$$\mathsf{Data} = \{v, \varrho, \rho\}$$

where v represents the quantitative set of the observation that can, at least in principle, be executed by some technical apparatus and ϱ is the qualitative set of the observation and ρ represents the position set of the observation [4].

Here ρ is regarded as a monotonically increasing sequence of natural numbers. Each position in ρ is a time index for the corresponding values in v and ϱ.

Definition 5. *If* $V = \{v, \rho\}$ *is called a* **quantitative set***. If* $Q = \{\varrho, \rho\}$ *is called a* **qualitative set***.*

Example. We now present an example to illustrate the concepts introduced above. Suppose a dataset $\mathcal{D}_t$ consists of 3 months of daily U.S. dollar exchange rate against Canadian dollar (e.g., 90 points):

$$1.318, 1.3215, 1.3235, 1.3181, \ldots, 1.3534, 1.3561, 1.3575, 1.3569, 1.3573$$

It can be transformed into state-space S as a qualitative sequence of the data (here we write i for $s_i \in S$):

$$Q = \{1, 3, \ldots, 1, 1, 3, 9, 7\} \tag{1}$$

Then we have $\mathcal{D}_t = \{d_1, d_2, \ldots, d_m\}$ in the form of both quantitative and qualitative:[5]

$$\mathcal{D}_t = \left\{ \begin{pmatrix} 1.318 \\ 1.3215 \\ 1.3235 \end{pmatrix} \times 1, \begin{pmatrix} 1.3215 \\ 1.3235 \\ 1.3181 \end{pmatrix} \times 3, \ldots, \begin{pmatrix} 1.3561 \\ 1.3575 \\ 1.3569 \end{pmatrix} \times 9, \begin{pmatrix} 1.3575 \\ 1.3569 \\ 1.3573 \end{pmatrix} \times 7 \right\}$$

We can also have $\mathcal{D}_t = \{d_1, d_2, \ldots, d_m\}$ in a natural way to form the sequence in both of the quantitative and qualitative forms:

$$\mathcal{D}_t = \{(1.318) \times 1, (1.3215) \times 3, \ldots, (1.3561) \times 9, (1.3575) \times 7\}$$

This is a principal representation of the sequence in both forms of quantitative and qualitative. It is clear that for any dataset there exist only one quantitative set and only one qualitative set. In other words the resolution of any dataset into its quantitative set and its qualitative set is unique. We will use this form to develop a time-changing feature selection method for data mining purposes in later sections.

---

[4] In fact, v, ϱ and ρ are vectors.

[5] Where the symbol "×" represents a relationship between the data quantitative and data qualitative.

2.2 Hierarchical Feature Selection

We assume that for each successive pair of time points in a DTS, we have $t_{i+1} - t_i$ = $f(c)$ (a uniformly distributed function). We consider the bivariate data (X_{t_1}, Y_{t_1}), ...,(X_{t_n}, Y_{t_n}), which forms an independent and identically distributed sample from a population $(\mathbf{X}, \mathbf{Y})$. For given pairs of data (X_{t_i}, Y_{t_i}), $i = 1, 2, \ldots, N$, we can regard the data as being generated from the model

$$\mathbf{Y}_{t_i} = m(\mathbf{X}_{t_i}) + \sigma(\mathbf{X}_{t_i})\varepsilon \tag{2}$$

where $\mathbf{E}(\varepsilon) = 0$, $\mathbf{Var}(\varepsilon) = 1$, and $\mathbf{X}_{t_i}$ and ε are independent [6].

In other words, the data model also corresponds to its submodels, which are called quantitative data model and qualitative data model, such as:

$$\mathcal{V}_{t_i} = m(\upsilon_{t_i}) + \sigma(\upsilon_{t_i})\varepsilon \tag{3}$$

$$\mathcal{Q}_{t_i} = m(\varrho_{t_i}) + \sigma(\varrho_{t_i})\varepsilon \tag{4}$$

Qualitative Time-Changing Feature Selection. Qualitative time-changing feature selection is based on finding time-changing features from data qualitative set, and the qualitative data set is based on state-space $\mathcal{S}$. We first suppose that a qualitative sequence on $\mathcal{S}$ as a set of structural vector sequences, such as $\{\mathbf{S}_1, \cdots, \mathbf{S}_m\}$, where each $\mathbf{S}_i = (s_{i1}, s_{i2}, \cdots, s_{in})^T$ denotes the n-dimensional time-changing attributes for each time-changing object $\mathbf{S}_i$ that is to be assigned to a prespecified distribution class.

Let $\{\mathcal{Q}_t : t \in \mathsf{N}\}$, where $\mathcal{Q}_t = \{\varrho_1, \varrho_2, \ldots, \varrho_k\}$ is the data qualitative sequence and (for $1 \leq j \leq k$) $\varrho_j \in \mathcal{S} = \{s1, s2, s3, s4, s5, s6, s7, s8, s9\}$, be an irreducible homogeneous qualitative sequence[7] on $\mathcal{S}$, with probability sequence $\Gamma = (\gamma_{ij})$, where for all qualitative states s_i and s_j and times t:

$$\gamma_{ij} = \mathsf{P}(\mathcal{Q}_t = s_{ij})$$

Also we define a probability sequence which is a correlated measure of the relationship of two time-changing features. It is called a correlation ratio sequence for all qualitative states si and sj and times t:

$$\varpi_{ij} = \mathsf{P}(\frac{\mathcal{Q}_t(sj)}{\mathcal{Q}_t(si)}).$$

For each $\mathcal{Q}_t$, there exists a unique, strictly positive, statistical distribution.

Quantitative Time-Changing Feature Selection. On the quantitative time-changing feature selection, we consider the relationship between the response time-changing featur variable $\mathcal{V}_t$ and the vector of time-changing featur variables $\upsilon = (t, \upsilon_1, \ldots, \upsilon_n)^T$. For a given dataset of generated data model 2, the unknown regression function $m(\mathbf{x})$

---

[6] We always denote the conditional variance of $\mathbf{Y}$ given $\mathbf{X} = \mathbf{x}_0$ by $\sigma^2(\mathbf{x}_0)$ and the density of $\mathbf{X}$ by $f(\bullet)$.

[7] $s(i+1)$ only depends on $s(i)$.

is obtained by applying a Taylor expansion of order p in a neighbourhood of $\mathbf{x}_0$ with its remainder ϑ_p,

$$m(\mathbf{x}) = \sum_{j=0}^{p} \frac{m^{(j)}(\mathbf{x}_0)}{j!}(\mathbf{x} - \mathbf{x}_0)^j + \vartheta_p \equiv \sum_{j=0}^{p} \beta_j(\mathbf{x} - \mathbf{x}_0)^j + \vartheta_p.$$

The first stage of methods for detecting the characteristics of those records is to use the linear regression analysis. We may assume linear model $\mathbf{Y} = \mathbf{X}\beta + \varepsilon$. The linear model based upon least square estimation (LSE) is $\hat{\beta} = (\mathbf{X}^T\mathbf{X})^{-1}\mathbf{X}^T\mathbf{Y}$. Then we have: $\hat{\beta} \sim N(\beta, Cov(\hat{\beta}))$. Particularly, for $\hat{\beta}_i$ we have $\hat{\beta}_i \sim N(\beta_i, \sigma_i{}^2)$, where $\sigma_i{}^2 = \sigma^2 a_{ii}$, and a_{ii} is the ith diagonal element of $(\mathbf{X}^T\mathbf{X})^{-1}$.

Now, for the set of pure values, we may fit a local linear model as above and parameters can be estimated under $\mathcal{LSE}$. Then the problem can be formulated as the data distribution functional analysis of discrete-valued time series.

Global Time-Changing Feature Selection. We combine the above two kinds of feature discovery to discover global time-changing features from a time-changing dataset. In the qualitative group, let the qualitative sequence $\{Q_t : t \in \mathsf{N}\}$ be data functional distribution sequence on the state-space $S = \{s1, s2, s3, s4, s5, s6, s7, s8, s9\}$. Then suppose the data quantitative sequence is a nonnegative random vector process $\{V_t; t \in \mathsf{N}\}$ such that, conditional on $S^{(T)} = \{Q_t : t = 1, \ldots, T\}$, the random vector variables $\{V_t : t = 1, \ldots, T\}$ are mutually independent. We give an example later to show how to mine global time-changing features from a dataset.

Suppose that, if $Q_t = si$, $\mathbf{Y}_t$ has a Poisson distribution with mean λ_i, let $E(Y_t \mid Q_t)$, the conditional mean of $\mathbf{Y}_t$ be

$$\mu(t) = \sum_{i=1}^{m} \lambda_i W_i(t),$$

where the random variable $W_i(t)$ is the indicator of the event $\{Q_t = si\}$. The state-dependent probabilities are then given for all nonnegative v by

$$\pi_{vi} = \frac{e^{-\lambda_i}\lambda_i^v}{v!}$$

The models $\{\mathbf{Y}_t\}$ are defined as Poisson hidden models.

3   Experiment of Diabetes Records

In this section, we first explain briefly the background of our application and then we present our time-changing feature selection techniques on the analysis of the medical service profiles of diabetes, a common disease in the senior population in Australia. We have applied our technique to the dataset and identified the distribution of time-changing features of the diabetes patients.

3.1 The Background of the Application

Medicare is the Australian Government's universal health care system. Each visit to a medical practitioner or hospital is covered by Medicare and recorded as a transaction in the Medicare Benefits Scheme (MBS) database. This data has been collected in Australia since the inception of Medicare in 1975. Such a massive collection of data provides an extremely rich resource that has not been fully utilised in the exploration of health care delivery in Australia. The HIC[8]. has a responsibility to protect the public purse and to ensure that taxpayer's funds are spent wisely and efficiently on health care. The knowledge discovered can be used to educate medical practitioners to improve their medical practice in order to achieve the best health outcomes while ensuring health costs remain under control. For this current exploration we use a subset of de-identified data (to protect privacy) based on Medicare transactions for the period 1997 to 1998. Our particular focus is on time-changing feature selection for data mining related to care models for diabetes. For example, we can ask ourselves questions like: Are there any distinct time-changing features of care for these diabetes patients? Are there any groups of patients receiving similar time-changing features of care? Are the time-changing features of care related to their doctor? Do patients of different ages or gender or location receive differing time-changing features of care to other patients? Answers to the above questions rely on a thorough analysis of the sequences of medical test of the patients and is the objective of our application.

In particular, the purpose of this experiment is to find a set of time-changing features for describing the patterns of care in the management of diabetes. These time-changing features will provide input to a model that will monitor behaviour by diabetic patients. The data used in this case study was extracted from the Medicare transactional database[9]. The data extracted from Medicare is raw transaction data which is stored on IBM main 370 frame computer running MVS operating system. It is a very large data set with millions of records and each record has more than a hundred attributes. There is a transaction record for each Medicare service. Each service record has its item number which is the most important field in the data set. The item number tells to a large extent what kind of service has been performed on the patient. The patients' medical service pattern is represented by a series of item numbers served during the year. The records include fields such as: Encrypted Provider number, Encrypted PIN number, Method of Payment, Item number, Date of service (DOS), Benefit, Reason code for rejection, Referal provider, Processing indicator, Date of referal and Hospital index. From each patients' medical service pattern, an EPISODE[10] dataset is generated:

Patient, DOS, Item1, Item2, refs, Item3, Item4, . . .

---

[8] The Health Insurance Commission of Australia: http://www.hic.gov.au

[9] The data consist of 10,000 diabetic patients using Medicare services paid by H.I.C. under the Medicare Benefits Schedule.

[10] The EPISODE is time period. The time a patient spends in the continuous care of consultants using Medicare services which paid by H.I.C. of one provider (e.g. GP) or, in the case of shared care, in the care of two or more consultants. Where care is provided by two or more consultants within the same episode, one consultant will take overriding responsibility for the patient and only one consultation EPISODE is recorded.

where the first item(s) have no referral date and the remaining items have a referral date same as the first item(s) DOS. In most cases, the episode is not the same for each time period. For example, there is a patient, whose episode sequence in the six Medical categories[11] (e.g., 1 is stand for category one) benefits schedule is:

1, 6, 6, 6, 1, 1
1
2, 1, 5, 1, 6, 6, 6, 1, 1, 3, 5, 5
1
2, 6, 6, 6, 2, 5, 1, 1,
1, 6, 6, 6, 6, 1, 6, 6, 1, 1, 2

From each medical category, the episode includes all medical items that have been used and associated with doctors, DOS and so on.

In this experiment, we use our new method to analyze the medical service profiles of diabetes. We have applied our technique to identify classes, in which the patterns of the diabetic patients were found. The event sequence data can be augmented with any available vector based data. There are three steps of time-changing feature selection from the time-changing sequences (databases):

1. Data quantitative time-changing feature selection,
2. Data qualitative time-changing feature selection, and
3. Data global time-changing feature selection by the above two steps.

Through this experiment, for example, we are interested in finding following time-changing features:

-   Does there exist any global time-changing feature T_{f_t} for doctor visits by all diabetic patients?
-   What kind of sub-time-changing features exist for all diabetic patients?
-   What kinds of time-changing features (models) are there for groups of diabetic patients?

3.2   Steps for the Application of Hierarchical Feature Selection

The main steps for applying Hierarchical Feature Selection within time-changing data mining are as follows:

-   The formalisation of the time-changing data mining problem for hierachical time-changing feature selection,
-   Selecting two different hierachical time-changing features from qualitative and quantitative parts, then selecting a subset of time-changing features for global time-changing feature set, and
-   The interpretation of the global time-changing feature informations.

---

[11] The six categories of medical services are: professional Attendances (PA); Diagnostic Services (DS); Approved Dental Practitioner Services (AD); Diagnostic Imaging Services (DI); and Pathology Services (PS).

3.3 On Qualitative Time-changing Feature Selection

The first experment is the selection of qualitative time-changing feature. We are investigating the data qualitative time-changing feature on state-space $S = \{s1, s2, s3, s4, s5, s6\}^{12}$ to test the naturalness of qualitative time-changing features. For selecting all levels of time-changing features, we use time gap functions with a distance function on state-space S.

In this qualitative time-changing feature selection experiment, all items have been grouping into six categories for each patient. To find the best subset of time-changing features, the key issue is that features between categories that are highly correlated or have mutual information will have similar weight values in categories. The selection process can be summarized in the following steps:

Step 1. Grouping episode sequence for each patient into six categories by its weighted probability values. Computing the sample correlation matrix for those six categories.
Step 2. Computing standard deviation on correlation ratio sequence to find degree of relationship between categories then grouping them into different feature classes.
Step 3. Clustering six categories according to above feature classes into sub-feature classes within each of six categories according to time gap distribution function.
Step 4. Choose qualitative time-changing features from those relationship classes. Those features can be represented by a path between categories.

Now we interpret three important (and smallest) subsets of time-changing features we have discovered from the qualitative time-changing sequences:

- There exists a moderate time-changing feature (similarity) relationship between MBS category one and MBS category six for all diabetic patients visiting their doctors regardless of whether they have folowed up their visits by any medical treatments (e.g., between Figure 1 and Figure 2).
- For non-diabetic medical treatments of diabetic patients, there does not exist any correlated time-changing feature between any of the categories. This means, for example, there are non time-changing related common features among diabetic patients other than problems related to the diabetes.

3.4 On Quantitative Time-Changing Feature Selection

We now illustrate our new method to analyse the quantitative sequence of health time-changing records for selecting time-changing features. In this health time-changing records, since each patient record length is different, we can only use their statistical value as variables in regression functions. In the light of our selected qualitative time-changing feature in first the experiment, we have the series

$$Y_t = f_t^{feature_i}(v_t) - f_t^{feature_j}(v_t)$$

where $f_t^{feature_i}(v_t)$ is a frequency distribution function of medical item numbers which have been used within feature i, its variable v_t is the time distance between the same

---

[12] There are only six categories in MBS Australia.

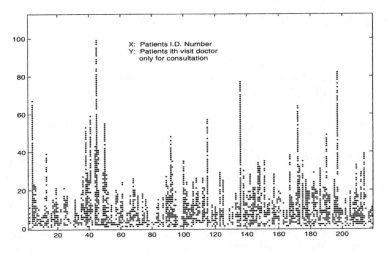

Fig. 1. Time-changing qualitative feature distribution: patients only use consultation item numbers

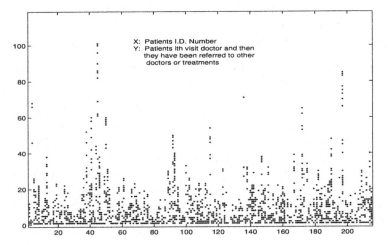

Fig. 2. Time-changing qualitative feature distribution: patients use consultation and medical item numbers

feature (e.g., $v_t = feature\ k_{t_1} - feature\ k_{t_2}$), in the same time-changing cluster. Then the observations can be modelled as a linear regression function, say

$$Y_t = f_t^{feature_i}(v_t) - f_t^{feature_j}(v_t) + \varepsilon_t, \qquad t = 1, 2, \dots, N$$

and we also consider the $\varepsilon(t)$ as an auto-regression $AR(2)$ model

$$\varepsilon_{t'} = a\varepsilon_{t'-1} + b\varepsilon_{t'-2} + e_{t'}$$

where a, b are constants dependent on sample dataset, and $e_{t'}$ with a small variance constant which can be used to improve the predictive equation.

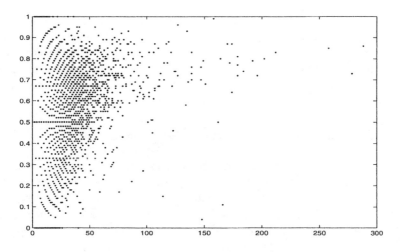

Fig. 3. Item frequency distribution in the different time-changing features

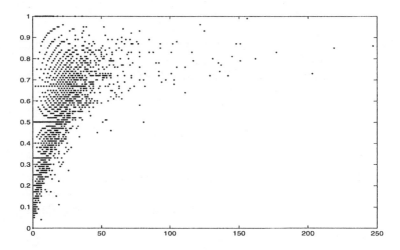

Fig. 4. Item frequency distribution in the same time-changing qualitative feature

For each of the time-changing qualitative features found there exist two important quantitative time-changing features. Some results of quantitative time-changing features experiments are explained as follows.

In Figure 3, the x-axis represents the number of each item number that has been used in different time-changing qualitative features and the y-axis represents the probability of the item within the time-changing cluster k. This explains two facts: (1) the distribution of the number of items the patients have received is periodic and similar for all the medical treatments related to all kinds of diabetic problems. And (2) that patients have received treatment according to the medical guidelines.

But in Figure 4, the x-axis represents the number of each item number that has been used in the same selected time-changing qualitative feature over all medical categories and the y-axis represents the probability of the item within the selected time-changing qualitative feature. This also explains two facts: for example, (1) the patients have received moderately similar medical treatments for diabetic problems, because doctors have different levels of knowlegde of diabetes problems. And (2) that patients have received a number of medical treatment items that relate to diabetes problems (e.g., the heart problems and eye problems) depending on their doctors knowlegde.

3.5   Time-Changing Feature Selection for Global Mining

According to the results from qualitative time-changing feature selection and quantitative time-changing feature selection in the health data records, let $\{S_t : S_t \in \mathcal{S}, t \in \mathsf{N}\}$ be a qualitative process representing $features$ occurrence, and $\{V_t : t \in \mathsf{N}\}$ be the corresponding to qualitative process which includes number of all item's medical number used sequence, then we have the global features of V_t conditional distribution on S_t given by

$$P(V_t = v | S_t = i) = p_{vi}^t$$

Then some results of global feature experiments can be explained as follows.

- feature 1: In state space $\mathcal{S}$, V_t^{state1} and V_t^{state6} both have Poisson distribution with means λ_i^{state1} and λ_i^{state5}. Two states satisfy the condition $V_t^{state1} = \alpha V_t^{state5} + \theta_t$. Then the conditional mean of V_t and state-dependent probabilities given for all non-negative integers v_t will be

$$\mu(t) = \sum_{i=1}^{m} \lambda_i W_t(t), \qquad P_{v_t, statek} = e^{-\lambda_{i,v_t}} \frac{\lambda_{i,v_t}}{v_t!}$$

- feature 2: For state 2, V_t^{state2} is an exponential distribution with parameters λ_i^{state2} and μ_i^{state2}. Then the conditional exponential distribution of V_t^{state2} and state-dependent probabilities given for all non-negative integers v_t will be

$$m(t) = \sum_{i=1}^{m} \lambda_i W_t(t), \qquad P_{v_t, test2} = \begin{cases} \lambda_{(i,v_t)} e^{(-\lambda_{(i,v_t)}(v_t - \mu))} & v_t > \mu \\ 0 & v_t < \mu \end{cases}$$

- feature 3: For state 3, V_t^{state3} is a geometric distribution with parameter p_i^{state3}. Then the conditional geometric distribution of V_t^{state3} and state-dependent probabilities given for all non-negative integers v_t will be

$$m(t) = \sum_{i=1}^{m} p_i W_t(t), \qquad P_{v_t, test3} = p_{i,v_t}^{state3} (1 - p_{i,v_t}^{state3})^{(v_t - 1)}.$$

- other feature: States 4 and 5 are independent. We found that there exist some similarity patterns between their states but non-related time-changing features exist between their clusters, this means the patients have received a number of treatments of time-changing features that are similar but for different time periods.

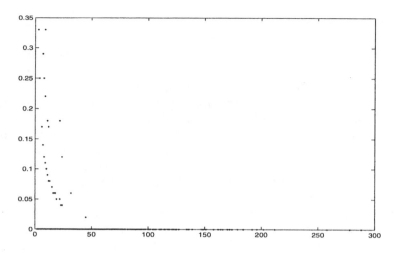

Fig. 5. Item frequency distribution in the time-changing qualitative feature 2

According to those important time-changing features, we can start mining the health data records. The main result from qualitative pattern search and quantitative pattern search is that the behaviour of doctor visits toward a pure diabetic (e.g., the patient has only one medical diabetic problem) is a Poisson distribution. The other main combined-results of time-changing data mining on the health dataset are as follows:

– According to time-changing feature 1, there exist some full periodic time-changing patterns among the diabetes patients, especially the patterns across over (MBS) category 1 and category 6.
– There exist some partial similarity patterns if time-changing feature 2 has been used over all MBS categories. This means that the patients have sub-common problems (for instance, they all have an eye problem) and the distribution of uncommon problems is non-stationary, etc.
– There does not exist any full periodic pattern of medical test item number for all diabete's patients, but there exist some similarity patterns with a small time gap shif for those item numbers.

4   Discussion and Conclusion

In recent years, various studies have been done in knowledge discovery from time-changing datasets for searching different kinds of and/or different levels of patterns, but the techniques are not for general cases. For example, most researchers use statistical techniques such as Metric-distance based technique, Model-based technique, or a combination of techniques (e.g, [6], [14]) to search different pattern problems such as in periodic pattern searching, e.g., [5, 7], in similarity pattern searching(e.g, [3]). In [1], R. Agrawal and others present a "shape definition language", called $\mathcal{SDL}$, for retrieving objects based on shapes contained in the histories associated with these objects. In [4],

Das with others describe adaptive methods which are based on similar methods for finding rules and discovering local patterns and in [12] Rohan and others have considered three alternative feature vectors for representing variable-length patient health records.

Our work is different from their work. First, we use a statistical language to perform all the search work based on time-changing features identified from the dataset. Second, we divide the data sequence or, data vector sequence into two groups for time-changing feature selection: data quantitative group and data qualitative group.

We have considered the use of data feature vectors of quantitative and qualitative groups for representing variable-length patient health records. The time-changing feature of the qualitative group is the simplest one found, but important since it does capture the distribution of patient care throughout the data window. For the time-changing data mining task for discovering diabetes care relationship patterns, the time gap feature within both quantitative group and qualitative group most directly represents in selected global time-changing features. We expect that our **Hierarchical Time-changing Feature Selection** method presented here for event sequence data for this health application will be applicable to other time-changing event sequence data such as market trading dataset.

This paper has presented a new approach based on hierarchical time-changing feature selection of application of time-changing data mining. The clusters of similarity patterns are computed in this level by the choice of certain time gap measures. The quantitative patterns are decided in the second level and the similarity and periodicity of a DTS are extracted. In the final level, we combine qualitative and quantitative features to obtain a global pattern picture and understand the patterns in a dataset better. Another approach to find similar and periodic patterns has been reported in [8, 9, 10, 11]; there the models used are based on hidden functional analysis. The use of time-changing feature selection in our framework makes mining time-changing patterns from time-changing health records easier and faster. Most importantly, it increases the quality of the discovered patterns.

References

1. Rakesh Agrawal, Giuseppe Psaila, Edward L.Wimmers, and Mohamed Zait. Querying shapes of histories. In *Proceedings of the 21st VLDB Conference*, September 1995.
2. C. Bettini. Mining temportal relationships with multiple granularities in time sequences. *IEEE Transactions on Data & Knowledge Engineering*, 1998.
3. G. Das, D.Gunopulos, and H. Mannila. Finding similar time seies. In *Principles of Knowledge Discovery and Data Mining '97*, 1997.
4. G. Das, K. Lin, H. Mannila, G. Renganathan, and P. Smyth. Rule discovery from time series. In *Proceedings of the international conference on KDD and Data Mining(KDD-98)*, 1998.
5. J.Elder IV and D.Pregibon. A statistical perspective on knowledge discovery in databases. In U. Fayyad, G. Piatetsky-Shapiro, P. Smyth, and R. Uthurusamy, editors, *Advances in Knowledge Discovery and Data Mining*, pages 83–115. The MIT Press, 1995.
6. J.B.MacQueen. Some methods for classification and analysis of multivariate observations. In *5th Berkeley Symposium on Mathematical Statistics and Probability*, pages 281–297, 1967.
7. Cen Li and Gautam Biswas. Temporal pattern generation using hidden markov model based unsuperised classifcation. In *Proc. of IDA-99*, pages 245–256, 1999.

8. Wei Q. Lin and Mehmet A.Orgun. Applied hidden periodicity analysis for mining discrete-valued time series. In *Proceedings of ISLIP-99*, pages 56–68, Demokritos Institute, Athens, Greece, 1999.

9. Wei Q. Lin and Mehmet A.Orgun. Temporal data mining using hidden periodicity analysis. In *Proceedings of ISMIS-2000*, University of North Carolina, USA, 2000.

10. Wei Q. Lin, Mehmet A.Orgun, and Graham Williams. Temporal data mining using multilevel-ploynomial models. In *Proceedings of IDEAL-2000*, The Chinese University of Hongkong, Hong Kong, 2000.

11. Wei Q. Lin, Mehmet A.Orgun, and Graham Williams. Temporal data mining using local polynomial-hidden markov models. In *Proceedings of PAKDD-2001*, The University of Hongkong, Hong Kong, 2001.

12. G. Williams R. Baxter and H. He. Feature selection for temporal health records. In *The Fifth Pacific-Asia Conference on Knowledge Discovery and Data Mining (PAKDD-01)*, Hong Kong, April 16-18, 2001. Springer-Verlag.

13. JF Roddick and M Spiliopoulou. A survey of temporal knowledge discovery paradigms and methods. *IEEE Transactions on Knowledge and Data Engineering*, 2002.

14. Z.Huang. Clustering large data set with mixed numeric and categorical values. In *1st Pacific-Asia Conference on Knowledge Discovery and Data Mining*, 1997.

A Data Mining Approach to Analyze the Effect of Cognitive Style and Subjective Emotion on the Accuracy of Time-Series Forecasting

Hung Kook Park[1], Byoungho Song[1], Hyeon-Joong Yoo[2], Dae Woong Rhee[1], Kang Ryoung Park[1], and Juno Chang[1]

[1] Division of Media Technology, College of Computer Software & Media Technology,
Sangmyung University, 7 Hongji-dong, Jongno-gu,
Seoul, Republic of Korea 110-743
{parkh, bhsong, rhee219, parkgr, jchang}@smu.ac.kr
[2] Division of Information Technology & Communication, College of Engineering,
Sangmyung University, San 98-20, Anseo-dong, Cheonan,
Chungcheongnam-do, Republic of Korea 330-720
yoohj@smu.ac.kr

Abstract. Data mining is finding hidden rules in given dataset using non-traditional methods. The objective is to discover useful or patterns from the given collection of data. This research investigates if the differences in accuracy of "time series forecasting" are related to the differences in one's cognitive style and subjective emotion. Two kinds of analyses were performed before applying data mining. Firstly, a statistical test was used to see if there was a positive correlation between a number of cognitive styles and subjective emotional states and the accuracy of time-series forecasting. This was not very revealing and the next step are to use a self-organizing neural network (SONN) to see if correlations between these variables could be discovered. The results showed that there were correlations but did not show whether the correlations were positive or negative. Finally data mining was applied to discover which cognitive styles and subjective emotions positively influence forecasting. It was found that subjects who have in analytic style and subjects who have a relaxed mode were more accurate in their judgments than those who do not these characteristics.

Keywords: data mining, neural network, self-organizing neural network, self-supervised adaptive neural network, cognitive style, emotion, intuitive forecasting, decision making.

1 Introduction

"Judgmental time series forecasting" is prediction of events based on the past data contained in the time series, as opposed to "rational choice," which is formed from causal relationship. The activities of judgmental time-series forecasting can be easily found in real life such as estimating the movement of stock exchange indices, weather forecasting and similar. Although statistical method is generally utilized in predicting

G.J. Williams and S.J. Simoff (Eds.): Data Mining, LNAI 3755, pp. 218–228, 2006.

an event, intuitive judgment is also used. Intuitive judgment is used widely since it can be applied in areas where statistical prediction cannot be used; however it is not without potential errors. The main factors that deter the accuracy of "judgmental time series forecasting" have not yet been closely studied. The research investigated whether the differences in accuracy of "time series forecasting" are related to the difference in one's cognitive style as well as one's subjective emotions.

1.1 Cognitive Style in Decision Making

Kuo [1] found from research into cognitive style that top economists rely on their intuition to solve problems. Knowledge necessary for problem solving is dispersed in one's inmost thoughts and environs, which explains why intuition may be able to more effectively solve dynamic and abstract problems. In addition, most of businesses rely on intuitive forecasting as their main tools in their business activities as research demonstrates that "judgmental forecasting" is more accurate and efficient compared to statistical forecasting [2]. Ruble and Cosier [3] studied on effects of cognitive styles and decision setting on performance based on 162 economic-majoring students. Davis, Grove and Knowles [4] divided 96 graduate students into categories of four decision making styles and put them through computer simulation, which situated them in an economic environment. The result confirmed significant differences in cost effectiveness among different decision making styles. Furthermore, it was discovered that intuitive decision making was more likely to be used when there is high uncertainty, no past data or experience is available, many variables are scientifically unpredictable, there is time constraint, or many alternatives exist [5].

Value Orientation

	Logical	Relational
Complexity Tolerance for Ambiguity	*Analytical*	*Conceptual*
	◆ Enjoys problem solving ◆ Wants best answer ◆ Thrives on control ◆ Uses large volumes of data ◆ Enjoys variety ◆ Innovative ◆ Uses great care in analysis	◆ Achievement oriented ◆ Generally broad outlook ◆ Creative ◆ Humanistic/artistic ◆ Regularly initiates new ideas ◆ Futuristic thinker
	Directive	*Behavioral*
Structure Need for Structure	◆ Expects results ◆ Aggressive nature ◆ Tends to react quickly ◆ Relies heavily on rules ◆ Intuitive in nature ◆ Verbal communicator	◆ Generally supportive ◆ Very persuasive ◆ Empathetic nature ◆ Good communicator ◆ Generally prefers meetings ◆ Relies on limited data for analysis
	Task/Technical	**People/Social**

(left axis: Cognitive Complexity)

Fig. 1. Decision style model (source: Adapted from [6])

As can be seen in figure 1, decision style is classified into four distinct categories using two component parts: cognitive complexity and value orientation. They are Directive, Analytical, Conceptual and Behavioral [6].

The directive decision style combines a high need for structure in the problem context with a relatively low tolerance for context ambiguity. The directive style decision makers tend to function best when they communicate verbally rather than through writing or other multi-channel media.

The analytical style demonstrates a much greater tolerance for context ambiguity and tends toward the need for greater volumes of information and the consideration of large sets of alternatives. The analytical style decision makers are best at coping with new, often unexpected, situation and problem context.

The conceptual manager demonstrates a high tolerance for ambiguity much like the analytical decision makers but tends to be much more of a "people person." The conceptual style decision maker is a long-term thinker and generally strongly committed to the organization.

The behavioral type falls low on the cognitive complexity scale. This style requires a relatively low amount of data input and, as such, generally demonstrate demonstrates a relatively short-range vision.

1.2 Emotion in Decision Making

A number of recent studies indicate that one's emotion may play a key role at every phase of decision making in the way (s)he utilizes decision aids [7] and selects decision strategies for the task [8]. A number of studies also suggest the effect of emotion on decision making which would certainly affect decision outcomes. Schwarz [9] reported that people tend to be intuitive in happy mood, whereas more analytical judgment was evident when people were in sad mood. Indeed, increasing task-related negative affect appeared to lead people to use scanning strategies, which increased choice accuracy in easy tasks but impaired it in hard tasks [10]. More directly addressing the role of emotion in the selection of decision strategies, Isen [8] argued that when induced to happy mood, people tended to simplify the problem space and employ short cuts in their decision making. In fact, emotion is a factor that may influence the accuracy of decision outcomes [10] and thus, should not be missed out in the relevant research. Despite its importance in the context of decision making, however, little evidence appears to exist as to the effect of emotion on judgmental forecasting.

The emotional representation takes literally the spatial metaphor for differences in emotional meaning. The dimensional approach to emotional meaning exploits the fact that some emotion terms can be directly construed with one another, while others seem to have more similar referents. For example, in some sense at least, people consider *happiness* as well as *joy* to mean roughly the opposite of *sadness*, and likewise *love* to mean the opposite of *hate*. It therefore seems feasible to chart a structural arrangement of the relations and oppositions between representations of different emotion names.

For example, Russell[11] analyzed similarity ratings of twenty-eight different affect adjectives to derive a consensual representation of their interrelations. As shown in figure 2, he found that these affect terms can be reliably arranged in a two dimensional representation with axes labeled 'pleasantness' and 'arousal'. The pleasantness dimension reflects the fact that affective states are thought to range in quality from highly unpleasant (negative) to highly pleasant (positive). Arousal refers to the contrast between states such as tranquility which are associated with low levels of arousal (relaxed), and conditions like astonishment or anger which are thought to involve high degrees of arousal (alert).

Alert (High arousal)

	shameful	strained	
Negative	angry	surprised	**Positive**
(Unpleasant)	fearful/uneasy	flutter	**(Pleasant)**
	painful	excited	
	sad	joyful	
	dislike	happy	
	gloomy	satisfied	
	lonely	comfort	

Relaxed (Low arousal)

Fig. 2. Two dimensional representation of emotion (Adapted from [11])

The research reported in this paper includes the results of experiments that analyzed the effects of decision makers' cognitive styles and subjective emotions on the accuracy of their intuitive time-series forecasting. Unfortunately meaningful relationships between the variables could not be easily revealed by the use of traditional statistical correlations. This then led to the use of a self-supervised adaptive algorithm [12] to see if correlations could be discovered between the variables. The results obtained showed correlations, but did not indicate if the correlations were either positive or negative. Data mining [13, 14, 15, 16] was then applied to see if meaningful associations between the variables could be found.

2 Research Methodology

2.1 Research Hypotheses

The following hypotheses were tested:

H1: Accuracy in "time-series forecasting" differs with different subjective emotions.

H2: Accuracy in "time-series forecasting" differs with different cognitive styles.

2.2 Experimental Design

IT junior and senior undergraduate students were used as the subjects for the research. The subjects had taken decision making related classes in the past. The researchers first evaluated cognitive styles of 29 students, and measured their forecasting error. Then 48 students were added to provide a better sized sample for the research to give a total of 77.

The experimental outcome was time-series forecasting. Time series data was derived from work done on forecasting competition [17]. The time–series data given to the test subjects was the number of PCs sold in a month and they were to assume that they were PC sales managers. A total of forty test scenarios were given and these gave information on the sales volume for each month for a period of three years and four months. The subjects were asked to predict the sales volume for next eight months. No other cause-and-effect data were provided to the subjects.

In order to minimize differences in the experiments, one person performed the entire test while standardizing the instructions given to the subjects.

The research was conducted as follows:

(1)   Read the instruction when the subject is seated in the room.
(2)   The researcher gives a brief summary of the experiment.
(3)   Prior to the experiment, measure subject's subjective emotions.
(4)   Collect the emotion survey.
(5)   Proceed with the test (app. 2 min.)
(6)   End the test.
(7)   Measure subject's cognitive styles

2.3 Measure and Observation

Independent Variables. These included each subject's subjective emotion and cognitive style:

- **Subjective Emotions**: The subjective emotion survey tool using five-point Likert scales developed by the researchers was used to measure the subjective emotions such as i(negative-alert), ii(negative-relaxed), iii(positive-alert) and iv(positive-relaxed).
- **Cognitive Styles**: This research adopted the decision style classification scheme, which is the basis for many measures of decision style including the popular Myers-Briggs Type Indicator test [18]. This research used Alan Rowe's Decision Style Inventory to measure the subjects' decision styles such as A(analytic), B(behavioral), C(conceptual), and D(Directive) [6].

Dependent Variable. Accuracy of time-series forecasting is measured by the mean absolute percent error (MAPE). MAPE is a universally used tool in time-series forecasting and represented in absolute percentage value of standard deviation of forecasted value form actual value. The range of possible MAPE values is 0 to 1. The lower the MAPE value is, the more accurate the judgment should be.

3 Results of the Analyses by Statistical Test and Neural Network

3.1 Statistical Hypothesis Testing

T test and ANOVA were used to determine the significance of the results of this experiment. SPSS 9.0 for Windows [19] was used for these tasks. Table 1 and 2 showed the results of the analysis as follows:

(1)   No differences were found between different subjective emotions and accuracy of time-series forecasting.

(2)   No differences were found between different cognitive styles and accuracy of time-series forecasting.

Table 1. ANOVA: Sujective Emotion vs MAPE

	Sum of Squares	df	Mean Square	F	Sig.
Between Groups	.014	3	.005	.556	.647
Within Groups	.373	44	.009		
Total	.392	47			

Table 2. ANOVA: Cognitive Style vs MAPE

	Sum of Squares	df	Mean Square	F	Sig.
Between Groups	.006	3	.002	.217	.884
Within Groups	.386	44	.009		
Total	.392	47			

3.2 Self-Organizing Neural Network

Since meaningful statistical relationships were not found between subjective emotions and cognitive styles and the judgmental task, a neural network that could inherently utilize the correlations between inputs was used to see if relationships could be found between the independent and dependent variables. The self-supervised adaptive neural network (SSANN) proposed by Luttrell [12] was used for this purpose. This is a self-organizing neural network [20, 21, 22, 23]. It has a unique feature that during the training, each neuron cluster in its self-organizing layer uses the information of training status of the other clusters. The winning frequencies of neurons in clusters are converted to probability density functions (pdf) and the pdf's are combined to construct the joint pdf. The neighborhood function of each cluster is determined based on the joint pdf. As a consequence, the network can have asymmetric neighborhood function.

Experiments were conducted with fixed, approximated asymmetric neighborhood functions with the networks by different research groups. These proved that the asymmetricity could help extract correlations between input vectors, and even compare the degrees of correlation. When there are correlations between input vectors, the degree of the asymmetricity and the reconstruction error show systematic relationships, i.e., the reconstruction error decreases with the increase of the asymmetricity; On the other hand, the asymmetricity has no adverse effect when there exists no correlation between the input vectors.

Figure 3 shows the mean squared errors after training the network for each cognition class and for each emotion class. Each bar shows the result for each style, and the marked line curve shows their averages over patterns. In this figure, W3 stands for the approximated 3-point ([.3 .4 .3]) symmetric neighborhood function; the asymmetricity of neighborhood functions W4 ~ W6 are in the increasing order. Based on the results in the figure 3 it was concluded that:

(1)   the decreasing reconstruction errors with the increase of the asymmetricity on the whole reveals that there are correlations between cognitive styles and time-series forecasting accuracy, and also between subjective emotions and this measure.

(2)   the comparison of the slopes of the average curves reveal that the correlations between cognitive styles and time-series forecasting accuracy is higher than that between subjective emotions and this measure.

(3)   the degree of correlation with time-series forecasting is in the order of D > B, C > A and i, ii > iii, iv.

Since there is no absolute reference data used, a property of the self-supervised adaptive neural network is that it inherently used the correlations between inputs to figure out the existence of correlations and to compare correlation degrees. We found that there were correlations between cognition characteristics and decision-making.

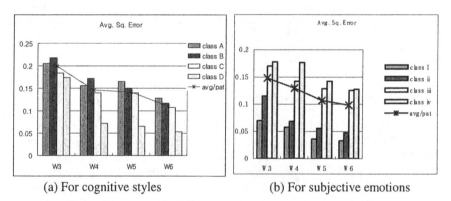

(a) For cognitive styles   (b) For subjective emotions

Fig. 3. The training results with the SSANN for each cognition style and subjective emotion

4   Data Mining

As described in the previous section, two kinds of analyses were performed in advance of applying data mining to tell whether the correlations between independent and dependent variables were positive or negative. Therefore, data mining was used to discover which ways the independent variables influence intuitive forecasting.

One approach to data mining is finding hidden rules in given dataset using non-traditional methods [4]. The objective is to discover some useful tendency or patterns from the given collection of data. This research discovered classification rules representing the effect that cognitive styles and subjective emotions have on the accuracy of the subjects' forecasting, and then attempted to find consistent tendencies in the frequent rules.

Several techniques have been proposed for this type of mining [24, 25]. In this research, the researchers used the "ROSSETA" which is a data mining tool for MS Windows developed by the Department of Computer and Information Science in Norwegian University of Science and Technology in 1999 [25].

4.1 Preparation for Data Mining

For each subject, we have his or her cognitive style value (A, B, C, or D), his or her subjective emotional values (in numeric) and his or her MAPE value (in numeric).

Mining the classification rule requires partitioning every continuous (numeric) value range into several zones to find a tendency because it is difficult to measure the frequency of each value in the continuous value domain due to the numerous numbers of the different values. The researchers partitioned all the numeric properties into three levels: high, low, and middle. Highest 30% was assigned to 'high'; Lowest 30% was assigned to 'low'; and the rest 40% was assigned to 'middle'. Thus 23 of 77 MAPE values were 'high', 31 of 77 MAPE values were 'middle', and 23 of 77 MAPE values were said to be 'low'. Values at any boundary were considered to be 'middle'.

4.2 Mining Results

Many rules (relationships) were found between arbitrary pair of properties. Infrequent rules were removed and any consistent tendencies in the rest frequent rules were then identified. The rest of this section consists of the observations. The portions of high accuracy (low MAPE), middle accuracy (middle MAPE), and low accuracy (high MAPE) will be written in this order in '(' and ')' at the end of any tendencies or rules.

Observations on the Effect of Cognitive Style

Observation 1: The subjects in style A had a tendency to make high accurate (low MAPE) forecasting *(10/25, 9/25, 6/25)*.

Observation 2: The subjects in style B had a tendency to make low accurate forecasting *(3/17, 8/17, 6/17)*.

Observation 3: There were no meaningful tendencies found in style C *(7/23, 9/23, 7/23)* and style D *(3/12, 5/12, 4/12)*.

Observations on the Effect of Subjective Emotion

Observation 3: There was a tendency that regardless of positive or negative emotion, the higher the relaxed level the subject shows at forecasting, the higher accuracy (s)he achieves, and when the lower relaxed level is shown, the lower accuracy is achieved. The evidence is:

negative-relaxed (low)
-> *(4/11, 1/11, 6/11)*
positive-relaxed (mid)
-> *(5/22, 9/22, 8/22)*
positive-relaxe (high)
-> *(6/12, 3/12, 3/12)*

Observation 4: In contrast, there was a tendency that regardless of positive or negative emotion, the higher alert level the subject shows at forecasting, the lower accuracy (s)he achieves, and when the lower alert level is shown, the higher accuracy is achieved. The evidence is:

negative-alert (high)
-> (3/12, 4/12, 5/12)
positive-alert (low)
-> (5/11, 4/11, 2/11)
positive-alert (high)
-> (2/10, 3/10, 5/10)

4.3 Analysis of Results

It was found that there are positive correlations for some styles and emotions. Subjects in analytic style showed more accurate judgments and the subjects in relax mode also showed this tendency as well.

- Subjects in style A (Analytic) seem to be more accurate, and subjects in style B (Behavioral) seem to be less accurate.
- Subjects in relaxed mode seem to be more accurate.

5 Discussion

Although judgmental forecasting is a commonly accepted method in business practice, we do not knowin details as to its cognitive processes and factors influencing the accuracy. And the emotion is the one that people always carry during their routine performance of tasks. Very scarce research on the effect of the cognitive style and the emotion on the the decision accuracy has been made. This research investigated the effect of the cognitive styles and the emotions on judgmental forecasting.

The results particularly the lack of correlations in the statistical analysis and the neural network analysis might be due to the uncontrolled external variables that were operating during the experiments as well as the small size of the samplea used in the research. Significant correlations may have been found in the first stage if the experimental environment was more strongly controlled and a larger sample was used.

In spite of the limitations, the data mining research results showed meaningful correlation for some styles and emotions. Especially, the finding that the analytic style tend to be more accurate is identical with the finding of the earlier study done by Lim [26]. The main findings of personality and psychology literature [8, 9, 10] that people in the negative emotion state tended to be more analytic than those in the positive emotion state. According to Lim's finding, people in negative emotion perfomed better than those in the positive emotion. It means that the more negative emotion brings about the more being analytic which results in the more being accurate. It implies that the analytical decision makers should be assigned to the forcasting tasks.

The result of this research may not be generalizable because the research was conducted with undergradute students. It would be fruitful to replicate this research with experts in their context. The further research is needed with a more refined methodology.

6 Concluding Remarks

This research analyzed in various ways of using cognitive style data and subjective emotion data to discover which of these styles and states positively influence forecasting. The results of the statistical test showed no significant differences exist in the accuracy of time-series forecasting between different cognitive styles and no significant differences also exist in the accuracy of time-series forecasting between different subjective emotions. Thus, the research could not find correlations between cognitive styles as well as subjective emotions in the accuracy of time-series forecasting.

The self-organizing neural network (SONN) was utilized for analyzing and comparing the relative degree of correlation between variables. The results showed that there were correlations between cognitive styles as well as subjective emotions in the accuracy of time-series forecasting but did not indicate whether the correlations were positive or negative.

However with the data mining, positive correlations were found for some styles and states. Table 3 summarizes the comparison of three analyses findings.

In conclusion, data mining discovered the more meaningful relationships between the accuracy of time-series forecasting and both the cognitive styles and the subjective emotions than did the statistical test and the SONN.

Table 3. Comparison of three analyses findings

	MAPE		
	Statistical Test	SONN	Data Mining
Subjective Emotion	no significant difference	correlated	positively correlated in parts
Cognitive Style	no significant difference	correlated	positively correlated in parts

References

1. Kuo, F. "Managerial intuition and the development of executive support systems," *Decision Support Systems*, 24 (1998) 89-103.
2. Lim, J., Whang, M., Park, H., Lee, H.: "A physiological approach to the effect of emotion on time series judgmental forecasting: EEG and GSR," *Korean Journal of the Science of Emotion and Sensibilty*, Vol. 1, No. 1 (1998) 123-133
3. Ruble, T., Cosier, R.: "Effects of cognitive styles and decision setting on performance," *Organizational Behavior and Human Decision Process*, Vol. 46, No. 2 (1990) 283-312
4. Davis, D., Grove, S., Knowles, P.: "An experimental application of personality type as an analogue for decision-making style," *Psychological Report*, 66-1 (1990) 167-184
5. Agor, W.: "The logic of intuition: How top executives make important decisions," *Organizational Dynamics*, 14-3 (1986) 5-23.
6. Rowe, A., Boulgarides. *Managerial Decision Making*. Englewood, Cliffd, NJ: Prentice Hall (1994).
7. Luce, M.F., Bettman, J.R. and Payne, J.W., "Choice Process in Emotionally Difficult Decisions," Journal of Experimental Psychology: Learn, Memory and Cognition, 23 (2) (1997) 384-405.

8. Isen, A.M. and Means, B., "The Influence of Positive Affect of Decision-Making Strategy," Social Cognition, 2 (1) (1983) 18-31.
9. Schwarz, N. and Bless, H., "Happy and mindless, but sad and smart?" The impact of affective affective states on analytic reasoning. In J. P. Forgas (ed.), Emotion and social judgments. Oxford: Pergamon. (1991) 55-71.
10. Stone, D.N. and Kados, K. "The Joint Effect of Task-Related Negative Affect and Task Difficulty in Multiattribute Choice," Organizational Behavior and Human Decision Processes, 70 (2) (1997) 159-174.
11. Russel, J.A., Weiss, A. and Mendelsohn, G.A., "Affect Grid: A Single-Item of Pleasure and Arousal," Journal of Personality and Social Psychology, 57-3 (1989) 493-502.
12. Luttrell S. P: "Self-supervised adaptive networks", *IEE Proceedings-F*, vol. 139 (1992) 371-377
13. Agrawal, R., Imielinski, T. and Swami, A. "Database Mining: A Performance Perspective," IEEE Transactions on Knowledge and Data Engineering, Vol. 5, No. 6, Dec. 1993.
14. Barson, A. and Smith, S. J. Data Warehousing, Data Mining, and OLAP, McGraw-Hill Pub. (1997).
15. Chen, M.-S. Han, J. and Yu, P. S. "Data Mining: An Overview from a Database Perspective," IEEE Transactions on Knowledge and Data Engineering, Vol. 8, No. 6, Dec. 1996, pp. 866-883.
16. Frawley, W. J., piatetsky-Shapiro, G. and Matheus, C. J. "Knowledge Discovery in Databases: An Overview," Knowledge Discovery in Databases, AAAI/MIT Press, 1991, pp. 1-27.
17. Makridakis, S.: Forecasting Competition, http://www.insead.fr/Research/ForecastCompet.
18. Myers, I.: *Manual for the Myers-Biggs Type Indicator, Princeton, NJ: Educational Testing Service* (1962)
19. Using SPSS For Windows (Data Analysis And Graphics), Springer-Verlag New York Inc, 2005.
20. Kohonen, T: *Self-Organizing Maps*, Springer (1995)
21. Srivastava, L. , Singh, S.N. , Sharma, J.: "Estimation of loadability margin using parallel self-organizing hierarchical neural network" *Computers & electrical engineering*, v.26 no.2 (2000) 151-167
22. Oh, S., Pedrycz, W.: "The design of self-organizing Polynomial Neural Networks" *Information Sciences*, v.141 no.3/4 (2002) 237-258
23. Oh, S., Pedrycz, W., Ahn, T.: "Self-organizing polynomial neural networks based on polynomial and fuzzy polynomial neurons: analysis and design," *Fuzzy sets and systems*, v.142 no.2 (2004) 163-198
24. Kdnuggets, "Software for Data Mining and Knowledge Discovery," http://www.kdnuggets.com/software/index.html, (May 3, 2000).
25. Knowledge Systems Group, Dept. of Computer and Information Science, Norwegian University of Science and Technology, Trondheim, Norway, "The ROSSETA Homepage," http://www.idt.unit.no/~aleks/rosetta/rosetta.html (May 3, 2000).
26. Lim, J.S, Whang, M.C., Park, H.K and Lee, H.S., "A physiological approach to the effect of emotion on time series judgmental forecasting EEG and GSR," Korean Journal of the Science of Emotion and Sensibility, 1 (1) (1998), 123-133.

A Multi-level Framework for the Analysis
of Sequential Data

Carl H. Mooney, Denise de Vries, and John F. Roddick

School of Informatics and Engineering,
Flinders University of South Australia,
PO Box 2100, Adelaide 5001, South Australia
{carl.mooney, denise.devries, roddick}@infoeng.flinders.edu.au

Abstract. Traditionally text mining has had a strong link with information retrieval and classification and has largely aimed to classify documents according to embedded knowledge. Association rule mining and sequence mining, on the other hand, have had a different goal; one of eliciting relationships within or about the data being mined. Recently there has been research conducted using sequence mining techniques on digital document collections by treating the text as sequential data.

In this paper we propose a multi-level framework that is applicable to text analysis and that improves the knowledge discovery process by finding additional or hitherto unknown relationships within the data being mined. We believe that this can lead to the detection or fine tuning of the context of documents under consideration and may lead to a more informed classification of those documents. Moreover, since we use a semantic map at varying stages in the framework, we are able to impose a greater degree of focus and therefore a greater transitivity of semantic relatedness that facilitates the improvement in the knowledge discovery process.

1 Introduction

Association rule mining, sequence mining and more recently text mining, in common with other knowledge discovery algorithms, have similar goals, namely to extract useful knowledge from large amounts of data. The techniques employed by association and sequence mining have been analogous and aim to elicit relationships within or about the data. In contrast, text mining, which has a strong link to information retrieval and classification for search engine purposes, largely aims to classify documents according to embedded/known knowledge. There has, however, been some research conducted into the application of data mining techniques for text mining based on the acknowledgement that text is sequential data [1–3] and it from this perspective that we have developed our framework.

Data mining has used constraints placed on the mining process to accomplish *inter alia* the reduction of the search space (through support thresholds etc.) and the focussing on what is relevant (through item constraints, etc.). By incorporating such constraint heuristics, in particular support, some information

G.J. Williams and S.J. Simoff (Eds.): Data Mining, LNAI 3755, pp. 229–243, 2006.
© Springer-Verlag Berlin Heidelberg 2006

may have been lost. The problem of what to do with lower level concepts (elements), that narrowly fail to meet a support threshold, can be ameliorated by the introduction of hierarchies that enable the failed items to be viewed within an encompassing concept. Inferences can then be drawn from both within or across levels of the hierarchy. However, if the reason for failure to meet support was due to a simple typographic error then a problem still remains. For example, if the term *accommodation* narrowly fails to meet the support threshold because some occurrences have been entered as *accomodation*. Correcting this would give an improved, and truer, picture or representation, of the data. Similar concepts expressed differently may also have a similar impact. For example, in medicine, there are often duplicate terms for the same illness or symptoms, dependent upon the branch of medicine, as well as the same or similar term for different conditions. For example, *scrapie, ovine spongiform, bovine spongiform encephalopathy, BSE, Mad Cow Disease, kuru, Creutzfeldt-Jakob disease, CJD, new variant Creutzfeldt-Jakob disease, nvCJD*, and *transmissible mink encephalopathy* or *TME*, all refer to (almost) the same disease in sheep, cattle and humans.

Some of these semantic similarities are highly context sensitive but the ability to 'compress' these two concepts for the purpose of mining[1] would necessarily maintain the intention of the data and perhaps produce otherwise unknown relationships, be they simple associations, or more complex temporal relationships.

The remainder of this paper is organised as follows. Section 2 presents related work in the areas that are encompassed by our framework, Section 3 discusses the framework that has been implemented thus far, and Section 4 concludes with some discussion of future work.

2   Related Work

2.1   Sequence Mining

Sequence mining is not limited to data stored in overtly temporal or longitudinally maintained datasets – examples include genome searching, web logs, alarm data in telecommunications networks, population health data, etc. In such domains data can be viewed as a series of events occurring at specific times and therefore the mining problem becomes a search for collections of events (episodes) that occur frequently together. Solving this problem requires a different approach to the more traditional market-basket domain, and several types of algorithm have been proposed for different domains. For example Manilla *et al.* [2, 3] have developed algorithms and evaluated them on alarm detection data. There is however no reason why text cannot be viewed in the same way and Ahonen *et al.* [1, 4] and Rajman and Besançon [5] have applied similar techniques, based on generalised episodes and episode rules, to text analysis tasks.

---

[1] We acknowledge the need to calculate a relevant support that would be indicative of the combined terms.

In a 'normal' sequence mining scenario based on generalised episodes, each of the tokens are generally independent of each other, e.g. a message from sensor A is independent of a message from sensor B, unless B is reacting as a consequence of A, and the mining process uses a *sliding window* to limit the length of the discovered episodes. At this level also there are no semantics associated with each input token. The following example will serve to illustrate this point.

Example 1. Given the following series of sensor readouts:

   A C B D F A C D F ...

there is no reason that a *sliding window* cannot partition this at every token, and in general this is what happens, resulting in the sequences below:

$\langle A \rangle$ $\langle AC \rangle$ $\langle ACB \rangle$ $\langle ACBD \rangle$ ...
$\langle C \rangle$ $\langle CB \rangle$ $\langle CBD \rangle$ ...
$\langle B \rangle$ $\langle BD \rangle$ ...

.

In a text environment, however, (text files, emails etc.) this does not necessarily make sense due to the semantics of language as the following example illustrates:

Example 2. Given the following sequence:

   Fred goes shopping on Tuesday. His cat is black.

it makes no sense if we use the traditional *sliding window* method, as is the case in Example 1, because at some point we would end up with the sequence:

   on Tuesday His cat is black

Although this may be grammatically correct, in the context of the sequence from which it came, it is not semantically correct. Furthermore this sequence may never be frequent, but may have to be processed anyway due the length of the *window* under consideration. This type of problem exists for all forms of text document and therefore there is a need to further constrain the window under consideration. In Section 3 a strategy will be outlined that deals with this specific problem.

One of the problems for any data mining task is how to handle the volume of data to be mined. Different strategies have been employed to improve the efficiency of the process and in the context of text mining this is of particular importance. There are obvious benefits to employ mappings of the data, especially when dealing with text. These mappings can be justified mainly by space and time benefits, but in some instances there may be an additional semantic benefit. However, in this work the utility of encoding the text, to more efficiently process the amount of data, is not feasible since we need to compare both typographical and semantic differences or similarities between episodes.

2.2   Approximate String Matching

Research in the area commonly known as 'string matching', or 'string edit distance' has been active for many years and includes not only algorithms for string matching using regular expressions [6, 7, 8, 9, 10, 11, 12, 13], but also algorithms in the related area of edit distance [14, 15, 16, 17, 18, 19, 20, 21, 22, 23, 24][2]. In particular, the work by Oommen et al. [17, 18] generated a *confusion matrix*. This matrix is used to determine the probability of striking a wrong key on a keyboard, which is then incorporated into the edit distance function. The implementation of this and the incorporation of it into our framework has been accomplished and can be used during a first pass of the data, or as a pre-processing step for data cleaning. It is envisaged that this will eliminate a considerable amount of typographic errors, but the problem of similar context sensitive concepts, eg *scrapie – ovine spongiform*, is also relevant, therefore processing to handle *semantic distance* is included in our framework.

2.3   Semantic Distance

There are many research areas, other than data mining and knowledge discovery, dealing with semantic distance, among them knowledge representation, statistical clustering, machine learning, medical informatics, and natural language processing. Semantic distance, in text, is a measure of the relationship between the *concepts* represented by words. How closely related they are depends upon their formal definition, their common usage and human psychology (where one term prompts us to think of the other). A thorough review of work done in these areas is beyond the scope of this paper, however, much of the work related to semantic distance relies on the linguistic or semantic similarity of terms that are based on a lexicographic definition of words or terms without reference to the application context. Approaches to measuring semantic similarity fall into three main types - thesaurus, dictionary and ontology based.

Thesaurus-based approaches use groups of related words and synonyms, usually arranged as a taxonomy, to determine similarity which is expressed generally a boolean value, *close* or *not close*. Synonymy judgement and semantic similarity research on pairs of words done by Rubenstein and Goodenough [26], Miller and Charles [27], Morris and Hirst [28] and Okumura and Honda [29] provide methods to calculate the degree of similarity as a number. A limited 'transitivity' measure was also introduced by Morris and Hirst to provide a metric to trace patterns of lexical cohesion in text.

Dictionary-based metrics using hierarchical schemata evaluate the similarity of terms based on spatial or mereological classifications (that is, part–whole relationships) of entities, or hypernyms and hyponyms (specialisation–generalisation relationships), and by edge counting methods in which the granularity of the description of entities and their classes affects the value of the distance.

---

[2] For an excellent survey on this field see "A Guided Tour to Approximate String Matching" by Gonzalo Navarro [25].

Kedad and Métais [30] propose using metadata, including a linguistic dictionary, in a hierarchical structure with no distance set by the user. In their model, values are considered close if they belong to the same class. The semantic distance is fixed by the dictionary definition. The semantic similarity dependent upon a particular context is not readily extracted. Kozima and Furugori [31, 32] present a method which computes the semantic similarity between words using a semantic network constructed from a subset of the Longman Dictionary of Contemporary English. This method relies on each word used in a definition of a word being present in the dictionary.

A much-used semantic network resource is *WordNet* [33], which comprises separate networks for nouns, verbs, adjectives and adverbs with the basic element being a set of synonyms (synset). These can be arranged in *IS_A* hierarchies of hyponyms/hypernyms or with the additional relationships of meronyms (part-of), holonyms (has-part) and antonyms (opposite) as a multi-relational network. Many similarity measures compute path lengths with variations to calculate similarity (qv. Rada *et al*, Hirst & St-Onge, Sussna and Leacock & Chodorow [34, 35, 36, 37]). However, none of these adequately solve the problems inherent in a hierarchy or caters for typographical errors. Approaches that include corpus analysis to refine similarity calculation (qv. Resnick, Jiang & Conrath [38, 39, 40] and Lin [41]) report results that come closer to human judgement. These measures however are dependent on the quality of the information source.

Richardson and Smeaton combine the lexical database WordNet with Resnick's measure of similarity to give a semantic similarity measure that can be used as an alternative to pattern matching [42]. They use *synsets*, collocations (connected words), and a hierarchical concept graph (HCG), with semantic pointers to hyponyms/hypernyms and meronyms/holonyms. Edges between concepts are given *weights* and the weight of a link is affected by the density of the HCG at that point, the depth in the HCG, and the strength of connotation between the vertices.

Spanoudakis and Constantopoulos [43, 44] investigate in depth the use of metrics to measure the distance between semantic descriptions of artefacts, particularly those developed at various stages of software development. Their model operates on semantic descriptions of objects using the modelling abstractions - *classification, generalization and attributes*. Objects are compared by four partial distance functions, which compare objects at different levels of detail. The results of the partial distance functions are aggregated into an *Overall Distance* measure which is then transformed into a *Similarity* measure. This model also introduces a *Salience* function, where salience is defined as the belief that an attribute is dominant, based on a compound of the properties *charactericity, abstractness* and *determinance*. It is unclear, however, at what point the salience function is calculated and applied to the similarity measure.

Weinstein and Birmingham measure syntactic correspondence between definitions of pairs of terms. Their work deals with artificial ontologies rather than real world complexities as ... *in the context of real-world applications, it is not possible to calculate the meaning of a term* [45]. Contexts restrict accessibility within an ontological structure and are used to hide concepts and relations (ie. a relationship with another concept). Contexts are partially ordered and accessibility among contexts is transitive and non-symmetric. In our model, by having a separate graph for each context, real world complexities can be accommodated, because the context itself, defined by the user, gives meaning to the terms used.

Miller and Yang apply clustering techniques and a discrete distance function to measure distances over interval data where the interval distance measures the degree of association [46]. However, all examples shown are quantitative intervals. Their method assesses whether a *semantically meaningful distance metric is available* in order to *consider those attributes together and apply clustering to the set of attributes*. It is unclear how non-numeric intervals are treated.

Rodríguez and Egenhofer [47] present an approach for semantic similarity across different ontologies based on the matching process of each of the specification components in the entity class representations. The similarity function determines lexical similarities with feature sets (functions, parts, attributes). The similarity function equals the weighted sum of each specification component. The work focuses on entity classes and on comparing distinguishing features in terms of strict string matching between synonym sets that refer to those features. It is interesting to note that when undertaking human testing, the subjects' answers varied on the number of ranks used to classify entity classes.

Rodríguez, Egenhofer and Rugg [48] combine feature mapping with semantic distance calculation to assess semantic similarities. Their model for measuring semantic similarity has a strong linguistic basis and takes into account synonyms and different senses in the use of terms. It also considers component-object relations with properties of asymmetry in evaluation of similarity. Their work outlines a model that assesses similarity by combining feature mapping with a semantic distance measurement defined in terms of the relevance of different features in terms of the distance in a semantic network. The global similarity function is a weighted sum of the similarity values for parts, functions and attributes and yields values between 0 and 1. Context, although recognized as a relevant issue for semantic similarity, is not addressed in this work.

Roddick *et al.* [49] present a unifying semantic distance model in which a graph-based approach is used to quantify the distance between two data values. This approach facilitates a notion of distance, both as a simple traversal distance and as weighted arcs. Transition costs, as an additional expense of passing through a vertex, are also accommodated. This model recognizes context as the most important factor in measuring distance.

3   Framework

3.1   Overview

Our multi-level framework for the analysis of sequential data is comprised of four levels, see Figure 1. Levels One and Two take user defined parameters and are not context dependent, since we are dealing with the frequent episodes at a individual character level. Levels Three and Four, which are concerned with

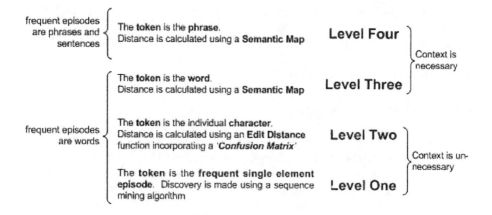

Fig. 1. Overview of the framework

complete words and phrases, are necessarily context dependent and as such allow the interaction by means of an accept and reject policy as well as the ability to alter the current support levels.

3.2 Level One – Discovering the Single Element Episodes

The algorithm we use as the basis for generating the frequent episodes was developed by the authors and detailed in a previous paper [50], however some modifications have been made to accommodate the fact that we are now primarily interested in text documents as input. Nevertheless the following definitions are still applicable.

Let the set of available input tokens (the alphabet), denoted T, be defined as $T = \langle t_1, \ldots, t_k \rangle \mid t_i \neq t_j, i \neq j, 1 \leq i, j \leq k$. A sequence S is then defined as a time ordered ($<$) sequence of input tokens and is denoted $S = \langle s_1, s_2, \ldots, s_m \rangle \mid s_i \in T, 1 \leq i \leq m$. An *episode*, denoted E, is a sequence of tokens, $\langle s_n, s_{n+1}, \ldots, s_{n+k} \rangle$, where $E \subseteq S$.

The user defined *lookahead*, l (similar to Mannila *et al.*'s window concept[3]), defines the maximum length episode to be mined, where $|E| \leq l \leq |S|$. A window, denoted w, is defined as the length of E, where $|E| \leq l$, at any point during the mining process. Therefore the maximum number of windows, *max_win* is given by $|S| - w + 1$ and the *frequency* of E in S is defined as the number of windows in which E appears. The minimum frequency required for an episode to be reported, *min_freq* denoted δ, is calculated using a support, σ_1 (user defined), multiplied by *max_win* at any given point in the mining run.

In addition to this *lookahead* the provision for a *delimiter_list* has been introduced; the period (.) and the comma (,) being two such examples, and these override the *lookahead* at any time they are encountered, even if it is before the maximum value of the *lookahead* has been reached. However, if a delimiter is reached, then the length of E when the delimiter was reached becomes the the window, w, for the purpose of calculating *min_freq*, δ.

Thus our problem for this level is to find all single element candidate episodes

$$E_i \text{ on } \{\mathbf{S} \mid E_i \leq l \text{ or } [delimiter\_list], freq(E_i) \geq \delta, \delta = (|S| - w + 1) \times \sigma\} \quad (1)$$

and have them available for Level Two.

3.3   Level Two – Edit Distance

There are two possible strategies for dealing with the incorporation of the edit distance metric for the removal of typographic errors; 1) as a pre-process data cleaning step or, 2) after the single element candidate episodes have been generated. There may be some argument with respect to which strategy is best[3], but in the context of this work, and since the methodology is the same regardless of the positioning, we have adopted the latter. This results in the need for two processes to be implemented on the generated single element candidate episodes:

1. Edit distance calculation and merge;
2. Semantic distance calculation and merge.

At this Level we are concerned with the edit distance calculation as follows. The current value of support, σ_1, is used to collect those episodes that meet threshold, while another list is collected for those episodes that fall between the primary support value and secondary support value, σ_2. A third support value, σ_3, is used for a cut-off that indicates those candidates that are not considered in any of the calculations[4]. Once this list has been compiled the edit distance algorithm, incorporating the *confusion matrix*, is used as per Algorithm 3.1.

In traditional mining tasks it is normal to have one support threshold, *min_supp* or θ, or in the case of hierarchical association mining it may be that there are two or more on a sliding scale. We have introduced a sliding support scale based on the lengths of the episodes being mined and this has proved to useful in detecting more interesting longer episodes. However, when dealing with context dependent measures it has become apparent that it may be necessary to have three *persistent* levels of support[5]:

- support, *min_supp* (θ), which is the same as any traditional support heuristic,
- distance support, *dist_supp* (θ_α). Currently this is calculated to be one standard deviation from *min_supp*. The purpose of this heuristic is that those elements that are between *min_supp* and *dist_supp* will be used as the seeds for any distance calculations that are performed, and

---

[3] eg. time, usefulness of the cleaned data for other purposes, etc.

[4] In our experimental work we used a static value for σ_2 that is 5% lower than that of σ_1 and a value that is 15% lower than σ_1 for σ_3. However, for datasets that are more normally distributed, values that are multiples of the standard deviation of the dataset can be used, i.e. 1SD for σ_2 and 2SD for σ_3.

[5] The term *persistent* here relates to the fact that they are always there, not that they are always the same value.

- lower bound support, *low_supp* (θ_β). Currently this is calculated to be two standard deviations from *min_supp*. Any elements that fall below this threshold will not be included in any distance heuristic and furthermore only those elements that fall between *dist_supp* and *low_supp* will be used in either Level Two, Three or Four distance calculations.

Algorithm 3.1. Pseudo code for using string edit distance

Input: a *list* L, of *episodes* e and a *support* σ_1, a *support* σ_2 and a minimum edit distance, ϵ.
Output: the collection of frequent single element episodes E.
1: **for all** α, in L **do**
2:     **for all** $\sigma_3 < \beta < \sigma_2$ **do**
3:         calculate the edit distance, ρ, between α and β
4:         **if** $\rho \leq \epsilon$ **then**
5:             merge α and $\beta \Rightarrow \alpha$
6:             *frequency* α = *frequency*($\alpha + \beta$)
7:             **if** the support for the merged α and β is $\geq \sigma_1$ **then**
8:                 remove both α and β from further processing
9:             **end if**
10:         **end if**
11:     **end for**
12: **end for**

The calculations of the standard deviation can be made after the first pass of the data when the total number of elements, the number of unique tokens[6] and the frequency of the elements is known. The standard deviation is calculated as:

$$\sigma = \sqrt{\frac{\sum x^2}{n} - \bar{x}^2} \text{ , and therefore, } \theta_\alpha = \theta - \sigma \text{ and } \theta_\beta = \theta - 2\sigma \qquad (2)$$

Some limitations of using supports based on standard deviations are:

1. If the *min_supp* has to be set very low, as is the case with our current synthetic datasets, then the values are meaningless. (Our current synthetic datasets use a *min_supp* that is just above 3σ),
2. the lower bound, *low_supp* may have to be cut at zero depending on the value of *min_supp* – negative values make no sense.

After this processing we have a set of frequent one element episodes, E, that has eliminated the majority of, if not all, typographic errors. The choice of the value for ϵ, see Algorithm 3.1 line 4, can be varied to accommodate a more or a less strict interpretation of what a typographic error is, but during this study we hard coded this value to be relatively small and therefore, two words were considered the same only if they contained a single typographic error. A more exhaustive study using documents from varied domains may show that this value

---

[6] Here the term tokens is used to represent the alphabet.

should be a user-defined parameter to the mining process that would take into account the domain knowledge of the users of the system.

This set of frequent one element episodes can now be processed in Level Three using the semantic distance measures.

3.4   Level Three – Semantic Distance Between Words

In this work, we use the semantic distance model developed by Roddick *et al.* [49] for its flexibility and ease of use. A separate semantic map is constructed for each context. The semantic map is stored in a directed graph with words (or phrases) in vertices and arcs connecting them weighted with agreed values. The graph may be populated using a dictionary, thesaurus or ontology with the weights calculated by any of the previously discussed distance measures, see Section 2.3, or by a domain expert. A value $d(n_i, n_j)$, between 0 and 1, representing the distance between each adjacent vertex, is associated with each directed arc indicating the uni-directional or bi-directional distance between vertices.

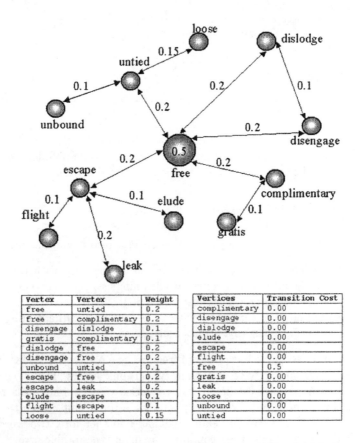

Vertex	Vertex	Weight
free	untied	0.2
free	complimentary	0.2
disengage	dislodge	0.1
gratis	complimentary	0.1
dislodge	free	0.2
disengage	free	0.2
unbound	untied	0.1
escape	free	0.2
escape	leak	0.2
elude	escape	0.1
flight	escape	0.1
loose	untied	0.15

Vertices	Transition Cost
complimentary	0.00
disengage	0.00
dislodge	0.00
elude	0.00
escape	0.00
flight	0.00
free	0.5
gratis	0.00
leak	0.00
loose	0.00
unbound	0.00
untied	0.00

Fig. 2. A portion of the Semantic Map surrounding the term 'free', with the associated input files below it

A distance may be calculated for any word or phrase pair, or alternatively, a set of words/phrases can be retrieved, each of which is deemed to be *close to* a given word by specifying a threshold value. Transitivity of semantics is enabled by arc weights, transition costs and a focussing factor. The number of arcs does not automatically increase distance as arc weights may be zero. A shortest path algorithm is used to calculate distances between vertices in a fully connected graph.

Words are easily added to the map by specifying an additional vertex and at least one arc connecting it to an existing vertex, see Figure 2. This allows abbreviations, slang and jargon terms to be included in subsequent mining, fully utilising the re-usability of the map. Moreover, multiple maps can be combined – thus domain specific jargon can be included into more or less common graphs.

To process the list of frequent one element episodes the same approach to that used in Algorithm 3.1 can be used. The choices for the cut-offs, see Line 2, can remain the same or be changed depending on the requirements of the user. Further to this, since this level is interactive, the user may or may not accept the terms presented for *compression* into a single term, for the purpose of meeting the support threshold.

Example 3. Distance value and 'compression'.

TERM	RELATIONSHIP	TERM
bush support 48%	*close to*	*president* support 32%

with a distance value of 0.05

Algorithm 3.2. Pseudo code for 'compression' options

1: **if** the distance value is less or equal to ϵ (Line 4 - Algorithm 3.1) **then**
2:    the 'compression' is automatic
3: **else if** the distance value is greater than ϵ **then**
4:    the user is prompted to 'compress' the two terms if they agree that they are synonyms.
     The second of the two terms, in this instance *president*, is displayed with its surrounding words from the document to assist with this decision.
5: **else**
6:    the term is rejected and the next term is assessed.
7: **end if**

Example 3 illustrates the degree of control on the finer points of semantic relevance that the user can impose, thus enhancing the usability of our framework.

3.5 Level Four – Semantic Distance Between Phrases

At this time we have not implemented this level, but we envisage that the processing would be very similar to Level Three. Any differences would be as a result of the type of Semantic Map that would be employed. The difficulty for this level is not necessarily in the processing phase, but rather in the creation and maintenance of any 'phrasal' semantic maps that are used. Currently we are investigating the use of ontologies for this purpose.

4   Discussion and Future Work

In this paper we have outlined a framework to mine text as a sequence of tokens in the first instance and to incorporate the detection and processing of, in the second instance typographic errors and in the third instance semantically related terms.

There are however some enhancements that can be made especially using the semantic distance of terms. At present we are only applying the semantic distance to single element episodes but there is no reason why the maps can not be expanded to handle phrases that are semantically similar and then these phrases can be processed as single element episodes. One benefit of such an approach is that the mining process becomes more tractable since potentially we would not be generating long sequences[7].

In addition to the above we are currently implementing the algorithms to fully realise the framework so that exhaustive tests can be conducted to validate and verify the concept.

References

1. Ahonen, H., Heinonen, O., Klemettinen, M., Verkamo, A.I.: Applying data mining techniques in text analysis. Tech Report C-1997-23, University of Helsinki, Department of Computer Science (1997)
2. Mannila, H., Toivonen, H.: Discovering generalized episodes using minimal occurrences. In: Proceedings of the Second International Conference on Knowledge Discovery and Data Mining (KDD'96), Portland, Oregon, AAAI Press (1996) 146–151
3. Mannila, H., Toivonen, H., Verkamo, A.I.: Discovery of frequent episodes in event sequences. Data Mining and Knowledge Discovery **1** (1997) 259–289
4. Ahonen, H., Heinonen, O., Klemettinen, M., Verkamo, A.I.: Applying data mining techniques for descriptive phrase extraction in digital document collections. In: Proceedings of the Advances in Digital Libraries Conference, IEEE Computer Society (1998) 2
5. Besançon, R.a.: Text mining — knowledge extraction from unstructured textual data. In: 6th Conference of International Federation of Classification Societies (IFCS-98), Rome (1998)
6. Hall, P.A.V., Dowling, G.R.: Approximate string matching. ACM Computing Surveys **12** (1980) 381–402
7. Aho, A.: Algorithms for finding patterns in strings. In van Leeuwen, J., ed.: Handbook of Theoretical Computer Science. Volume A: Algorithms and Complexity. Elsevier (1990)
8. Breslauer, D., Gąsieniec, L.: Efficient string matching on coded texts. In Galil, Z., Ukkonen, E., eds.: Proceedings of the 6th Annual Symposium on Combinatorial Pattern Matching, Espoo, Finland, Springer-Verlag, Berlin (1995) 27–40
9. Bentley, J.L., Sedgewick, R.: Fast algorithms for sorting and searching strings. In: Proceedings of the Eighth annual ACM-SIAM Symposium on Discrete Algorithms, New Orleans, Louisiana, United States, Society for Industrial and Applied Mathematics (1997) 360–369

---

[7] This benefit would be more fully realised when using a candidate generation and prune approach.

10. Landau, G.M., Myers, E.W., Schmidt, J.P.: Incremental string comparison. SIAM Journal on Computing **27** (1998) 557–582
11. Sankoff, D., Kruskal, J.B.: Time warps, string edits, and macromolecules / The theory and practice of sequence comparison. Reissue ed. edn. David Hume series. Center for the Study of Language and Information, Stanford, Calif. (1999)
12. Chan, S., Kao, B., Yip, C.L., Tang, M.: Mining emerging substrings. Tech Report TR-2002-11, HKU CSIS (2002)
13. Amir, A., Lewenstein, M., Porat, E.: Faster algorithms for string matching with k mismatches. In: Proceedings of the Eleventh annual ACM-SIAM Symposium on Discrete Algorithms, San Francisco, California, United States, Society for Industrial and Applied Mathematics (2000) 794–803
14. Wagner, R.A., Fischer, M.J.: The string-to-string correction problem. Journal of the ACM (JACM) **21** (1974) 168–173
15. Tichy, W.F.: The string-to-string correction problem with block moves. ACM Transactions on Computer Systems (TOCS) **2** (1984) 309–321
16. Bunke, H., Csirik, J.: Edit distance of run-length coded strings. In: Proceedings of the 1992 ACM/SIGAPP Symposium on Applied Computing, Kansas City, Missouri, United States, ACM Press (1992) 137–143
17. Oommen, B.J., Loke, R.K.S.: Pattern recognition of strings with substitutions, insertions, deletions and generalized transpositions. In: Proceedings of the IEEE International Conference on Systems, Man and Cybernetics. Volume 2. (1995) 1154–1159
18. Oommen, B.J., Zhang, K.: The normalized string editing problem revisited. IEEE Transactions on Pattern Analysis and Machine Intelligence **18** (1996) 669–672
19. Cole, R., Hariharan, R.: Approximate string matching: a simpler faster algorithm. In: Proceedings of the Ninth annual ACM-SIAM Symposium on Discrete Algorithms, San Francisco, California, United States, Society for Industrial and Applied Mathematics (1998) 463–472
20. Arslan, A.N., Egecioglu, O.: An efficient uniform-cost normalized edit distance algorithm. In: 6th Symposium on String Processing and Information Retrieval (SPIRE'99), IEEE Comp. Soc (1999) 8–15
21. Arslan, A.N., Egecioglu, O.: Efficient algorithms for normalized edit distance. Journal of Discrete Algorithms **1** (2000) 3–20
22. Cormode, G., Muthukrishnan, S.: The string edit distance matching problem with moves. In: Proceedings of the Thirteenth annual ACM-SIAM Symposium on Discrete Algorithms, San Francisco, California, Society for Industrial and Applied Mathematics (2002) 667–676
23. Batu, T., Ergün, F., Kilian, J., Magen, A., Raskhodnikova, S., Rubinfeld, R., Sami, R.: A sublinear algorithm for weakly approximating edit distance. In: Proceedings of the Thirty-Fifth ACM Symposium on Theory of Computing, San Diego, CA, USA, ACM Press (2003) 316–324
24. Hyyrö, H.: A bit-vector algorithm for computing levenshtein and damerau edit distances. Nordic Journal of Computing **10** (2003) 29–39
25. Navarro, G.: A guided tour to approximate string matching. ACM Computing Surveys **33** (2001) 31–88
26. Rubenstein, H., Goodenough, J.B.: Contextual correlates of synonymy. Computational Linguistics **8** (1965) 627–633
27. Miller, G.A., Chalres, W.G.: Contextual correlates of semantic similarity. Language and Cognitive Processes **6** (1991) 1–28
28. Morris, J., Hirst, G.: Lexical cohesion computed by thesaural relations as an indicator of the structure of text. Computational Linguistics **17** (1991) 21–48

29. Okumura, M., Honda, T.: Word sense disambiguation and text segmentation based on lexical cohesion. In: 15th Conference on Computational Linguistics. Volume 2., Kyoto, Japan (1994) 755–761

30. Kedad, Z., Métais, E.: Dealing with semantic heterogeneity during data integration. In Akoka, J., Mokrane, B., Comyn-Wattiau, I., Métais, E., eds.: Eighteenth International Conference on Conceptual Modelling. Volume 1728 of Lecture Notes in Computer Science., Paris France, Springer (1999) 325–339

31. Kozima, H.: Text segmentation based on similarity between words. In: 31st Annual Meeting of the Association for Computational Linguistics. (1993) 286–288

32. Kozima, H., Furugori, T.: Similarity between words computed by spreading activation on an english dictionary. In: 6th Conference of the European Chapter of the Association for Computational Linguistics, Utrecht, Netherlands (1993) 232–239

33. Fellbaum, C., ed.: WordNet: An Electronic Lexical Database. Bradford Books (1998)

34. Rada, R., Bicknell, H.: Ranking documents with a thesaurus. Journal of the American Society for Information Science (JASIS) **40** (1989) 304–310

35. Hirst, G., St-Onge, D.: Lexical chains as representations of context for the detection and correction of malapropisms. In Fellbaum, C., ed.: WordNet: An Electronic Lexical Database. MIT Press, Cambridge, MA, USA (1998) 305–332

36. Sussna, M.: Word sense disambiguation for free-text indexing using a massive semantic network. In: Second International Conference on Information and Knowledge Management, Arlington, Va, USA (1993) 67–74

37. Leacock, C., Chodorow, M.: Combining local context and wordnet similarity for word sense identification. In Fellbaum, C., ed.: WordNet: An Electronic Lexical Database. MIT Press, Cambridge, MA, USA (1998) 265–283

38. Resnik, P.: Using information content to evaluate semantic similarity in a taxonomy. In: 14th International Joint Conference on Artificial Intelligence, ,, Montreal (1995) 448–453

39. Resnik, P.: Semantic similarity in a taxonomy: An information-based measure and its application to problems of ambiguity in natural language. Journal of Artificial Intelligence Research **11** (1999) 95–130

40. Jiang, J.J., Conrath, D.W.: Semantic similarity based on corpus statistics and lexical taxonomy. In: International Conference on Research in Computational Linguistics, Taiwan (1997) 19–33

41. Lin, D.: An information-theoretic definition of similarity. Proc. 15th International Conf. on Machine Learning, Morgan Kaufmann, San Francisco, CA (1998) 296–304

42. Richardson, R., Smeaton, A., Murphy, J.: Using wordnet as a knowledge base for measuring semantic similarity between words. Technical Report Working Paper CA-1294, School of Computer Applications, Dublin City University (1994)

43. Spanoudakis, G., Constantopoulos, P.: Similarity for analogical software reuse: A computational model. In: 11th European Conference on Artificial Intelligence(ECAI '94), Amsterdam, The Netherlands (1994) 18–22

44. Spanoudakis, G., Constantopoulos, P.: Elaborating analogies from conceptual models. International Journal of Intelligent Systems **11** (1996) 917–974

45. Weinstein, P., Birmingham, W.: Agent communication with differentiated ontologies: eight new measures of description compatibility. Technical report, Department of Electrical Engineering and Computer Science, University of Michigan (1999)

46. Miller, R., Yang, Y.: Association rules over interval data. In Peckham, J., ed.: ACM SIGMOD Conference on the Management of Data, Tucson, Arizona, USA, ACM Press (1997) 452–461

47. Rodríguez, M.A., Egenhofer, M.J.: Putting similarity assessment into context: Matching-distance with the user's intended operations. In Bouquet, P., Serafini, L., Brézillon, P., Benerecetti, M., Castellani, F., eds.: 2nd International and Interdisciplinary Conference on Modeling and Using Context, CONTEXT-99. Volume 1688 of Lecture Notes in Artificial Intelligence., Trento, Italy, Springer (1999) 310–323

48. Rodríguez, M., Egenhofer, M., Rugg, R.: Assessing semantic similarities among geospatial feature class definitions. In Vckovski, A., Brassel, K., Schek, H.J., eds.: Second International Conference on Interoperating Geographic Information Systems, INTEROP'99. Volume 1580 of Lecture Notes in Computer Science., Zurich, Switzerland, Springer (1999) 189–202

49. Roddick, J.F., Hornsby, K., De Vries, D.: A unifying semantic distance model for determining the similarity of attribute values. In Oudshoorn, M., ed.: 26th Australasian Computer Science Conference (ACSC2003). Volume 16., Adelaide, Australia, ACS (2003) 111–118

50. Mooney, C.H., Roddick, J.F.: Mining relationships between interacting episodes. In Berry, M.W., Dayal, U., Kamath, C., Skillicorn, D., eds.: Proceedings of the Fourth SIAM International Conference on Data Mining, Lake Buena Vista, Florida, SIAM (2004)

Hierarchical Hidden Markov Models: An Application to Health Insurance Data

Ah Chung Tsoi[1], Shu Zhang[2], and Markus Hagenbuchner[2]

[1] Monash University, e-Research Centre, Vic. 3800
[2] Faculty of Informatics, University of Wollongong, NSW 2522

Abstract. This paper provides a constructive algorithm in which a hierarchical tree of hidden Markov models may be obtained directly from data using an unsupervised learning regime. The method is applied to health insurance transaction data such that profiles with similar local temporal behaviours are grouped together. By judicious incorporation of limited additional prior information, it is found that profiles can be separated into various sub-behavioural groups thus providing a technique for large-scale automatic labelling of data. In the application to the health insurance transaction data set, by incorporating limited information concerning the medical functions used in a medical procedure, it is possible to label some individual medical transactions as to whether they are related to a particular medical condition or not. This automatic labelling process adds values to the collected transactional database for possible further applications, e.g. public health studies.

1 Introduction

The study undertaken in this paper is motivated by the following common data mining problem: Given a large number of temporal profiles with unknown classifications, can we classify them into various behavioural groups? In general this problem is solvable as there are a number of unsupervised learning algorithms which can classify the data into various behavioural groups. For example, we may be given a database of credit card transaction records. It is possible to use various unsupervised learning methods, e.g. K-mean clustering to classify the records into clusters of behavioural groups; in this case, profiles of credit card usage by their temporal behaviours over a particular period. However, often such grouping of data is of limited practical applications, as it is not possible to label the clustered data. If however in addition, we are given some labelled data then it may be possible to generalize the underlying information captured by the labelled data to the entire set of temporal profiles. Such labelled data set will be of much practical value. For instance, in the credit card example, if we are given some "ground truth" information, e.g. profiles which are known to be "fraudulent" (through forensic examination of the profiles, and successfully validated through expert opinions), then it is possible to use supervised techniques to train a model and then use the trained model to classify the entire data set into labelled data. However, often the "ground truth" data is very expensive or impossible to obtain. In the credit card example, it is known that it is expensive to obtain a small set of curated "ground truth" validated training examples. Secondly, in a supervised

G.J. Williams and S.J. Simoff (Eds.): Data Mining, LNAI 3755, pp. 244–259, 2006.

training regime, often for good generalization accuracy, the number of training data required needs to be carefully chosen, so that (a) they cover most of the common behavioural patterns which the user wishes to capture in the data set, (b) they are sufficiently varied as to cover all "eventualities" in the data set. This implies that a human is capable of choosing exemplars from a large number of data, and has sufficient domain knowledge as to know that a particular profile represents a typical behaviour which is to be captured, and secondly, knows that the selected profiles will have sufficient diversity or "richness" so that the supervised training of the model would converge to a model capable of generalizing well. Obviously the choice of suitable training exemplars from a large set of data is very much an art rather than a science.

In many practical examples, it may be too expensive to obtain a large set of training examples, or have a limited understanding of the underlying system and this prevents human experts from assessing the suitability of particular data for training purposes. This is especially true in cases where there is a large amount of data. As an example, a computer system administrator in a large organisation can capture the network traffic through say a border router. The aim may be to detect any intrusion attempts into the computer system under study. The advance of the art of intrusion detection has not progressed to such an extent that a human system administrator can look at such traffic record and determine whether a particular record is a suitable training example.

In this paper we are interested in a particular domain application which involves routinely collected and unlabelled data. More precisely, we are given detailed transactional records of a large health insurance vendor. The transactional record contain de-identified claimant details, e.g. unique personal identifier (which cannot be reverse engineered to ensure privacy), time of claim, amount of claim, and brief description of the purpose of the claim which is provided in the form of an *item*. The item only pertains to the medical procedure performed on the claimant by the medical service provider. It does not pertain to diagnostic information on the medical condition of the claimant. Often the same item is used for a variety of (related) ailments, thus without access to the diagnostic information of the medical service provider, it is very difficult to associate the items used with a particular course of treatment as a "proxy" indicator of the medical condition suffered. Our challenge is to *label* a sub-group of the large amount of such transactional records. In particular, the question which we wish to answer is: can we label some transactional records as representing cases featuring particular ailments. It is obvious that it will not be possible to label all transactional records into unique sub-groups, say, claimants suffering from the common cold, as there is simply insufficient information to allow us to do so. On the other hand, some items are specific to particular ailments, e.g. stroke sufferers often are provided with treatments represented by item numbers 63130, 63218, 63850 [1]. The question becomes: can we label sub-groups of medical transaction records using such item numbers. A naive answer would be: search all medical transaction records for all occurrences of such

---

[1] These items are related to magnetic resonance imaging scans or magnetic resonance angiography. They relate to investigation of the occurrence of stroke in the claimants, or the monitoring of claimants who have been diagnosed as suffering from strokes.

item numbers. However, an indication of a stroke sufferer is someone who uses one or all of these items as well as a large number of other items. In other words, even if a person uses item 62130, the person might not be suffering from a stroke. The item is used if an investigation is being carried out to ascertain if the claimant might be suffering from a stroke. Secondly the medical service providers may use many other items to determine if the person is suffering from a stroke or not. Hence by searching through the database for occurrence of these records may not capture all possible sufferers of the illness. The question is that there needs to be a way in which we can with some confidence indicate that a person is suffering from strokes. A fundamental assumption underpinning our work is: claimants suffering from the same ailments would have similar temporal behaviours as exhibited by their Medicare claim behaviours over a period of time. This assumption is demonstrated to be valid *ex poste* from our results.

The value to the data set is enormous as if we can overcome this challenge, as it would be possible to automatically label sub-groups of these transactional records into various sub-groups as sufferers of diabetes, stroke, etc. Once labelled as such, the database may be used for other purposes, e.g. the geographical distribution of stroke sufferers in the country, at a particular moment in time, and its variation over a period of time. In combination with data from other sources, e.g. general dietary information from supermarkets, amount of exercise of small scaled surveys, it may be possible to derive some general conclusions on the cause and effect of stroke illness.

In this paper, we will only consider the first part, i.e. how to label a sub-group of transactional records as claimants suffering from various illnesses. We will not be concerned with the second part, viz., its possible public health applications once such labelling can be performed.

Our data consists of 180 GB of de-identified transactional records which covers seven consecutive quarters of transactions [2]. Our task is: label a sub-group of such records into claimants suffering from diabetes, stroke, etc.

Faced with such task, we proceed as follows:

(1) **Feature extraction** to extract representative features of the underlying temporal behavior of the claimant. In our case, we extracted the following information: unique personal identifier, date of claim, age of the claimant, total claims per day.

(2) **Creation of cohorts** considers the fact that a claimant's medical records change dramatically with age. Claimants of similar age range form an age cohort. Steps (1) and (2) are pre-processing steps which prepare the data for the application of pattern discovery techniques.

(3) **Clustering.** Gaussian mixture clustering is applied to identify clusters in the data for each age cohort. This step gathers profiles together according to an Euclidean norm based on the entire temporal profile, rather than based on temporal variations within the profile.

---

[2] This data set has been provided by the Health Insurance Commission (HIC), Australia, a national medical insurance vendor which provides universal health cover to all Australian citizens and permanent residents.

(4) Pattern discovery is accomplished by using hidden Markov models (HMM), a stochastic model commonly used in temporal behavioral pattern discovery [3]. Steps (3) and (4) are executed recursively until convergence occurred. This recursive process yields a set of HMMs which are hierarchically organised.

(5) Automatic annotation. Without any additional information, the clusters from recursive applications of steps (3) and (4) will contain temporal behaviours of claimants who might be suffering from various ailments. In other words, different ailments will produce similar temporal behavioral patterns. In order to disambiguate these similar patterns, additional information on the medical treatments received by claimants in the form of items used by the medical service providers is used to further separate the patterns within the same cluster as obtained in steps (3) and (4) into ailments which the claimant might be suffering[4]. Thus, by utilizing the information on medical items used by the medical service providers, we are able to obtain an automatic annotation technique which can annotate large scale medical transaction records.

The organization of this paper is as follows: Section 2 describes the techniques used in the pre-processing steps. A general discussion of pattern discovery is given in Section 3. Our method will be presented in Section 4. Experimental results are shown in Section 5. Conclusions are drawn in Section 6.

2 Representation of Temporal Sequences

As indicated in Section 1, we will use the total claim per day from a claimant, the date when the service was rendered, and the age of the claimant to construct a profile. In addition, we smooth out the fluctuations (as not everybody sees a medical service provider every day) by using a sliding window of 14 days to compute the total claim made over that period. *Ex poste* this was found to be appropriate as a sick person is often required to see a medical service provider a number of times over a short period. We use an annual cycle of 365 days, and account for boundary effects as benefit claims often are not lodged on the same day as they are rendered. This results in temporal profiles such as those shown in Figure 1.

A claimant's medical condition can change dramatically with age. We analysed the data and observed that there are abrupt changes between certain age groups. Consequently, we segmented the profiles into age cohorts as shown in Table 1. Segmenting the profiles into cohorts of claimants of similar age gives two advantages: First, it reduces the size of the dataset for later analysis tasks, and secondly it reduces the impact of age related medical issues on the learning tasks.

In Table 1 we find that for both male and female claimants the amount of benefit paid and the frequency of medical services decrease until the claimants reach adolescence.

---

[3] HMMs are not particularly suited for large scale data mining tasks given the high computational demand associated with the training of these models. This problem is alleviated through the recursive training of HMMs on small portions of the data set; a step which will be addressed in greater detail later in this paper.

[4] Note that we do not have access to medical service providers' diagnosis nor notes.

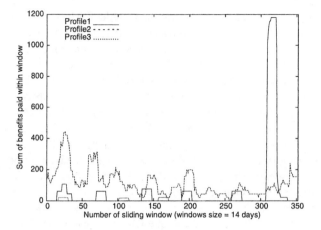

Fig. 1. Three profiles from the dataset

Table 1. Cohort groups and sizes

	Female			Male		
Age cohort	Number of claimants	Av. num. of claims	Av. value of claim	Number of claimants	Av. num. of claims	Av. value of claim
0-3	460,548	7.65	229.94	489,403	8.29	257.56
4-6	347,328	5.58	166.34	368,972	5.79	179.33
7-15	957,225	4.47	158.04	997,945	4.39	161.58
16-24	1,053,985	7.41	308.14	946,464	4.77	196.22
25-35	1,498,662	9.04	437.98	1,257,976	5.29	227.97
36-44	1,221,511	8.59	448.24	1,074,617	6.09	285.41
45-55	1,287,334	9.82	524.06	1,199,845	7.38	388.57
56-70	1,101,022	12.73	684.27	1,068,311	11.21	654.19
>70	862,858	16.97	875.29	556,972	15.07	715.07

Then these values experience a rapid increase before slowing down until retirement age for female claimants; a similar trend can be observed for male claimants but at a much slower rate.

In summary, a dimension reduction of the dataset is achieved by setting up a one-dimensional profile for each claimant, and the dataset is segmented into age cohorts. The pattern discovery techniques will be applied to each age cohort separately.

3   Pattern Discovery Techniques

This section gives a general introduction to Gaussian Mixture models and hidden Markov models which will be employed in the pattern discovery task later in this paper. We will also describe a method to obtaining a hierarchical tree of hidden Markov models from the set of claimant profiles. This is a two step process:

Step 1. Clustering of the entire profiles. In this step, we will group profiles together according to their overall pattern. This is achieved by using a clustering technique such as a Gaussian mixture model.

Step 2. Use a hidden Markov model to further divide the clusters obtained in Step 1 into clusters of similar temporal behavioral patterns.

3.1 Gaussian Mixture Model as a Clustering Tool

The task of discovering temporal patterns could be initialized by clustering because of its ability to segment data into clusters according to a similarity criterion. There are a number of possible algorithms which can be employed for this purpose, e.g., K-means clustering algorithm [4], Gaussian mixture algorithm [5], mixture of HMMs [11], self organizing map method [6]. Mixture of HMMs and Self-Organizing Maps are computationally expensive to be used given the size of the dataset. The K-means algorithm has been tried but the results obtained indicated that "sparse" vectors are not clustered well. Sparse vectors are common occurrences in the given dataset as most claimants do not visit a medical service provider frequently. Consequently, we did not use the K-means algorithm in any further experiments. In this respect, Gaussian mixture (GM) models are more practical in terms of computational demands [3].

With GM, it is assumed that the data observed are generated by a $\mathcal{D}$-dimensional GM of N components (N clusters) with the following probability density function [3]: $f(\mathbf{x}|\Psi) = \sum_{n=0}^{N-1} p_n g(\mathbf{x}|\Theta_n)$ where Ψ denotes the vector encompassing all the mixture parameters (Θ_n and p_n), p_n ($\geqslant 0$, $n = 0, 1, 2,...$, N-1, $\sum_{n=0}^{N-1} p_n = 1$) is the weight of the $n-th$ component in the model, or the possibility that the pattern $\mathbf{x}$ was generated from the $n-th$ component. Θ_n stands for all the parameters (μ_n and $\mathbf{V}_n$) of the $n-th$ $\mathcal{D}$-variate Gaussian distribution $g(\mathbf{x}|\Theta_n)$ of probability density function: $g(\mathbf{x}|\Theta_n) = \frac{exp^{-\frac{1}{2}(\mathbf{x}-\mu)^T(\mathbf{V})^{-1}(\mathbf{x}-\mu)}}{\sqrt{(2\pi)^D \det(\mathbf{V}_n)}}$ with mean vector μ_n and covariance matrix $\mathbf{V}_n$.

In general, the parameters of the model are typically trained using expectation maximization (EM) algorithm [3] which is used to produce the maximum likelihood estimates $\hat{\mu}_n$ and $\hat{\mathbf{V}}_n$ to parameters μ_n and $\mathbf{V}_n$, respectively. More importantly, the parameters can be improved through some EM iterations [7] with respect to the dataset $\mathbf{x} = \{\mathbf{x}_m, m = 0, 1,...$, M-1$\}$ so that the model will fit the data better. The updating of parameters in the k-th EM iteration is as follows [7]:

$$h_n^{(k)}(\mathbf{x}_m) = \frac{p_n^{(k-1)}(\mathbf{x}_m)g(\mathbf{x}_m, \Theta_n^{(k-1)})}{f^{k-1}(\mathbf{x}_m)} \qquad \hat{p}_n^{(k)}(\mathbf{x}) = \frac{\sum_{m=0}^{M-1} h_n^{(k)}(\mathbf{x}_m)}{M}$$

$$\hat{\mu}_n^{(k)}(\mathbf{x}) = \frac{\sum_{m=0}^{M-1} \mathbf{x}_m h_n^{(k)}(\mathbf{x}_m)}{M\hat{p}_n^{(k)}(\mathbf{x})} \qquad \hat{\mathbf{V}}_n^{(k)}(\mathbf{x}) = \frac{\sum (\mathbf{x}_m - \hat{\mu}_n^{(k)}(\mathbf{x}))h_n^{(k)}(\mathbf{x}_m)(\mathbf{x}_m - \hat{\mu}_n^{(k)}(\mathbf{x}))^T}{M\hat{p}_n^{(k)}(\mathbf{x})}$$

where $\hat{p}_n^{(k)}(\mathbf{x})$, $\hat{\mu}_n^{(k)}(\mathbf{x})$ and $\hat{V}_n^{(k)}(\mathbf{x})$ are the maximum likelihood (ML) estimators for the unknown parameters p_n, μ_n and $\mathbf{V}_n$.

The EM iteration will stop when one of the following criteria is satisfied: (i) not enough improvement, $1 \leq \frac{L(\hat{\psi}^{(k)})}{L(\hat{\psi}^{(k-1)})} \leq 1 + \gamma$, where $\gamma > 0$ is given by user, and

$L(\hat{\Psi}^{(k)}) = \sum_{m=0}^{M-1} \log[\sum_{n=0}^{N-1} \hat{p}_n^{(k)} g(\mathbf{x}_m|\hat{\Theta}_n^{(k)})]$, or (ii) $k = K$, K is the maximum number of EM iterations.

After the updating of parameters through the EM algorithm, a Gaussian mixture model is able to group each $\mathbf{x}_m$ (m = 0, 1, 2,..., M-1) into a cluster c if $\beta_n(\mathbf{x}) = \log[\hat{p}_n g(\mathbf{x}|\hat{\Theta})]$ and $c = \arg\max_{n=0,1,2,...,N-1} \beta_n(\mathbf{x})$.

With the GM model, a problematic issue is the choice of the number of components N. The number of components could be assigned based on some prior knowledge of the dataset, or obtained by applying some information criteria (IC) [8, 9], which provides a rational choice of the number of components based on Bayesian or similar arguments. In our work, we chose the number to be 6 through some preliminary experiments on the dataset while IC will be considered in future work.

3.2 The Hidden Markov Model

A hidden Markov model (HMM) is a system of states with a probabilistic state transition model which can model a given sequence of events. A number of variants of HMMs are available [10], such as discrete HMM, continuous observation HMM, input-output HMM. In our case, a continuous HMM is deployed. It is assumed that the observations $y_1, y_2, \ldots, y_T$ are generated by a multivariate probability density function. For simplicity, we will assume that this is generated by a Gaussian mixture as follows:

$$f_{\mathbf{y}|\mathbf{x}}(\xi|i) = \sum_{m=1}^{P} c_{im} \mathcal{N}(\xi; \mu_{im}, C_{im}) \tag{1}$$

where $\mathcal{N}(\xi; \mu_{im}, C_{im})$ denotes a Gaussian probability density function with mean μ_{im} and covariance matrix C_{im}. The notation $f_{\mathbf{y}|\mathbf{x}}(\cdot)$ denotes the probability of observing $\mathbf{y}$ given the hidden state sequence $\mathbf{x}$. The constants c_{im} are known as mixing coefficients. In order to be a probability density function, we must have $\sum_{m=1}^{P} c_{im} = 1$ for $1 \leq i \leq S$, and S is the size of the alphabet (the dimension of the state space).

It is further assumed that the observation probability density functions are generated by a hidden state $\mathbf{x}$, $\mathbf{x}$ is a S dimensional vector which follows the evolution equation:

$$\mathbf{x}(t+1) = A\mathbf{x}(t) \tag{2}$$

where A is the state transition matrix, with initial condition $\mathbf{x}(0) = \pi_0$. The parameters in the model are then $\mathcal{M} = \{S, \pi_0, A, \{f_{\mathbf{y}|\mathbf{x}}(\xi|i), 1 \leq i \leq S\}\}$.

The problem in HMM estimation can be divided into two sub-problems: (1) given a series of training observations for a given entity, say, a label, how do we train a HMM to represent this label? This problem becomes the finding of a procedure for estimating an appropriate state transition matrix A, and observation probability density function $f_{\mathbf{y}|\mathbf{x}}$ for each state. (2) given a trained HMM, how do we find the likelihood that it produced the incoming observation sequence.

The HMM estimation algorithm is readily available in e.g., [1, 2, 10]. We will use the training algorithm presented in [10]. For the problem of finding class labels given a set of observations, the Viterbi algorithm [10] is used.

4   The Proposed Method

Our approach to the task of pattern discovery is presented in this section. A two-step approach is used which is then applied recursively to obtain a hierarchical tree of HMMs. In the first step, GM is engaged to detect clusters among the profiles. The second step trains a set of HMMs, one for each cluster of profiles. To reduce the computational burden, the HMMs are trained recursively on relatively small subsets. In each iteration, the HMMs are trained on a different subset of randomly selected profiles from the cluster until the classification error reaches a minimum. Note that this approach to training is similar to the k-fold cross validation approach [12], except that it is not as formal. In our approach, we do not divide the data formally into k equal groups. Instead we divide the data into two groups, which may not be equal in size. Then, we randomly select the profiles in one group for training. The evaluation is performed on other groups of data not used in the training data set. Then the data set is further refined using the HMM. The number of profiles in each group may be different. We do not report the average generalisation error. Instead we report the error obtained on a particular set of testing data set. The use of k-fold cross validation process may improve our proposed methodology, as it provides a formal method for training and evaluating data. Furthermore some convergence results have been proved [12]. This will be an issue for further research as it will be interesting to see how different would the results be using our ad hoc method compared with the more formal cross validation methods [12].

4.1   Gaussian Mixture Clustering

It was mentioned in Section 2 that cohorts of claimants of similar age are considered for the pattern recognition task. In this section we choose age cohort 56-70 to illustrate the approach. There are a total of 2,169,333 profiles in this age cohort; we will divide them into a training data set and a validation data set. The GM clustering approach addressed in Section 3.1 is employed on 91,219 randomly selected profiles from the data pool. We employ this relatively small subset of data rather than the full data set available in this cohort group as it suffices for illustration purposes and it allows us to reduce the turn around time for experiments. The subset was obtained by selecting all claimant profiles from a number of postcode areas. Special care was taken to ensure that patients from rural areas and metropolitan areas are proportional to the entire dataset. The list of postcode areas was hand-picked. Postcode areas were obtained by looking up on a geographical map. It was then decided to whether or not to include this postcode area in for the subset. This procedure was tailored to reduce the risk of possible side affects which may arise out of randomly choosing patient profiles. Since both, GM and HMM scale linearly with the number of training data, the training time required for the full dataset is easily estimated through a linear adjustment of the training times stated in this paper. It is important to note that the size of this subset has been chosen so that it contains a good representation of the features available in the full data set.

Out of 91,219 profiles, 64,553 are used for the training process; all remaining profiles are used for testing purposes. Again, the size of the training set is influenced by

Table 2. The clustering results of Gaussian mixture model with 6 components

Cluster:	A	B	C	D	E	F	Total:
Size:	10780	10225	17762	11105	10315	4366	64553

a proportional selection of rural and metropolitan postcode areas. All claimants whose residential addresses that fall within the selected postcode areas are selected (not just some of them). We assume that the dataset is generated by a Gaussian mixture model of $N = 6$ components [5]. The parameters of the model will be first estimated by utilizing the EM algorithm, and then updated through a few EM iterations as shown in Section 3.1 for a better representation to the dataset. The updating ends when improvement of the log likelihood of the posterior probability is less than 1% or the number of EM iteration reaches 50. We applied the GM algorithm to segment the 64,553 profiles into 6 clusters as shown in Table 2.

These clustering results are not suitable for the task of temporal pattern discovery in the sense that it only provides a clustering based on the entire profile using say an Euclidean norm. Thus, two profiles with different temporal differences but similar Euclidean norm would be grouped together in the same cluster. The coarse segmentation will be refined through the application of HMMs.

4.2 Recursive HMM Modeling

As a widely used pattern discovery technique, HMMs are capable of classifying profiles with similar temporal patterns into the same class. The clustering results of GM could serve as training sets so that 6 HMMs, one for each cluster, are trained. However, the computational efforts of training hidden Markov models render them not particularly suitable for data mining tasks, e.g., it takes about 250 minutes to train a HMM on 10,780 profiles using a workstation with a 2GHz XEON processor, and 2 GB RAM. We propose to take a recursive training-recognizing cycle on subsets of data to ease this computational burden:

Training phase: No more than 2000 profiles are randomly chosen from each cluster to train a corresponding HMM. By doing so it takes about 13 minutes to train a HMM.

Recognition phase: All 64,553 profiles are classified by the trained HMMs. The classification re-distributes the profiles between the 6 clusters as shown in Table 3. The rows in Table 3 refer to the clusters obtained by GM whereas the columns are the classifications produced by the set of HMMs. The result will be used for further processing.

The off-diagonal numbers of the confusion Table 3 describe how GM segments different profiles from the HMM. For example, the number of profiles in Class E fell from 10,315 to 6,948. Thus, the recognizing phase provides an adjustment to the grouping of profiles by considering temporal patterns discovered in the training set.

The result may not be optimal since only a relatively small number of profiles were engaged during the training process. The quality of HMMs is improved through a

---

[5] We had tried a number of values for N and found that $N = 6$ produces well behaving hierarchical trees of HMMs as is shown later in this paper.

Table 3. Classification results by the hidden Markov model

Class	A	B	C	D	E	F	Total
A	**9485**	1285	10	0	0	0	10780
B	4055	**3516**	2224	430	0	0	10225
C	957	7002	**9146**	657	0	0	17762
D	0	0	2019	**5701**	2787	598	11105
E	0	0	186	6207	**3282**	640	10315
F	0	0	0	0	879	**3487**	4366
Σ	14497	11803	13585	12995	6948	4725	64553

Table 4. Classification results by the trained HMMs when reaching the stopping criteria

Class	A	B	C	D	E	F	Total
A	**9030**	0	0	0	0	0	9030
B	14	**14227**	11	0	0	0	14252
C	0	1	**16457**	0	0	0	16458
D	0	0	64	**13952**	0	0	14016
E	0	0	0	8	**8853**	0	8861
F	0	0	0	0	3	**1933**	1936
Σ	9044	14228	16532	13952	8856	1933	64553

recursive application of training-recognition cycle by adopting the grouping results from the recognition phase of the previous cycle. This iterative process ensures that more and more data from the training set is eventually considered in the training process, and that mis-classifications are reduced.

The recursive application of training-recognizing cycle stops when there are no mis-classifications or when a maximum number of iterations is reached. Here we allow it to run for up to 50 cycles. The resulting confusion matrix as shown in Table 4 shows that the classification of profiles is vastly improved.

In summary, the recursive training of HMMs significantly reduces the computational burden since it provides a mechanism to detect redundancy in the data set. This is due to the fact that mis-classifications will approach zero faster if the dataset contains many redundant data.

4.3   Building a Hierarchical Tree of HMMs

In the previous 2 steps of GM-HMM pattern discovery process, we have successfully trained HMMs as a representation of patterns. Here we show how the quality of the HMM representations can be further enhanced. At the 40-th cycle it is observed that this is still a gross segmentation of the set of profiles since it is impossible to be certain about the number of clusters which can be used to describe the dataset. The refinement of classification starts with another GM-HMM pattern discovery process for each of the classes obtained so far unless the size of a class is too small to proceed, say, less

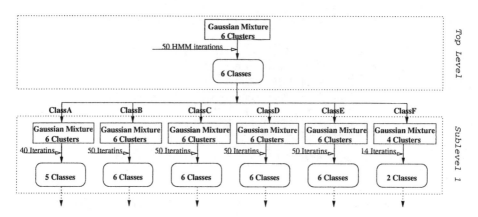

Fig. 2. A flowchart of the iterative GM-HMM refinement process

than 300 profiles[6]. Figure 2 explains the process in a visual manner. The first iteration of the GM-HMM process at the top level ends up with 6 classes after 50 iterations of training of HMMs which reaches the best performance at the 40-th cycle. At the 40-th cycle, another iteration of GM-HMM process at sub-level 1 has proceeded to each of the classes (A to F) for further refinement of the classification results. It is noted that instead of 50, there are only 40 iterations of HMMs training conducted in Class A, i.e., the HMMs trained at the 39-th and the 40-th cycles respectively classify the profiles of Class A in the same manner therefore the HMM training stops. The early exit of HMM training indicates that the HMMs trained on the 2000 randomly chosen profiles from the classes are robust especially when the size of the data set is relatively large. A similar observation can be made on the GM-HMM process to Class F, where only 14 iterations have been run before the mis-classification to the profiles converges to zero. Another observation is that the GM algorithm only provides 4 classes to the profiles in Class F rather than the default number of 6. This implies that the GM algorithm is able to reduce the number of clusters, given the default value. As it is pointed out in Section 4.2, the quality of HMMs can be improved through the recursive deployment of training and recognition cycles to the profiles until the stopping criterion is reached. Then, yet another GM-HMM process is about to start to further refine the classifications when the mis-classification reaches a minimum as long as the size of class is large enough. Figure 3 uses Class A to provide a detailed example of the tree-like recursive application of the GM-HMM process.

Through this refinement process, we decompose the bigger classes into smaller ones so that each HMM is more specialized on the patterns it represents. Our tree-like approach to pattern discovery ends up with 76 classes (A_1 to A_{10}, B_1 to B_{17}, C_1 to C_{20}, D_1 to D_{16}, E_1 to E_{10} and F_1 to F_3). The average benefit paid for each claimant in a class provides a way for us to 'name' clusters: the higher the average value, the higher the class order. e.g., the average benefit paid for claimants in class B_1 is lower

---

[6] We set 300 as the threshold since we find that a HMM cannot be properly trained on less than 300 training data. No HMM will be trained on clusters that contain less than 300 profiles. Affected profiles are considered in the recognition phase to ensure that no profile is discarded.

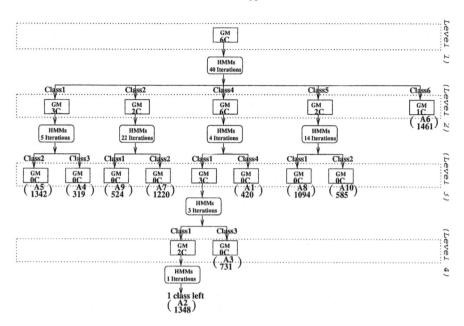

Fig. 3. Applying GM-HMM iteratively to profiles in Class A. The values in the brackets give the class label, and the number of profiles in the sub-class.

than that of class B_2. But it does not guarantee that the value of a subclass from class A, say A_{10}, is lower than that of a subclass of B, say, subclass B_1. The alphabetical order of the classes is decided by the maximum average value of all its subclasses.

5   Experimental Results

Note that the profiles are unlabeled, and the HMMs were trained in an unsupervised fashion. In order to give a meaning to the classes and patterns represented by HMMs, and in order to assess the quality of the results we extract properties on the claimants in the training set and determine how these claimants are classified. For example, it is interesting to see how claimants suffering from a given illness are distributed across the classes. It may be expected that claimants suffering from similar ailments are classified into the same class. This arises from the assumption that the treatment of a particular ailment requires a particular course of treatment, and hence, a "signature" pattern may be present within a profile which can help to classify claimants with similar medical condition into the same class.

We found that this assumption is true *ex poste*, and that the proposed method works particularly well in this respect. In this paper, we will demonstrate this by considering a given ailment, say, stroke, and investigate how the hierarchical HMM models classify affected profiles. Medical items 63130, 63218, and 63850 specifically refer to investigation of whether the claimant is suffering from stroke. There were no other medical

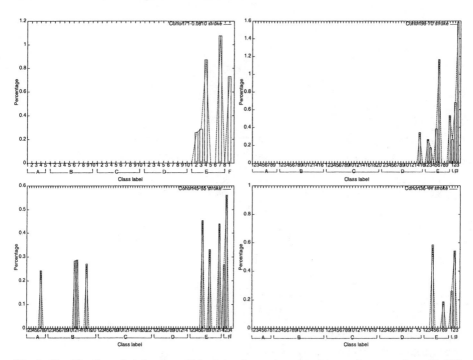

Fig. 4. Classification of claimants which claim for stroke related items for ago cohort 71-110 (upper-left), ago cohort 56-70 (upper-right), age cohort 45-55 (lower left), and age cohort 36-45 (lower right)

items containing the keyword "stroke" when we performed a keyword search on the Medicare Benefits Schedule [7]. Claimants claiming one or more of these items were classified as presented in Figure 4. It is observed that affected profiles are classified into a relatively small set of classes. We also found that for other cohort groups that cases of stroke are rarely observed, and hence were omitted in Figure 4. A closer investigation into the classification for age cohort group >71 shows that only five classes collect such profiles. As is observed, profiles classified as E7 are most likely to feature the property "stroke", while the nearby class E8 did not capture any such claimants.

Creating a histogram of item usages for those two classes, and then subtracting the usage count from each class resulted in a histogram shown in Figure 5. Shown are the differences in item usage between the two classes, where a line pointing in the negative direction indicates that the associated item was used more frequently by claimants in class E8, otherwise, if the line points in the positive direction then the associated item was used more frequently by claimants in class E7. The longer the line, the greater the difference. For example, a value of -163 for item 17603 shows that this item was claimed 163 times more often by claimants in E8 than by claimants in E7.

---

[7] Note that this does not mean that there are no other items which are related to stroke management. It merely indicates that no other item description contained this specific keyword.

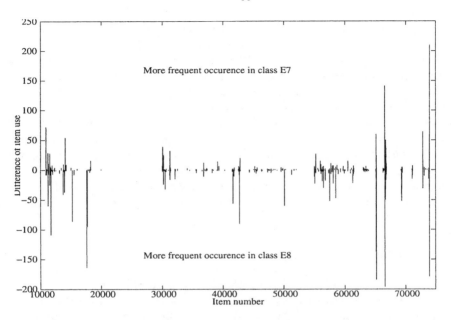

Fig. 5. Difference of item usage for claimants in class E7 and class E8

It can be observed that the greatest differences between the two classes were for items 11700, 17603, 17711, 42702, 65120, 66500, 66515, 73907, and 73910. When taking the relative frequency of item usage into account, then the most significant differences between the two classes were for items 17711, 42702, and 66500. For these items the two classes differed by up to 800% (e.g. item 17711 was claimed 14 times in E7 and 109 times in E8).

From the Medicare Benefits Schedule such observations is interpreted as follows:

Item	Description
17711	Anesthetic, 11 units
42702	Lens extraction & insertion of artificial lens
66500	Lipid studies: cholesterol

Items 17711 and 42702 were used much more frequently by claimants classified into a class which did not collect stroke related item users, whereas item 66500 was claimed much more frequently by claimants classified as E7 (indicating a likelihood that they suffer from stroke). It seems evident that item 66500 is stroke related since cholesterol can contribute to stroke. In contrast, claimants in class E8 seems to be more related to operations on eyes which may be unrelated to stroke.

This is a particularly interesting finding as it is shown that the proposed method introduced in this paper segments profiles into behavioural groups where each group represents a given ailment, property, or course of treatment. The example demonstrated that by judicious incorporation of limited prior information, it is possible to effectively label profiles. In this example, we have shown that class E7 indicates a likelihood that claimants classified in E7 suffer from a stroke related illness. This was confirmed by finding that many of the other profiles from the same class indicate stroke related (e.g. cholesterol studies) treatments even though a claimant has never claimed an item specifically addressing "stroke". In contrast, there is no confusion with claimants from other classes since it was shown that classes unrelated to stroke detection or stroke treatment address ailments completely unrelated to stroke. Hence, it is demonstrated that the proposed method generalizes, and discriminates well.

We also note that more than a single class is typically activated when classifying claimants with a known ailment. This is due to the fact that some ailments may not be isolated instances but are rather embedded courses of treatments within other "signatures" indicating another ailment. For example, there are claimants who receive treatment for a stroke, and at the same time receive treatment for another illness such as diabetes. Thus, some classes collect claimants who suffer from a combination of ailments.

6   Conclusions

In general, hidden Markov models are not particularly suitable for data mining applications as the computational loads are high when the training datasets are large. We have developed an effective method to overcome this limitation. Our approach first decomposes the dataset into groups of claimants of similar age since the age contributes significantly to a claimant's medical conditions. Then the approach applies recursively the Gaussian mixture clustering and HMM procedures on randomly selected samples from the training set until the classification errors converge to a prescribed minimum threshold is observed. This method is effective in detecting redundancies in the dataset and hence can contribute significantly to the reduction of the computational effort of the HMMs. Secondly, by using some limited prior information we obtain a model which is suitable for large scale automatic labeling of profiles. It was demonstrated that the model generalizes well, and is capable of assessing whether medical transactions refer to a related medical condition. This is an interesting attribute given that the model is trained unsupervised, and the underlying medical condition is not used as an input during training. The approach provides a fertile area for further studies and applications such as public health studies which can include prediction of developing ailments, geographic distribution of specific ailments, and many more.

Acknowledgement

The second and third authors wish to acknowledge financial support provided by the Australian Research Council through a SPIRT grant.

References

1. Juang, B. H., Levenson, S. E., Sondhi, M. M. "Maximum likelihood estimation for multivariate mixture observations of Markov chains", *IEEE Trans on Information Theory*. Vol 32, pp 307-309, 1986.
2. Liporace, L. A., "Maximum likelihood estimation for multivariate observations of Markov sources". *IEEE Trans on Information Theory*, Vol 28, pp 729-734, 1982.

3. McLachlan, G. J., Peel, D. "Finite Mixture Models", *Wiley* New York, 2000.
4. Duda, R.O., Hart, P.E., "Pattern recognition and scene analysis", *J Wiley*: New York, 1972.
5. Banfield, J. D., Raftery, A. E. "Model-based Gaussian and non-Gaussian clustering", *Biometrics* Vol 49, pp 803-821, 1993.
6. Kohonen, T., "Self-Organizing Maps", *Springer*, Second Extended Edition 1997, 1995.
7. J.J.Verbeek, N.Vlassis, B. Krose. "Efficient Greedy Learning of Gaussian Mixture Model", *Neural Computation* Vol 15, Issue 2, pp 469-485, 2003
8. Bierens, H. J. "Information criteria", http://econ.la.psu.edu/~hbierens/INFCRIT.PDF, November 2004.
9. Hastie, T., Tibshirani, R., Friedman, J. "The Effective Number of Parameters". The Elements of Statistical Learning, Data Mining, Inference and Prediction, Springer Verlag, pp 203-205, 2001.
10. Deller, J. R. Jr., Proakis, J. G., Hansen, J. H. L. "Discrete-time Processing of Speech Signals", *MacMillan Publishing Company*:New York, 1993.
11. Smyth, P. "Clustering Sequences with Hidden Markov Models", *Advances in Neural Information Processing Systems*, Vol.9, pp 648-, The MIT Press, 1997.
12. Wahba, G. "Spline models for observational data". *CBMS-NSF Regional Conference Series in Applied Mathematics Volume 59*. SIAM, 1990.

Identifying Risk Groups Associated with Colorectal Cancer

Jie Chen[1], Hongxing He[1], Huidong Jin[1], Damien McAullay[1],
Graham Williams[1,2], and Chris Kelman[3]

[1] CSIRO Mathematical and Information Sciences,
GPO Box 664, Canberra ACT 2601, Australia
Firstname.Lastname@csiro.au
[2] Current address: Australian Taxation Office,
51 Allara Street, Canberra ACT 2601, Australia
Graham.Williams@togaware.com
[3] National Centre for Epidemiology and Population Health,
The Australian National University, Canberra ACT 0200, Australia
Chris.Kelman@anu.edu.au

Abstract. In this paper, we explore data mining techniques for the task of identifying and describing risk groups for colorectal cancer (CRC) from population based administrative health data. Association rule discovery, association classification and scalable clustering analysis are applied to the colorectal cancer patients' profiles in contrast to background patients' profiles. These data mining methods enable us to identify the most common characteristics of the colorectal cancer patients. The knowledge discovered by data mining methods which are quite different from traditional survey approaches. Although it is heuristic, the data mining methods may identify risk groups for further epidemiological study, such as older patients living near health facilities yet seldom utilising those facilities, and with respiratory and circulatory diseases.

1 Introduction

Colorectal cancer (cancer of the colon or rectum, abbreviated as CRC) is the second leading cause of cancer-related deaths in the United States for both men and women combined. The disease surpasses both breast and prostate cancer in mortality, and is second only to lung cancer in cause of cancer deaths. Despite the fact that it is highly preventable, approximately 146,940 new cases of colorectal cancer was diagnosed in 2004 and more than 56,000 people will die from the disease in USA [1]. An almost equal number of men and women are diagnosed each year.

In Australia, colorectal cancer is the third most common cause of death from cancer in women (after breast and lung cancer) and men (after lung and prostate cancer). The exact cause of colorectal cancer is unknown, in fact it is thought that there is not one single cause. It is more likely that a number of factors, some known and many unknown, may work together to trigger the development of

G.J. Williams and S.J. Simoff (Eds.): Data Mining, LNAI 3755, pp. 260–272, 2006.
© Springer-Verlag Berlin Heidelberg 2006

colorectal cancer. Previous studies have identified risk factors which may increase a person's risk of developing colorectal cancer. The following factors are widely accepted risks:

- **Age.** Increasing age is considered a major risk factor for developing colorectal cancer. Colorectal cancer is rare in people under 40. The risk increases after the age of 40, rising sharply and progressively after the age of 50.
- **Dietary factors.** It is estimated that rates of colorectal cancer could be reduced in western populations by up to 35% through changes to the food we eat. A diet that is high in fat and low in fibre and vegetables has been linked with an increased risk of colorectal cancer. There has also been an association between heavily browned or charred meat and colorectal cancer. Excessive alcohol intake and a diet low in calcium have also been implicated.
- **Behavioural and lifestyle factors.** An inactive lifestyle, obesity and smoking have been associated with an increased risk of developing colorectal cancer.
- **Regional factors.** People in western countries have a higher incidence of colorectal cancer than people in Asian or African countries. This may be partly due to differences in diet.

This paper aims at studying the relationship between CRC prevalence and various attributes of the patients. These attributes include demographics, medical service history etc. We use large administrative data sets instead of data from survey. The advantages are large coverage of population, low cost and less selection bias. In our case, our dataset covers the medical records of more than one million people. The disadvantage is that we can not design what information we get from individual patients as in designed survey data. Since the transaction data is collected for administrative purposes only, some important information regarding patients' diet and lifestyle is missing. Therefore some well known risk factors can not be verified using administrative data. Nevertheless, it is a good practice to discover unexpected and interesting relationships from this dataset. Since data to be explored is large, and most traditional methods dealing with small samples are not working well, therefore we employ various data mining techniques in our analysis. Exploratory tools of data mining on large dataset may be able to find some factors previously unnoticed. Furthermore, we may identify a few groups of patients with some common characteristics who are at risk of colorectal cancer.

Exploratory health data mining is a rewarding but highly challenging area [14,3]. Recently there have been a few data mining projects initiated for the surveillance and analysis of colorectal cancer patients. A Bayesian framework to extract recurrence, the key outcome for measuring treatment effectiveness for colorectal cancer patients, has been built in [13]. Logistic regression [11] and survival analysis [15] have been applied to identify recurrences and to model the prognosis of colorectal cancer patients. Different from these studies, this paper aims at identifying and describing risk groups rather than single risk factors efficiently. This paper applies various data mining techniques on linked administrative health dataset QLDS. In [2,4], adverse drug reaction has been successfully identified from the same dataset using association and classification algorithms.

The rest of the paper is organised as follows. Section 2 describes the dataset and features selected for the mining process. Sections 3, 4 and 5 describe the methods and mined results for association rule discovery, scalable cluster analysis and association classification analysis respectively. Section 6 discusses the advantages and limitations of the methods. Section 7 concludes the paper.

2   Data Preparation

2.1   QLDS

We use the Queensland Linked Data Set (QLDS) [17] for this exploratory data mining study. The Queensland Linked Data Set (QLDS) was made available to CSIRO under an agreement between Queensland Health and the Commonwealth Department of Health and Ageing (DoHA). The data set contains de-identified and confidentially linked patient level hospital separation data (1 July 1995 to 30 June 1999), Medicare claims data and Pharmaceutical Benefits Scheme (PBS) data (both 1 January 1995 to 31 December 1999). All data were de-identified, and actual dates of service were removed, so that time sequences are indicated by time from first admission. This process provided strong privacy protection, consistent with the requirement of the relevant Federal and State legislations.

The QLDS is based on the collection of patients hospitalised in Queensland between 1 July 1995 to 30 June 1999, with linked PBS and MBS data. Because the linkage relied on a valid Medicare number, around 30% of hospital records (those without a valid Medicare Number associated) were discarded. The QLDS therefore contains 3,087,454 hospital records, corresponding to 1,176,294 individuals, which represents about 35% of the Queensland population. The issues of selection bias and data quality of the QLDS are discussed in the report [18].

2.2   Population Selection

A patient is flagged as a CRC patient if they have ever had a hospital separation between July 1995 and June 1999 with a diagnosis indicating CRC. The ICD9 (The International Classification of Diseases, 9th Revision) codes included are those beginning with 153 (for malignant neoplasm colon) or 154 (malignant neoplasm of rectum/anus). All ten diagnosis flags in hospital separation data are considered. There are 8,104 such patients. In our analysis, the CRC patients are classified into class 1, all the other patients are classified into class 0.

2.3   Feature Selection

Table 1 lists the features selected for the study. The postcode is based on the patients' MBS records. Those patients who do not have any MBS records or their postcode does not fall in Queensland have the field value "NO" as a missing

Table 1. Features selected for the study

Feature	Description	Data Type
Linkid	Encrypted link id	ID variableSymbol
Gender	m:male, f:female	Binary
Age	Age at 1995	Integer
Age Group	Discrete age group	00-43,44-53,54-63,64-73,74-00
Postcode	Postcode of Patient	categorical
Aria Continuous	Access to health facility	Continuous
Aria Discrete	Access to health facility	HA, A, MA,R, VR
Seifa Continuous	Postcode's average household income[1]	Continuous
Seifa Discrete	Postcode's average household income	High, Medium, Low
Consultation Continuous	Number of physician consultations	Continuous
Consultation Discrete	Number of physician consultations	High, Medium, Low
Diagnostic Continuous	Number of diagnostic items in MBS	Continuous
Diagnostic Discrete	Number of diagnostic items in MBS	High, Medium, Low
Procedure continuous	Number of procedure items in MBS	Continuous
diabetes	diabetes flag	0,1
mental	mental flag	0,1
circulatory	circulatory flag	0,1
heart	heart flag	0,1
respiratory	respiratory flag	0,1
asthma	asthma flag	0,1
musculoskeletal	musculoskeletal flag	0,1
Class	0:non-crc 1:crc	Binary

value. For the patients who have more than one MBS record, the majority value is used to decide the value of postcode. The Seifa (Social Economic Index for Areas) data are mapped from postcodes according to the 1996 Australian Census data. The Aria (Accessibility/Remoteness Index of Australia) data are derived from postcodes to reflect the accessibility to health care facilities.

Consultation and diagnosis record the average number of physician consultations and diagnostic items per year respectively. This is calculated for the period prior to the first CRC hospital event for CRC patients and for the entire five years (1996–1999) for non-CRC patients. Consultation is discretised to Low ($c < 4.8$), Medium ($4.8 \leq c < 9.2$) and High($c \geq 9.2$). Diagnostic is discretised to Low ($d < 2.0$), Medium ($2.0 \leq d < 5.43$) and High($d \geq 5.43$). These cutoff values are chosen based on results from running an association algorithm (Magnum Opus). The discretised Seifa values are Low ($s \leq 856.86$), Medium($856.86 < s \leq 1032.15$) and High($s > 1032.15$) so that the population of Queensland has 25% belonging to High, 50% to Medium and 25% to Low.

3   Association Rule Discovery

3.1   Method

The aim of association analysis is to discover the association between available variables and the colorectal cancer prevalence. Magnum Opus was first applied to the whole population in the QLDS. Magnum Opus is an ease to use association rule discovery tool with excellent flexibility. It finds rules from both transaction

---

[1] Year 2000 survey result from Australian Bureau of Statistics.

data and attribute-value data efficiently [16]. It can discretise the numeric attributes automatically.

3.2   Feature Selection

The selected features used for analysis are listed as follows:

- Gender: m, f
- Age: numeric 3
- AriaDis: categorical
- Seifa: numeric 3
- Consultation: numeric 3
- Diagnostic: numeric 3
- Procedure: numeric 3
- Seven Diagnosis flags: 0,1
- Class: 0, 1

All numeric features are discretised into three sub-ranges, each of which contains approximately the same number of cases.

3.3   Results for All Patients

A rule has two parts: a Left Hand Side (LHS) and a Right Hand Side (RHS). The strength of a rule is the proportion of examples covered by the LHS of the rule that are also covered by the RHS. The lift of a rule is the strength divided by the RHS coverage proportion. This indicates how much more frequent the RHS is than normal if the LHS occurs. Table 2 shows a part of the association rules sorted by lift in descending order. Magnum Opus took 21.12 seconds to generate sorted best 100 association rules. Our observations are as follows.

Table 2. Part of the rules identified by Magnum Opus on all patients

Rule No	LHS	RHS(Class 1)	Lift
1	Gender=m Age > 50 AriaDis=HA Consultation < 5.80	806	4.75
2	Age > 50 AriaDis=HA Consultation < 5.80	1299	4.61
3	Age > 50 Consultation < 5.80 $2.40 \leq$ Diagnostic ≤ 6.40	767	4.55

- Rule 1 is interesting, covering about 10% of the 8,104 CRC patients. This group of patients include males aged above 50, with high accessibility to health facilities and having consultation counts less than 5.8. Patients identified by the rule are 4.75 times more likely to have CRC than the general population.

- Rule 2 is a more general rule covering 16% of the CRC population and retaining a lift of 4.61. Rule 3 is similar.
- These rules all suggest that older patients (50+) with accessibility to health care facilities but low utilisation rates are more than four times more likely than the general population to develop colorectal cancer.

3.4   Results for Patients Over 44

Since most CRC patients are older than 40, we selected patients over 44 years of age to form a new dataset for analysis. Magnum Opus was applied to this dataset with selected features and parameters for discretisation as above. Table 3 shows a part of the association rules sorted by lift in descending order. Magnum Opus took 4.57 seconds to generate sorted best 100 association rules. Our observations are as follows.

- Patients aged between 55 and 68 with circulatory disease and a low utilisation of consultations are more than twice as likely as the general population to have colorectal cancer.

Table 3. Part of the rules identified by Magnum Opus on all patients over 44

Rule No	LHS	RHS(Class 1)	Lift
1	55 ≤ Age ≤ 68 Consultation < 8.00 circulatory=1 heart=0	565	2.82
2	AriaDis=HA Consultation < 8.00 respiratory=1 asthma=0	486	2.55
3	55 ≤ Age ≤ 68 Consultation < 8.00 circulatory=1	714	2.41
4	AriaDis=HA Consultation < 8.00 respiratory=1	572	2.35
5	Consultation < 8.00 heart=0 respiratory=1	711	2.28
6	Consultation < 8.00 respiratory=1 asthma=0	726	2.22
7	AriaDis=HA Consultation < 8.00 circulatory=1 heart=0	760	2.20
8	Gender=m 55 ≤ Age ≤ 68 Consultation < 8.00 musculoskeletal=0	906	2.15
9	55 ≤ Age ≤ 68 AriaDis=HA Consultation < 8.00 musculoskeletal=0	863	2.12
10	Consultation < 8.00 circulatory=1 heart=0 musculoskeletal=0	1052	2.10

– Patients with circulatory disease and a low utilisation of consultations living in regions highly accessible to health care facilities are more than twice as likely as the general population to have colorectal cancer.

4 Scalable Cluster Analysis

4.1 Method

Clustering is one of the most widely used techniques in data mining. It is used to reveal patterns in data that can be extremely useful to data analysts. The task of clustering is to partition a data set into clusters in such a way that the data records within each cluster are more similar among themselves than data records in other clusters [5,8]. A scalable clustering system, the computational time of which grows linearly or sub-linearly with the number of data records, bridges the gap between the limited computational resources and large databases [9,7].

We employed a scalable clustering algorithm, BIRCH [19], to identify the groups of patients who are more likely to suffer from CRC. First we normalised each continuous attribute into the interval [0,1]. Then BIRCH with default setting was used to generate 100 clusters based on these continuous attributes. After that, CRC patients within each cluster was used to identify high risk clusters in comparison with the whole data set. For example, the lift is defined as the proportion of CRC patients covered by a cluster divided by the proportion of non-CRC patients covered by this cluster. It roughly indicates to what degree this cluster of people are more likely to suffer from CRC than the whole population. The clusters that have less than 200 patients are left out since they are too small compared with the whole data set.

4.2 Feature Selection

The selected features are listed as following.

– Age: numeric
– AriaCon: numeric
– Seifa: numeric
– Consultation: numeric
– Diagnostic: numeric
– Class: 0, 1

4.3 Clusters for All Patients

We first applied BIRCH to generate 100 clusters for all the 1,176,294 patients. It took about 8.19 seconds in total and about 52,608 patients were not clustered and viewed as outliers.

Table 4 lists typical clusters with high proportions of CRC patients. The clusters are listed in descending order with respect to their lift. The clusters with lift less than 2.0 are omitted from the table. Each row indicates an interesting

Table 4. Typical clusters with high risk for CRC patients identified from all the 1,176,294 patients

Cluster ID	Age	Aria-Con	Seifa	Consu-ltation	Diag-nostic	Class 1	Coverage Cardinality	Coverage %	Lift
0	81.7	0.12	859.6	11.9	5.7	45	1623	0.144	4.17
82	71.7	4.23	967.2	13.2	8.5	236	9485	0.844	3.73
98	71.5	4.97	1014.6	11.8	7.2	38	1696	0.151	3.35
12	79.4	0.55	965.7	16.0	8.5	821	38625	3.437	3.18
43	65.4	0.02	1048.5	43.8	62.1	62	2934	0.261	3.16
63	77.5	2.84	963.8	13.7	7.9	377	18120	1.613	3.11
46	78.2	0.13	1164.3	15.1	9.0	65	3146	0.280	3.09
39	78.0	5.92	950.0	11.9	6.7	68	3298	0.293	3.08
72	67.7	0.32	969.3	15.1	9.5	1293	62716	5.581	3.08
83	64.7	11.46	943.8	8.2	4.2	15	728	0.065	3.08
37	67.9	2.74	882.5	10.8	6.3	58	2820	0.251	3.07
55	62.1	7.89	922.1	9.8	6.1	23	1128	0.100	3.04
86	78.2	0.06	1049.2	16.2	9.3	559	27477	2.445	3.04
6	78.4	10.64	923.3	9.3	3.5	19	948	0.084	2.99
95	65.6	0.11	1045.6	14.4	9.1	750	37627	3.349	2.97
53	80.8	3.54	897.7	11.9	5.3	45	2345	0.209	2.86
79	60.5	3.09	995.7	11.4	7.8	266	14073	1.252	2.82
47	61.1	2.64	941.2	11.3	7.6	424	22693	2.020	2.79
76	64.7	4.15	907.8	10.4	6.3	63	3396	0.302	2.76
97	60.9	10.17	1020.7	6.5	3.9	12	655	0.058	2.73
58	72.9	1.70	1020.4	12.9	7.8	54	3011	0.268	2.67
75	64.7	5.79	953.2	10.4	7.0	97	5566	0.495	2.59
78	55.9	0.36	869.4	11.6	7.2	72	4145	0.369	2.59
13	78.0	8.12	921.3	9.8	4.2	7	411	0.037	2.53
21	60.8	0.16	1168.3	12.3	8.6	102	6417	0.571	2.36
74	62.4	10.47	892.7	8.7	5.0	24	1521	0.135	2.35
66	57.9	1.76	1035.7	10.7	6.9	43	3191	0.284	2.00

cluster described by a cluster centroid. For example, as listed in the first row of Table 4, Cluster 0 has a centroid of Age: 81.7, Aria: 0.12, Seifa: 859.6, Consultations: 11.9, and Diagnostics: 5.7. There are 1,623 patients in the cluster, and 45 CRC patients. The lift is 4.17, i.e., the patients within the cluster are 4.17 times more likely to suffer from CRC. It indicates that this cluster of patients are more likely to suffer from CRC, compared with the whole data set. Similar interesting results can be found in Table 4.

4.4 Clusters for Patients Over 44

We also conducted cluster analysis on the patients over 44 years of age. BIRCH took about 2.39 seconds to generate 100 clusters from the 453,645 patients and generated 27,955 outliers.

Table 5 lists some typical clusters with high proportions of CRC patients from these old patients. They are sorted by lift in descending order, while those with lift less than 1.30 are omitted. A typical example is Cluster 31 as listed in Table 5. Its cluster centre is Age: 65.1, Aria: 5.41, Seifa: 896.3, Consultations: 41.3, and Diagnostics: 54.0. There are 284 patients in the cluster, and 11 CRC patients. The lift is 2.50, this cluster of patients are significantly different from other patients over 44 years of age. Similar results can be observed from other clusters.

Table 5. Typical clusters with high risky of CRC patients on 453,645 patients elder than 44

Cluster ID	Age	Aria-Con	Seifa	Consu-ltation	Diag-nostic	Class 1	Coverage Cardinality	%	Lift
31	65.1	5.42	896.3	41.3	54.0	11	284	0.063	2.50
88	62.9	7.17	886.8	26.6	35.0	11	296	0.065	2.39
29	75.2	8.40	922.0	37.7	49.3	7	216	0.048	2.08
30	81.1	3.64	861.0	25.8	33.9	13	423	0.093	1.97
65	69.1	11.03	938.3	33.8	44.1	12	416	0.092	1.84
71	68.2	4.98	1016.0	31.1	40.6	34	1295	0.285	1.67
2	73.3	0.31	1199.2	14.5	19.0	26	996	0.220	1.66
76	72.9	4.74	907.5	31.2	40.7	34	1338	0.295	1.62
37	65.3	0.14	887.2	28.0	36.6	152	6040	1.331	1.60
81	68.0	3.62	981.7	38.2	49.9	126	5133	1.132	1.56
67	74.5	3.72	981.9	40.5	52.8	85	3487	0.769	1.55
4	82.0	5.93	952.1	26.3	34.3	43	1774	0.391	1.54
13	79.0	0.06	866.1	35.7	46.7	49	2061	0.454	1.51
26	81.9	3.59	991.3	35.5	46.4	82	3540	0.780	1.47
15	66.1	0.31	1197.0	31.9	41.7	20	867	0.191	1.46
86	73.6	0.09	1133.6	37.3	48.7	22	985	0.217	1.42
16	71.5	0.39	966.4	41.0	53.5	355	15943	3.514	1.41
79	76.1	0.66	945.5	37.7	49.2	284	12816	2.825	1.41
90	80.8	4.10	933.4	33.6	43.9	39	1766	0.389	1.40
78	75.9	0.10	1044.1	28.3	36.9	420	19294	4.253	1.38
39	80.6	0.31	1198.2	30.5	39.8	11	514	0.113	1.36
44	65.6	2.58	945.7	35.2	45.9	212	9921	2.187	1.35
46	77.3	2.69	944.4	36.0	46.9	98	4628	1.020	1.34
94	61.3	3.12	997.6	32.7	42.6	160	7569	1.668	1.34
34	69.1	0.09	1049.0	34.5	45.0	424	20059	4.422	1.34
82	71.0	2.82	940.2	32.5	42.4	188	9016	1.987	1.32
54	58.4	0.34	869.3	20.7	27.1	40	1942	0.428	1.30
51	73.5	1.75	1032.9	33.5	43.7	34	1654	0.365	1.30
27	66.3	3.24	887.3	37.4	48.8	24	1168	0.257	1.30
74	81.7	10.53	903.4	32.3	42.3	6	292	0.064	1.30

5   Association Classification

5.1   Method

The association classification algorithm developed in [10] generates the optimal class association rule set. The experimental results in [10] show that the optimal class rule set achieves a very high classification accuracy.

However, our dataset has very unbalanced classes. Our main interest is in finding rules (or cohorts) which lead to higher occurrences of colorectal cancer patients than the average occurrence. As a result, the original algorithm has been modified to increase classification accuracy of class 1 patients. The modification is that, instead of using the minimum global support as a criterion for rules to be included, local support is introduced to find the rules describing the small class (class 1). *Local Support* is defined by Equation 1.

$$lsup(A \rightarrow c) = \frac{sup(A \rightarrow c)}{sup(c)} \tag{1}$$

Here $sup(c)$ and $sup(A \rightarrow c)$ represent the support (or proportion or relative frequency) of class c in the whole population and the support of pattern A in class c respectively. The algorithm will identify rules which give high "lift" values for class 1. Lift is defined in Equation 2.

$$lift(A \rightarrow c) = \frac{lsup(A \rightarrow c)}{sup(A)} \qquad (2)$$

5.2 Results for All Patients

Example rules identified are listed in Table 6. Features selected are similar to Section 3 except that some features are discretised to categorical variables. Rule 1 identifies patients with the following characteristics:

- Aged between 64 and 73.
- Living in areas highly accessible to medical facilities.
- Having small number of doctor's consultations.
- No heart and musculoskeletal diseases.

Table 6. Part of the rules identified by association classification algorithm for all patients

Rule No	Rule	Class 1	Lift
1	Age = 64-73 Aria = HA Consultation = Low heart = 0 musculoskeletal = 0	273	6.74
3	Age = 54-63 Aria = HA Consultation = Low heart = 0 musculoskeletal = 0	317	6.28
10	Age = 64-73 Consultation = Medium diabetes = 0 circulatory = 1 heart = 0	255	6.19
62	Gender = m Aria = HA mental = 0 circulatory = 1 heart = 0 respiratory = 1 asthma = 0	260	5.05
66	Gender = m Age = 64-73 heart = 0 respiratory = 1 asthma = 0	269	4.97
79	Age = 74-00 circulatory = 1 heart = 0 respiratory = 1 musculoskeletal = 0	278	4.89
91	Consultation = Low circulatory = 1 respiratory = 1 asthma = 0	283	4.77

There are a total of 273 CRC patients in this group. The lift of the group is 6.74. It implies that the individuals who have these characteristics are 6.74 times more likely to have CRC than general population. Rule 62 indicates that for males, living in highly accessible area with circulatory and respiratory diseases, but no heart and asthma diseases, the likelihood of CRC is 5.05. Rules 62, 79 and 91 all suggest that CRC is correlated with circulatory and respiratory diseases.

5.3   Results for Patients Over 44

Results for patients over 44 are shown in Table 7.

Table 7. Part of the rules identified by association classification algorithm for patients older than 44

Rule No	Rule	Class 1	Lift
1	Age Group = 64-73 Consultation = Low heart = 0 musculoskeletal = 0	475	2.62
2	Consultation = Low heart = 0 Respiratory = 1	414	2.48
4	Aria = HA Consultation = Low circulatory = 1 heart = 0	385	2.51
6	Age = 54-63 Consultation = Low musculoskeletal = 0	568	2.35

6   Discussion

The results obtained by the three data mining techniques are consistent with aggregation results based on CRC and non CRC patients profiles [6]. Most of the interesting results are agreeable in terms of high lift value, especially for the results by using association rule and association classification techniques. For instance, Rules 5 and 7 in Table 3 agree with Rules 2 and 4 in Table 7. The results from scalable clustering analysis are not as expressive as those from the former two techniques, but it can efficiently draw a big picture about the characteristics of CRC patients against whole population.

Logistic regression in R has been tried on the dataset [12]. Risk factors highlighted include Age, "Gender = m", "AriaDis" except for "AriaDis=R" and "AriaDis=VR", "Consultation", "Diagnostic", and seven diagnosis flags (mental flag was not highlighted for patients over 44). Nonetheless, it is not trival to identify risk groups through the statistical method.

Our current feature selection is based on domain knowledge and the limitations of each techinque. For instances, the scalable clustering algorithm can only handle continuous features. It will be interesting to apply automatic feature selection methods to this health data mining problem since there are a large number of variables in our data to be explored.

7 Conclusion

Three different data mining techniques have been used to explore possible risk groups for colorectal cancer. The analysis was performed on two populations in this study. The first population comprises the population who have developed colorectal cancer during the period of study. The second population consists of patients who have not developed colorectal cancer. The analysis explored the main differences between the two populations to identify risk groups for colorectal cancer. Each technique has been applied to the two datasets with demographic and socio-economical variables and variables extracted from patients' health care history.

These heuristic results from data mining explorations may help health care professionals in identifying areas for further study of the causes and preventative factors of colorectal cancer. Typical risk groups identified for colorectal cancer have the following potential characteristics:

- Older patients.
- People living near health facilities yet seldom utilising those facilities.
- Patients with respiratory and circulatory diseases.

As mentioned before, limitation of the data (in particular the lack of lifestyle factors including diet, physical exercise, smoking, and drinking) severely limits the scope of detailed analyses. The study is not intended to identify the most important factors leading to colorectal cancer. Rather it can only explore through the variables included in the data sets.

Acknowledgements

The authors acknowledge the Australian Government Department of Health and Ageing and the Queensland Department of Health for providing data for this research. The authors also would like to thank their colleagues, Ross Sparks, Jisheng Cui and Lifang Gu, as well as Jiuyong Li of University of South Queensland and the anonymous reviewers for their comments and suggestions.

References

1. Colorectal cancer: The importance of prevention and early detection. Division of Cancer Prevention and Control, National Center for Chronic Disease Prevention and Health Promotion, Centers for Disease Control and Prevention, U.S. Department of Health and Human Services, 2004.
2. J. Chen, H. He, G. Williams, and H. Jin. Temporal sequence associations for rare events. In *Proceedings of PAKDD04, Lecture Notes in Computer Science (LNAI 3056)*, pages 235–239, Sydney, Australia, May 2004.
3. K. J. Cios and G. W. Moore. Uniqueness of medical data mining. *Artificial Intelligence in Medicine*, 26(1-2):1–24, 2002.

4. L. Gu, J. Li, H. He, G. Williams, S. Hawkins, and C. Kelman. Association rule discovery with unbalanced class. In *Proceedings of AI03, Lecture Notes in Artificial Intelligence*, pages 221–232, Perth, Western Australia, December 2003.

5. J. Han and M. Kamber. *Data Mining: Concepts and Techniques*. Morgan Kaufmann Publishers, San Francisco, CA, USA, 2001.

6. H. He, J. Chen, H. Jin, S. Hawkins, G. Williams, D. McAullay, R. Sparks, J. Cui, and C. Kelman. QLDS: Colorectal cancer data mining analysis. Technical Report 04/92, CSIRO Mathematical and Information Sciences, Canberra, 2004.

7. H.-D. Jin, K.-S. Leung, M.-L. Wong, and Z.-B. Xu. Scalable model-based cluster analysis using clustering features. *Pattern Recognition*, 38(5):637–649, May 2005.

8. H.-D. Jin, W. Shum, K.-S. Leung, and M.-L. Wong. Expanding self-organizing map for data visualization and cluster analysis. *Information Sciences*, 163:157–173, Jun. 2004.

9. H.-D. Jin, M.-L. Wong, and K.-S. Leung. Scalable model-based clustering by working on data summaries. In *Proceedings of Third IEEE International Conference on Data Mining (ICDM 2003)*, pages 91–98, Melbourne, Florida, USA, Nov. 2003.

10. J. Li, H. Shen, and R. Topor. Mining the optimal class association rule set. *Knowledge-Based Systems*, 15(7):399–405, 2002.

11. D. McClisha, L. Penberthyb, and A. Pughc. Using medicare claims to identify second primary cancers and recurrences in order to supplement a cancer registry. *Journal of Clinical Epidemiology*, 56:760–767, 2003.

12. R Development Core Team. *R: A language and environment for statistical computing*. R Foundation for Statistical Computing, Vienna, Austria, 2004. ISBN 3-900051-00-3.

13. R. B. Rao, S. Sandilya, R. S. Niculescu, C. Germond, and H. Rao. Clinical and financial outcomes analysis with existing hospital patient records. In *Proceedings of the ninth ACM SIGKDD international conference on Knowledge discovery and data mining*, pages 416 – 425, 2003.

14. J. Roddick, P. Fule, and W. Graco. Exploratory medical knowledge discovery : Experiences and issues. *SIGKDD Exploration*, 5(1):94–99, 2003.

15. A. E. Smith and S. S. Anand. Patient survival estimation with multiple attributes: adaptation of coxs regression to give an individuals point prediction. In *Proceedings of European Conference in Artificial Intelligence in Intelligent Datamining in Medicine & Pharmacology*, pages 51–54, Berlin, 2000.

16. G. I. Webb. Efficient search for association rules. In *Proceedings of SIGKDD'00*, pages 99–107, 2000.

17. G. Williams, D. Vickers, R. Baxter, S. Hawkins, C. Kelman, R. Solon, H. He, and L. Gu. The Queensland Linked Data Set. Technical Report CMIS 02/21, CSIRO, Canberra, 2002.

18. G. Williams, D. Vickers, C. Rainsford, L. Gu, H. He, R. Baxter, and S. Hawkins. Bias in the Queensland Linked Data Set. Technical Report 02/117, CSIRO Mathematical and Information Sciences, Canberra, 2002.

19. T. Zhang, R. Ramakrishnan, and M. Livny. BIRCH: A new data clustering algorithm and its applications. *Data Mining and Knowledge Discovery*, 1(2):141–182, 1997.

Mining Quantitative Association Rules in Protein Sequences

Nitin Gupta[1], Nitin Mangal[2], Kamal Tiwari, and Pabitra Mitra

[1] Bioinformatics Group, Dept. of Computer Science,
University of California, San Diego,
3859 Miramar Street #D, La Jolla, CA 92037, USA
nitiniitk@yahoo.com
[2] Department of Computer Science and Engineering,
Indian Institute of Technology Kanpur - 208016, India
mangal_iitk@yahoo.com, pmitra@cse.iitk.ac.in

Abstract. Lot of research has gone into understanding the composition and nature of proteins, still many things remain to be understood satisfactorily. It is now generally believed that amino acid sequences of proteins are not random, and thus the patterns of amino acids that we observe in the protein sequences are also non-random. In this study, we have attempted to decipher the nature of associations between different amino acids that are present in a protein. This very basic analysis provides insights into the co-occurrence of certain amino acids in a protein. Such association rules are desirable for enhancing our understanding of protein composition and hold the potential to give clues regarding the global interactions amongst some particular sets of amino acids occuring in proteins. Presence of strong non-trivial associations suggests further evidence for non-randomness of protein sequences. Knowledge of these rules or constraints is highly desirable for the in-vitro synthesis of artificial proteins.

Keywords: Data mining, quantitative association rule mining, protein composition.

1 Introduction

Proteins are important constituents of cellular machinery of any organism. Recombinant DNA technologies have provided tools for the rapid determination of DNA sequences and, by inference, the amino acid sequences of proteins from structural genes [1]. The proteins are sequences made up of 20 types of amino acids. Each amino acid is represented by a single letter alphabet, see Table 1. Each protein adopts a unique 3-dimensional structure, which is decided completely by its amino-acid sequence. A slight change in the sequence might completely change the functioning of the protein.

The heavy dependence of protein functioning on its amino acid sequence has been a subject of great anxiety. Research has been done to determine the information content per amino acid in proteins by Yockey [2] and Strait & Dewey [3].

G.J. Williams and S.J. Simoff (Eds.): Data Mining, LNAI 3755, pp. 273–281, 2006.

Table 1. Single letter codes of amino acids

S.No.	AA Code	Full-Name
1	A	Alanine
2	C	Cysteine
3	D	Aspartic Acid
4	E	Glutamic Acid
5	F	Phenylalanine
6	G	Glycine
7	H	Histidine
8	I	Isoleucine
9	K	Lysine
10	L	Leucine
11	M	Methionine
12	N	Asparagine
13	P	Proline
14	Q	Glutamine
15	R	Arginine
16	S	Serine
17	T	Threonine
18	V	Valine
19	W	Tryptophan
20	Y	Tyrosine

There has been a continuing debate on whether the amino acid seqeunces of proteins are random or have statistically significant deviations from random sequences. White & Jacobs [5] have shown that any sequence chosen randomly from a large collection of nonhomologous proteins has a 90% or better chance of having a lengthwise distribution of amino acids that is indistinguishable from the random expectation regardless of amino acid type. They claimed that proteins have evolved from random sequences but have developed significant deviations from randomness during the process of evolution. Pande et al [4] mapped protein sequences to random walks to detect differences in the trajectories of a Brownian particle. They found pronounced deviations from pure randomness which seem to be directed towards the minimization of energy in the 3D structure.

In this study, we take a further step in this direction by trying to predict if there are any co-occurrence patterns among the 20 amino-acids. We have attempted to find out rules that can tell that occurrence of one amino-acid is more likely when another amino-acid is present or absent. Such rules are called "association rules", and the corresponding technique is called "association rule mining" (ARM). In ARM terminology, the amino- acids may be considered as items, and the protein sequences as "baskets" containing items. See the next section for a introduction to association rule mining. Proteins are polymers of length usually in hundreds. Since the length is much larger, all the 20 amino acids are present in majority of proteins, and thus we will not be able deduce any significant rule just based on presence or absence. To obtain more meaningful association rules in this context, we have incorporated the normalized frequencies of amino-acids observed in each protein, and also discovered "quantitative association rules", which tell that if one amino-acid A is present with a f_1 frequency, another amino-acid B is likely to be present with f_2 frequency. Our quantitative association rule mining procedure [8] enables us to find these numbers f_1 and f_2.

The organization of this paper is as follows; the next section gives an overview of association rule mining. Section 3 describes how we have implemented association rule mining for finding quantitative rules in proteins. Section 4 shows the rules that we have obtained. The next section discusses these results and concludes the outcomes of this study, followed by future work describing how this study can be extended.

2   Association Rule Mining

Before we begin with the description of our algorithm, it will be helpful to review some of the key concepts of association rule mining. We use the same notation as used in [9]. Let $I = \{i_1, ..., i_k\}$ be a set of k elements, called *items*. Let $B = \{b_1, ..., b_n\}$ be a set of n subsets of I. We call each $b_i \subseteq I$ a *basket* of items. For example, in the market basket application, the set I consists of the items stocked by a retail outlet and each basket is the set of purchases from one register transaction. Similarly, in the "document basket" application, the set I contains all dictionary words and proper nouns, while each basket is a single document in the corpus. Note that the concept of a basket does not take into account the ordering or frequency of items that might be present. An association rule is intended to capture a certain type of dependence among items represented in the database B. Specifically, we say that $i_1 \rightarrow i_2$ if the following two hold

1. i_1 and i_2 occur together in at least $s\%$ of the n baskets (the *support*).
2. Of all the baskets containing i_1, atleast $c\%$ also contain i_2 (the *confidence*).

This definition is also extended to $I \rightarrow J$, where I and J are disjoint sets of items instead of single items. Let us consider an example of a document basket application. The baskets in this case are many short stories that are available at our disposal, while the items within each basket are the words. A reader might observe that stories which contain the word "sword" also frequently contain the word "blood". This information can be represented in the form of a rule as:

$$sword \rightarrow blood$$

$$[support = 5\%, confidence = 55\%] \qquad (1)$$

Rule support and confidence are the two measures of rule interestingness [10]. They respectively reflect the usefulness and certainty of discovered rules. A support of 5% for an association rule means that 5% of stories under analysis show that "blood" and "sword" occur together. A confidence of 55% means that 55% of the stories that contain the word "sword" also contain the word "blood". Typically, associations rules are considered interesting if they satisfy both minimum support threshold and a minimum confidence threshold. Such threshold can be set by users or domain experts. As pointed out in [9], it should be noted that the symbol $\rightarrow$ is misleading since such a rule does not correspond to real implications; clearly, the confidence measure is merely an estimate of the conditional probability of i_2 given i_1.

2.1   The Apriori Algorithm

The most commonly used approach for finding association rules is based on the Apriori algorithm [6]. Apriori employs an iterative approach known as a level-wise search, where k-itemsets (sets containing k items) are used to explore $(k + 1)$-itemsets. First, the set of frequent (i.e. having more than the minimum support) 1-itemsets is found. This set is used to find set of frequent 2-itemsets, which is used to find the set of frequent 3-itemsets, and so on, until no more frequent k-itemsets can be found. The efficiency of the level-wise generation of frequent itemsets is improved by using the Apriori property which says that all nonempty subsets of a frequent itemset must also be frequent. This is easy to observe, because if an itemset I does not satisfy the minimum support threshold, then the set $I' = I \vee \{i_{new}\}$, containing all elements of I and an extra element i_{new}, cannot occur more frequently than I, and thus cannot satisfy the minimum support threshold.

2.2   Quantitative Association Rules

While the association rule model described above suffices for many applications, it is not adequate when the frequency of each item in the basket is variable and cannot be ignored. For example, in the previously considered example, a user might be interested in the rules of the form:

$$sword_{30-35} \wedge war_{14-16} \rightarrow blood_{50-52} \tag{2}$$

This rule represents that a story that contains between 30 to 35 occurrences of "sword" and 14 to 16 occurrences of "war", is also likely to contain 50 to 52 references of "blood". Such rules are called quantitative association rules.

The ARCS system [11] for mining quantitative association rules is based on rule clustering. Essentially this approach maps pairs of quantitative attributes onto a multi-dimensional grid, with the number of dimensions equaling the number of quantitative attributes considered. The grid is then searched for clusters of points, from which the association rules are generated. Techniques for mining quantitative rules based on x-monotone and rectilinear regions were presented in [7]. Approach proposed in [8] works by fine-partitioning the values of the quantitative attributes, and then generating rules of interest.

3   Algorithm

Our implementation is based on the partitioning approach described in [8]. We consider 20 attributes in proteins, each related to an amino acid. The value of each attribute in a basket (here protein) is the frequency of the corresponding amino acid in the protein. Since the proteins are of varying lengths, we normalize this frequency by dividing by the length of the protein.

The main steps in the algorithm are as follows:

1. Partition the attributes: We have divided each of the 20 attributes into 10 intervals. In [8], the authors have discussed the notion of partial complete-ness to quantify the amount of information lost due to partitioning. It has been further shown that for a given number of partitions, equi-depth par-titioning (each partition having equal support) gives the minimum loss of information, and is thus optimal. Thus, we have used equi-depth partition-ing in our method. For the sake of completeness and comparison, we have also experimented with equi-distant partitioning, in which all intervals are of equal length.

2. The intervals/partitions are mapped into consecutive integers, which are used to represent the intervals. The order of intervals is preserved in the mapping.

3. Find the support for each of the intervals. Also the consecutive intervals are combined as long as their support is less than a predetermined maximum support. This is actually needed in case of equi-distant partitioning when some of the intervals may have very small support and thus it makes sense to combine them with the adjoining intervals. In equi-depth partitioning, all intervals have equal support, and thus this problem does not arise. We identify the set of all intervals which have more than a minimum support *minsup*. This is called the set of *frequent* items.

   Next we find all sets of items whose support is greater than *minsup*. These are called the frequent itemset, and the algorithm is based on the Apriori algorithm, discussed in the previous section.

4. The frequent itemsets are used to generate association rules. each itemset can give rise to number of association rules by dividing into two parts: an-tecedents and consequences. For example, an itemset {P,Q,R} can lead to the following rules

   - $P \rightarrow Q \wedge R$
   - $Q \wedge R \rightarrow P$
   - $P \wedge Q \rightarrow R$
   - $R \rightarrow P \wedge Q$
   - $Q \rightarrow P \wedge R$
   - $P \wedge R \rightarrow Q$

   The confidence *conf* for each of the rules is determined as the conditional probability of conclusion given precedent. For example, for the rule

   $$P \wedge Q \rightarrow R, conf = support\{P, Q, R\}/support\{P, Q\}$$

If the confidence is greater than a pre-determined minimum confidence, *min-conf*, the rule is kept, otherwise it is removed.

4 Results

The protein sequences are taken from the SCOP Astral File v1.63 [12], containing only those sequences which are less than 40% homologous to each other. This reduces the bias in favour of highly populated families as compared to sparse ones. The sequences with length less than 100 or more than 500 are not considered. This gives us a set of 3728 non-homologous amino-acid sequences representing the different types of proteins. In this study our focus is on deriving associations applicable to all proteins in general.

Figure 1 shows the rules obtained with minimum support of 30 proteins. We have obtained 12 association rules, which have confidence more than 50%. The universe of chains that can be built from 20 amino acids is extremely large and diverse. In light of this fact, the confidence and support of the rules presented in Figure 1 are quite significant.

As an example, the eighth rule indicates that proteins containing large amounts of Arginine(R) and very low amount of Serine(S) are likely to contain no Cysteine (C). Cysteines are the amino acids that participate in the formation of disuphide bonds in the amino acids. This rule implies that presence of large amounts of Arginine without compensating Serine will hinder the ability of a protein to form the disulphide bonds. Such rules provide some insight into the interaction and role of these amino acids in proteins, and have important consequences in the emerging field of *synthetic biology* where biological entities are designed and synthesized in the lab.

Rule	Confidence(%)	Support
<G,52..500> ^ <S,45..500> => <E,0..16>	64.7	33
<E,0..16> ^ <L,0..26> => <T,40..500>	60.9	39
<E,0..16> ^ <M,0..2> => <T,40..500>	59.6	31
<L,0..26> ^ <S,45..500> => <T,40..500>	55.0	38
<E,0..16> ^ <L,0..26> => <G,52..500>	54.6	35
<I,0..13> ^ <R,39..500> => <N,0..8>	54.4	43
<K,0..11> ^ <S,45..500> => <E,0..16>	54.2	32
<R,39..500> ^ <S,0..14> => <C,0..0>	53.5	30
<K,0..11> ^ <N,0..8> => <R,39..500>	53.4	31
<P,35..500> ^ <R,39..500> => <N,0..8>	52.6	30
<L,64..500> ^ <P,35..500> => <N,0..8>	51.7	30
<I,0..13> ^ <N,0..8> => <R,39..500>	50.5	43

Fig. 1. Associations obtained using equi-depth partitioning. Each interval (contained in angular brackets) has an amino acid, and frequency range with protein length scaled to 500. The support is the number of proteins in our dataset of 3728 proteins containing all the intervals present in the association rule.

Rule		Confidence(%)	Support
`<I,40..49> ^ <R,20..29> => <W,0..9>`		94.5	139
`<C,0..9> ^ <F,10..19> ^ <P,10..19> ^ <V,40..49> => <W,0..9>`		94.4	102
`<C,0..9> ^ <I,40..49> ^ <N,10..19> => <W,0..9>`		94.1	112
`<I,40..49> ^ <L,40..49> => <W,0..9>`		93.6	118
`<A,60..79> ^ <P,20..29> ^ <W,0..9> => <C,0..9>`		93.6	103
`<C,0..9> ^ <H,0..9> ^ <S,20..29> ^ <Y,0..9> => <W,0..9>`		93.6	104
`<D,20..29> ^ <P,10..19> ^ <V,40..49> => <W,0..9>`		93.5	101
`<A,60..79> ^ <T,20..29> ^ <W,0..9> => <C,0..9>`		93.3	126
`<H,0..9> ^ <N,10..19> ^ <Y,0..9> => <W,0..9>`		93.2	151
`<Q,10..19> ^ <S,20..29> ^ <Y,0..9> => <W,0..9>`		93.2	110
`<H,0..9> ^ <V,40..49> ^ <Y,0..9> => <W,0..9>`		93.1	108
`<C,0..9> ^ <S,20..29> ^ <T,20..29> ^ <V,40..49> => <W,0..9>`		93.1	109
`<C,0..9> ^ <H,0..9> ^ <N,10..19> ^ <Y,0..9> => <W,0..9>`		93.0	121

Fig. 2. Associations obtained using equi-distant partitioning. Representation is same as in Figure 1. Note that consequence part in all the rules contains either Cysteine (C) or Tryptophan (W). See results section for the discussion of this behavior.

To see how the performance of the algorithm changes when equi-distant rules are used, we created 10 intervals of equal length with frequency ranges 0-9, 10-19,..., 80-89 and 90-500. Note the last interval has been stretched to accommodate any arbitrarily high frequency, which is extremely rare. The proteins lengths are scaled to 500 and the frequencies are increased or decreased in proportion. The association rules obtained from this approach are shown in Figure 2. As expected, the method gets heavily biased in favour of those intervals which have very high supports. For example, Cysteine(C) and Tryptophan(W) are the less frequent amino acids in proteins; in most proteins the frequency of these amino acids is close to zero. Thus the lowermost intervals for these two amino acids get very high support value, and thus generate association rules with very high support and confidence. Note that these rules, inspite of high confidence and support, are not useful to biologists. The consequence part of these rules say that Cysteine and Tryptophan occur in range 0-9, which is trivially known for majority of the proteins.

5   Discussions and Conclusion

We have used quantitative association rule mining to discuss global associations between amino acids in proteins. We call the associations global because the rules are not forced to be based on contiguous set of amino acids, and thus can capture global correlations as well.

The amino acid frequencies are divided into intervals to build the rules. We observe that equi-depth partitioning gives 12 association rules involving various amino acids. The use of equi-distant partitioning gives skewed results, because the relative frequencies of amino acids in the proteins are highly different and equi-distant partitioning results in some very highly populated and some very sparsely populated partitions. This is in line with the conclusion about supremacy of equi-depth approach drawn from the concept of partial completeness in [8].

An important property of our approach is that it can discover rules based not only the presence of amino acids, but also on absence. For example, the eighth rule in Figure 1 has the consequence which says C is likely to be absent. This is a significant difference from the standard motif based works, which are framed only the basis of presence of an amino acid. We acknowledge the fact that absence of a particular amino acid can also be important in the structure and/or function a protein.

To the best of our knowledge, this is the first systematic study to discover global associations between amino acids. The rules obtained here present the constraints in the composition of proteins, and will prove very important in the design and synthesis of artificial peptides, outside the cell. The pharmaceutical industry is gradually shifting from *small molecule* drugs to *biologics* which are synthetic peptides, and is likely to benefit from the availability of knowledge about the rules governing the composition of peptides found in the nature.

This work can be extended in following ways:

- The rules generated in this study are very interesting, and non-trivial. Experimental verification of these methods is a big challenge, and there is no easy way to do that. One strategy could be to design synethetic amino acid chains that violate the rules obtained here, and study their physico-chemical properties in-vitro to see if they behave differently.
- Our approach has been based on partitions approach proposed in [8]. It is possible to use other approaches as well, and it is to be seen if they result in some more interesting rules.
- Instead of finding rules based on whole set of proteins, specialized rules can be found for different classes of proteins. This, however, requires a larger protein dataset containing sufficient number of distinct and non-homologous represenentatives in each class.

Acknowledgment

We thank Dr. Somenath Biswas (Computer Science, IIT Kanpur) for valuable discussions.

References

1. Branden, C. and Tooze, J. *Introduction to Protein Structure* (Garland Publishing, New York, 1991).
2. Yockey, H. P. (1977). On the information content of cytochrome. *J. Theor. Biol.* 67, 147-151.
3. Strait, B.J.& Dewey, G.(1996). The Shannon information entropy of protein sequences. *Biophys. J.* 71, 148-155.
4. Pande, S. V., Grosberg, A. Y. & Tanaka, T. (1994). Non-randomness in protein sequences: evidence for a physically driven stage of evolution? *Proc. Natl. Acad. Sci. U.S.A.* 91, 12972-12975.

5. White, S. H. & Jacobs, R. E. (1993). The evolution of proteins from random amino acid sequences - I. Evidence of proteins from the lengthwise distribution of amino acids in modern proteins. *J. Mol. Evol.* 36, 79-95.

6. Agrawal, R. and Srikant, R. (1994). Fast algorithms for mining association rules. In *Proc of the 20th Int'l Conference on Very Large Databases*, Santiago, Chile, September'94.

7. Fukuda, T., Morimoto, Y., Morishita, S. and Tokuyama, T. (1996) Data mining using two-dimensional optimized association rules: Scheme, algorithms, and visualization. In *Proc. 1996 ACM-SIGMOD Int. Conf. Management of Data*, pp 13-23, Montreal, Canada.

8. Srikant, R. and Agrawal, R. (1996). Mining quantitative association rules in large relational tables. *Proc. ACM SIGMOD*.

9. Brin, S., Motwani, R., and Silverstein, C. (1997). Beyond market basket: Generalizing association rules to correlations. In *Proc. 1197 ACM SIGMOD*, pp 265-276. Tuscon, AZ.

10. Han, J. and Kamber, M. Data Mining: Concepts and Techniques. *Morgan Kaufmann Publishers*, San Francisco, 2001.

11. Lent, B., Swami, A. and Widom, J. (1997). Clustering association rules. In *Proc. Int'l Conf. Data Engineering (ICDE'97)*, pp220-231, England.

12. http://scop.mrc-lmb.cam.ac.uk/scop/

Mining X-Ray Images of SARS Patients

Xuanyang Xie, Xi Li, Shouhong Wan, and Yuchang Gong

Department of Computer Science and Technology,
University of Science and Technology of China,
Hefei 230027, Anhui, China
shiehxy@mail.ustc.edu.cn

Abstract. Severe Acute Respiratory Syndrome (SARS) has infected more than 8,000 persons [1] after it first broke out in Guangdong China. As there was no fast and effective detection method of suspected SARS cases,this paper proposes a computer aided SARS detection system (CADSARS) based on data mining techniques.'Typical pneumonia' and SARS X-Ray chest radiographs were collected.Feature extraction of these images was performed after segmenting out pulmonary fields. Feature vectors were then constructed to build rules for the discrimination of SARS and 'typical pneumonia'.Three methods were used to classify these images: C4.5, neural network and CART.Final results show that about 70.94% SARS cases can be detected. ROC charts and confusion matrix by these three methods are given and analyzed.Association rules mining was used to find whether there exists difference of lesions' location between SARS and pneumonia cases.

1 Introduction

SARS,also known as 'Atypical Pneumonia' in China,was first found in Guangdong, China,2002. By July 31,2003,5327 patients had been infected with it in China, accounts to 65.6% of all the cases reported in the world[1]. Four newly confirmed SARS cases were reported in China last year.It's important to detect suspected SARS cases early and exactly,the same to the diagnosis of this disease.There is a pressing necessity of developing a computer aided detection of SARS system,especially for the countries or regions that have no experience in dealing with this disease.

As said in [2][3],besides the epidemiology, diagnostic examination and laboratory test,one of the most important factors of judging a SARS case is the patients X-Ray chest radiographs.Because of the high resolution of X-Ray images($2K \times 2K$ or higher with 12 to 14 bits gray level),confirmation of SARS cases is decided by using X-ray images,especially the Posterior-Anterior(PA) images[4].

Medical Image analysis in combination with data mining yields the possibility of advanced computer-assisted medical diagnosis systems[5].As many of the research fields are focused in lung cancer[6],breast cancer[7],functional brain image analysis[8],etc.,few literatures were found to deal with SARS images[9].

In this paper,a data mining based scheme of Computer Aided Detection of SARS (CADSARS) is introduced.The architecture of CADSARS will be given

G.J. Williams and S.J. Simoff (Eds.): Data Mining, LNAI 3755, pp. 282–294, 2006.

in Sect. 2.In Sect.3,the data cleaning process is described to construct the high quality training set for future usage.The definition of Region of Interest(ROI) and how to segment out this area are given in Sect. 4.The window of lung fields,a important new concept will be introduced in this section too.Section 5 will focus on the feature extraction from ROI and the establishment of feature vectors,which will be used as samples in training set.Detailed mining results will be presented in Sect. 6.Future works and some researches in progress are shown in Sect. 7.

2   The CADSARS System

Availability of Picture Archiving and Communication System(PACS) raises the possibility of massive digital medical image processing and analyzing.Because

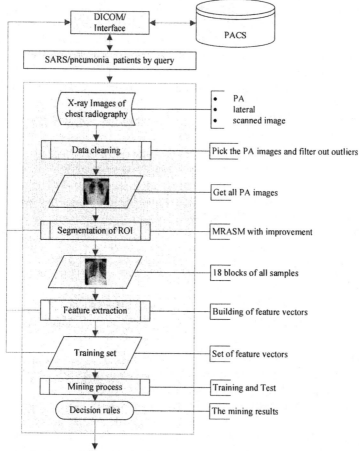

Fig. 1. Architecture of CADSARS

there are variety modalities of images stored in PACS,first we should focus our attention on PA X-ray chest radiography images.This brings the data cleaning procedure.In the literature of pulmonary analysis,each lung field(the left and the right) is divided into 9 blocks.So we need to define the ROI and segment out these blocks.Feature extraction and mining process will be relatively easy if the pre-steps are carried out in high quality. Fig.1 shows the architecture of CADSARS,which also include comments of all steps.

All images are stored as DICOM(Digital Imaging and COmmunication in Medicine) compatible format in PACS.For our mining purpose,only the gray level images are needed.The DICOM/Interface will accomplish the task of exchanging data format, the window level/height convert between 12-14 bits bitmap and the ordinary 8-bit gray level image.Though various modality images are stored in PACS,only DX(digital X-ray) images of chest radiographs are needed for our purpose.The selection of this type of images can be easily done by query one property of DICOM.

Three classes of images are included during one examination:PA,the Lateral images and the examine reports scanned from paper version.Automatic classification method of these three classes is developed.Thus the data cleaning process is completed and a high-quality subset of PA X-ray chest radiographs containing typical pneumonia and SARS images is constructed.

Segmentation of ROI is performed in most image analysis systems.In this paper, we use the Multi Resolution Active Shape Model(MRASM) which is an extension of ASM[10].Also noted by [10],a good starting approximation is important for the convergence of the algorithm and for the efficiency.The concept *window of lung fields* is introduced to initialize the starting approximation [19].As used by radiologist,the left/right lung field is divided into 9 blocks separately.The dividing criterion is *outer/middle/inner* × *upper/middle/lower*.One radiologist helped us to delineate which of the 18 blocks are considered abnormal. Association rule mining was then launched to find the relations.

Each block's features are extracted to construct the feature vector.Data mining techniques were invoked to build decision rules.The mining process is a supervised one since part of the training set is used to train and the other part is used to validate.

3   Data Preparation

Since real-life data is often incomplete, noisy and inconsistent,pre-processing becomes a necessity[11].In our case,the data cleaning process consists of two types of cleaning:the selection of PA X-ray chest images from PACS database and deleting outliers.The last step is carried out manually for some reason explained below.

Three types of images:the PA,the lateral and scanned images of reports were selected from PACS randomly.The scanned images of reports are only for the digitalized storage,so this type of images should be deleted firstly.A good survey in[6] analyzed lots of papers to show that almost all chest radiography diagnosis

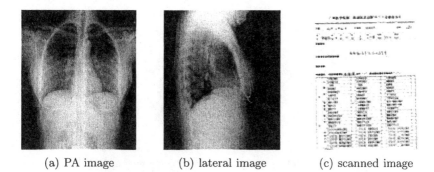

| (a) PA image | (b) lateral image | (c) scanned image |

Fig. 2. Three Types of Images

were performed in PA images.Although the lateral chest images are needed for their specific purpose,they have little usage for our mining goal.All 3 types of images are demonstrated in Fig.2 (a-c). It's obvious that all scanned images are brighter than the other types. So a simple gray level threshold can filter out the scanned images.

To separate the PA images,it is observed that if we scale the image smaller,say 50×50,then for a lateral image,either the left column or the right column is black mainly.This feature can be used to justify whether a image is PA or lateral.To carry out the separation, four features are calculated:

- $mean_L$:mean gray level of the first column
- $mean_R$:mean gray level of the last column
- std_L:standard deviation of the gray level of the first column
- std_R:standard deviation of the gray level of the last column

Then C4.5 was used as the mining tool to obtain decision rules.These rules from C4.5 show that using this method, about 99.12% PA images can be selected successfully[14].

Outliers are defined as the images of bad quality,which maybe caused by improper exposure or position when photographed.The children' images are considered as outliers.A few PA images are also deemed as outlier if the images contain pacemaker or other medical attachments.The outliers are filtered out manually to ensure the good quality of samples.

4   Segmentation of ROI

Automatic segmentation the Region of Interest(ROI) is virtually mandatory before any computer analysis of X-ray images takes place because the lung fields X-ray image contain so much information.We observed that some gray level based methods are not suitable for the segmentation of ROI in X-ray images,even hybrid methods are inappropriate.Knowledge based segmentation is suitable for the indistinct edge of lung filed.Active Shape Model(ASM)[10] and its extension version are used widely in medical image segmentation.An accurate initial position

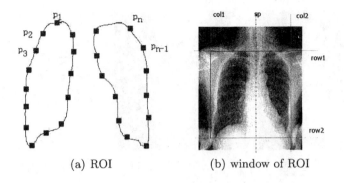

(a) ROI   (b) window of ROI

Fig. 3. Definitions of ROI and the Window of ROI

placement influences the segmentation result badly.We present our improvement of setting the initial parameters smartly by defining the *window* of ROI.

4.1   Definition of ROI

Each PA X-ray of chest radiography comprises two main parts:the left and right lung field as showed in Fig.2(a).We define the ROI as a vector of coordinates of n landmark points.

Definition(ROI). If there are n key points,a vector in $\mathbb{R}^{2n}$:

$$\mathbf{x} = (x_1, y_1, x_2, y_2, \ldots, x_n, y_n)^T$$

can be used to represent the ROI.Each x_i, y_i, stands for the x and y coordinates of key point i.

Definition(window of ROI). The *window* of ROI is ideally defined as the bounding-box of $\mathbf{v}$ which is a 4 parameters vector $\mathbf{w}$:

$$\mathbf{w} = (row_1, row_2, col_1, col_2)^T$$

$row_1 = \min y_i$ and $row_2 = \max y_i$ denote the upper and lower bound,$col_1 = \min x_i$ and $col_2 = \max x_i$ denote the left and right bound,respectively.We will use $\mathbf{w}$ to set the initial parameters of ASM.The definitions of ROI and the *window* of ROI are depicted in Fig.3.Another parameter named SP in Fig.3 defines where the spine column is located in the image.

4.2   MRASM Algorithm with Improvement

The authors of [10] and a series of related papers give the knowledge based algorithm of ASM,a widely used segmentation method.To improve the robustness of ASM, Multi Resolution ASM(MRASM)[12][13] is proposed.In order to use MR search,a pyramid of images with different resolutions should be generated.At the base of the pyramid (Level 0), we have the original image and on higher levels (Level 1 to L-1) we decrease the resolution by a factor of two.MRASM is a supervised model,so a training set is mandatory.

Definition(training set for MRASM). Let N be the total number of samples,each sample is a ROI $\mathbf{v}^i, 1 \leq i \leq N$,then the training set is defined as:

$$\text{traing set} = \left\{ \mathbf{v}^i \,\middle|\, \mathbf{v}^i \text{is ROI of the ith sample}, \mathbf{v}^i \in \mathbb{R}^{2n} \right\}$$

Three kinds of shape-invariant operators are enforced upon each $\mathbf{v}^i$ to make sure that all $\mathbf{v}^i$ in the same coordinate.All these operations can be written in one formula.If $\mathbf{v}^i = (x_1, y_1, x_2, y_2, \ldots, x_n, y_n)^T \in \mathbb{R}^{2n}$, then $\mathbf{v}_i$ is translated by $t = (dX, dY)$,rotated by θ and scaled by s of $\mathbf{v}^i$ can be expressed by $M(s, \theta)[\mathbf{v}^i] - t$.The alignment task is to find these parameters:$t = (dX, dY), \theta, s$ that minimize the distance between source$\mathbf{v}^i$ and target$\mathbf{v}$:

$$Err = (\mathbf{v} - M(s, \theta)[\mathbf{v}^i] - t)^T \mathbf{W} (\mathbf{v} - M(s, \theta)[\mathbf{v}^i] - t)$$

where $\mathbf{W}$ is weight matrix to give significance to those points which tend to be most 'stable' over the training set.The task of alignment is to align all $\mathbf{v}^i \in$ training set with respect to a target ROI.Normally the target ROI is the mean shape over training set. Detailed alignment process and results are in [14].

The first and important step in segmentation is how to find initial parameters. If we put the initial guess of ROI far away from where the destination ROI is, the hope of ASM converges to ideal edge becomes uncertain.There are 4 parameters to be initialized before MRASM algorithm:translation by $t = (dX, dY)$, rotation by θ and scaling by s.Because we choose $\overline{ROI}$ as the target of alignment step,set the rotation parameter $\theta = 0$ is well enough.The translation and scale parameters can be calculated by the following formula provided the *window* of ROI:$w = (row_1, row_2, col_1, col_2)^T$ has been deduced:

$$(dX, dY)^T = (X, Y)^T - (\overline{X}, \overline{Y})^T$$
$$s = f(s_w, s_h)$$

where:

- $(X, Y)^T$ is the ideal centroid of ideal ROI which can only be approximated by (X', Y'):

$$X' = \frac{1}{2}(col_1 + col_2) \qquad Y' = \frac{1}{2}(row_1 + row_2)$$

- $(\overline{X}, \overline{Y})^T$ is the centroid of $\overline{ROI}$ defined by:

$$\overline{X} = \frac{1}{n}\sum_{i=1}^{n} \overline{ROI}_{xi} \qquad \overline{Y} = \frac{1}{n}\sum_{i=1}^{n} \overline{ROI}_{yi}$$

- define the width and height of $\overline{ROI}$ as:

$$\overline{W} = \max\{x_1, x_2, \ldots, x_n\} - \min\{x_1, x_2, \ldots, x_n\}$$
$$\overline{H} = \max\{y_1, y_2, \ldots, y_n\} - \min\{y_1, y_2, \ldots, y_n\}$$

– define the width and height of *window* of ROI as:

$$W = col_2 - col_1 \quad H = row_2 - row_1$$

– set the scale parameters of X and Y axis,s_w, s_h, as:

$$s_w = W/\overline{W} \quad s_h = H/\overline{H}$$

A function $s = f(s_w, s_h)$ is used to combine s_w, w_h into one s because there should be only one scale parameter s.Finally,$f = 0.9s_h$ is chosen. Details of calculation can be found in [14].

4.3   Segmentation Result

Using $\mathbf{w} = (row_1, row_2, col_1, col_2)^T$ to set initial parameters will improve the convergence rate of MRASM.For example,in Fig.4,the first 8 iterations of MRASM are showed. Fig.4(a) shows that after about 6 iterations,the algorithm converges to the ideal contour of ROI.But when *window* of ROI: $\mathbf{w}$ is used to initialize translation,scale and rotation parameters, Fig.4(b) reveals that only 1 iteration is needed for the convergence.

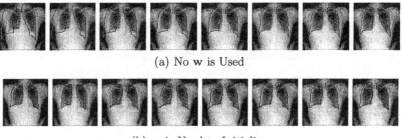

(a) No $\mathbf{w}$ is Used

(b) $\mathbf{w}$ is Used to Initialize

Fig. 4. Comparison of Convergence Rate Between Whether *window* is Used or Not

5   Feature Extraction for Mining

Having obtained the ROI,which is a vector $\mathbf{v}^i \in \mathbb{R}^{2n}$,our next task is to divide ROI into individual blocks so that meaningful features for each block can be extracted for mining purpose.According to the common stand used by radiologists,each lung field is divided into 9 blocks,totally 18 blocks for each image.This is demonstrated in Fig.5.Splitting criterion is to divide ROI according to Cartesian product:

$$\{upper, middle, lower\} \times \{left, intermediate, right\}.$$

Further split can be found in [16] but our test shows that 18 block is a fairly balance between computation payload and mining results.

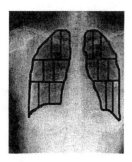

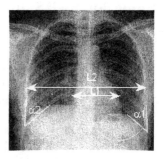

Fig. 5. Block Dividing   **Fig. 6.** CTR and CPA

Texture features are then extracted from each block.Let $\mathbf{P}^{ij}_{m \times n}, i \in \{0, 1\}, 1 \leq j \leq 9$ where $i = 0$ or 1 denotes the left or right lung field;$j = 1, 2, \ldots, 9$ denotes each block;$m \times n$ represents the size of block $\mathbf{P}^{ij}$.Only the pixels in ROI is used for feature extraction.Moment based and co-occurrence matrix based features are extracted for each one of 18 block.These features include:

1. mean, standard deviation, skewness and kurtosis grey level to describe the average data distribution of each block;
2. energy, entropy, correlation, inertia and local calm generated from the co-occurrence matrix of four directions, say $0, 1/4\pi, 1/2\pi, 3/4\pi$ in radian, to describe the texture of each block;

Thus for each block, 24 features are extracted.So for each image, there are $24 * 18 = 432$ features generated.Finally, other three features are added to represent the overall condition of lung fields, see Fig. 6.

1. Cardiothoracic ratio (CTR): the ratio between the maximal transverse diameter of the heart and the thoracic cage at the same level. A cardiothoracic ratio of more than 50% is considered abnormal. For clarity, we draw the two diameters in different horizontal levels in Fig. 6. CTR can be simply calculated as $CTR = L_1/L_2$;
2. Costophrenic angles(CPA):normally, a obliterated angle reminds abnormality. There are two costophrenic angles in PA X-ray radiography: the left one and the right one. These two angles are annotated as α_1 and α_2 in Fig.6.

Let $\mathbf{f}^j \in \mathbb{R}^{28}, j = 1, 2, \ldots, 18$ denotes feature vector of block $\mathbf{P}^j$,then for each X-ray image X^i,the feature vector is $\mathbf{F}^i, i = 1, 2, \ldots, N$:

$$\mathbf{F}^i = \left(ID\#, Imageid, \mathbf{f}^1, \mathbf{f}^2, \ldots, \mathbf{f}^{18} \right)^T, i = 1, \ldots, N$$

where

$$\mathbf{f}^j = \left(MEAN, STD, SKEW, KURT, \underbrace{\cdots}_{0°} \ \underbrace{\cdots}_{45°} \ \underbrace{\cdots}_{90°} \ \underbrace{\cdots}_{135°} \right)^T, j = 1, \ldots, 18$$

and N be the total number in training set.

6 Mining for SARS and Experiment Results

6.1 Association Rules

Because our 'simplicity first principle', association rules mining was chosen at first. We want to find whether there exist differences of lesions' locations between SARS and pneumonia cases. One radiologist helped us to delineate which of the 18 blocks are considered abnormal. An image set contains 75 SARS images and 125 pneumonia cases, was presented to the expert. Let $R_1\tilde{\ }R_9, L_1\tilde{\ }L_9$ denote the 9 blocks of right and left lung fields respectively.Then the expert just tick off each block to indicate it is abnormal. For direct comparison of the two classes, total number of each position is normalized in percentage. Figure 7 shows that there seems no significant difference of the locations of abnormal between SARS and pneumonia.$t_{test}(p_{value} \rightarrow 1)$ confirms this observation. Association rules mining was performed on the tick matrix resulted from the expert.

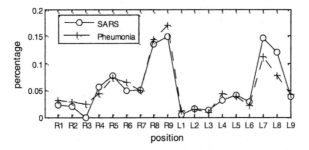

Fig. 7. Occurrence frequency of SARS and pneumonia

Table 1. Association Rules Mining Results

SARS				PNEUMONIA			
CONF.	SUPT.	LIFT	RULE	CONF.	SUPT.	LIFT	RULE
100	64.38	1.28	$L_8 \rightarrow L_7$	100	40.00	1.74	$L_8 \rightarrow L_7$
100	53.42	1.28	$L_8\&R_9 \rightarrow L_7$	100	36.00	1.74	$L_8\&R_9 \rightarrow L_7$
100	49.32	1.28	$L_8\&R_8 \rightarrow L_7$	100	33.60	1.74	$L_8\&R_8 \rightarrow L_7$
100	45.21	1.28	$L_8\&R_9\&R_8 \rightarrow L_7$	100	32.00	1.74	$L_8\&R_9\&R_8 \rightarrow L_7$
100	27.40	1.28	$R_7 \rightarrow R_8$	100	22.40	2.66	$R_4 \rightarrow R_5$
100	24.66	1.28	$R_9\&R_7 \rightarrow R_8$	100	20.80	1.74	$L_8\&R_5 \rightarrow L_7$
100	24.66	1.28	$L_8\&R_5 \rightarrow L_7$	100	20.00	2.50	$L_9\&L_7 \rightarrow L_8$
100	23.29	1.28	$L_8\&R_8\&R_5 \rightarrow L_7$	100	20.00	1.74	$L_9\&L_8 \rightarrow L_7$
100	21.92	1.28	$L_8\&R_9\&R_5 \rightarrow L_7$	100	20.00	1.74	$L_8\&L_9\&R_5 \rightarrow L_7$
100	20.55	2.03	$L_7\&R_7 \rightarrow L_8\&R_8$	100	20.00	1.74	$L_8\&R_8\&R_5 \rightarrow L_7$
100	20.55	1.70	$L_8\&R_7 \rightarrow L_7\&R_8$	100	19.20	2.66	$R_9\&R_4 \rightarrow R_5$
100	20.55	1.55	$L_7\&R_8\&R_7 \rightarrow R_8$	100	18.40	1.74	$L_8\&L_4 \rightarrow L_7$
100	20.55	1.55	$L_7\&R_7 \rightarrow L_8$	100	18.40	1.34	$L_7\&L_4\&R_9 \rightarrow L_8$
100	20.55	1.38	$R_7\&R_5 \rightarrow R_8$	100	17.60	3.13	$R_8\&R_4 \rightarrow R_9\&R_5$
100	20.55	1.38	$L_8\&R_7 \rightarrow R_8$	100	17.60	2.66	$R_8\&R_4 \rightarrow R_5$

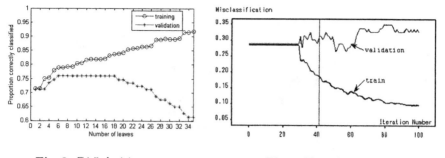

Fig. 8. C4.5 decision tree   **Fig. 9.** Neural network

Table 1 gives the results in percentage. We sort the rules descending by their confidence (CONF.),support (SUPT.). Then first 15 rules generated were presented in Table 1. Many rules are identical. This again confirms that association rule cannot be used to classify SARS and pneumonia.Classifier based on the feature vector was built and results are given below.

6.2 Building the Classifier

To make the classification results more credible, the sample set is partitioned into training, validation and testing sets in the ratio of 6:1:3 by simple stratified partition.Three mining techniques are used to build the classifier for the detection of SARS:

1. C4.5 decision tree:C4.5 with Gini reduction as the splitting criteria was used because of the 'simplicity first' principle. Figure 8 gives the success rate versus the number of leaves. It can be noticed that a 6-leaf tree can reach about 75% success rate. As the tree grows larger, say with 18 leaves, the success rate of validation will decrease. This is called over fitting.
2. Neural network:standard back propagation multilayer perceptron neural network (Fig.9) was used. A good trade-off between misclassification rate of training and validation can be chosen after 42 iterations. The success rate is about 73%, a good lift compared to decision tree.
3. CART:classification and regression tree, a robust and advanced data analysis algorithm. Ten fold cross validation is used to ensure more reliable results. Figure 10 shows how the cost related to number of leaves needed during training. Though compared to Fig.8, CART uses more leaves (21 leaves is chosen) to reach about 70% overall success rate. However CART performs the best as analyzed hereafter.

Total success rate for these three methods are 75.9%, 73.0% and 69.32%, respectively.It seems that C4.5 decision tree performs best. But further analysis reveals that contrary to this, CART is the best one. Figure 6.2 gives the receiver operating characteristic (ROC) curves of C4.5 and NN. Roughly speaking, the NN performs better than C4.5. But the CART performs the best as can be

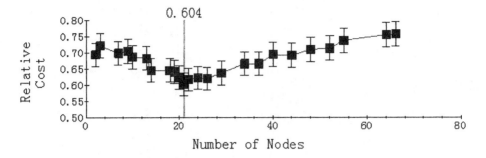

Fig. 10. CART

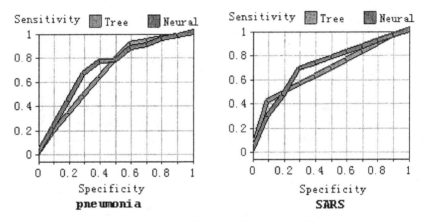

Fig. 11. ROC Charts of C4.5 and NN

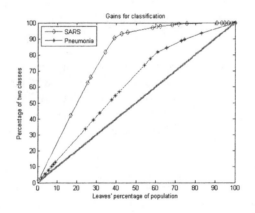

Fig. 12. ROC Charts of CART

Table 2. Confusion Matrix for C4.5/NN/CART

Actual class		Predicated class					
		SARS			Pneumonia		
		C4.5	NN	CART	C4.5	NN	CART
	SARS	41.67	45.83	**70.94**	58.83	54.17	**29.06**
	Pneumonia	10.17	15.25	**31.34**	89.83	84.75	**68.66**

observed from Fig. 6.2, which is drawn separately for clarity. Confusion matrix confirmed these observations numerically (Table 2).All rows in the table are presented in percentage to make them comparable. As noted previously, although the C4.5 makes the highest total success rate,it detects 41.67% of SARS cases. This is not applicable to use. NN performs better but not well enough to match the 70.94% success rate given by CART.The bold faced data are results provided by CART.

7 Conclusion and Future Works

Mining X-ray images of SARS patients for the detection, including detailed techniques for each key procedure is presented in this paper. Because simple location association rules cannot distinguish between SARS and normal pneumonia,we built classifier based on image texture. Experiment results from three classification methods of data mining are presented and analyzed. Final conclusion is that CART performs well: 70.94% of SARS cases can be detected.

SARS detection plays a central role in our project though the following works are important for further research,some of which are in progress:

1. We have detected SARS images from typical pneumonia images with an acceptable correct rate of 70.94%.More analysis should be made to improve this rate, at the same time to reduce false negative of misclassification.
2. Pinpoint where lesions of SARS located in a X-ray image of chest radiography.As mentioned in this paper,lung fields are divided into 18 blocks,9 blocks of each field.This task is to automatically position in which block lesion(s) located.This work is under progress.
3. Only images are used in present research,no diagnosis information of doctors is used.Besides images stored in PACS,examines and diagnosis are also stored in structured report(SR)[17] format.Expert's description makes the automatic diagnosis possible if used properly.For example,text mining technique applies to mining SR data.Combined with feature vectors from images,text feature extraction makes the semi-automatic description generators possible.
4. Image registration and fusion should be used to make the best use of PACS[18]. Only X-ray images(DX) used in present works,but computerized tomography(CT) is also widely used in medical image analysis.Different modalities of images take different aspects of lesions.Image registration and fusion can bring this information seamlessly together to lay the foundation for data mining and make a promising research area.

References

1. Summary of SARS case by country, World Health Organization,http://www.who.int/csr/sars, 2003.9
2. SARS Reference book (ver.3), Kamps Hoffmann, Flying Publisher, 2003.10
3. Early Advise of Monitoring the Infectious Atypical Pneumonia. the Ministry of Health of China,http://www.moh.gov.cn, 2003.11
4. Radiological Appearance of Recent Cases of Atypical Pneumonia in Hong Kong, Anil T. Ahuja et.al.Radiological Department of Chinese Univerisity of Hong Kong.http://www.droid.cuhk.edu.hk,2003.10
5. Struggle against cancer inspires PACS data-mining methods. Douglas Page.PACS web http://www.diagnosticimaing.com/pacsweb, April 2004
6. Computer-Aided Diagnosis in Chest Radiography: A Survey, Bram van Ginneken et.al, IEEE transactions on Medial Imaging, Vol.22, No.12,December 2001
7. Mammography Classification by an Association Rule-based Classifier. Osmar R.Zaiane et.al, Proceedings of the MDM/KDD 2002, July 2002
8. Data Mining from Functional Brain Image, Mitsuru Kakimoto et.al, Proceedings for MDM/KDD 2000, August 2000
9. A computerized cheme of SARS detection in early stage based on chest image of digital radiograph.Zhong, Z., L. Rihui, et al. Medical Imaging 2004:Image Processing 5370(Proceedings of SPIE): 904-914
10. Active Shape Models-Their Training and Application.T.F.Cootes,C.J.Taylor, D.H.Cooper,etc.al.. Computer Vision and Image Understanding.Vol.61,No.1,pp.38-59,1995
11. Data Mining,Concepts and Techniques. Jiawei Han and Micheline Kamber. Morgan Kaufmann, 2001.
12. T. Cootes, C. Taylor, A. Lanitis, Active Shape Models: Evaluation of a Multi-Resolution Method for Improving Image Search. Proceedings of the British Machine Vision Conference, 1994, pp.327-336.
13. Active Shape Models-Part II:Image serach and classification.Rafeef Abu-Gharbieh etc.al. Proceedings of the Swedish Symposium on Image Analysis, SSAB 1998.
14. Data mining on PACS.Xie Xuan-yang.Technical report of the project(within our team,not published).2004.8
15. Application of Data Mining Techniques for Medical Image Classification.Maria-Luiza Antonie,Osmar R. Zaiane, Alexandru Coman.Proceedings of the Second International Workshop on Multimedia Data Mining (MDM/KDD'2001)
16. Computer-Aided Diagnosis in Chest Radiography.Bram van Ginneken.Thesis of the author.2001
17. About SR,Features:The Next Digital Frontie.David J. Vining. 2003-06.Avialible at http://www.imagingeconomics.com/library/200306-07.asp.
18. International Society of Information Fusion, ISIF, http://www.inforfusion.org/
19. The window of lung fields:Automatic determination and its applications in chest radiographs processing. Xie Xuanyang, Li Xi, Zhang jin,et. al. The Third IASTED International Conference on Biomedical Engineering.2005-2,p 458-86, ISBN:0-88986-476-4

The Scamseek Project – Text Mining for Financial Scams on the Internet

Jon Patrick

Sydney Language Technology Research Group,
School of Information Technologies,
University of Sydney
Capital Markets Co-operative Research Centre
jonpat@it.usyd.edu
http://www.usyd.edu.au/~jonpat

Abstract. The Scamseek project, as commissioned by ASIC has the principal objective of building an industrially viable system that retrieves potential scam candidate documents from the Internet and classifies them as to their potential risk of containing an illegal investment proposal or advice. The project produced multiple classifiers for different types of data, and achieved higher than expected performance statistics on classifications. The development of the system required the solution of two major problems in document classification, namely accurate identification of classes with very small footprints, $<.1\%$, and classification using meaning intention rather than word strings. The approach taken used Systemic Functional Grammar to model the semantics of the scam classes and used unigrams with significant language pre-processing to assist in separating irrelevant documents. Litigations have been initiated by ASIC from classifications made by the system[1]. ASIC operates the system on a 24/7 basis. The estimate of savings in human effort in its monitoring role is the order of 100-fold. The estimate in savings to the community cannot be estimated readily but is likely to be of the order of tens of millions of dollars.

1 Introduction

Text Classification has a tradition of treating documents to be processed as a "bag-of-words" or n-grams, that is, the words or word groups within a text are treated as independent and uncorrelated with each other. Such a model of language is exceedingly simple but has been proven to satisfy many researchers.

The Scamseek project has sought to separate itself from the bag-of-words tradition of text classification. In particular the model of language used in the project was Systemic Functional Grammar (SFG) [1]. This model takes the position that language usage is a matter of choice set in a configuration of hierarchically layered strata of graphetics, graphology, lexicogrammar, semantics and context. Systemic grammar is a network of "systems" that interact with each other rather than a set of rules as with generative grammar.

---

[1] See ASIC Media Release 04-178: Grammax Investment Club operating unlicensed investment club is believed to have moved over $10M overseas in the prior year.

G.J. Williams and S.J. Simoff (Eds.): Data Mining, LNAI 3755, pp. 295–302, 2006.
© Springer-Verlag Berlin Heidelberg 2006

The project was executed as a systematic research program with an important constraint. Much of the research is restricted from publication by confidentiality agreements with the Commonwealth of Australia, which carry severe penalties. Hence we are not able to report on the specifics of the research we conducted on language models that describe various forms of financial scams, the machine learning methods to cope with unbalanced classes, and the nature of some of the data channels we built classifiers for. For these reasons the paper does not refer to specific references that informed our research strategies.

In computing classifications, texts of a given class, apart from a small number of very common topic words, are more closely related by the minute intricacies of a weak network or chains of correlations that persist at low levels across small sub-sets of the class and the persistent meaning they represent, rather than by large persistent clusters of resoundingly dominant word sets that trumpet the presence of their class. In this case, the use of SFG states that the social context of the text's composition dictates choices of meaning intentions which in turn influences the form of the text. The linguist's task is to make sense of the decision making process and render it in a manner that might be suitable for computation. The computational linguist then has to convert the linguist's model into a computable representation in the context of his target analytical methods which in this case is the procedures of machine learning.

2 Scamseek Project Specifications

The Scamseek project was devised in two stages. The first stage had the aim of producing a production system for retrieving and classifying web pages. The client provided a manually classified corpus of about 8000 documents. The delivery time was 6 months from project commencement. The project team consisted of 1 linguist, 1 computational linguist and 3 software engineers.

The second phase ran for 9 months to 30 June 2004 and had the objectives of improving the accuracy of the web page classifier and the development of new classifiers for a number of other Internet data types. In Phase 2 the contract had more data sources to be scrutinized, entity recognition and performance requirements, plus in each case retrieval mechanisms had to be developed and for one source the corpus had to be compiled. The team was expanded with another linguist and computational linguist. Other part-time staff and consultants also made contributions.

3 Project Operations

The Scamseek team was set up with a clear operational model that was effective throughout the life of the project, but adapted as work patterns developed to maturity. The operational model represented the task as consisting of 4 groups with different job functions; the client, linguists, computational linguists, and software engineers. The client was in contact with the linguists to deal with the classification of data. The linguists had the task of preparing the linguistic models of the data and passing that to the computational linguists who in turn had to prototype computational methods to compute the language models and devise machine learning experiments to optimize the classifiers. The computational linguists would pass their prototype code to the software engineers for efficient industrial quality implementation. This configuration operated effectively throughout the project development phases.

4   Computational Linguistic Research Topics

4.1   Linguistic vs. Administrative Classes

One of the early problems to emerge with the project requirements was the difference between the classification scheme of the client designed to conform to an administrative perception, that is, there are three types of scam under the law (unlicensed advisors, unregistered fundraising, and share ramping), and the linguistic manifestation of those three types. After a significant amount of linguistic analysis a set of registers (scam document sub-types based on their linguistic characteristics) were created representing subdivisions of the 3 scam types. This configuration was changed a number of times and expanded in phase 2 when the client opted to create different subdivisions in the data. The 3 scam types were treated as 1 document class with sub-classes or registers and the remaining part of the corpus was classified by the client into three more classes, Other-Agency-Scams, Scam-like and Irrelevant. These classes were also divided into registers to capture the linguistic variation within the classes. In all, over 50 registers were created with more than 20 in the scam class.

4.2   Linguists' Compilation Procedures

The linguists conducted their work by a two part strategy. Firstly they read the documents and collated them into registers and at the same time created register descriptions. In the latter stages of the work the linguists were able to scrutinize documents that were incorrectly classified and attempt to adjust their ontologies for both the register of the misclassified document and the register it was computed to belong to.

4.3   Specification of Linguistic Model

From the outset a decision was made to use a strong linguistic model to govern the direction of the work. This position was taken because the problem of identifying specialist content very thinly distributed and written in a particular manner was not believed accessible automatically by any other strategy.

The development of the linguistic model of the registers went hand in hand with the creation of the registers. The linguists read the documents and developed small scale characterizations of them. As the work developed documents of similar ilk were paired together until all scams were assigned to a register and described for their features of differentiation and "scaminess".

It was decided to represent register descriptions in an ontology rendered by XML. The upper part of these ontologies conformed to the SFG grammar as generally published, and the lower part is an ever increasing delicate rendition of the detail of the relevant content in the documents of the register. An objective of the work that was never achieved was the capacity to view a document and render it with an overlay of a register ontology and allow the linguists to do their extraction directly from the document image on the screen rather than their laborious hand collation.

The register descriptions and allocations resulted in a final list of more than 20 scam registers and 40 other registers spread across the 4 classes. At the same time the linguists with increasing understanding of the nature of the corpus advocated that greater amounts of the most structural components of the SFG model needed to be introduced into the assessment. Hence, the SFG networks for specific grammatical concepts were introduced as separate ontologies.

4.4 Small Footprints of Target Classes

The scam class as a whole represented less than 2% of the corpus in phase 1, however with the development of the register model of the data there became registers with sizes <.1%. This represented significant problems with underrepresented classes and led to an experimental program to alleviate its effects. In phase 2 the client changes doubled the size of the scam class, however it also triggered a need to redevelop the whole set of scam registers to disperse a heterogeneous register into a homogeneous set. This also caused more small registers to be created and thereby not particularly improve the overall problem of the small footprints of registers.

Ultimately the small footprint problem was resolved by the development of the SFG ontologies for each register. The amount of effort spent on each individual register was related to some degree to the difficulty of separating it from other registers and therefore de facto addressed this problem.

4.5 Hybrid Language Model

The linguistic model can be considered to be designed in two parts. The first part was the register descriptions of the most important subdivisions of the corpus either on client needs basis, the scams, or for processing efficiency, that is, the largest groups of non-scam documents. The second part was the collection of all the non-scam classes and the completely irrelevant material which was the largest class (about 60%). These parts were in turn grouped into the four classes of the client. The task required was to develop classifiers for the major classes as well as the scam registers. The solution chosen was to develop ontologies for separating registers and use an n-grams approach to support the separation of the larger classes. This lead to multiple lines of experimentation, namely, developing language processing functions for the ontologies, exploring the optimum feature selection for the classes independently of the registers, and, finally bringing the two solutions together to construct a combined classifier.

The SFG ontologies consisted of words and phrases from the texts organised in an SFG hierarchy, the upper parts reflect the theory of SFG and the lower parts represent the greater delicacy of the documents under analysis. The leaves of the ontologies were initially strings chosen from the texts classified in the given register. Over time the ontologies were developed and they became rich representations of the total document collection in the respective registers.

4.6 Machine Learning – Classifier Development Programme

The program for optimising the classifiers in the first phase concentrated on the problem of developing a single optimal classifier for web pages. In phase 2 separate classifiers were required for each data source and so experiments followed multiple strategies for all sources. SVMs were quickly identified as the best classifier for the data set.

Investigations were made of the selection of features from the collection of registers vis-à-vis the set of classes. While there was a significant overlap in the features chosen by an Information Gain metric there was still an appreciable improvement by using the feature set chosen from the registers in the small classes and between the classes in the large classes thus giving a blend of feature selection methods.

Selection of features from register ontologies required an extensive series of experiments. The register ontologies performed well independently of other feature sets once they were developed to a very mature stage. Later the four grammatical ontologies were added which made various levels of contributions in intriguing ways. For example the Modality grammatical ontology performed particularly poorly by itself on some occasions classifying no documents correctly, yet when it was added to other models it consistently improved their scores. This result indicated clearly that there is an interaction effect within the grammatical ontologies that exploits a weak correlation not recognizable within the individual systems themselves. It is their union with other systems that created their strength. This result is entirely predictable with the SFG model of language and further justifies its use for this task.

4.7 Mapping Features to Attributes

We use the terminology of *feature* for the linguistic phenomena that is the target of interest, and *attribute* for its numerical instantiation, and *mapping* for the computational transformation of the frequency count of the feature into its attribute representation. This distinction is unimportant for n-gram methods as the difference between features and attributes is inconsequential since the mapping transformation is trivial. This position cannot be taken in our work as the mapping transformation is different depending on the theoretical origin of the feature.

Feature representation for the ontologies was created by accumulating scores up the ontology tree. SFG in principle argues that the language is choice and therefore the important aspect of understanding the difference between two texts is the choice made by the authors. Hence by this principle the relative proportions of the choice to use one part of the tree over another should be the best differentiating feature. This is the case for the grammar ontologies but however does not apply to the register ontologies. The reason is that the register ontologies represent the most common semantic phenomena of a given register type, rather than choices between competing ways of expression. Hence, the attributes of domain register features are mappings to accumulative scores which are unnormalised, and grammar register features are mapped to proportional scores, whereas the n-gram word tokens are frequency counts normalized by document length.

5 Software Engineering Issues

5.1 Regulating Experimental Practices

In the background, the engineers created an architecture that was intended to automate as much as possible the roll-out of the production system. As the production system required the use of the specific language processing methods and parameters of the very best machine learning experiment, the experimental programme had to be fully integrated into the engineers' software production process. Hence all computational linguists were coerced by the engineers into producing their code within the CVS system. This ensured that all the computational linguists' code was designed, at least architecturally, to fit the current production system.

5.2 Automatic Roll-Out of Production Classifiers

The integration of the computational linguists work into the CVS system ultimately enabled the complete automatic generation of the production system merely by supplying the number of the experiment which had produced the "best" classifier. With this number all the language models, all the language processing code and all the background system code (database schema, user interfaces, data retrieval, etc.) were automatically assembled into a single system for shipping to the client.

5.3 Use of Open Source Software

The project used open source software for all aspects of its operations. The underlying operating system was Linux. Programming was in Python and interfaces were constructed using GTK with GLADE and CVS was used for code management and Bugzilla used for software revision requests. Postgres was used for database management, and all machine learning experiments used the Weka suite.

6 Results – Phase 1

The results of the first phase of the web page classifier for the scam classes as applied to an audit corpus have performance values of: Precision=.75, Recall=.41, and F-value=.53 and are to be contrasted with the laboratory results of the completed system on the training corpus using 10-fold cross validation of: Precision = .74, Recall = .35, F=.48. A baseline of 1000 single words has F=.21. ASIC was entirely satisfied with these results and made a commitment to a larger project in Phase 2.

This corpus was unseen by the development team and made available by ASIC at the time of delivery of the system. The processing was conducted by the ASIC staff and the project team was given one week in which to request revisions to ASIC's manual classifications. The Scamseek classifier in this instance identified 4 scams that had been manually misclassified by ASIC.

7 Results – Phase 2

The results of the second phase of the classifier for the scam classes applied to the web page corpus are presented in figure 1. ASIC was satisfied by the performance of the system in phase 1 not to require a second audit corpus assessment. Figure 1 provides results for 3 separate corpora, web pages as in the phase 1 experiments, and two other corpora developed for phase 2. The Web Pages(1) result represents the system delivered to ASIC as of 30 June, 2004, and Web Pages(2) represents results produced at the close of the project, from investigating further solutions to the problem of a large class of irrelevant documents, but they have not been fully explored experimentally. The exact nature of the other corpora cannot be presented due to security obligations. The performance figures are determined by 10-fold cross-validation. Column 4 provides the classifier performance when using a bag-of-words or unigram model for the Web Page data. Likewise the figures in the fifth and sixth columns provide the SFL model statistics first and the unigram model results second. In all cases the unigram results are an over estimate of the true performance of the model. The language processing used in all experiments has a significant amount of pre-processing for such anomalies as alternative orthographies, entity recognition, multi-word expressions, crafted stop lists and admission lists, and spelling inconsistencies. Removal of this atypical processing would diminish the performance of the unigram models by up to 10%. The closeness of the results for corpus 2 are likely to be an artifact of a small balanced corpus and we would not expect the unigram model to perform anywhere near as well for a larger corpus.

	Web Pages(1) SFL	Web Pages(2) SFL	Unigram (5000 atts.)	Corpus 2 SFL/Unigram	Corpus 3 SFL/Unigram
Precision	.744	.767	.520	.850/.803	.852/.797
Recall	.528	.655	.480	.834/.818	.639/.312
F-value	.618	.707	.499	.844/.810	.730/.449
Scam/non-scam texts	373/6391	373/6391	373/6391	686/1483	1395/13716

Fig. 1. The performance results from the web pages classifier and 2 other classifiers for identifying scams on the Internet as delivered to ASIC

8 Conclusions

The Scamseek project is a success for ASIC in that it is operable 24 hours a day 7 days a week. In its first operational run it discovered an activity that has since been taken to the stage of litigation. The estimate of savings in human effort in its monitoring role is the order of 100-fold, as previously ASIC had to read 80 documents to find one of interest they now read 5 documents to find 4 of interest. The estimate in savings to the community by bringing speedier detection and intervention of scams cannot be estimated readily but is likely to be of the order of tens of millions of dollars. ASIC is not prepared to release all details about the technology but has released the following summary statement: "The Scamseek technology is deployed in such a way that any scam proposal on any Internet channel that is generated in Australia or directed at Australians is highly likely to come under scrutiny".

The research contribution has been significant in that it is the first project that has used Systemic Functional Grammar for automated text classification. Solutions to serious problems in practical text classification, namely unbalanced classes, and the integration of semantic and n-gram language models have also been developed.

The project has also made a significant contribution to the issues of software engineering in language technology in that it has shown that computational linguistics research can be performed in the context of reaching industrial objectives.

Acknowledgements

The following people worked on the Scamseek project and made contributions to the final solutions, Michele Wong, Kathryn Tuckwell, Stephen Anthony, Tim Yeates, Dr. James Farrow, Neil Balgi, Jian Hu, Carlos Aya, Will Radford, Mathew Honnibal, David Smoker, Naomi Carter. The following doctoral students contributed to the work Maria Couchman, Casey Whitelaw, David Bell. The following people acted as advisors: Prof Christian Matthiessen, Prof Jim Martin, and Prof Vance Gledhill. Participating organizations were Australian Securities & Investment Commission (ASIC), Capital Markets Co-operative Research Centre (CMCRC), University of Sydney, Macquarie University, and the Australian Centre for Advanced Computing and Communications (AC3).

Reference

1. Halliday, M. (1994). *Introduction to Functional Grammar*. 2nd Edition. London: Arnold.

A Data Mining Approach for Branch and ATM Site Evaluation

Simon C.K. Shiu[1], James N.K. Liu[1], Jennie L.C. Lam[2], and Bo Feng[1]

[1] Department of Computing, The Hong Kong Polytechnic University, Hong Kong
{csckshiu, csnkliu, csbfeng}@comp.polyu.edu.hk
[2] Hong Kong and Shanghai Banking Corporation, Hong Kong

Abstract. In the past, some sites selected for closure by a large international bank in Hong Kong were based on personal experience of a group of experts by formulating a set of evaluation guidelines. The current 300 existing sites are therefore considered to represent a set of rules and expert decisions which are manually recorded on paper files and de-centralized. In order to validate the guidelines/rules and discover any hidden knowledge, we employ a data mining approach to examine the data comprehensively. Several modeling techniques including neural network, C5.0 and General Rule Induction systems are used to determine the significance of those attributes in the data set. Various models based on the historical data set of sites in different forms are constructed to deduce a rule-based model for subsequent use. Promising result has been obtained which can be applied in future Branch and ATM Site Evaluation with a view of providing a better solution. The useful patterns and knowledge discovered will further add benefit to exploring customer intelligence and devising marketing planning strategies.

Keywords: Datamining, rule induction, branch and site evaluation, model analysis.

1 Introduction

In a service industry like banking, meeting and satisfying customer needs is of prime importance. Providing multiple distribution channels for them to perform banking transactions as part of the business objectives and marketing strategy is often found in retail banking. Also, the distribution strategy, as one of the marketing mix strategies, forms part of the planning process as outlined in Mary Ann Pezzullo's model [1].

Since early 1980's banks have realized the benefits of lowering operating costs resulted from the migration of counter transactions from branches to these unmanned machines, by introducing automatic teller machine (ATM) in high-pedestrian traffic areas, such as along mass transportation lines, big shopping centers, etc. Nowadays, more customers prefer being able to perform bank transactions any time at home, in office and anywhere. Banks and financial institutions have therefore sought to develop e-banking services in recent years. The reliance on branches and ATMs is diminishing. As a result, not only are there more ATMs in the market; today these machines can do more than accept deposits and dispense funds. Some machines can cash checks, issue money orders, and accept loan payments. Enhanced, web-enabled ATMs are essentially electronic kiosks, providing access to bank's Internet site and information

G.J. Williams and S.J. Simoff (Eds.): Data Mining, LNAI 3755, pp. 303–318, 2006.
© Springer-Verlag Berlin Heidelberg 2006

services ranging from financial planning to investment products. This has created an opportunity for the Bank to conduct a similar site evaluation project with a view of further reducing costs. However, the use of existing set of site evaluation criteria derived from past personal experience is questionable, due to the fact that there is no change or modification to such criteria for some time and in particular taking into account of recent technology innovations.

Apart from exploring the applicability of previous unstructured knowledge in site evaluation, it is undoubted that using the latest technology, such as data mining ([2], [3]), will give new insights into the ways of evaluating the sites. Another main challenge is knowledge discovery [4] that is a new and rapidly evolving discipline which uses tools from artificial intelligence [5], mathematics and statistics to extract useful knowledge out of corporate data. The new technologies allow relatively efficient, rapid collection and analysis of enormous amounts of ATM information. The present study has provided substantiation on the basis and criteria used for optimizing the banking services. Section 2 will describe the problem domain, namely distribution channel of retail banking. Section 3 outlines the system architecture of conceptual components and methodology for knowledge discovery process. Section 4 gives an analysis of the results. Section 5 gives a conclusion and the future work.

1.1 Background of Site Evaluation

With the advent of Internet and telephone banking since late 1990's, the routine transactions, except those involving physical cash can further be migrated away from manned and unmanned ATMs. The ability to effectively market an integrated variety of delivery channel options is always the key to the banking industry's long term profitability and survival as mentioned in the special report: Channel Deliver Strategies (Chartered Institute of Bankers, October 1998 [6]). In order to remain competitive, the bank has to provide more cost-effective alternative delivery systems for customer convenience and reduce the number of costly labor intensive branches. Offsite remote banking, whether it be ATM, telephone banking or PC-based services, costs less in the long run than conventional branch banking operations because of the proportionately leverage saving on salaries and rent.

The Bank is well known for maintaining an extensive network of manned branches and unmanned ATMs (about 300) in Hong Kong. Although the increasing cost in branch resources did not adversely affect the overall cost/income ratio, the huge customer base made the undifferentiated marketing mix cost ineffective. Therefore, a segmentation strategy was introduced in the 1980's. Since early 1990's, with this strategy on banking products, promotion tactics and policy, the Bank started to review the "distribution" segmentation in a more defined and structured manner.

Over the past years, the formulated strategy was to reduce the number of retail sites (branches and unmanned ATM sites) gradually. It has been extended to branch sites which are smaller sites manned by 3 sales persons only and equipped with self-service machines such as ATMs, or branch sites with financial service centres serving higher customer segment profile. The strategic decision of reducing and re-configuring the sites is based on 3 main evaluation criteria, namely:-

i.   Site overlapping effect: The farther away the distance between 2 sites is, e.g. more than 15-minute walk, it is more worthwhile to keep them.
ii. Cash withdrawal count per ATM: The higher the count at a site is above the threshold, i.e. the mean value of 12,000 counts per ATM per month, it is worthwhile to maintain it.
iii. Customer segment profile: The higher the profile of customers is above the threshold, i.e. the proportion of preferential customers (those maintaining a high deposit and/or loan portfolio with the Bank and this yardstick may change from time to time) is constituting more than 10% of total transacting customers per ATM, it is more worthwhile to maintain the site.

The above criteria form the basis of site evaluation and the decision process (see Figure 1).

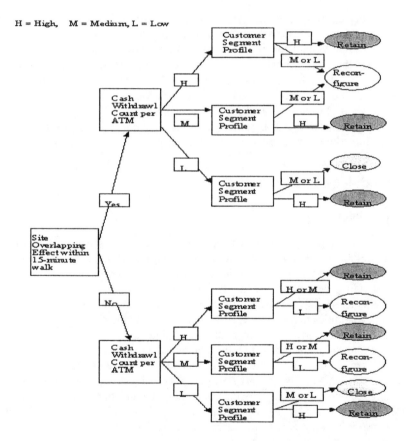

Fig. 1. Site evaluation in the past – decision process

As can be seen from the decision process, those sites recommended for closure are those having low level of cash withdrawal counts AND the customer segment profile is not high. In other words, the existing branch and ATM sites are supposed not to have such negative characteristics. As a result of previous site evaluation, the existing sites are classified into 4 categories namely: -

i.   Traditional branch site;
ii. Financial Service Centre site;
iii. Off-station ATM (unmanned) site;
iv. Self-service Centre site.

Regardless of their classifications, each site is equipped with at least one ATM and therefore has same set of data properties, such as cash withdrawal count/amount, balance inquiry count, transfer count/amount, cheque book order request, etc. These transaction records are stored in ATM transaction data files and aggregated on a monthly basis. We will be doing empirical tests to explore some interesting and important questions such as the followings:-

•   How many existing sites are there having the characteristic of "site overlapping effect" (which is defined as a distance of 15-minute walk between 2 sites). What are other important attributes e.g. cash withdrawal counts?
•   Which are the decisive attributes in the site evaluation? How are they inter-related?
•   What are the characteristics of the existing 300 sites? Are there any useful patterns that could be discovered and used for site evaluation?
•   Are there any clusters of sites sharing same characteristics? If the "site overlapping effect" is relaxed to say 20-minute walk, what is the target group of sites that could be considered for closure and/or re-configuration?

3   Methodology

3.1   Data Mining

Data mining techniques are being considered to automate discovery of non-trivial, previously unknown, and potentially useful knowledge embedded in databases. It can help identify the correct number, optimal location, and type of branches and ATM distribution points needed to effectively serve the customer base and grow market share. This is increasingly important that banks are exploiting business intelligence and controlling capabilities to try to understand better the structure of their client bases, the crucial factors that drive customer attitudes, and the parameters of effective customer-relationship management. In general, data mining techniques can be classified based on the characteristics of the data to be mined and knowledge users try to find out, which can be divided into six kinds of techniques [7]. The knowledge from data mining techniques include a) Multilevel data generalization, summarization, and characterization [8], b) Mining association rules [9, 10, 11, 12], c) Data classification [13], d) Clustering analysis [14], e) Pattern-based similarity search [15], f) Discovery and analysis of time series or trends [16].

The software package Clementine[1] is used to facilitate knowledge discovery and site evaluation. It supports :-

---

[1] A datamining toolkit developed by Integral Solutions Limited: http://www.isl.co.uk/

- investigating the data using visualization, statistics, etc.
- identifying a promising set of attributes
- dividing the data into training and test sets
- deploying the machine learning facilities on the training set
- testing the trained neural nets and induced rules on data set
- analyzing the results, and repeat the above steps where necessary

3.2 Selection of Training and Testing Data Sets

The data set is a set of variables of data samples for 290 sites, out of the 300 records including the prior knowledge on the important factors from July 1998 to June 1999 (Table 1). The remaining 10 unused site records are those sites which have been opened or closed for a period of time less than 12 months. Specific attributes were derived for data manipulation, analysis, building models and knowledge discovery. This data set was divided into a training set (220 sites) and a testing set (70 sites). Random sampling technique was employed in the selection of data sets.

Table 1. Training and testing data sets

Type of Data Sets	Type of Distribution Channels				
	BR	FC	OS	SC	Total
Training	119	9	72	20	220
Testing	50	0	20	0	70
Total	169	9	92	20	290

where

FC_Site : It is referred to any branch (BR) site having a Financial Centre (FC) site accommodated within a traditional branch (usually a large and strategic branch), so as to denote its importance.

BR_OS : It is referred to any branch (BR) site which requires a nearby unmanned site to provide sufficient coverage.

OS_BR : It is referred to any unmanned site (OS) maintained purely for the purpose of supplementing the nearby branch site.

SC: It is referred to any self service site in this study.

Data preprocessing includes basic operations such as the removal of noise, if appropriate. Those active sites, e.g. the flagship branch in headquarters and those unmanned sites dedicated for use by staff, are excluded so as to minimize distortion. The pre-processing steps include: -

i. Those closed sites are excluded and used as example cases to cross-validate the rule-based models. They are expected not to meet the criteria (the rules) contained in the models.

ii. Other non-monetary transactions, such as pay-in book request, personal PIN requests are excluded purposely, since the counts are extremely small in values (are ranged between few counts to 100 counts). Also, the data items itself are of less interest in the decision-making process by the managers.

iii. New sites having transactions for less than 3 months are excluded. These are also used as example cases for validating the discovered rules, even though the average figures are based on a few months as opposed to 12 months.

In addition, dimensionality reduction or transformation methods are used to reduce the effective number of variables under consideration. Certain data attributes transformed into more meaningful values for subsequent data analysis and predictive modeling are listed as follows:

-   Average cash amount per count (withdrawal amount divided by withdrawal count)
-   Overall average amount per transaction count
-   Total inquiry count (inquiry count * number of ATM)
-   Cash withdrawal count to inquiry ratio
-   Sum of total cash withdrawal count and total inquiry count

Answers to the following questions are also explored to see whether there is any hidden knowledge which are of interest to the decision-making process: -

•   Can the attribute "total cash withdrawal count" provide any justification of site existence?
•   Which zones/regions have the highest cash withdrawal counts?
•   Which sites have nearby sites within 15-minute walking distance? What are the characteristics of these sites?
•   Which sites have total cash withdrawal counts greater than 40,000 counts per month?
•   Are all zones having at least one traditional branch?

4 Experimental Analysis

While all decision tree algorithms undergo a similar type of process, they employ different mathematical algorithms to determine how to group and rank the importance of different variables as follows.

4.1 Descriptive Analysis on Transactions at Sites

Table 2 summarizes the statistical properties of some important attributes, the numeric numbers represent the counts or dollar terms per ATM. Results indicate:

-   Total cash withdrawal count (T_CWd_Ct) is the type of transaction having the highest mean value (26,926 monthly average counts per site), followed by inquiry count (19,541 counts per site).
-   The mean value of cash withdrawal average monthly count per ATM (machine utilization) is 12,441 counts which are comparable with the one (12,000 counts) obtained a few years ago based on expert knowledge. It means that the level of cash withdrawal count performed at each ATM remains rather steady throughout the

past years. This type of transaction cannot be performed via other distribution channels, e.g. phone banking. However, this needs to be closely monitored because of the likely impact brought about by the emerging Internet banking, mobile phone banking and electronic commerce.

- The mean values for other types of transactions per ATM not included in the Table 2 ranked in descending order are transfer count (2,457), credit card settlements (319), electronic cash deposit (6), electronic cash withdrawal (220), PIN inquiry (59) and cheque book ordering (25). New types of transactions performed via chip-card (i.e. electronic cash withdrawal and deposit transactions) are still not popular, given the low transactions.

- There is poorly positive correlation between all other types of transactions with the number of ATMs, except the electronic cash withdrawal count (0.345 medium positive correlations).

- The walking distance between the manned sites has poor correlation with all the raw and derived attributes.

- The attribute "cash withdrawal count (CWd_Ct)" per ATM can be interpreted as the level of machine utilization. The maximum figure is 33,199, implying about 70 counts per hour (based on 30 days a month and 16 hours a day) or about 110 counts per hour (based on 25 days a month and 12 hours a day). Using the selected node to define this figure (33,199), the site ID (3011P) is identified and its site name is Trade Department Tower in Mongkok, Kowloon. This site is installed with 2 machines only, but is located within 10-minute walk from a main branch site "Mongkok" (site ID 3001B).

Table 2. Statistical analysis results on numeric attributes

Attribute	Min	Max	Mean	Standard Deviation
Cash withdrawal count (CWd_Ct)	169	33,199	12,441	6,046
Inquiry count (Inquiry)	643	21,884	9,643	4,093
Total cash withdrawal count per site (T_CWd_Ct)	169	103,032	26,926	19,841
Cash withdrawal amount per count (AvgCashAmt)	$875	$3,575	$1,543	$375
Total inquiry count per site (T_Inq)	643	79,155	19,541	12,414
Cash withdrawal count to inquiry count Ratio (CWdVs Inq)	0.26	4.10	1.32	0.60
Summation of cash withdrawal count & inquiry (T_CWd&Inq)	812	182,187	46,468	31,161
Overall average amount per transaction count (OvAvgAmt)	$1,505	$13,087	$2,786	$1,426

4.2   Analysis on Attributes with Visualization Interface

Interesting and important features, relationships and patterns have been mined. As seen in Figure 2, over 74% of the sites have the number of ATMs less than or equal to 2. Such data analysis does support that branch sites can accommodate more ATMs because of their relatively larger premises.

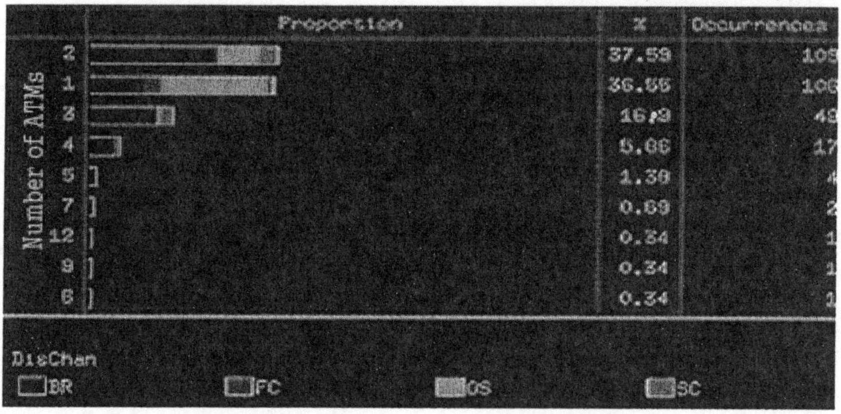

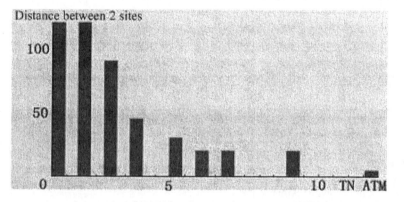

Fig. 2. Distribution of number of ATMs

Fig. 3. Relationship between distance and number of ATMs

Figure 3 shows that the larger the number of ATMs (implying higher transaction demand from customers) are found in the branch sites (with the number of ATMs greater than or equal to 5), the shorter walking distance of the nearest sites is from them to provide sufficient coverage of customer demands. By using the select node and specifying the criterion, "number of ATMs > 4", the 9 largest sites are identified and located. The properties for this data set are uncovered and shown in Table 3.

Table 3. The 9 largest sites – data properties

DisChan	Site_ID	TM_ATM	CWd_Ct	Region	Zone	S_Type	Nrt_Site	Dist	T_CWd_Ct	AvgCashAmt	T_Inq	CWdVisInq	T_CWd&Inq	OvAvgAmt
BR	30013	9	11440	KLN	KTN	MIX	34728	20	103032	1535.8	73155	1.3	182187	2478.34
BR	30628	12	8544	HKI	HOA	COM	36018	5	102528	1475.1	77508	1.32	180086	3158.18
BR	30343	5	20350	NTT	NTH	MIX	35433	15	101750	1420.48	53090	1.52	154840	2079.43
BR	31818	7	13402	KLN	NTS	COM	30183	10	93814	1249.07	67172	1.4	160986	2055.36
BR	30303	7	10799	KLN	KKY	MIX	30768	20	75593	1595.73	54866	1.38	130459	2405.55
BR	30128	6	12308	KLN	KTK	MIX	35318	20	73848	1331.18	50706	1.46	124554	2292.59
BR	31108	5	13111	HKI	HMC	NTH	30628	15	65555	1390.42	47695	1.37	113250	2640.91
BR	35918	5	10353	KLN	KTK	REP	34573	30	51765	1448.24	37190	1.39	88945	2776.43
BR	31268	5	9935	KLN	KKY	MIX	35382	20	43675	1857.36	49600	1.0	99555	2948.57

By selecting the number of ATMs greater than 4 for the unmanned sites (OS) and Self-Service Centre sites (SC), data properties are discovered as Table 4 shows.

Table 4. Data Analysis on OS and SC sites

DisChan	Site_ID	TM_ATM	CWd_Ct	Inq	Zone	S_Type	Nrt_Site	Dist	OS_BR	T_CWd_Ct	AvgCashAmt	T_Inq	CWdVisInq	T_CWd&Inq	OvAvgAmt
OS	3546P	3	24574	11886	RLK	TRS	34838	10	N	73722	1293.9	35858	2.07	109380	1926.34
OS	30180	3	19763	10547	KTS	COM	30183	1	Y	59387	1293.4	31541	1.87	90943	2049.71
OS	3018P	3	12367	11381	KTS	TRS	30183	15	N	37101	1112.4	35943	1.03	73044	1710.27
OS	3583P	3	8465	5650	KTS	TRS	36308	1	Y	25395	1433.58	16950	1.5	42345	2177.35
SC	3532C	4	16226	13040	KTT	MIX	30813	20	N	64904	1463.43	52160	1.24	117064	2309.37
SC	3510C	4	15331	12216	NFM	MIX	35392	10	N	63324	1489.23	48864	1.25	110188	2402.22
SC	3514C	3	17229	11547	NFM	MIX	31068	15	N	61687	1486.76	34641	1.49	88328	2297.01
SC	3513C	3	14629	9418	NTS	EST	35440	45	N	43887	1554.38	28254	1.55	72141	2046.6
SC	3523C	3	11180	7728	NFM	EST	3514C	30	N	33540	1535.51	23184	1.45	56724	2190.81
SC	3529C	4	8330	8746	HCJ	MIX	34833	20	N	35320	1571.64	34984	0.95	68304	2813.47
SC	3521C	3	10030	8778	KTS	COM	31813	10	N	30090	1716.13	26334	1.14	56424	2834.33
SC	3527C	3	6945	6853	HCA	COM	31723	8	N	20838	1647.9	20673	1.01	41517	3267.23
SC	3524C	3	5555	10821	HCA	COM	30629	1	Y	16685	1293.75	32463	0.51	49128	2979.02

In Table 5, it is interesting to see that the walking distance between branches is within 20 minutes, except one branch site (Whampoa Garden). These discovered information do give the answer to the hypothesis testing in the way that this group of sites is considered to have "site overlapping effect" (refer to question 1 in Section 2), because of extremely higher transaction counts (the total cash withdrawal counts are ranged from about 50,000 to 103,000).

312   S.C.K. Shiu et al.

Table 5. Data Analysis on largest sites with ranking

Site Name	Ranking in Descending Order			Distance (minutes)
	Machine Ultilization	Total Cash Withdrawal Count	Overall average amount	
China Building (3062B)	9 (8,544)	2	1 ($3,158)	5
Wayfoong House (3181B)	2	4	8	10
Hay Wah Building (3110B)	3	7	4	15
Yuen Long (3034B)	1 (20,350 cts)	3	9 ($2,079)	15
Mongkok (3001B)	5	1 (103,032 cts)	5	
Kwun Tong (3030B)	6	5	6	
Hung Hom Commercial Centre (3012B)	4	6	7	
Telford Garden (3126B)	8	9 (49,675 cts)	2	20
Whampoa Garden (3591B)	7	8	3	30

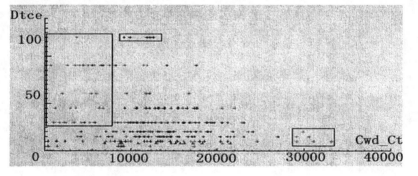

Fig. 4. Distance vs. total sum of cash withdrawal count and inquiry

Further analysis on the unmanned sites (OS) and Self-Service Centre sites (SC) has been carried out and a typical example is shown in Figure 4. The points are:

- Kowloon Tong KCR (site ID 3546P) unmanned site recorded a higher level of total cash withdrawal transactions (73,722 counts) which are even higher than those for some of the 9 large branch sites. Recently, a site named Festival Walk has been opened and located in close proximity (say 5 to 10 minutes) to supplement the transaction demand.

- The unmanned sites (OS) are all located in mass transportation lines.
- Those sites with the distance (value = 1) are maintained for the purpose of providing coverage (Y value under the attribute name "OS_BR) to the nearby branch sites which do not have sufficient space to accommodate more ATMs due to physical constraint.
- The 3 self-service centre sites (SC) with walking distance within 15-20 minutes, but with total cash withdrawal counts can be considered for closure in future site evaluation. They are Henning House (site ID 3529C) and Kimberly Road (site ID 3521C).
- The financial centre (FC) sites have a distinct set of features with predictions very close to expert's experience. These sites aim to serve a very small target group (lowest transactions) of up-market customers (highest dollar value per transaction).
- Some interesting relationships are:
- The sites with the highest cash withdrawal counts (machine utilization) are mainly those unmanned off-sites located at KCR stations (Kowloon Tong, Tai Wo, Tai Po, Sheung Shui). Each of them has its own manned sites located in close proximity (within 10-minute walk).
- Those sites with "distance" value in range of 90 to 120 minutes are treated as remote sites, whether they are located in outlying islands (e.g. Cheung Chau) or in prestige areas (e.g. the Peak). All remote sites are of branch (BR) type for filling the geographic gap, in addition to one unmanned (OS) site in a remote island - Cheung Chau. Further examination on the transaction volume on both manned (2 ATMs) and unmanned (1 ATM) site in Cheung Chau appears not exceptionally high, with the average count of about 9,500 per ATM which is below the network average of 12,441 counts.
- A cluster of unmanned sites (OS) are not busy in terms of lowest transaction counts for cash withdrawal or summation of cash withdrawal and inquiry, irrespective of distance (ranged from 10 to 120 minutes).
- No obvious pattern between branch (BR) and self service centre (SC) sites in this study.

The mean values for those important numeric attributes are analyses by types of distribution channels and results shown in Table 6. The figures represent counts of dollar value per ATM and indicate that the traditional branch (BR) and self-service (SC) sites share very similar data properties in terms of mean values per site. There is no obvious distinction between them. Also, the financial centre (FC) sites have a distinct set of features with predictions very close to expert's experience. These sites aim to serve a very small target group (lowest transactions) of up-market customers (highest dollar value per transaction).

Table 6. Statistical Analysis by types of distribution channels

Distribution Channel	All (290)	BR (169)	FC (9)	OS (92)	SC (20)
Cash withdrawal count (CWd_Ct)	12,441	13,700	440	11,400	12,000
Inquiry count (Inquiry)	9,642	9,800	1,300	10,300	9,200
Total cash withdrawal count per site (T_CWd_Ct)	26,926	34,300	440	16,600	36,576
Average Cash Amount (AvgCashAmt)	$1,543	$1,500	$3,000	$1,470	$1460
Cash Withdrawal Count to Inquiry Count Ratio (CwdVsInq)	1.32	1.49	0.35	1.14	1.24
Summation of cash withdrawal count & inquiry (T_CWd&Inq)	46,468	56,500	1,700	30,600	54,700
Overall average amount per transaction count (OvAvgAmt)	$2,786	$2,600	$9,800	$2,500	$2,670

4.3 Analysis on Attributes Relating to Site Information

Transactions performed at an ATM machine can be analysed in terms of numeric data whereas site location in terms of symbolic data. The following interesting features have been identified by executing the web node:

- A strong association is that the unmanned sites are not the category of the branch sites to supplement another unmanned site (marked by "N" for the attribute "BR_OS"), nor the Financial Centre sites (marked by "N" for the attribute "FC_Site").
- The "Y" values of the above-mentioned attributes are associated with the branch sites. These mean that some branches are codified to make differentiation from other branch sites for 2 specific reasons. The first one is that due to physical branch configuration constraint, one or more ATMs cannot be installed in a branch, and therefore, an unmanned site in its close proximity has to be established to overcome the limitation. The second differentiation is to classify those branch sites accommodating the Financial Centre sites which are located on different floors or in dedicated areas within the branch premises.
- Most of the branch (BR) sites are located in mixed areas, for instance, Mongkok is classed as a mixed area where shops, commercial / residential buildings, etc can be found. There is a strong link between these 2 attributes, namely branch (BR) site and mixed (MIX) type.

-    Another obvious link is that there are more unmanned sites in dedicated areas (DSC). These sites are usually located in restrictive areas and maintained for use by staff working in reputable companies, e.g. the sites in Tap Shek Kok and in Ocean Park.
-    The Financial Centre (FC) site can only be found in commercial and industrial area.
-    Only unmanned sites (OS) are located in the large public hospitals (HOS).

4.4 Model Evaluation and Analysis

Apart from finding manually the associations using visualization techniques such as the web node, using the APRIORI and Generated Rule Induction (GRI) modeling techniques provided by the software tool can generate the associations automatically. The advantage of association rule over the more standard decision tree algorithms (BuildRule and C5.0) is that associations can exist between any of the attributes. There are some strong association rules using APRIORI which are very similar to those displayed by the web node as mentioned above.

When using GRI technique, all attributes are fed into the model to identify relationships. Surprisingly, the numeric attributes, electronic cash withdrawal counts, and its dollar value, these 3 specific attributes have strong association rules. Using this unrefined model to induce further rules, the accuracy of the results has been improved to 95% and 92.85% correct cases for the training and testing data sets respectively. By connecting the association rules and the ruleset in series, the agreement between these results are 83.64% and 87.14% respectively (see Table 7). An alternative approach is to train a network and use the Sensitivity Analysis feature (analysis node) to rank the different fields by their relevance to the outcome.

Table 7. Summary of results for decision tree and ruleset

Scenario	C5.0 Decision Tree		C5.0 Rule Set	
	Training	Testing	Training	Testing
1	83.64%	78.57%	83.64%	80.00%
2	83.64%	78.57%	83.18%	78.57%
3	84.09%	80.00%	84.09%	80.00%
4	**85.91%** (189 sites)	**84.29%** (59 sites)	**86.36%** (190 sites)	**87.14%** (61 sites)
5	79.09%	80.00%	77.73%	**87.14%**
6	80.45%	82.86%	80.45%	80.00%
7	85.00%	74.29%	84.09%	77.14%
8	83.18%	**84.29%** (59 sites)	83.64%	84.29%

316 S.C.K. Shiu et al.

Table 8. Summary of results – neural networks

Scenario	Quick Method		Prune Method	
	Training	Testing	Training	Testing
1	70.00%	77.14%	76.36%	82.86%
2	70.00%	78.57%	70.91% (156 sites)	**90.00%** **(63 sites)**
3	**69.55%** **(153 sites)**	**84.29%** **(59 sites)**	69.55%	77.14%
4	67.73%	82.86%	**77.27%** **(170 sites)**	87.29% (61 sites)
5	70.00%	84.29%	73.64%	84.29%
6	65.00%	71.43%	67.73%	82.86%
7	68.64%	81.43%	73.16%	82.85%

As seen in Table 8, Scenario 4 is considered to be the best in terms of highest confidence level under the prune method training (77.27%), even though its testing result is not as good as Scenario 2 testing (87.29% vs. 90.00%). The attributes used in Scenario 4 are Distance (Dtce), Overall amount per transaction (OvAvgAmt), Summation of cash withdrawal count and inquiry (T_CWd&Inq). The best result is from the rule model which is connected to a trained Knet (clustering). The accuracy of the results has been improved to 82.73% and 88.87% correct cases for the training and testing data sets respectively.

5 Conclusion and Future Work

After the data mining process, new knowledge have been discovered in this study. We summarize the knowledge discovered K1 to K6 in Table 9 below. The prior knowledge can be re-affirmed by this study in the following:

- Cash withdrawal count and distance are important factors for site evaluation based on rule and net results on the data set (around 80% accuracy as demonstrated in Scenarios 1 and 2 in Section 4.4).
- For those sites with lowest transactions (e.g. below 10,000 cash withdrawal counts), they are located either in prestige areas (in Repulse Bay) or maintained for corporate customer relationships (Tap Shek Kok in Tuen Mun) because of geographical gap.
- All FC sites appear to be located correctly as supported by site segment profile analysis.
- A site may be considered for opening in close proximity to new or existing MTR/KCRC station by virtue of the cash withdrawal count.

Possible extensions include the evaluation of distribution channels of the Bank's subsidiary company as well as quantifying tangible benefits of applying the acquired knowledge base. Some extra features, e.g. trend analysis (change in transaction count), transaction customer and preference analysis [2], [7], Web information and multimedia data analysis [17], fuzzy relationship and association [9] are to be added into any future enhancement

Table 9. Knowledge being discovered

	New Knowledge
K1	Cash withdrawal count and distance are thought to be the decisive factors for site evaluation in the past. However, under Scenario 4 in the machine learning results (decision tree, rule set and neural network) detailed in Section 4.4, the 2 decisive attributes are indeed *overall amount per transaction count* and *summation of cash withdrawal count and inquiry count.*
K2	The unmanned site (3167P) should not have been opened, if the induced rules are followed. The transaction demand is extremely low (1,350 counts) and the dollar value is also low ($981) while the site (Palace Mall in Tsimhatsui) is within 10-minute walk from another manned site. This is also found to be inconsistent with previously believed knowledge.
K3	The traditional branches in remote areas, such as Yung Shue Wan, may be re-configured into "SC" site, given the low site segment profile.
K4	The sites in Shun Tak Centre and Shenzhen recorded the highest dollar value per cash withdrawal transaction. This is quite understandable because commuters to Macau and China normally carry cash as opposed to using credit card. Contrarily, the site with lowest dollar value is located in University of HK ($875), as the majority of the users performing the transactions at this site are undergraduates and not full time income earners.
K5	The analysis on the transaction of "cash withdrawal" alone (with counts exceeding 40,000 per site) shows that the top ranked sixty sites scattered across the twenty defined zones with Tseung Kwan O.
K6	Special attention should be given to those potential sites located near to large shopping complex or large private housing estate. This is supported by the largest branch sites located in these areas.

Acknowledgement

We extend our gratitude to the bank which has helped in providing useful data for this research, and also grateful to the partial support of research grant A-PF83 of The Hong Kong Polytechnic University.

References

1. Koch, T.W. and MacDonald, S.S.; Bank Management. 5th Edition, South-Weastern College Pub (2002)
2. Keim, D.A.; Information visualization and visual data mining. IEEE Transactions on Visualization and Computer Graphics, Vol.8, Issue 1, pp.1 - 8 (2002)
3. Liu, J.N.K. and Sin, D.K.Y.; A datamining approach for maintenance scheduling. International Journal of Engineering Intelligent Systems, pp. 119-126 (2000)
4. Pazzani, M.J.; Knowledge discovery from data? IEEE Intelligent Systems and Their Applications, Volume 15, Issue 2, pp.10 – 12 (2000)
5. Wu, X.D.; Data mining: artificial intelligence in data analysis. IEEE/WIC/ACM International Conference on Intelligent Agent Technology, pp.7 (2004)
6. Standard Chartered Bank. http://www.standardchartered.com/global/index.html
7. Liu, J.N.K. and Leung, F.; A framework to investigate consumer preference on using new interactive media for electronic Banking. International Conference on Electronic Commerce, pp.28-34 (2000)
8. Durkee, D.P.; Pohl, E.A. and Mykytka, E.F.; Input data characterization factors for complex systems affecting availability estimation accuracy. Annual Symposium on Reliability and Maintainability, pp.80 - 89 (2002)
9. Chung, S.M. and Mangamuri, M.; Mining association rules from relations on a parallel NCR teradata database system. International Conference on Information Technology: Coding and Computing, Vol.1, pp.465 - 470 (2004)
10. Jin, D. and Ziavras, S.G.; A super-programming approach for mining association rules in parallel on PC clusters. IEEE Transactions on Parallel and Distributed Systems, Vol.15, Issue 9, pp.783 - 794 (2004)
11. Shi H.; Zhang, J.F. and Zheng, L.; Mining association rule oriented data cube and its application. International Conference on Machine Learning and Cybernetics, Vol. 2, pp. 705 – 709 (2002)
12. Yen, S.J. and Chen, A.L.P.; A graph-based approach for discovering various types of association rules. IEEE Transactions on Knowledge and Data Engineering, Vol. 13, Issue. 5, pp. 839 – 845 (2001)
13. Jia, X.P. and Richards, J.A.; Cluster-space representation for hyperspectral data classification. IEEE Transactions on Geoscience and Remote Sensing, Vol. 40, Issue. 3, pp. 593 – 598 (2002)
14. Bin, X.; Aimeur, E. and Fernandez, J.M.; PCFinder: an intelligent product recommendation agent for e-commerce. IEEE International Conference on E-Commerce, pp.181 - 188 (2003)
15. Wang, H.X.; Perng, C.S.; Fan,W. and Yu, P.S.; An index structure for pattern similarity searching in DNA microarray data. IEEE Computer Society on Bioinformatics Conference, pp. 256 - 267 (2002)
16. Angelov, P.P. and Filev, D.P.; Flexible models with evolving structure. International IEEE Symposium on Intelligent Systems, Vol. 2, pp. 28 - 33 (2002)
17. You, J.; Liu, J.; Li, L. and Cheung, K.H.; On data mining and data warehousing for multimedia information retrieval. IASTED International Conference on Artificial and Computational Intelligence, 130 – 135 (2002)

The Effectiveness of Positive Data Sharing in Controlling the Growth of Indebtedness in Hong Kong Credit Card Industry

Vincent To-Yee Ng, Wai Tak Yim, and Stephen Chi-Fai Chan

Department of Computing, The Hong Kong Polytechnic University,
Hung Hom, Hong Kong
cstyng@comp.polyu.edu.hk

Abstract. In order to cut down on soaring personal loan bankruptcies, the Hong Kong government had unveiled a plan in early of 2002 to allow banks to share more credit information about their customers. This paper analyses how effective the positive data sharing scheme will be and examines whether any other personal credit attributes can serve the same purpose. In our work, a survey was conducted to verify industry's perception on what attributes was essential for credit risk assessment. The result was compared with the implication from the neuro-fuzzy data mining on real transaction data. The comparison suggests that the perception on positive data is not absolutely correct and the positive data sharing cannot always achieve its purposes.

1 Introduction

Data mining is the task of discovering interesting patterns from large amounts of data where the data can be stored in databases, data warehouses, or other information repositories. It is a decision support analysis process to find buried knowledge in corporate data and delivers useful information and knowledge to business professionals [4]. Thawornwong and Enke used data mining to uncover the relevant variables with higher predictive ability [12]. Neural network techniques including probabilistic and feed-forward neural networks were employed to predict the directions of future excess stock return.

Unlike the quantifiable data methods, Peramunetilleke and Wong used data mining technique on textual data to forecast the currency exchange rate [11]. Textual data like the news headlines provide richer information. It contains not only the effect (e.g. currency goes up or down), but also the possible causes of the event. Another example of data mining application was done by Zhang *et al.* [13]. It was to investigate the money laundering crimes by using the link hypothesis and clustering technique to analyse the correlations between financial transaction data.

In this paper, we are interested to apply data mining technologies the effectiveness of positive data sharing. The proposal for banks to be allowed to share positive consumer credit data in Hong Kong through a credit reference agency has attracted a lot of attention. There is considerable support for the proposal, particularly among banks, because the sharing of positive consumer credit data will enable them to conduct better assessments of the creditworthiness of individual borrowers. However, there

G.J. Williams and S.J. Simoff (Eds.): Data Mining, LNAI 3755, pp. 319–329, 2006.

are strong reservations, not only in view of the need to provide adequate safeguards to the privacy of bank customers but also arguing the effectiveness of sharing of the positive consumer credit data to control indebtedness rate.

In the public discussion so far, it was noticed a few persistent conceptions, where this paper would particularly like to address. The first is that after the introduction of positive consumer credit data sharing, the ability to determine the potential risky customers will be tremendously improved. Banks can use on these attributes to prevent issue credit cards indiscriminately; as a consequence the growth of bad debt can be inhibited in a better manner. This will benefit to most consumers as it helps to mitigate the problem of over-indebtedness by some borrowers. However, this phenomenon is not absolutely true as elaborated by the research result of this paper.

The second misconception is that the credit scoring system currently used by banks will be much accurate if consumer positive data sharing scheme is introduced. Without positive consumer credit data sharing, as at present, consumers with good credit have been subsidizing those with doubtful credit [5]. The costs of bankruptcies to the banks have been passed on, in one way or another, to all borrowers. This unfair sharing of the burden among borrowers takes the form of higher charges for banking services and higher borrowing costs for consumers. With positive consumer credit data sharing, the banks would be able to introduce differential pricing on the basis of credit quality. As a consequence, those with good credit, who are in the majority, will benefit, possibly through more favorable terms for borrowing and for the use of banking services. This again is not necessary true. Credit scoring is already widely used by banks in Hong Kong. In other jurisdictions this is a proven statistical method, which helps banks to assess a borrower's creditworthiness. This study reaffirms that the current consumer credit data (what banks are using now) are also significant attributes for credit rating, in particular the delinquent information.

The third is that the rapid increase in personal bankruptcies is entirely the responsibility of lack of positive consumer credit data; as a consequence banks are unable to be prudent in the issue of credit cards. There is some truth in this allegation, but there is also reservation. The paper has conducted data mining on some real transactional records from a major financial institution. The result revealed that with the aims of positive data, indeed, it did not have substantial contribution in credit assessment in the credit scoring processes. Though it is recognised that the more information available to banks, the better control could be implemented, the amplitude of the effectiveness of positive consumer credit data sharing is an unknown generally. Also, excessive data introduces overhead in the processes of data collection, data entry, consistency check, and data analysis.

2 Study Objectives

Provision for bad debt is a serious problem in the banking industry. The number of bankruptcy orders increased ten-fold from 893 in 1998 to 9,151 in 2001 [9]. The rising trend continued into the first two quarters of this year, with 3,737 bankruptcy petitions presented and 2,251 orders granted (http://www.infogov.hk/oro/statistics/statistics.htm).

There are many reasons that cause over-indebtedness, in particular, credit cards contribute a significant portion. The solution to tackle delinquency became the first priority for most banks in Hong Kong. Though there are a number of measures that can be taken to deal with these growing problems, there are limits to what banks can do in the absence of fully utilizing of consumer credit data to deal with the problem. Negative data is certainly useful, but it does not allow a full picture to be built up of the borrower's total indebtedness and of his overall credit history (including the extent to which debt payments have been made on time as well as having gone overdue). In particular, negative data does not help with the situation of a borrower who builds up large amounts of debt and services it on time (perhaps by utilising other credit facilities) before suddenly defaulting and going into bankruptcy [1]. It is perceived that positive data sharing is the exit to the problem.

The bank industry in Hong Kong proposed the sharing of positive consumer credit data in order to enhance their ability to assess the creditworthiness of the borrowers in early 2002. This paper aims, by using of statistical analysis and neuro-fuzzy data mining technique, to determine:

- whether the positive consumer credit data sharing can improve the ability to determine the potential risky customers;
- whether the credit scoring system currently used by banks will be much accurate if positive data sharing scheme is introduced; and
- whether the rapid increase in personal bankruptcies is entirely the responsibility of lack of positive consumer credit data.

3 Our Approach

Hypothesis testing and neuro-fuzzy data mining technique were adopted for analysis in this study. Initially, mail survey and personal interview were conducted to collect the perceptions on essential attributes for credit risk assessment [2]. Of the 58 respondents, all were experienced bankers in the credit card industry, with at least 3-years experience in the field, who actively provided their opinion regarding the essential attributes in the credit risk assessment process. The collected survey was then input to the system and tested for the significance for the credit risk assessment attributes [3]. The testing result revealing that most bankers perceived the positive data attributes weighting a significant portion in predicting a risky customer.

Next, neuro-fuzzy data mining was applied on the real transactional data. It is employed in this study because of the uncertainty of dependent variables in the dataset. The primary focus here is to reveal the delinquent pattern from the dataset. The information regarding the customer credibility attributes from the statistical analysis and data analysis was then made a comparison, and aimed to give the clue for the followings:

1. Identify what attributes are optimal for credit scoring
2. The actual effect on the positive data sharing
3. Any gap between industry's perception on Positive Data sharing and the actual transactional data pattern

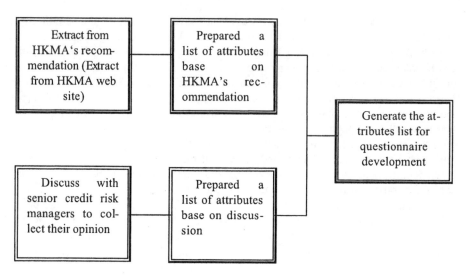

Fig. 1. The attribute selection process

Our work has two phases. Phase one is the collection of industrial perception. We analysed what attributes are perceived to be essential for credit risk assessment. Phase two is the transformation of transactional data for data mining. We collected the transactional data and transformed the data to the format for data mining. We then deduced the implication from the mining outcomes. Finally, the results from phase one and two are compared.

3.1 Phase One – Collecting Industrial Opinion

105 questionnaires had been sent out to the bankers for conducting the survey. Approximately 9 financial institutions were picked for sampling purpose, and all candidates were selected from each of these financial institutions credit risk, credit card or consumer loan department for collecting the most significant information. These 9 financial institutions, in total owed over 95% market share and having average 20 years in credit card industry at Hong Kong. Each candidate selected for the survey should have at least 3-years experience, and possessed a minimum of a university qualification. This ensures a better quality of answers to questionnaire. The sample set represents a strong consensus of the financial sector, which also reflects their concerns over the present problem of over-indebtedness. In order to achieve a better response rate and data quality, personal interviews were also conducted, which aimed to improve the overall reliability and validity of the survey result [6,7].

The selection of the attributes, as shown in Figure 1, was based on the monetary authority standards and recommendations from some senior credit risk managers in various credit agencies. Each attribute ranking for the credit scoring process was collected based on a 5-point Likert Scale, ranging from (1) most important to (5) least important [6]. The following table listed the credit risk assessment attributes that came up from the selection process.

Table 1. Credit Risk Assessment Attributes Selected

Attributes	Positive Attribute	Attributes	Positive Attribute
Employer's Name	No	Type of facilities used	No
Monthly Income	No	Credit limited approved	Yes
Resident Area	No	Outstanding balance	Yes
Properties Information (Rent/Owned)	No	Amount owed	Yes
Gender	No	High Credit	Yes
Education Level	No	Over due amount	Yes
Occupation	No	Full Payment History	Yes
Current Position	No	Previous delinquency	No
Marital Status	No	Public – Litigation Record	No
Professional Designation	No	Other loan	Yes
Household Income	No	Account balance	Yes
Personal Account Information	Yes	Payment behaviour	Yes
Credit card receivables for the last 3 months	Yes	Acquisition type	No
Rollover amount for the last 3 months	Yes		

The development of the questionnaire followed the criteria recommended by Fowler [2]. The questionnaire was initially distributed to a sample of five respondents for pre-testing. Based on feedback received the questionnaire is then further modified. The survey instrument comprised of three parts. Part I focused on the respondent's background, including personal information, demographics and respondent's skill set evaluation. Part II focuses on the attributes ranking, and only closed questions are included, which based on a 5-point Likert Scale, ranging from (1) most important to (5) least important. Part III of the questionnaire is to obtain ideas or recommendations on the attributes that to be included for credit assessment.

3.2 Phase Two – Data Mining on Consumer Credit Data

In our work, the NEFCLASS-J, a new implementation of NEFCLASS – a neuro-fuzzy data mining package was adopted. NEFCLASS-J is written in Java, a platform-independent object-oriented programming language. The neuro-fuzzy classification model NEFCLASS offers learning algorithms to create the structure (rule base) and the parameters (fuzzy sets) of a fuzzy classifier from data. The aim of the NEFCLASS approach is to create interpretable classifiers.

The sample dataset was extracted from an archived credit card transactional database of year 1999 (July – December). In order to ensure the neuro-fuzzy system being trained in an unbiased manner, the training dataset covered both negative and positive data. The distribution of data also included various kinds of customer classes, and that the rules generated would be representative. The training dataset approximately had 9,235 records, with 32 attributes per record. The database consisted of 20 kinds of banking products / facilities; for simplicity in the analysis process, only common consumer products are selected for analysis. They are Personal Loan, Credit Card, Overdrawn, and Tax Loan. Prior to the extraction, the transaction records were aggregated to the customer-account level, which assured that customers with multiple accounts would be grouped under a single entry. Thanks to the private ordinance, the customer's name and Hong Kong Identity number were removed from the record.

In NEFCLASS-J model, the validation feature offers automatic random division of the dataset and there does not require separating data into training and validation sets [10]. However, before the data could be plug-in for training, it needs to transform to a format, which could be readable by the system. A simple mapping program was developed to transform the dataset to an input file for training.

The NEFCLASS system can be built from partial knowledge about the patterns, and can be refined by learning, or even with empty rule base that is filled by creating rules from training data. In our analysis, as no partial knowledge is inserted, the rule base is learned from "scratch" (the Training Set). In the training process, which is also named the "training of network", weights are changed, such that at the end the classifier is created. So in the first learning step the structure of the classifier is created that fits the credit transactional database, and builds up few numbers of rules and fuzzy sets. In the second learning step the classifier is to be completed by determining the parameters of the system in an iterative training process to improve the accuracy without losing the interpretability.

The neuro-fuzzy model generated a set of rules for identifying potential risky customers. The association rules that generated from this phase then be translated to a list of attributes that considered highly correlated to the high-risk customers, and identifying these kind of customers' behaviour.

The final step is to compare the attribute lists generated from Phase One and Phase Two. By which, conclusion would be drawn regarding on the actual effect of positive data sharing. If the attributes in both Phase 1 and Phase 2 are ranked essential, it should be strong indicators to predict a high-risk customer; in contrast, the attributes that do not appear neither in Phase 1 or Phase 2 implied that the attributes were indeed insignificant. If the attributes appeared in either one phase, it might indicate that the bankers' perception did not match with the practical result.

4   Results

As planned, 103 questionnaires were sent out to the pre-selected financial institute. 63 responses were obtained. 5 questionnaires were discarded due to either incompletion of the questionnaire, or respondent's background did not match for the research. Of the 58 respondents, all were experienced bankers in credit card industry, with at least 3-years experience in the field, who had solid experience on using or developing the credit scoring model. All respondents are aware that credit risk assessment is essential to the cut down the over-indebtedness rate.

Attributes were tested for significance of credit rating. With that if the bankers' rating mean was less than or equal to 2, the attribute would be considered as a significant factor for credit assessment. Compare the rating mean with 2 is referring to the 5-point Likert Scale. Hypothesis test is applied with the hypothesis H_o: The rating mean less than or equal to 2. If it fails to reject the hypothesis, the attribute is considered essential, in contrast, the attribute is considered insignificant.

Table 2. Top 17 Factors that Considered Essential for Credit Assessment

Rank	Attributes	Positive Attribute	Mean
1	Previous delinquency	No	1.17
2	Full payment history	Yes	1.31
3	Payment behaviour	Yes	1.39
4	Amount owed	Yes	1.40
5	Litigation record	No	1.41
6	Overdue amount	Yes	1.45
7	Other loan	Yes	1.52
8	Household Income	Yes	1.54
9	High credit	No	1.65
10	Outstanding balance	Yes	1.74
11	Account balance	Yes	1.75
12	Personal Account Information	Yes	1.76
13	Rollover amount for the last 3 months	No	1.76
14	Occupation	No	1.81
15	Credit Card receivables for the last 3 months	No	1.84
16	Monthly Income	No	1.95
17	Education Level	No	1.96

The testing is a one-tailed test since it aimed to test the significance of the attributes. The smaller the mean the more significant the attribute represented. For 5% level of significance, the calculated test statistic should be compared with the z-values of 1.645. Table 2 presents the top 17 factors that most respondents considered significant for credit risk assessment. Positive attributes like payment history, payment behaviour, amount owed, overdue amount, other loan, and personal account information were having the rating mean well below 2.0. This implied that the majority of respondents perceive that positive data is playing a vital role for credit risk assessment, which also reveals that the majority of positive data attributes are considered important in the assessment process.

On the other hand, when we applied the neuro-fuzzy technique, the credit card transactional dataset has 4 different classes to represent different customer status. There is a proper surveillance process and a credit risk assessment guideline for assigning the class to the customer by the risk analysis in the credit risk department. The four classes are 'Good Standing', 'Satisfied', 'Filed', and 'Suspended', and their assessment guideline is as follow:

- Class 1: *Good Standing* – The customer has a clean record, and having the highest credit score so far.
- Class 2: *Satisfied* – With a single overdue record in the last 36 months, but with no overdue or rollover amount currently.
- Class 3: *Filed* – With multiple overdue records in the last twelve months, and the overdue balance have not been settled yet.
- Class 4: *Suspended* – Decided by the credit analysis or the customer relationship manager. If the customer status has suspended, all credit line will be terminated accordingly.

Table 3. Result of Attributes and Class Relationship

Classifier	Good	Satisfied	Filed	Suspended
Product Type	Insignificant	Insignificant	Insignificant	Insignificant
Facilities	Insignificant	Insignificant	Insignificant	Insignificant
Occupation	Insignificant	Significant	Significant	Significant
Title	Insignificant	Insignificant	Insignificant	Insignificant
Gross Annual Income	Insignificant	Medium	Medium	Insignificant
Income Proof Type	Insignificant	Insignificant	Insignificant	Insignificant
Gender	Significant	Significant	Significant	Insignificant
Education Level	Insignificant	Insignificant	Insignificant	Insignificant
Marital Status	Medium	Medium	Medium	Insignificant
Credit Limit	Insignificant	Insignificant	Insignificant	Insignificant
Age	Significant	Significant	Significant	Significant
Residential Type	Insignificant	Insignificant	Medium	Insignificant
Last Balance	Insignificant	Insignificant	Insignificant	Insignificant
High Credit	Insignificant	Insignificant	Insignificant	Insignificant
Last Payment Amount	Insignificant	Insignificant	Insignificant	Insignificant
Payment Method	Insignificant	Significant	Significant	Significant
Past Due 30 Days	Insignificant	Significant	Significant	Insignificant
Past Due 45 Days	Insignificant	Insignificant	Significant	Insignificant
Past Due 60 Days	Insignificant	Insignificant	Insignificant	Insignificant
Past Due 90 Days	Insignificant	Insignificant	Insignificant	Significant
Past Due 120 Days	Insignificant	Insignificant	Insignificant	Significant
Past Due 150 Days Plus	Insignificant	Insignificant	Insignificant	Significant
Rollover Flag	Insignificant	Significant	Significant	Significant
Rollover Amount	Insignificant	Insignificant	Insignificant	Insignificant

Pruning the rule base is to improve the interpretability of the classifier [8]. Pruning tries to get the same or better classification results with a smaller rule base. Initially, 129 rules were created with the data, with 2363 misclassifications, and 2715 errors. From the rule editor, some classifiers were removed, such as, the product type and facilities. After restarting the pruning, the misclassification drops to 777, and error has reduced to 1366.

At each round of training and pruning the classifier, the fuzzy sets also be trained automatically to achieve the best result for the rule base. Ultimately, 12 rules are remained, which is reduced significantly from original. Table 3 presents the attributes and class relationship suggested by Neuro-Fuzzy system.

From the generated rules, each attribute would have a specific relationship with the 4 Classes. The attribute would Significant, Medium or Insignificant related to the classes. For example, the attribute "Occupation" is a significant indicator to the class of "Satisfied", "Filed", and "Suspend". Table 4 presents the attributes and class relationship suggested by Neuro-Fuzzy system. In summary, the relationships are:

- For Class 1, attributes Gender, Marital Status and Age are significant indicators.
- For Class 2, Occupation, Gross Annual Income, Gender, Marital Status, Age, Payment Method, Past Due 30 days, and Rollover Flag are the significant indicators.

Table 4. Attributes for different classes (Over30 = overdue 30 days; Over45 = overdue 45 days; Over90 = overdue 90days; Over120 = overdue 120 days; Over150 = overdue 150 days; Roll = rollover flag)

Class / Attribute										
Suspended	Occupation	Age	Payment Method	Over90	Over-120	Over150	Roll			
Filed	Occupation	Age	Payment Method	Gender	Marital Status	Residential Type	Gross Income	Over-30	Over-45	Roll
Satisfied	Occupation	Age	Payment Method	Gender	Marital Status		Gross Income	Over-30		Roll
Good Standing		Age			Marital Status					

- For Class 3, Occupation, Gross Annual Income, Gender, Marital Status, Residential Type, Age, Payment Method, Past Due 30 days, Past Due 45 days, and Rollover Flag are the significant indicators.
- For Class 4, Occupation, Age, Payment Method, Past Due 90 days, Past Due 120 days, Past Due 150 days and Rollover Flag are the significant indicators. Interpretation of the Result:
- Occupation, Payment Method, Age, Rollover Flag are the attributes that likely to determine Class 2 to Class 4, these are the classes that consider potential delinquent account. It also revealed that the longer balance overdue, the higher chance to become delinquent.

5   Discussion

Table 5 summarizes the comparison result.

Table 5. Comparison of Results

Classifier	Survey Implication	Neuro-Fuzzy Implication	Positive attribute
Product Type	Not Significant	Not Significant	No
Facilities	Not Significant	Not Significant	No
Occupation	Not Significant	Significant	No
Title	Not Significant	Not Significant	No
Gross Annual Income	Significant	Medium	No
Income Proof Type	Not Significant	Not Significant	No
Gender	Not Significant	Significant	No
Education Level	Not Significant	Not Significant	No
Marital Status	Not Significant	Medium	No
Age	Not Significant	Significant	No
Residential Type	Not Significant	Medium	No
Payment Method	Not Significant	Significant	No
Past Due 30 Days	Significant	Significant	No
Past Due 45 Days	Significant	Significant	No

Past Due 60 Days	Significant	Not Significant	No
Past Due 90 Days	Significant	Significant	No
Past Due 120 Days	Significant	Significant	No
Past Due 150 Days	Significant	Significant	No
Proposed Positive Data			
Rollover Flag	Not Significant	Significant	
Rollover Amount	Significant	Not Significant	Yes
Last Balance	Significant	Not Significant	Yes
High Credit	Significant	Not Significant	Yes
Last Payment Amount	Significant	Not Significant	Yes
Credit Limit	Significant	Not Significant	Yes
Other Loan	Significant	N/A	Yes
Previous delinquency	Significant	N/A	No
Litigation record	Significant	N/A	No
Acquisition type	Significant	N/A	No

- Result 1: NF considers Occupation, Gender, Age, and Payment Method are factors that strongly influencing the classification, while the bankers perceive in a different way that these factors are insignificant for credit assessment. For instance, NF rules indicating that with the occupation is risk profession, the tendency to be classified in class 3 or class 4 (Filed and Suspended) is relatively higher. Furthermore, if the customer to settle the bill via "Direct Debit", the tendency to be classified in class 1 or class 2 is also relatively higher. Obviously, what the industry perceived could be quite different from the transactional data implication.
- Result 2: Survey says Rollover amount, Last balance, High credit, Last payment amount are significant, while NF system implies these factors are not significant. The gap revealed here also illustrating industrial perceptions indeed did not match the actual transactional record behaviour.
- Result 3: Both Survey and NF considered significant factors are: Gross Income, Number of days overdue.

6 Conclusion

Result 1 and 2 indicated a major gap between industry's perception and the actual transactional data behaviour, which also implied that the use of Positive data for predicting risky customers should not be as powerful as expected. Essentially, result 2 also revealed an extreme dimension that with the aim of positive data sharing, might not improve the prediction accuracy very much, as those positive attributes which considered essential for credit assessment by the bankers indeed were not significant in the NF classification.

The proposal on positive consumer credit data sharing is a measured and targeted approach to enhancing the efficiency and risk management of one important aspect of financial intermediation by the banks. Intuitively, the scheme is undeniably an effective tool to help restraining the problem of over-indebtedness, but with the findings in this study, it is not a panacea for tackling indebtedness. Other personal data attributes like payment method, delinquent information, occupation, age and gender should also be important information for credit risk assessment. In summary, this study recommends:

- With the aim of positive consumer credit data sharing, the ability to determine the potential risky customers may not be improved tremendously;
- Sharing positive data will improve the prediction accuracy is not entirely true. In contrast, the NF result implies the other way. For instance, date on which the last payment was made, last statement balance, last payment amount, high credit used are not considered significant from the neuro-fuzzy system implication. Therefore the effort in data collection and analysis is over-committed. The collection of undesirable data is a waste of efforts;
- The urge for greater sharing of credit data is becoming a matter of pressing urgency in the light of the rise in bankruptcies and the associated delinquencies; the introduction of positive data sharing indeed is not the sole solution to tackle the high level of delinquencies. For instance, the negative data, and some other existing information such as payment method, age, and occupation are also essential attributes for credit scoring.

References

1. Barron JM and Staten M (2000) The Value of Comprehensive Credit Reports: Lessons from the US Experience. Credit Research Center, McDonough School Business, Georgetown University, February, 2000.
2. Fowler FJ (1993) Survey research methods, 2nd edn. Newbury Park: Sage Publications.
3. Glazier JD and Powell RR (ed) (1992) Qualitative research and information management. Colorado: Libraries Unlimited, pp. 238.
4. Goodman SK (1993) Information needs for management decision making. Records management Quarterly, October, pp. 21-22.
5. Hong Kong Consumer Council, Choice Magazine. August, 2000.
6. Howells JM (1972), A Quantitative Analysis on research question.
7. Kervin JB (1996) Methods for Business Research. Harper Collins, New York.
8. Kruse R (1999) Design and Implementation of Neuro-Fuzzy Data Analysis Tool in Java. Technische Universität Brauschweig, Brauschweig.
9. McKinsey & Co Report, November 2001.
10. Nauck D and Kruse D (1996) Designing neuro--fuzzy systems through backpropagation. In: Pedrycz W (ed) Fuzzy Modelling: Paradigms and Practice. Kluwer, Boston, pp. 203-228.
11. Peramunetilleke D and Wong RK (2002) Currency Exchange Rate Forecasting from News Headlines. In: Proceedings of the thirteenth Australasian conference on Database technologies - Volume 5, Melbourne, Victoria, Australia, pp. 131-139.
12. Thawornwong S and Enke D (2004) The adaptive selection of financial and economic variables for use with artificial neural networks. Neurocomputing, vol. 56, pp. 205-232.
13. Zhang Z, Salerno JJ and Yu PS (2003) Applying Data Mining in Investigating Money Laundering Crimes. In: SIGKDD '03, August 24-27, 2003, Washington, DC, USA.

Author Index